T0385079

[QUINTILIAN]

THE MAJOR DECLAMATIONS

III

LCL 549

[QUINTILIAN]

THE MAJOR DECLAMATIONS

VOLUME III

EDITED BY

ANTONIO STRAMAGLIA

TRANSLATED BY

MICHAEL WINTERBOTTOM

WITH NOTES BY
BIAGIO SANTORELLI AND
MICHAEL WINTERBOTTOM

HARVARD UNIVERSITY PRESS
CAMBRIDGE, MASSACHUSETTS
LONDON, ENGLAND
2021

LOEB CLASSICAL LIBRARY® is a registered trademark
of the President and Fellows of Harvard College

Library of Congress Control Number 2021932924
CIP data available from the Library of Congress

ISBN 978-0-674-99742-4

*Composed in ZephGreek and ZephText by
Technologies 'N Typography, Merrimac, Massachusetts.
Printed on acid-free paper and bound by
Maple Press, York, Pennsylvania*

CONTENTS

DECLAMATION 12

INTRODUCTION

Plagued by a famine, a city (A) sends an envoy to buy a load of grain from a neighboring city (B), setting a deadline for his return. The envoy reaches city B, makes his purchase, and sets sail; on his way back to city A, a storm drives him onto the shores of a third city (C). Here the envoy sells his cargo at twice the purchase price, then goes back to city B and buys a double amount of grain. Finally, the envoy returns to city A on the agreed day; meantime, however, the famine has reached its peak and the citizens have fed on the corpses of their dead. The envoy is accused of harming the state.

Our declamation is the speech for the prosecution, delivered by an unspecified speaker on behalf of the whole city. The speaker's task is to prove that the envoy, while meeting the deadline set by the city, has in fact betrayed his mandate: he was not authorized to act as a merchant in search of profit (e.g., 19.5), since he was sent to save his city in a moment of crisis; therefore, he should have returned to city A immediately after purchasing the first cargo (as he had promised when he was appointed: 6.2–3). By his actions the envoy has damaged his city, as he has caused the death of many fellow citizens and, even worse, has driven the survivors to pollute themselves with cannibalism (e.g., 19.3–4); hence the charge of harming the

[QUINTILIAN]

state. It is not certain whether this charge was an invention of the rhetorical tradition or an actual practice in Greek and Roman courtrooms;[1] in any case, it was usually applied to cases of physical damage to public property (11.3–5). The prosecutor has to prove that this specific case falls under the law on harm to the state (12.1);[2] on the other side, the defendant will maintain that he should instead be tried under the law on misconduct of an embassy, thus facing a milder penalty (12.2).[3] Given this uncertainty on the legal side, and the fact that the envoy has not been caught in the act (he had *not* exceeded the deadline), our prosecution speech relies much more on pathetic than on judicial arguments: its main aim is attaining indignation, rather than systematic persuasion.[4]

We have here a case of collective cannibalism. The idea of feeding on the corpse of one's own kind had been addressed in a long-standing mythological and historiographical, as well as rhetorical, tradition.[5] Our speaker exploits the commonplaces normal in this topic: the sufferings of the starving people are described in macabre tones, down to the most gruesome details (e.g., 9.2–3);[6] the act of cannibalism is portrayed as a loss of the innocence of the entire community (18.6), which drags peo-

[1] Cf. Quint. 7.4.37; Stramaglia (2002, 92n3); Ravallese (2021, 331).

[2] Cf. Stramaglia (2002, 128–29n109, 130–31n114).

[3] Cf. Quint. 7.4.36; Stramaglia (2002, 131–32n118).

[4] Stramaglia (2019, *7ff.).

[5] An overview is given by Stramaglia (2002, 13–22); add now Cappello (2016), Faber (2020), and Ravallese (2021).

[6] See van Mal-Maeder (2007, 74–81) on the "aesthetics of horror" displayed in this speech.

4

ple down to a lower level than the wildest animals (26.7–27.5); and the horror of these actions makes the most tragic myths believable (26.4–5).

The speech can be analyzed as follows:[7]

> PROEM 1.1–3.6
> NARRATION 3.7–11.2
> ARGUMENTATION
>   *Propositio causae* 11.3
>   *Confirmatio* 11.3–19.1
>   *Refutatio* 19.2–26.1
> EPILOGUE 26.2–28.6

Linguistic and stylistic features suggest a dating of *DM* 12 to the early decades of the second century AD; this would make it almost contemporary with Juvenal's fifteenth satire, which also concerns a case of cannibalism: the two pieces have several images and *topoi* in common,[8] and Juvenal may well have drawn on our declamation, which could then be datable more precisely around 127 AD.[9] The only other extant ancient declamation on cannibalism is Libanius' *Decl.* 13.[10] A modern reply to the *Cadaveribus pasti* is found in Patarol's *Antilogies*.[11]

---

[7] Stramaglia (2019, *5ff.). But the amplified recapitulation in the epilogue (26.2–27.5) might perhaps be labeled as a second narration proper (*epidiegesis*; cf. Introduction to *DM* 5, n. 4).

[8] Detailed below, in the notes to the translation.

[9] See General Introduction, §4.

[10] See Stramaglia (2002, 21–22 and n. 35), with a list of passages in which this speech resembles *DM* 12.

[11] (1743, 326–51).

12

Cadaveribus[1] pasti

Cum civitas fame laboraret, misit ad frumenta legatum, praestituta die intra quam rediret. Profectus ille emit et ad aliam civitatem tempestate delatus duplo vendidit et duplum frumenti modum comparavit. Illo cessante corporibus suorum pasti sunt. Reversus ad praestitutam diem rei publicae laesae accusatur.

1. Quamvis, iudices, innumerabiles me indignandi causae initio statim actionis strangulent, quia nec dicere universas semel possum nec gregatim erumpentes differre gemitus (levior est enim dolor qui disponitur), primum tamen ille sibi adserit locum, qui est ex hoc iudicii tempore et tam lentae vindictae dilatione ortus animi mei prope dixe-

---

[1] -ribus *Gryph.* (*ut vid.*): -ris *codd.*

---

[1] I.e., (arguably) at city B where he had made the original purchase, as opposed to city C where he had sold it.

[2] A metarhetorical allusion to the orderly organization of the

12

The people who fed on corpses

A city afflicted by famine sent an envoy in search of grain, fixing a day by which he should return. He went off and made the purchase. Driven ashore by a storm at another city, he sold the grain at double the price, then bought a double amount of it.[1] While he was dallying, the citizens fed on the bodies of their own people. The envoy came back on the prescribed day. He is accused of harming the state.

(Speech for the prosecution)

1. Judges, I am stifled right at the start of these proceedings by countless reasons for indignation, for I can neither do justice to them all at once nor defer the groans that burst from me en masse: a grievance has to be lighter than this to be susceptible of orderly treatment.[2] But first place is claimed by what I might almost call the madness arising in my mind from the time taken up by this case[3] and the

speech (*dispositio*), in which "groans" would be delayed until the peroration.   [3] We should have torn him apart and eaten him immediately on his return (12.1.3–4). Cf. also the complaint of the speaker in 11.1.1.

rim furor, quod hominem tam sceleratum, ut nos quoque
fecerit nocentes, legibus accersimus; quod defendi patimur; quod ut puniatur precamur; quod damnatus quoque
vel morte defungetur, quam nos in illa funestissima fame,
dum sepeliri licuit, optavimus, vel exilio, quod hic quan-
topere contemnat apparet, qui tam lente in patriam rever-
2 titur. Quamquam de quo exilio loquor?[2] Quantalibet igno-
3 minia dimittite domo noxium: habet quo eat. Non publicis
manibus exeuntem discerpsimus, non, quoniam semel
consueramus et bona fide ferarum esse civitas coeperat,
hic primus nobis ex tam tardo commeatu placuit cibus? Sic
enim istum laniari, sic confici, sic consumi oportuit iure
4 nostro. Quis credat? Ego me ab hoc abstinere potui, cum
et esurirem et irascerer. 2. Sed frumento occupati sumus,
nec quicquam aliud videmus. O quanta es, fames, quae
tam grandem iram vicisti!
2   At ego, etiamsi talis ultio contigisset, si me a nefario
grassatore rei publicae non lingua sed dentibus vindicas-
sem, nihil tamen irae, nihil vindictae praestiteram: hoc et
3 meis feci. Aestuant adhuc intra pectus sepulta ventribus
nostris cognata viscera, et tumescere intus atque indignari
videntur et sera paenitentia redundant. Iam enim vacat

---

2 -quor *Wint.*[7] *153 post Warr*: -quar *codd.*

---

[4] To city C, grateful to him because he sold there the grain
from city B.   [5] Cf. 12.9.4. Now that they have embraced
cannibalism, the people feel entitled to continue on this path, as
if sanctioned by their laws.   [6] Cf. Juv. 15.129–31.

[7] Had we eaten the envoy to punish him, his fate would have
been no worse than that of our relatives, as we ate them too.

[8] Cf. Sen. *Thy.* 999–1001. See also n. 40.

delay that is making punishment so slow. For we have summoned to court a man so wicked that he has made *us* guilty as well. We are allowing him to defend himself. We are begging for him to be punished. Even if he is found guilty, he will suffer either death, which we longed for during that appalling famine while burial was still possible, or exile: and it is quite clear how much he despises *that*, considering how slow he is in coming home. (2) Yet what exile am I talking about? Drive the guilty man from his home with as much dishonor as you like, he has somewhere to go.[4] (3) Did we really not make a general attack on him and tear him limb from limb as he disembarked? Did we really not enjoy him as hors d'oeuvre for the provisions he brought us so late in the day? We had after all grown used to such food, and the city had become in effect a community of wild animals. This is how he should, by our rules,[5] have been butchered, have been prepared for the table, have been consumed. (4) Who would believe it? I was able to refrain from eating him, though I was both hungry and angry.[6] 2. But we were intent on the grain, and had eyes for nothing else. How powerful you are, hunger, to have overcome such a degree of anger!

(2) On the other hand, if such a punishment had taken place, if I had avenged myself upon this wicked robber of the republic with my teeth, not my tongue, I should not have done this out of anger, or to take revenge: I did this to my family, too.[7] (3) There still seethe, buried in my stomach, organs related to mine. It is as though they were swelling inside me, displaying their indignation; they strive to overflow with tardy remorse.[8] For *now* I have

nobis lugere, iam cibos nostros efferimus, residua[3] crema-
mus; nam cetera nobiscum sepelientur. O fames inaudita,
4 in qua levius est quod esurimus! Ignoscite tamen, violati
manes meorum—hic vos adloquor—, ignoscite quod ora
temeravimus, quod ab homine descivimus. Non ut infelicem animam sustineremus, non ut invisum spiritum pro-
duceremus, fecimus; una causa mortem distulimus: quod,
si expirassemus, idem timebamus.
5   Et ego quidem me consumptis excuso, qui mihi ipsi
⟨nisi⟩[4] irasci non possum. At iste interim stat, ut videtis,
longa via saginatus et satur atque habundans publico commeatu; ad mentionem ciborum nostrorum plenum fastidio vultum trahit et exsangues ac pallidos ad calculum
vocat, quasi ego non confitear illum etiam nimium multum
6 attulisse tam paucis.[5] Rari per vias interlucent, et, quamvis
odio eversoris nostri evocatus e latebris suis, populus sub-
sellia non implet. Pauci sceleribus pasti, alienis mortibus
salvi, quod vivunt, ipsi sibi rei, graves, aegra et tabida
7 membra in publicum protulerunt. Hae sunt civitatis reli-
quiae, quas videtis; sic tabuimus, ut miseri nec vivos
habeamus nec mortuos. Hic est populus, hae vires, hae
spes, hae opes. Nisi tandem ad vadimonium, legate, venisses, non multorum dierum commeatum habebamus.
3. Quo nunc tantum frumenti, quo classem commeatu

---

3 residua *Håk. coll. 12.13.6*: viscera *codd.*

4 *add. Håk.*: irasci *del. Sh. B.*[2] *205*

5 paucis. *Gron. (praeeunte Du Teil 245)*: pauci *codd. (unde
post* attulisse *dist. edd. vett.*): -sse. tam [pauci] rari *Dess.*[1] *84*

---

9 Cf. Juv. 15.105–6.
10 Cf. 12.7.4.

time to grieve, *now* I can conduct the funeral of those who fed me, can burn what is left over—the rest will be buried when *I* am buried. O unparalleled famine, where our hunger was the least of it! (4) Forgive me though, you violated spirits of my family (it is you I address here), forgive me for polluting my mouth, for failing to behave like a human. I acted as I did not to give sustenance to my unfortunate soul, not to extend a life I loathe. One motive alone made me delay my death: if I passed away, I was afraid I would meet the same fate.

(5) So I ask to be excused by those I consumed[9]—with *myself* I cannot <but> be angry. Yet meanwhile this man stands here, as you can see, plump after his long trip, replete, richly fed on public provisions. At the mention of what we ate, he pulls a face, full of distaste, and asks his pale and bloodless hearers to do some sums,[10] as though I do not freely admit that he brought more than enough to so few. (6) They show up here and there in the streets, at wide intervals, and the citizenry, though summoned from their hiding places by hatred of the man who ruined us, cannot fill the benches in court. A few, fed on acts of wickedness, their lives saved by the deaths of others, feeling guilt for still being alive, have dragged into the public gaze limbs sick and wasted. (7) These are the remnants of the city that you see; in our wretched plight, we are so worn away that we have neither dead nor living to put on show. This is the people, this our strength, these our hopes, these our resources. If you had not in the end come as you promised, Mr Ambassador, we had food[11] for only a few days. 3. What is the use now of so much grain, of a

[11] I.e., corpses to eat, as the food supplies had run out long before the envoy's return.

gravem? Multum hercule negotiatione tua actum est: frumentum habeo, populum non habeo. Nusquam prodest,
nusquam opus est: iam licet vendas.

2   Dum tu salutis publicae nundinator proximum quem-
que emptorem admittis,[6] dum aut funera nostra vendis aut
scelera, dum populo tuo fame moriente alienae civitati
legatus es factus, nos interim cibos ex malis invenimus, et
fames se ipsa pavit, et miseriae nostrae crudeles factae
sunt. Patiamur te defendi, si absolvi saltem nos possumus.

3   Haec nunc, iudices, ego solus queror, ad me magis pertinent, aliquid proprie passus sum? Non communem do-
4   lorem accusator habeo cum iudice? Quisquam in hac vin-
dicta alteri cedit? Non publica inopia, non totius populi
una mendicitas fuit?—Nisi, quia funestas epulas et nefa-
5   rios invenimus cibos, non putamus famem fuisse. In omnes gentes, in omnia ventura saecula proscripti sumus,
omnes haec prodigia narrabunt, omnes execrabuntur—
nisi qui non credent. Famem ipsam infamavimus, et, quod
miseris ultimum est, miserationem quoque perdidimus.

6   Adhuc tamen una defensio fuit, quod videbamur in haec
omnia istius opera impulsi; si hic innocens est, nostra
culpa est!

7   Etiamne publica mala narrabo et miseriis nostris convi-

---

6 adm- *Sch.* (*cf. 12.19.9*): dim- *codd.*

---

12 As you did at city C.
13 Cf. 12.19.9.
14 Cf. 1.6.6.
15 Metarhetorical: *narrabo* signals the beginning of the narration.

fleet heavily laden with provisions? The result of your
business dealings is indeed highly impressive: I have grain,
but a people I do not have. The wheat does no good anywhere, there is no need of it anywhere; *now* you may sell
it.[12]

(2) While you, the trafficker in the public well-being,
were opening the door to one buyer after another,[13] while
you were dealing either in our funerals or in our crimes,
while, at a time when your people were dying of hunger,
you became envoy for another city, we, in the meantime,
found food from doing evil, hunger nourished itself, and
our miseries became cruelties. We may allow *you* to
mount a defense, so long as *we* can be acquitted. (3) Am
I, judges, the only person now complaining of these
wrongs, do they concern me rather than others, have I
suffered something peculiar to myself? Do not I, the accuser, have a grievance in common with the judge? (4) Is
one person less interested than another in punishing this
man? Was the food shortage not general, was not there a
single state of beggardom that affected the whole people?
Unless we believe there was no famine, since out of our
wicked food we devised *banquets*—tainted by death. (5)
We have become outlaws among all peoples and for all
ages to come, everyone will tell of these monstrous hap-
penings, everyone will lay them under a curse—except
those who will refuse to believe them. We have made
famine itself infamous, and have lost what is the last resort
for the wretched—the ability to excite pity.[14] (6) Up to
now we have at least had one defense: we came to this
pass—it seemed—by *his* doing; but if he is judged innocent, ours is the guilt!

(7) Shall I then even narrate[15] the public ills, and abuse

13

cium faciam? Exibunt verba, subsequetur sermo? Non
alligabitur lingua? Plane nihil non possumus: 4. expona-
mus[7] ordinem cladis nostrae, et simpliciter omnia indicen-
2 tur; decet ista nostro ore narrari! Sed novimus et nimium
meminimus. Iudex doceri non debet, opinor; reo indi-
canda sunt, qui a malis publicis afuit, qui hoc certe maximum debet patriae suae beneficium, quod a fame solus
3 dimissus est. Audi itaque, audi, frumentum istud, quod
lucri fecisti, quanti nobis constet.

4   Aliqui[8] fortasse, iudices, miratur, etiamsi huius feralis
anni fructus cessavit, quod tamen illa superior longi temporis beata fecunditas tabuerit, et secum ipse[9] dubitat
quid sit in causa, cur civitas opulenta quondam nihil fru-
5 menti, nisi in spe, habuerit. Sic fit ubi vicinis civitatibus
vendimus et, undecumque offulsit lucrum, sine respectu
salus publica addicitur:[10] in vacuam possessionem fames
venit. Etiam si quid residui erat, ut carius quidam ven-
6 derent, ad annonae incendium suppressum est. Testor tamen conscientiam vestram: non sumus questi quamdiu
duplo emebamus. Non enim vulgaris illa labes[11] frumenti
fuit, nec qualis alias[12] ab agricolis accusari solet perfidia

7 -pona- δ β (def. Håk.[2] 98–99): -poni- A: -plora- cett.
8 -is E δ*   9 ipse Sh. B.[4] 203 (firm. Str.[4]): iste codd.
10 sic—addicitur dist. Wint.[9]
11 ta- Bur. coll. 12.4.4, 12.4.7
12 -ias Gr.-Mer.: -iis codd. (quod deleverit Håk.)

16 A dark joke about his mouth used for eating as well as
speaking. Cf. 12.2.2, and also 12.26.6.

17 Because we all remember what happened. Usually, the defendant knows the facts of the case, and the judge has to be told

our own miseries? Will words come out, will sense result? Shall I not be tongue-tied? Well, I cannot say nothing whatever: 4. let me explain the stages of our disaster, let everything be set out straightforwardly; it is fitting for these things to be narrated by my *mouth*![16] (2) In fact we know them, and remember all too well. The judge, I think, does not have to be informed;[17] it is the defendant who needs the details, for he was away when the city was suffering, and certainly owes this immense debt of gratitude to the city, that he was the only one to be given leave from the famine.[18] (3) Hear, then, hear how much this grain, on which you made a profit, costs *us*.

(4) Someone, judges, may perhaps be surprised that, though the crops of this disastrous year failed, the earlier surplus, built up over a long period of prosperity, had dwindled away; he may have his private doubts how it was that a once rich city had no grain except in hope. (5) This is what happens when we sell to neighboring cities, and the public weal is recklessly knocked down anywhere there is a gleam of profit: famine moves in unchallenged. Even if there was something left over, it was concealed to give a boost to the price of grain, so that some might sell at a profit. (6) But I ask you to bear witness that we did not complain so long as we were paying double.[19] This was not a normal dip in the grain supply, not the sort of thing that leads farmers on other occasions to upbraid the faith-

them; in this exceptional situation, the defendant was away while cannibalism happened, and the judge took part in it (12.3.3).

[18] Cf. 12.7.3, 12.12.6.

[19] I.e., *only* double the usual price; but it got higher than that . . .

terrarum et ingratae messis inritus labor. Nova et inaudita
abominanda lues, quae nihil homini reliquit praeter homi-
7 nem. Aut astricta citra conatum sata sub ipsis tabuere sul-
cis, aut levi rore evocata radix in pulverem incurrit, aut
perustis torrido sole herbis moribunda seges palluit. Nullus imber sitientis soli pulverem tersit, nulla super arentes
8 campos saltem umbra nubium pependit. Calidi spiravere
venti, maturitatem praecepit aestus. Etiam sicubi forte
ieiunae herbae solum vicerant,[13] vanis tantum aristis spem
fefellerunt, et inanis culmos tristis agricola iactavit ventis
nihil relicturis. 5. Levia queror: prata exaruerunt, perierunt frondes, germina non exierunt, nuda terra et rudes
glebae et aridi fontes erant. Nisi haec omnia inter scientes
dicerem, poteram videri falso questus de hoc anno, quo
2 tantum frumenti vendidimus. Utinam saltem nobis rudem
victum silvae ministrassent, et carpere arbuta,[14] concutere
quercum, legere fraga licuisset, et, quaecumque primi
mortales ante traditos divinitus mitiores cibos contra famem obiecerunt, pestifer annus reliquisset! Non eram
3 delicatus. Sed o tristis recordatio, <o>[15] funesta necessitas:

[13] so- vi- he- V
[14] -uta *Beck.*[2] *37–38 (et vd. Der. 109–10):* -usta *codd.*
[15] *add. Scheff. 451 (corrob. Watt*[3] *53–54)*

---

[20] Sc., to eat.

[21] Winnowing: no grain was left, all was husk, that blew away.
See Verg. *G.* 3.132–34.

[22] Sc., from the rich harvest of the previous years—without
realizing the impending famine (12.4.4–5).

[23] I.e., before the gods gave mankind fire, with which food

lessness of the land and the labor wasted on a thankless harvest. It was a plague novel and unheard of, a curse that left man nothing[20] except man. (7) Either the crops shriveled away before germination and rotted away beneath the very furrows, or roots that had been summoned forth by a sprinkling of dew encountered nothing but dust, or the crop, doomed to die, grew pale as the blazing sun burned up the green shoots. No rain laid the dust of the thirsty soil, not even a shadow of a cloud hung over the dry plains. (8) The winds blew warm, and the heat brought on premature ripeness. Even where meager blades had chanced to win their battle with the soil, they flattered hope with ears that proved empty, and the farmer gloomily tossed the empty stalks at winds that would carry everything away.[21] 5. But those are the least of my complaints. The meadows dried up, leaves died, shoots failed to appear, the earth was bare, the soil uncultivated, the springs failed. If I were not telling all this to people in the know, I might be thought to be *making up* my complaints about a year in which we sold so much grain.[22] (2) If only the woods had at least furnished us with a primitive means of life, and we could have gathered arbutus berries, shaken down acorns, picked strawberries! If only the plague year had left us all that the first mortal men could find to ward off hunger before softer food was vouchsafed by the gods![23] I was not a fussy eater.[24] (3) But how bleak a memory, ‹how› dire a

could be cooked and made more palatable. For such primitive food gathering cf. Ov. *Met.* 1.103–6, with Russo (2019, 235).

[24] = I'd have eaten anything. But this remark sounds sinister, considering what the speaker will eat shortly thereafter.

4 nihil habuimus quo viveremus, praeter famem. Nec tamen in totum queri de numinibus possumus, maria certe secunda experti. Si voluisset servare legatus diem, quem illi felicitas temporis dederat, potuit nobis frumentum bis adferre.

5 Ut primum tanti mali sensus in civitatem percrebruit, cum iam urgente inopia cotidie malum artius premeret et praesente fortuna peior tamen esset futuri[16] metus, apparuit nullum ex propinquo esse praesidium, cum finitimas 6 quoque civitates incendium nostrum adussisset. Erat quidem aliquid in vicino adhuc frumenti, sed iam nemo vendebat. Ergo, ut vidimus salutem publicam trans mare petendam, se in curiam quisque cogunt. 6. Ut arma bello, ut aqua incendio inclamari publice solent, ita uno quodam consensu non aetatibus spectatis,[17] non honoribus,[18] pariter rettulimus, probavimus, decrevimus, pedibus manibus ruimus[19] in sententiam necessitatis, nec ordo nos officio- 2 rum moratus est. Legationem multi pollicebantur, nec innocentiae iste beneficio vel auctoritatis meritorumque respectu electus est; una causa nos movit: quod se cito

---

[16] -rae *Franc.*   [17] sp- ⟨: exp- *codd.*
[18] pedibus manibus ruimus (ruum- P) *hic add.* β
[19] ruimus *Håk.*[2] 99 e β *supra laud.*: imus B[pc] V: iimus *vel* ivimus *cett.* (β *quoque, cum h.l. verba iterantur*)

---

[25] I.e., the bodies of those who had starved to death.
[26] The speaker takes no account here of the storm mentioned in the theme; later, it will be openly labeled as a lie (12.23.1–2).
[27] Cf. 12.4.5.   [28] Referring to some city close on land: the decision to seek food overseas will be taken later, because nobody was selling nearby.

necessity!—we had nothing to live on except the famine.[25] (4) Yet we cannot altogether complain of our treatment by the gods: after all, we experienced good conditions at sea. If the envoy had cared to come on the day made possible to him by the clement weather,[26] he could have brought us grain twice over.

(5) When the impact of so great a disaster first made itself more widely felt in the city, when the shortage began to bite and calamity pressed closer every day, and however bad the present yet worse were our forebodings for the future, it was quite obvious that no help could be looked for from nearby: our explosion in grain prices[27] had singed adjoining cities too. (6) There was indeed still some grain available nearby,[28] but no one was selling now. So when we saw that it was imperative to seek the public salvation overseas, everyone thronged into the senate house. 6. Just as everyone cries out for arms when there is a war, or for water if there is a fire, so now, unanimously, with no distinction of age or rank, we all put the question, approved it, passed the decree. Off we rushed, "hand and foot," to vote[29] for what necessity dictated, and no procedural concerns held us up. (2) Many offered to act as envoys, and the defendant was *not* chosen by virtue of his clean record or out of respect for his authority and deserts; one thing and one only motivated us: he promised he would return

[29] An allusion to the voting *per discessionem*, which could be adopted by the senate to speed up decisions: omitting the debate, the senators would move toward two opposite parts of the senate house, representing the alternative motions; thus, the number of the supporters of each one would show the decision of the majority. Cf., e.g., Cic. *Phil.* 3.24; Gell. 14.7.9–13.

rediturum pollicebatur. Pecuniam sine numero infudi-
mus, frumentum sine modo[20] mandavimus: quantum po-
3 tuisset, adferret, festinaret modo. Hoc una voce supplices
acclamabamus, ac, ne moraremur, ne hoc quidem diu
rogavimus; una tantum vox fuit, quam iste pro quodam
praeiudicio amplexus est: "Nihil agis adferendo frumen-
4 tum, si post illum diem veneris." Nostris manibus legatum
in navem tulimus, ac, ne quid morae esset, pro sua quisque
portione etiam commeatum dedimus, retinacula incidi-
mus et litus ingressi classem publicis manibus impulimus.
Inde fugientia vela longo visu prosecuti facilem emptio-
nem, secundos ventos, placidum mare, non secus ⟨ac si⟩[21]
ipsi navigaremus, precati sumus.
5 Quis credat hoc de tam miseris? Omnia a diis impetra-
vimus. Scilicet unum superest, ut pro aliena civitate vota
6 solvenda sint. Cito pervenit, cito emit, cito rediit—quo
voluit. Quid prodest [expectare]?[22] Alia civitas prior est, et
sane religiosus legatus diem expectat.
7 Nos interim coacta primo ex agris pecora diripuimus
et, ne venturo saltem anno prospici posset, non reliqui-
8 mus, qui ararent, boves. Iam servis fugas imperavimus,
iam procumbentes ante limina principum pauperes in ipsis precibus expirant. Plorantibus liberis legatum promit-
9 timus. Iam tantum sibi quisque cura[23] est. Nihil tamen

---

20 -dio *Bur.*[1]
21 *suppl.* ς
22 *del. Håk. utpote e seq. sententia ortum*
23 -ae *Håk., sed cf. ThlL IV.1455.10ss.*

---

30 He claims that, by setting a deadline, we authorized him to
return on the very last day.

quickly. We thrust money on him without troubling to count it, and commissioned the purchase of grain without limit: he must bring back as much as he could, but fast. (3) This was what we shouted with a single cry of supplication, and in order not to waste time we didn't even ask this for long. All we said—something he has seized upon as a kind of prejudgment[30]—was: "It's no use you bringing grain if you come after that day." (4) We carried the envoy on board ship, and to avoid delay, we all gave him provisions too, each contributing his share. We cut the cables and went down to the waterline: everyone gave the fleet a push. Then we watched the sails as they disappeared into the distance, praying for easy negotiations, favoring winds, calm sea, just as though we were sailing ourselves.

(5) Who could believe this, of people so wretched?— we got all we asked from the gods. One thing remains, of course: paying vows of gratitude on behalf of a foreign city.[31] (6) He arrived quickly, bought quickly, returned quickly—to where he wanted to go. To what good? Another city comes ahead of us, and of course our scrupulous envoy is waiting for the set day.

(7) We, meanwhile, first of all drove herds in from the countryside and massacred them; to make any provision even for the coming year impossible, we did not leave oxen to do the plowing. (8) Now we ordered our slaves to run away,[32] now the poor kept dying in midprayer before the doors of the great. To our wailing children we promised— the envoy. By now everyone thought of himself alone. (9)

[31] Ironic—i.e., city C, which he had "saved" by selling them grain (cf. 12.25.7).

[32] So that we would not have to feed them.

horum etiam nunc in invidiam legati queror: adhuc prior cursus est; 7. hactenus nostra mala tulimus: in reliqua le-
2 gatus nos vicarios dedit. Si quicquam tibi humani sangui-nis superest, nisi nimia saturitate alienae fortunae cogi-tatio excidit, respice patriae casum, respice gravissimam fortunam. Miseri te misimus, expectant pallidi exsangues-que cives tui, et quicquid extremi spiritus adhuc superest,
3 spe tui trahitur. Figura tibi exesos vultus, decrescentem populum, iam praemortuas vires. Nec quicquam horum potes ignorare: si quid tibi credimus, fame laborantem
4 civitatem vidisti. Festina, dum supersunt quibus legatio-nem renunties; festina, dum mori ultimum est, ‹dum›²⁴ frumento digni sumus. Quid in nos convertis etiam alienae civitatis famem? Quatenus nobis computandum est, prop-ter te duplum mali tulimus.
5 Tu supra frumentum publicum stertis, et omnes maris circumvectus oras litora portusque cognoscis; tu, inter duas civitates fatorum arbiter, alienae conditor, tuae ever-sor, salutem nostram peregrinis admetiris, et secunda tempestate²⁵ in patriam ferente²⁶ contrarios ventos exop-
6 tas. Nos, per arentes effusi campos, morientium herbarum

²⁴ add. Str.⁴: ‹festina dum› fru- fere Wiles 69: est ‹et› Sch.
²⁵ an -ate ‹te›?   ²⁶ -te O: -tes cett.

³³ Suffering what the other city (C) should have suffered: the envoy chose to supply grain to a foreign city earlier than to his own.
³⁴ City C, whose sufferings he says he acted to alleviate (with the implication that he has made the whole story of their suf-ferings up). He has not seen the famine in his city (A), as he had left before it reached its peak (12.4.2, 12.12.6).

Even now, however, I am not making any of these complaints to arouse feeling against the envoy: he is still on the first stage of his journey; 7. so far the troubles we have endured are our own: for the *remaining* ones the envoy supplied us as substitutes.[33] (2) If you have any drop of human blood left in your veins, if your sated belly has not driven away all thought of how others are faring, have regard for the fate of your homeland, for its disastrous lot. We were pitiable creatures when we sent you; now your fellow citizens await you pale and bloodless, and we draw whatever last breath remains in hope of you. (3) Picture our gaunt faces, our diminishing numbers, our strength dead before we die. You cannot fail to know any of all this: if we can believe you, you have seen a city suffering from famine.[34] (4) Make haste, while there are people left for you to report back to; make haste, while death is the last resort, ‹while› we still deserve grain.[35] Why do you divert on to us the famine of a foreign city too? Since we are asked to do sums[36]—we have had twice the suffering to put up with, thanks to you.

(5) You lie snoring there on deck, while down below is the grain that belongs to the state. You have traveled around all the seacoasts, and are getting to know the shores and ports. You are arbiter of destiny between two cities, savior of a foreign one, destroyer of your own. You are doling out to aliens what should be our salvation, and though favorable conditions are ready to bear you home,[37] your prayer is for contrary winds. (6) We, dotted across

[35] I.e., before we pollute ourselves with cannibalism, which makes us unworthy of the food of civilized man (grain).

[36] Cf. 12.2.5.   [37] Cf. n. 26.

radices vellimus omnes [radices vellimus],[27] eo quidem
fortius ut, si fieri possit, in venenum incidamus subeuntes
insolitis cibis.[28] Et sicubi forte uberius paulo pabulum
contigit, de pascuis rixa est. Amaros fruticum cortices
et ramorum male arentium pallidas frondes decerpimus
morbidi; nam[29] quicquid fames coegit, corpus admisit.

7 Iam passim moriuntur, et pestilentium more pecudum
subinde aliquis ex populo in ipsis pascuis procumbit. Cre-
brior cotidie interitus et latior strages, et—me miserum!—iam fames desinit. 8. Quos tester deos? Superosne,
quos per tantum nefas fugavimus, an inferos, quos nobis

2 permiscuimus? Adde[30] nostram malam conscientiam omnia nos ante fecisse, quae nemo praeter nos fecit: pecora
cecidimus, campos evolsimus, silvas destruximus; novissime nihil relictum est, praeter esurientes et mortuos.

3 Si qua est fides, libenter hanc partem accusationis subinde differo: adeo, ubi tantum nefas narrandum est, etiam
exigua temporum lucra sectari libet. At[31] necesse est reo
indicare, qui a[32] malis publicis afuit, quam multis non ad

4 diem venerit. Ignoscite, dii hominesque, sceleri quidem

---

[27] herbarum—vellimus[2] B V A δ, *unde* radices vellimus[2] *secl.*
Str.[4]: h. omnes (*om.* ψ β) r. v. *cett.*

[28] -tos -bos π E, *sed cf. OLD*[2] subeo §7.*a*

[29] -bidi nam M: -bi nam B V δ: -bida γ β

[30] adde (*vel* adice) *coni. et post* fecit *sic dist. Russ.*[3]: ad B V γ
β: an δ   [31] at (*ex* et) D: et *cett.*   [32] qui a β: quia *cett.*

---

[38] Cf. Juv. 15.99–103.

[39] As they turn to cannibalism.

[40] A reference to the *manes* of the people whose corpses have
been devoured: the survivors now carry them buried in their

our parched plains, tear up every single dying plant by the root, pulling at them the harder on the chance of meeting with some poison, as we come upon unusual foods. If there chances to be a place where some slightly richer vegetation grows, there is a dispute about grazing rights. In our sickness we strip bitter-tasting bark off bushes and pale leaves off unnaturally dry branches—yes, our bodies granted entry to anything that hunger forced upon them.[38] (7) Now people are dying wholesale, and one after another of us drops where he feeds, just like animals in a pestilence. Every day the mortality increases and the carnage is wider spread—and now (alas!) the famine comes to an end.[39] 8. What gods am I appeal to? Those above, whom we have put to flight by such an appalling crime, or those below, whom we have blended with ourselves?[40] (2) And then there is our own bad conscience, the knowledge that we did beforehand everything that no one besides us has ever done—slaughtered herds, torn up plains, destroyed forests;[41] in the end nothing was left, except the hungry and the dead.

(3) Believe me, I should be only too glad to defer the succeeding part of my accusation, if only for a short time: so true is it that, when so dreadful a crime has to be related, one is glad to gain even a small period of respite. But it is necessary to inform the defendant, who was away during the public woes,[42] how many people there were for whom he came too late. (4) Forgive, gods and men, a

stomachs (cf. 12.2.3, 12.11.1, 12.26.3; Lib. *Decl.* 13.18 and *passim*).

[41] Cf. 12.13.4.
[42] Cf. 12.4.2.

ultimo, sed tamen quod fecisse miserrimum est. Non ha-
bitant una pudor et fames, et, cum semel intrarit impotens
5 domina, feras etiam et ingentes beluas subigit. Terram
morientes momorderunt. Memet ipsum,[33] si nil fuisset
aliud, comedissem; sed confitendum est: legati beneficio
non defuit.

6   Postquam omnem patientiam vicerat ignea fames,
postquam spes quoque, quae miseris ultima est, omnis
abierat, et frumentum totiens sibi frustra promissum animus iam ne cupere quidem audebat, subiit furor et alie-
natio mentis, et tota sui arbitrii fames facta est. Animus
malis deriguerat, os insolitis cibis stupebat, feris invidere
7 coepimus. Primo tamen furtim et intra suas quisque late-
bras admisit hoc monstrum, et, si paulo citius venisses,
potuisset hoc negari; si quid[34] ex strage corporum defue-
rat, sepultum putabamus. Nec tamen indicavit quisquam,
8 nec deprehendit aliquis. Nemo, ut hoc faceret, exemplo
impulsus est: se quisque docuit, omnes scire coepimus
postquam omnes fecimus. Quotiens tamen, antequam in-
ciperem, in portum cucurri, quamdiu in altum intentus, si
9 quae essent in conspectu naves, oculos fatigavi! Tibi, legate, tempus differre facile est, qui tuam tantum partem
non vendidisti. Tu, quem habeas diem, videris; ego septi-
mum expectare non possum.

---

[33] me me ip- B V, *fort. recte*   [34] -id V: -i B: -is Φ

---

[43] Cf. Juv. 15.105–6.   [44] Hunger.
[45] Cf. Juv. 15.102–3.   [46] I.e., of dead bodies.
[47] Because they do not feed on their kind: cf. 12.26.7–27.1.
[48] To city C: he kept back enough for himself (and the crew)
(DAR).
[49] For the medical doctrine—here presupposed—that death

crime which is indeed the ultimate—but is such that to
have committed it is the most pitiable fate.[43] Shame and
hunger do not dwell together, and once that irresistible
mistress[44] has entered on the scene, she subdues even wild
and enormous monsters. (5) The dying gnawed at the
earth. I would have eaten myself, if there had been nothing else;[45] but it has to be admitted: thanks to the envoy,
there was no shortage.[46]

(6) After the fire of famine had overcome all our powers of endurance, after even hope, last refuge of the unhappy, had quite departed, and one did not even venture
to long for the grain that had so often been promised in
vain, people went mad, out of their minds, and hunger
could do whatever it wanted. The intellect had grown
numb with all the suffering, the mouth was baffled by
unaccustomed food, we began to envy wild animals.[47] (7)
But at first it was only stealthily that people committed this
monstrous act, each in his own secret place, and, if you
had come a little more quickly, all this might have been
denied. If anything went missing from the mass of corpses,
we supposed that it had been buried. No one laid information, or caught anybody in the act. (8) No one was led by
example to act like this: each man taught himself; we all
learned how to do it after we had done it. Yet how often,
before I began, I ran to the harbor, how long I looked out
to sea, straining my eyes in case any ships were in the off-
ing! (9) For you, Mr Ambassador, it is easy enough to delay
your return: for yours is the only portion you have not
sold.[48] What day *you* have been assigned, is your business;
I cannot wait a week.[49]

comes on the seventh day without food, cf. Plin. *HN* 11.283; Gell.
3.10.15.

9. Ergo rabidi supra cadavera incubuimus et clausis oculis, quasi visus conscientia acerbior esset, tota corpora morsibus consumpsimus. Subit interim horror ex facto et taedium ac detestatio sui et planctus, sed, cum ab infaustis fugimus cibis, urit iterum fames, et quod modo ex ore
2 proiecimus colligendum est. Nunc mihi illa foeda videntur, nunc abominanda, laceri artus et nudata ossa et abrepta cute intus cavum pectus; nunc occurrunt effusa praecordia et lividae carnes et expressum dentibus tabum et exhaustae ossibus medullae (quantulum enim corporis
3 fames relinquebat!). Nunc illud horreo tempus, si quando aut manus incidit aut facies aut aliquid denique, quod hominem propria nota signat; nunc cibi succurrunt, quos imponere in mensam non ausus sum. Confitendum est enim: devoravimus homines et quidem avide, qui diu nihil ederamus.[35]

4 Et tamen coepisse difficillimum fuit. Postquam ius factum est, postquam nemo erat in civitate quem confiteri puderet, tum vero iam[36] in posterum prospicimus et fu-
5 nera horreis condimus. Retro aguntur exequiae, aut citra[37]
6 aut ad rogos pugna est. Heres cadaver cernit. Novum et incredibile, nisi nossemus, monstrum habuimus: sine rogis pestilentiam. Mortium[38] ratio non constitit; perisse

---

[35] *gravius dist. Wint.*[9]   [36] fami *Bur.*
[37] citra Φ (*def. Str.*[4]): circa B V: circa <corpora> *Håk.*[2] 99–100
[38] -tium 5 (*vind. Bur.*): -tui *codd.*

---

[50] *Now,* he can feel disgust for what he has done, for he is not starving any longer; but *at that time,* all he felt was hunger. Cf. 12.23.10.   [51] He remembers with horror some body part that identified a particular corpse he ate.

9. Accordingly, we fell upon the corpses like mad things. Closing our eyes, as if seeing was worse than knowing, we kept on biting, and ate them up. At times there ensued horror at the deed, disgust, self-loathing, wailing; but after we had fled from the ill-omened food, hunger began to torment us again, and we had to collect up what we had just spat out of our mouths. (2) *Now*[50] I see the foul, abhorrent sight—the torn limbs, the stripped bones, the cavity of the chest with the skin ripped off. *Now* in front of me are the vitals poured out, the livid flesh, the diseased blood spurting up beneath our teeth, the marrow sucked from the bones (how little of the body did hunger leave behind!). (3) *Now* I shudder at the thought of that time, if ever there comes to my mind a hand or a face or anything else marking off a particular person.[51] *Now* I have a picture of the food I could not bring myself to serve at table. Yes, I must admit it: we devoured human beings, and greedily too, for we had not eaten anything for many a day.

(4) Yet it was *starting* that was the hardest part. When the practice became the rule, when no one in the city felt ashamed to confess, that was the point when we began to plan for the future, and stockpiled bodies in the granaries. (5) Attempts are made to turn back funeral processions: before they reach the pyres, or at them, there are fisticuffs. An heir comes into possession of—a body.[52] (6) Here before us was a novel prodigy, incredible if we had not known of it: plague, but no burning of bodies.[53] The body count

[52] In such desperate conditions, heirs do not want the estate of the deceased, but his corpse to eat.

[53] For the corpses were stolen or diverted first (cf. 12.9.5).

cives scio tantum quia inter viventes non video. 10. Aegri
adsidentes timebant et labentem animam ⟨a⟩[39] supremis
domesticorum osculis[40] reducebant. Primo tamen nihil
rogabant suos nisi tantum[41] sepulturam; ut maior urgere
necessitas coepit, beneficium factum est expectare dum
2 moritur. Nemo adeo adfinis fuit, nemo tam coniunctus,
quem[42] pietas abstineret. Nostros comedimus, nostros:
nam si alienos vellemus, nemo [audebat][43] cedebat.
3   Nihil est tamen quod indignari velitis; narravi vobis
lucrum vestrum: frumentum duplo vendidimus et callidissimus legatus vicinae civitati imposuit. Plena nunc horrea,
bonae rationes, onustae naves sunt, et, quo magis gaudea-
4 mus tanto bono, pauci sumus. Nam quod ad temporis
excusationem pertinet, nihil est—opinor—quod aestuet:[44]
in desertum non incidit populum, nec sane fuit cur festinaret; etiam nunc expectare poteramus, sola est nostra
5 civitas, quae fame perire non possit. Dissimulaturum me
putatis istius patrocinia? Confiteor, venit ad ultimum
diem, adtulit frumentum; gratulemur, quod iam nulla civitas fame laborat.

[39] add. Bur.   [40] oscu- Sch.: ocu- codd.
[41] tantum Beck.[2] 82: totam codd. (at vd. Russ.[1] 45): solam
Håk.: an tostam (cf. CLE 960.3 cinis en et tosta favilla sum)?
[42] quo 5, sed cf. ThlL I.193.30ss.
[43] del. Plas. 38–39 (obest enim 12.9.5)
[44] -uet ⟨aliquis: fames⟩ in Håk.[4] 155–56, sed vd. Str.[4]

---

[54] They were aware that these same lips were about to devour
them (and perhaps feared that they would start right away).
[55] I.e., for at least some form of burial of what would remain
of them after being devoured (cf. 12.2.3, 12.14.3) (AS).
[56] Cf. 12.27.4.   [57] Citizens.

did not tally: I knew that people had died only because I could not see them among the living. 10. The sick went in fear of those who watched over them: when their breath was slipping away, they tried to take it back <from> the last kisses of their household.[54] In the early days, indeed, they asked their relatives for nothing but some burial;[55] when necessity pressed harder, it became an act of kindness to wait till death took place.[56] (2) No one was so closely related, no one so akin, that family ties made them abstinent. We ate our relatives, yes, our relatives; for if we wanted to dine outside the family, no one would let us take their place.

(3) Still, you[57] don't need to be angry; I have described something from which you profited: we sold the grain for twice the price, and our so cunning envoy cheated our neighbor city. Now the granaries are full, the accounts healthy, the ships laden, and, to add to our joy at such good fortune, there are only a few of us. (4) As to his excuse for being late, he has no need—I think—to fret: he did not have to do with a populace without resources,[58] and indeed he had no need to hurry: even now we could have waited; ours is the only city that cannot die of hunger.[59] (5) Do you think that I will try to suppress his lines of defense? I admit it: he came on the last possible day, he brought the grain; let's be glad that now no city is suffering famine.[60]

---

[58] Ironic: the envoy was sent out precisely because his city was short of food, and he was instructed to hurry (12.6.1–2). The "resources" are the stock of people to be eaten.

[59] Unlike city C, which he had succored; they were *not* cannibals.   [60] Neither city A nor city C—but (AS) the latter thanks to grain, the former to cannibalism!

6   O si vires sufficerent, latera durarent, aliquid ex aridis
diu faucibus residuae vocis exiret! Quanta indignatione
opus erat, ubi pro omnibus dolendum est! Quodsi[45] universi qui adsumus proclamemus, haec tota contio in unam
vocem consentiat, non esset tamen futura par crimini in-
7   vidia: ut[46] omnes accusemus, quota pars queritur! Secum
quisque reputet quae tulerit, quid admiserit. Plane immanis belua est et non tantum necessitatis causa per nefas pastus, qui, quod comederit hominem, non irascitur.
11. Succurrite, dolor et seri vomitus et ultrix paenitentia;
ades, longi ieiunii imperiosa necessitas; et vos intus impli-
citae, si quid potestis, admonete, animae, et a ferali ventre
prorumpite, dum commissum nefas devoto capite ex-
piamus et quasi lustrata urbe feralem victimam violatis
2   manibus mittimus. Decent nos tales hostiae. In iudicium
perduxi publicum scelus, et infamatae civitati quaero vela-
mentum. Nemo non commisit aliquid; habetis tamen, si
vultis, unum et pro omnibus nocentem.
3   Rei publicae laesae accuso. Mirari vos certum habeo,
cum civitas tota consumpta sit, cum populus in se tabuerit,

---

45 quodsi π (*def. Str.*[4]): qui`o´d cum si B: quod cum V: quod
cum sit Φ
46 ut ς: aut *codd.*

---

61 I.e., he liked the taste (DAR).
62 Cf. n. 40.
63 Sacral imagery: the envoy is seen as a scapegoat, whose
punishment will cleanse the city from the pollution of its collective crime, over which the speaker wishes to draw a merciful veil.
64 Ambiguous between "destroyed" and "eaten."

(6) O if only I had the strength, if only my lungs were still capable of it, if only I had some voice left to issue from a throat so long parched! How much indignation would be needed, when one has to grieve on behalf of everyone! Yet if all of us here were to cry aloud, if this whole assembly spoke in unison, there still could be no reproach sufficient to match the crime: even if we all were to accuse, how small a part of the citizen body is here to voice our complaint! (7) Let every one of us think back on what he endured, on what he did. Surely anyone who has fed on a human being is a hideous beast, and one that has fed on forbidden food not for need only,[61] if he is not angry to have eaten human flesh. 11. Come back to mind, the pain, the vomiting all too late, the penitence that took its revenge. Let the all-powerful necessity arising from long days of starvation come before our minds. And you too, if you can, remind us, you souls now inextricably part of us:[62] burst forth from our funerary stomachs, while by sacrificing a single life we expiate the wickedness we have perpetrated, and as though by purification of the city send down a funeral victim to the spirits of our ancestors we have violated. Such are the sacrifices that are fitting for us. (2) What I have brought to court is a *collective* crime, and now I am looking for some veil to draw over our disgraced city. Everyone without exception has done something wrong: but here before you, if you are willing, is one man, guilty for us all.[63]

(3) I am bringing a charge of harm to the state. I am sure you are wondering why, when the whole city has been consumed,[64] when the people has rotted away inside it-

hanc verbi[47] segnitiam, quo perstricta tantummodo patria
et leviter,[48] quod aiunt, manu offensa intellegi possit; sed
ferenda est, ut in ceteris, haec quoque rerum naturae iniuria, quod non tam immanibus factis paria verba accom-
modavit. Et fames nostra fames dicitur, et cibi nostri cibi

4   vocantur, et res publica nunc laesa. Nec scilicet nisi pe-
racto legitimo ordine reus non[49] punietur. Omnia, rogo,
scrupulose agantur. Videte ut iure irascamur, qui contra

5   ius viximus. Immo etiam, si libet, defensionem audiamus,
etiam nunc nos moretur. Neget laesam rem publicam quia
plus quam laesa est: non enim discussos alicuius operis
angulos nec recisas lucorum frondes nec publicarum ae-

6   dium dispersos parietes obicimus. Ac, si videbitur, adiciet
forsitan non esse rem publicam, quae perierit. Id enim
superest, ut iam hoc nomen extinctum audiamus. Procedet eo usque fortasse, ut esurisse nos neget! 12. Non in-
fitior autem parum[50] proprie hoc legis verbo nefas istius
signari non posse. Maiores enim ne laedi quidem rem
publicam impune voluerunt, ideoque existimo etiam hoc
esse comprehensum. Nemo autem verebatur ne absolvi
posset crimen lege maius.

---

[47] hanc verbi *h.l. habet* π (*vind. Reitz.[2] 45*): *post* certum habeo
(*supra*) *cett.*   [48] levi *Gron., sed vd. Str.[4]*
[49] non B V (*def. Str.[4]*): *om.* Φ
[50] ⟨nisi⟩ parum *Sch., sed vd. Str.[4]*

---

[65] The eaten bodies are now rotting in the stomachs of their
surviving fellow citizens (n. 40). Cf. Lib. *Decl.* 13.43, "Was it not
enough . . . that the greatest part of the people had been consumed—in the people?"
[66] Because we had enough (corpses) to eat.

self,[65] I use a word so feeble, one that might suggest a land merely grazed and (as one says) scratched with a light touch. But, here as elsewhere, one has to bear with the deficiencies of nature in not supplying us with words to match such appalling deeds. *Our* famine is still called "famine," *our* food is still called "food"—and now the state is said to have been "harmed." (4) And, to be sure, the defendant will only be punished after due process of law. Let everything be done meticulously, I beg you. We have survived unlawfully: see to it, that we are angry lawfully. (5) Indeed, let us, if you like, go so far as to listen to his defense; let him keep us waiting, now as before. Let him say that the state was not harmed—for indeed it was *more* than harmed: we are not after all making a charge out of damage to odd corners of a building, or the cutting of leaves in a sacred grove, or the demolition of the walls of a public shrine. (6) He will also perhaps add, if he thinks fit, that there *is* no state where the state has been destroyed: for it yet remains for us to hear the argument that the very word "state" is dead and gone. Maybe he will go so far as to say that we did not feel hungry![66] 12. Yet I am not saying[67] that the wording of the law cannot properly be thought to cover this man's dreadful crime. In fact the intention of our ancestors was that the state could not even be "harmed"[68] without a penalty; and so—I think—even this crime was covered. But no one was afraid that, if a crime was greater than the law envisaged, it might go unpunished.

[67] As I might be thought to be, after saying "harm" is so feeble a word.
[68] I.e., let alone subjected to such a horror.

2   Quid, quod actionem rei publicae laesae temptat in legem male gestae legationis deflectere? Eligit reus cri-
3   men, hoc est, noxius crucem optat! Non sustineo, iudices, in tanto animi motu argumenta conquirere, nec impetus irae meae in digitos descendit; hoc tamen scio: non cadit in formulam publicus dolor, nec, si adeo iudicibus quid passi sint[51] exciderit, ut has ferant cavillationes non diluentis crimen sed differentis,[52] populus quoque impu-
4   nitum nefas sine lapidibus praeteribit. Non praescribes. Accusare te male gestae legationis possum?[53] Age porro, si occisos obiecero homines, non tu es causa mortium? Si violata sepulcra, non propter te rogos fraudavimus?
5   Sed legatus fuisti. Quod tamen ipsum quid est aliud quam rem tractare? Rem[54] autem qui male agit, ut arbitror, lae-
6   dit. An existimas hanc legatis dari peccandi licentiam, ut, quaecumque scelera in eo officio commiserunt, cum his omnibus hac una lege decidant? O nimium invidendam huius legationis condicionem, si tibi et famem remisit et

---

51 sint ⟨ (def. Håk.): sunt codd.
52 diluentis . . . differentis V: -tes . . . -tes B Φ
53 sic dist. Reitz.[2] 69   54 rem . . . rem codd.: rem ⟨publicam⟩ (bis) ⟨, sed cf. Wint.[7] 153–54

---

69 Cf. 11.8.2.
70 An allusion to the practice of listing the arguments to be developed in the subsequent speech, while counting them on the fingertips: such a rationally ordered method would not be suited to the emotional involvement of the speaker in this case (see Quint. 4.5.24, 11.1.53, 11.3.114).
71 Cf. 11.10.3: stoning is the means for the angry people to take justice into their own hands.

(2) What of his attempt to divert an action for harm to the state by bringing it under the law on misconduct of an embassy? Here is a defendant selecting the charge to be brought against him: that is to say, a guilty man is choosing his own cross![69] (3) I am in such distress, judges, that I have no patience to hunt up arguments, and my urgent anger does not stoop to ticking off points on my fingers.[70] But this I do know: the grievance of the public does not fall under a legal formula; and if the judges have so far forgotten their own suffering that they are prepared to tolerate this logic-chopping from someone who is not answering the charge but putting it off, that does not mean that the people in their turn will let so appalling a crime go unpunished without a stoning.[71] (4) You will *not* be able to "prescribe."[72] Can I accuse[73] you of misconduct of an embassy? Consider: if I accuse you of killing persons, are you not the cause of their deaths? If I accuse you of violating tombs, have we not thanks to you robbed the funeral pyres?[74] (5) But you were an envoy. What else is *that* but to be on business? Now if someone conducts a piece of business badly, he is, in my view, harming it. (6) Or do you imagine that envoys are issued a license to do wrong, so that whatever crimes they have committed in their period of office, they can settle for all of them under a single law? Your embassy is on enviable terms indeed, if it let you

[72] I.e., to claim that the case does not fall under the law that is being invoked.   [73] = *simply* accuse . . .

[74] A warning to the envoy: if he escapes the accusation of harming the state with quibbles, there will be more serious charges, such as causing the death of people and the desecration of their tombs.

7   legem! Sed erraverim sane, et, quia nullum in foro nostro iudicium[55] fuit, desuetudine ipsa iura exciderint: quomodo legem meam effugis?[56] 13. Nam, nisi malis stupeo, duo sunt omnino quae in eiusmodi crimine quaeri soleant: an laesa sit res publica, an ab eo qui arguitur laesa. In quibus si quid tibi fiduciae fuisset, non a criminibus crimina appellares, nec ad alteram poenam transfugeres, sed te ab hac, quae intenditur, tuereris.

2   Dico laesam esse rem publicam. Oratione hic opus est, aut[57] reliquorum more accusatorum hoc nunc mihi quae-

3   rendum, quomodo res verbis adgravetur? Adeo infirma est calamitatium memoria? Quae si posset excidere, non tamen narranda vobis, sed ostendenda erat ruina publica.

4   Agedum, si videtur, extra portas prospicite squalida arva et spinis obsitas segetes et semesos arborum truncos. Viduis cultore agris errant a fame nostra[58] innocentes ferae, inanes villae sunt et deserta horrea in ruinam procum-

5   bunt. Nullus inversis aratro glebis campus nitet, nullum solum opere renovatur. Iam et in sequentem annum fa-

6   mem timeo. Redite in domos vestras: videbitis noxios focos et ignes tabo cadaverum extinctos et tecta mortibus

---

55 ⟨diu⟩ iud- *Håk.*
56 -ies *vel* -ias *Håk.*
57 *fere* = et (*OLD*² aut *§4*)
58 -ae *Håk.* (*mendo videl. typoth.*)

---

75 The former during the time of hunger (12.4.2), the latter now.
76 Sc., in the way I am conducting my case.
77 Cf. 12.8.2.

escape from both famine and law![75] (7) Suppose however
that I am in error,[76] suppose that, in the absence of hearings in our courts, legal principles themselves have been
forgotten from disuse: all the same, how can you escape
the law I am invoking? 13. For, unless misfortune has
deprived me of my wits, there are just two normal subjects
of inquiry in crimes of this type: whether the state has
been harmed; whether it has been harmed by the accused.
If you had any confidence in your case under these heads,
you would not be invoking one crime against another, or
taking refuge in a second penalty: you would be trying to
ward off the one that threatens you now.

(2) I assert that the state has been harmed. Is a *speech*
needed on this point? Have I now, like every other accuser, to look for a way to make words add weight to facts?
(3) Is the memory of our disaster so feeble? And even if
that memory could slip your minds, I should still not have
to narrate the ruin of our country, but only point to it. (4)
Look, if you will, at the unkempt fields outside the city
gates, the crops overgrown by thorn bushes, the tree
trunks half eaten.[77] In fields bereft of anyone to till them,
there range wild animals, innocent of what our hunger
brought about.[78] The farms are empty, the granaries deserted and falling into ruin. (5) There is no stretch of plain
shining from the plowshare, no soil reinvigorated by man's
labor. Already I fear famine for the coming year too. (6)
Go back to your homes, and you will see guilty hearths,[79]
fires put out by rotting corpses, buildings packed with

[78] Cf. 12.26.7–27.1.
[79] The bodies were cooked there. Contrast Juv. 15.82–87.

gravia;[59] cum maxime inferimus in tumulos ossa insepulta, ducimus opertas exequias et ad sepulturam residua con-
7 feruntur, et tandem cadavera igni permittimus. Ubi vero universas familias fames extinxit—quae pars maxima est—, inanes domus situm ducunt, iacent relictae sine herede sarcinae. Invenitur interim clusa domo conditus dominus, si cuius mors famem evasit, quem rimantes non
8 invenere proximi, qui[60] inter suos ultimus decessit. Quo vos mitto? Ipsam intuemini contionem, unius deficientis speciem tota civitas habet: cavum macie caput et conditos penitus oculos et laxam cutem, nudos labris trementibus dentes, rigentem vultum et destitutas genas et inanes faucium sinus; prona cervix, tergum ossibus inaequale, infernis imaginibus similes, foeda etiam[61] cadavera. Aut si quis talis non est, confiteatur[62] se usque ad saturitatem comedisse. 14. Sua quisque consulat misera praecordia, suum ventrem conscientia gravem. Dic nunc, legate: "Innocens sum, quod ad illum diem veni." At ego propter te nocens sum, quod ad illum diem vixi!
2   Quae comparata nobis mala non delicatas lacrimas habent? Aliquem populum hostilis exercitus intra portas coegit; solet venire ultima obsessis inopia, sed everti certe

---

59 -ida *Franc., sed cf. ThlL* VI.2.2277.9–12
60 ‹aut›/‹vel›/‹sive› qui *Sh. B.*[2] *205, sed* si cuius—decessit *asyndeton trimembre est*
61 iam (*"already"*) *Russ.*[2] *154, sed cf. ThlL* V.2.949.53–70
62 -tet- *Wint.*[7] *154*

---

80 And not to stomachs.
81 Cf. 12.27.5.
82 The members of the assembly.

bodies. This very moment we are carrying unburied bones to burial mounds and conducting covert funerals: remains are being assembled for burial, and at last we are able to commit corpses to the flame.[80] (7) But where whole families have been wiped out by famine (and this is what has happened to most), empty houses are going to rack and ruin. Chattels lie about with no one to inherit them. Sometimes an owner is to be found, hidden away in a shuttered house: one whose dead body eluded the famished, one whom his neighbors did not find when they rummaged about, one who died last of his family.[81] (8) But where am I asking you to go? Look at the people assembled *here*; the whole city has the look of a single dying man: head thin and gaunt, eyes sunken, skin baggy, teeth bared behind trembling lips, expression fixed, cheeks withered, gullet shrunken and empty; neck bowed, back knobbled by protruding bones. They[82] are like ghosts in hell—foul corpses, indeed. Or, if there is an exception, let him confess he has eaten until he could eat no more![83] 14. Let each man consult[84] his own pitiable vitals, his own stomach that is laden with guilty knowledge. Now say, Mr Ambassador: "I am innocent, because I came in time for that day!" For my part, thanks to you, I am guilty because I *lived* until that day!

(2) What misfortunes, when compared to ours, do not call forth tears that are merely a luxury? Suppose a hostile army has confined the citizen body within its gates; the besieged often suffer extreme shortage of food, but at least

[83] I.e., not just enough to stay alive: this person would be then even more guilty than the others.

[84] I.e., as to whether he is guilty.

licet: victor captivum aut occidet aut pascet. Tormenta
quidam piratarum tulerunt; felices, quibus contigit inno-
3 centia! Mors certe finis est, nec saevitia ultra fata procedit.
Aut etiamsi quis adeo hominem exuit, ut ibi poenam quaerat, ubi sensus doloris non inveniat, nempe tamen cada-
4 vera feris obiciet. Circumdati sunt quidam flammis, ipsa
tamen poena habuit sepulturam. Nos incendii cinerem
perdidimus, nostra etiam ruina tabuit. Nostra mala nunc
latent: non ignis defunctos cremavit, non ferae lacera-
verunt, non aves attigerunt, et tamen cadavera mortibus
5 adnumerare non possumus. Citra spem convalescendi
adflicti sumus, immo etiam citra votum. Gravior in dies
facti paenitentia est, pudet vitae, lucem ac sidera intueri
6 non audeo. Cotidie felices mortuos clamo, et malae conscientiae facibus agitatus nihil fortunatius in aeterna sede
utcumque compositis puto. Adeo mors placet: iam etiam
7 cibis nostris invideo! Praeterita differo; ipsa ex nimia cupiditate nocet habundantia. Desideratos diu cibos avide
haurimus, et lassam famem saturitate strangulamus. Morimur adhuc etiam frumento tuo.

15. Atqui ceterae rei publicae partes, quae sunt ad
usum populi comparatae, et leviore cum damni sensu
pereunt et facile remedium accipiunt, cum reparari possit
amissum: opera restituam, aerarium replebo, naves, arma

---

85 I.e., if he does seek to exercise his cruelty on the dead.

86 And not to (be eaten by) other human beings.

87 As we ate the corpses, rather than commit them to the funerary pyres.

they can allow the place to be sacked: the victor will either kill or feed his prisoner. Some have suffered torture from pirates; lucky people—they kept their innocence! (3) Death is certainly the end, and cruelty cannot go further than one's natural term. Even if someone so casts off his humanity that he looks to punish where he does not find a feeling of pain,[85] surely he will throw the bodies to the beasts.[86] (4) Some people have been encircled by flames; but the penalty itself involved burial. *We* have lost the ashes left behind by the funeral fire,[87] even our ruin has disappeared. Our ills are now hidden: fire did not burn up the dead, wild animals did not rip them apart, birds did not touch them; yet we cannot make the number of bodies tally with the number of deaths. (5) We have been afflicted without hope of recovery, even without any wish for it. Heavier by the day grows the burden of remorse; I am ashamed to live, I do not venture to look upon the sunlight or the stars at night. (6) Every day I cry aloud that the dead are the lucky ones: as the brands of a bad conscience harry me, I think none more fortunate than those laid, by whatever means, in their everlasting abode. See how much the thought of death pleases me: now I envy even what fed us! (7) Putting aside the past: even our present plenty does us harm, for it makes us overgreedy. We avidly gulp down the food we were without for so long, and throttle our weary hunger by filling ourselves too full. We still go on dying, even thanks to your grain.

15. Now, all other parts of the state that are put in place for the public use cause less sense of loss if they perish, and are easier to remedy, for what has been lost is capable of being repaired: I shall rebuild public works, replenish the treasury, renew the stock of ships and weap-

2 reficiam. Hic vulnus altissime penetrat, hic ipsa vitalia
feriuntur, ubi populus ruit, ubi continuis funeribus omnis
3 sexus atque aetas semel[63] sternitur. Exhausta est civitas et
desolatae domus, triste florentis quondam fortunae indicium laxi muri. Quam multi in civitate nostra perierint
quaeritis? Minima quidem portio est, sed etiam ex hoc
intellegi potest: esurienti populo satis fuerunt.
4 Plurimum tamen interest quomodo perierint. Felix
pestilentia, felix proeliorum strages, denique omnis mors
facilis! Fames aspera vitalia haurit, praecordia carpit,
animi tormentum, corporis tabes, magistra peccandi, du-
5 rissima necessitatium, deformissima malorum. Haec ad
humile opus nobiles manus mittit, haec alienis pedibus
mendicantes prosternit, haec saepe sociorum fidem fregit,
haec venena populis publice dedit, haec in parricidium
6 pios egit. Adhuc tamen unum videbatur remedium, non
expectare mortis diem et tabescentem cotidie spiritum
supervenientibus malis subducere; iam[64] in fame ne
mors[65] quidem mortis[66] immunis est.
7 At non tua culpa fames coepit; sed vulneratum iugu-
lasti, titubantem stravisti, fumantem incendisti. Ne quid
inique faciam, dividenda sunt mala: primam famem fortunae imputo, ultimam tibi; moram tuam itineribus separo;

[63] simul *vDorp 41b, sed cf. OLD*[2] semel §5

[64] iam *scripsi* (*cf. e.g. ad sensum 13.11.2, ad mendum 3.18.7*):
nam *codd.*: nunc *Str.*[4]

[65] ne mors *Str.*[4]: nemo *codd.*

[66] mortis ⌐ (*vind. Wint.*[7] *154*): mortibus *codd.*: (nunc in f.
nemo q.) morsibus *Pas.*[1] *571*

ons. (2) The wound goes deepest, the very vitals are struck, when the *populace* succumbs, when men and women, old and young, are mown down together in an endless succession of funerals. (3) The city is exhausted, homes made desolate, the walls—sad evidence of a once flourishing state—are too wide for it. Do you ask how many died in our city? Only a tiny proportion is left; but one can also judge from the fact that those who died were enough to feed a hungry people.

(4) Yet what makes all the difference is *how* they perished. Fortunate is an epidemic, fortunate carnage in war, in fact every easy death! Cruel hunger drains the vitals, preys on the innards; it is the mind's torture, the body's destruction, teacher of wrong doing; of necessities the harshest, of evils the ugliest. (5) It is this that dispatches noble hands to do humble work, this that forces beggars to grovel at the feet of strangers, this that has often made allies break faith, this that has poisoned whole peoples, this that has driven dutiful children to commit parricide. (6) But till now *one* cure seemed to be available:[88] to refuse to await death, to withdraw one's spirit, daily wasting away, from the ills that threatened to follow; now instead, in a famine, not even death is exempt from death!

(7) True, it was not your fault that the famine began; but you cut the throat of one already wounded, felled one already staggering, set on fire one already smoldering. To play fair, I shall divide up our misfortunes. The first famine I blame on fortune, the final one on you. I distinguish

---

[88] Suicide was an honorable option before our city set this precedent; from now on, killing oneself will only lead to cannibalism.

denique ex eo inopiam tibi obicio, ex quo propter te tuli.
8 Itaque caritas annonae, rarum frumentum, caedes ac di-
reptio pecorum fuerint fortunae, fuerint anni, fuerint
temporum; aliam condicionem habent civium mortes et
cadaverum dira laceratio et peiores inopia cibi. Haec fames iam tua est!

16. Puta me nihil in praesentia dicere[67] nisi hoc unum:
tardius quam potueras venisti. Nondum tibi obicio dupli-
cata tempora nec remensum totiens mare nec graves anco-
2 ras, nondum tantam moram quanta legationi satis esset. Si
innocentes essemus, populum septem diebus perdidisses:
3 angustos humani spiritus terminos fames fecit. Morimur,
defecimus;[68] festina misericors, omnes excipe auras;
etiamsi tota secundis flatibus vela tetenderint venti, tamen
remis adiuva. Salutem publicam vehis, spiritum populi tui
reportas, omnium nostrum in ista classe navigant animae.
4 Iuramus per tuum reditum, effusi per gradus templorum
vota suscipimus, tendimus manus—nam quas feriamus
hostias non habemus. Quid spem publicam ad ancoras
alligas? Non stat interim dies, et plenis velis mors venit.
5 Festina; merita tua non conditores aequaverint, non ipsi

[67] in praesenti adicere Φ
[68] -fec- V AD HJO[ac]: -fic- cett. (quo tamen anticlimax fit)

[89] The journeys were those from A to B and from B to C; the
(culpable) delay was at C.
[90] The final delay at city C (which was, in fact, an additional
mission that his original assignment did not include).
[91] A reason for the envoy to hurry: starvation would have
killed his people in seven days (12.8.9 with n. 49), if they had not
fed on human corpses.

between your journeys and your delay.[89] In sum, I accuse you of causing the shortage from the moment I began to suffer from it because of you. (8) So let the high price of food supplies, the shortage of grain, the wholesale slaughter of animals be put down to fortune, to the season, to circumstances; in a different category are the deaths of citizens, the dreadful butchering of corpses, food worse than lack of food. Now this is *your* famine!

16. Suppose I say nothing for the moment beyond this one thing: you came later than you could have done. I am not yet accusing you of taking twice the time, or of the crisscrossing of the sea, or of weighing anchor so reluctantly; not yet of a delay that would have sufficed for a complete embassy.[90] (2) If we had remained innocent, you would have destroyed the people in seven days: starvation contracts the bounds of human life.[91] (3) We are dying, our strength has failed; hurry, for pity's sake, ensure you catch every breeze. Even if favorable winds billow out your sails to the full, help them with oars. You carry with you the safety of the state, you are bringing back with you your people's breath of life, the souls of every one of us sail in that fleet of yours. (4) We are swearing oaths by your return; spread about on the steps of the temples, we are taking vows and raising our hands in supplication—for as to animals to sacrifice, we have none. Why do you tie your people's hopes to your anchors?[92] Time is not standing still, and *death* is approaching under full sail.[93] (5) Hurry: your services will prove to surpass those of our founding

92 Cf. 12.16.1.
93 Unlike you.

dii plus praestiterint. Tibi nos, tibi liberos nostros, tibi
quicquid homini iocundum est, tibi debemus[69] quicquid
6   vicinae civitati praestitisti. Non dico illa quae poteram:
"Puta caerulus imber in naves ruit, classis inter fluctus
latet, nec inter canentes collisarum aquarum spumas vela
dinoscimus; egerit ex fundo harenas mare, micant ignes,
intonat caelum, scissis rudentibus tempestas sibilat, denique sidus hibernum conditur; tu tamen persevera: frumentum vehis." Nihil horum necesse est feliciter navi-
7   ganti. Festina; quererer, si naves[70] commeatu tardasses:
dum velocitatis ratio haberetur, mallem accipere dimi-
dium. 17. Non delicati sumus, non luxuriae quaeritur
abundantia: unde spiritum sustineamus, unde mortem
differamus in praesentia quantulumcumque; si plus opus
fuerit, redibis.
2   Siccae fauces sunt, aeger anhelitus os tendit. Iam frustra in sinu parentium liberi plorant, et nondum editi
conceptus intra uterum famem sentiunt; iam nemo dives
est. Auras captamus et rore vescimur, et iam spirare[71] tor-
3   mentum est. Cotidie vires deficiunt: iam non imus in litus,
sed repimus;[72] in editis scopulis populus sedet dum naves
expectat, in pascua non redit. Aquas ingredimur et unus

[69] -ebim- *Reitz.*[2] *17, sed vd. Håk. et Str.*[4]
[70] <nimio> na- *Reitz.*[2] *17*
[71] spir- A[pc] (*cf. 12.18.9*): sper- *cett.*
[72] repi- *Håk.*[2] *101–2*: redi- *codd.*

94 City C. Sarcastic: cf. 12.6.5.
95 I.e., the stars that guide the navigator in winter, when
storms are more frequent. If the sky is clouded, those stars are
not visible and sailors lose their only guide.

48

fathers, not even the gods themselves will have done more for us. We are indebted to you for ourselves, for our children, for everything that is dear to men; we are indebted to you for everything you did for—our neighbor city.[94] (6) I am not saying what I might have said: "Suppose a grim storm falls on your ships, suppose the fleet disappears in the waves and we cannot catch sight of the sails amid the white foam of the clashing waters; suppose the sea stirs sand up from the bottom, lightning flashes, the heavens thunder, the storm whistles as the rigging snaps, and—on top of it all—the winter constellation is out of sight:[95] carry on for all that, your cargo is *grain*." None of this need be said to someone on a *fortunate* voyage. (7) Hurry! I should complain if you had slowed up the ships by the weight of provisions. So long as speed was your priority, I should rather have received a half. 17. We are not fussy, we aren't looking for a surfeit of luxury: just for a little, now, to keep us alive, to delay death. If more is needed, you will go back there again.[96]

(2) Throats are dry, laboring breath makes the mouth hang open. Now children cry in vain in their parents' arms, and fetuses not yet come to birth feel hunger in the womb; now no one is rich. We gasp for air, and feed on dew: and now it is an agony to breathe. (3) Every day our strength decreases: now we do not walk down to the shore, we crawl. The populace sits on the cliff-tops while they wait for the ships; they go back no more to the pastures.[97] We

[96] But more will *not* be needed, as there are now so few to feed (DAR).

[97] I.e., looking for some last root to eat (cf. 12.7.6).

ad te spectantium rictus est, et, cum defecerunt omnia,
expirant. Te, te expectantes intentis oculis morimur;[73] in
4   mare mortui cadunt.[74] Quotiens sole percussa nubes re-
fulsit, navem putamus; quotiens fractus vento fluctus in-
canuit, vela interpretamur. O mobiles miserorum spes:
ad unaquaeque solacia ab unoquoque quomodo nutant![75]
5   "Haec certe navis est; ecce vela panduntur, propius appel-
litur et accedendo crescit. Nostra est, suos in utramque
partem ventos habuit, nostris votis gubernati flatus sunt."
6   Haec dicimus, at illa interim transvolat. Fletus inde et
desperatio et lucis odium; nihil enim gravius quam desti-
7   tutae spes torquent. Ne interrogare quidem licuit aut
quaerere: nemo applicabat. Ergo incerti omnium rerum
pependimus, nihil quisquam cognovit. Saltem si scire li-
8   cuisset ubi frumentum vendidisses, ipsi petissemus. Iam
quomodo ad singula momenta temporum mutabantur
animi! "Bene est, serenus sol occidit, purus se dies tollit,
ad nos venti ferunt; iam veniet." 18. Pendet interim fames,
et illud, quod iam diu cogitat, differt, ita tamen, ut subinde
2   computet quot dies ad mortem supersint. "Numquid[76]
profecit?"[77] Meministis, cum contrarii venti flare coe-
pissent et in altum fluctus a terra volarent, quanta complo-

---

    [73] *sic dist. Wint.*[7] *154.2*

    [74] *personarum grammat. vices* (ingredimur . . . expirant . . .
morimur . . . cadunt) *def. Wint.*[7] *154*

    [75] mu- A (*unde* mutantur *Håk. post Bur.*), *sed vd. Str.*[4] *et Pas.*[1]
570

    [76] numquid *Sch.*: num quidem B V δ: nam quidem (quid E)
π γ β

    [77] *verba personata agn. Sh. B.*[2] *206*

wade into the water, and the mouths of those watching for
you gape open as one; when all remaining strength is gone,
men breathe their last. As we wait for you, yes, you, straining our eyes, we die; the dead fall into the sea. (4) Whenever a cloud glints in the sun, we think it is a ship; whenever a wave shines white as the wind breaks it, we make it
out to be sails. How changeable the hopes of the wretched,
how they waver from one means of comfort to another! (5)
"This is a ship, surely. Look, the sails are full set, it is getting nearer: the closer it comes, the bigger it is. It is one
of ours, it has had fair winds both ways, they have blown
as our prayers steered them." (6) That is what we say—but
meanwhile the ship goes past. Hence laments, despair,
loathing of life: for there is no worse torture than frustrated hopes. (7) We could not even ask questions and seek
information: no one put in. So we were in suspense, in
complete uncertainty; no one knew anything. If we could
at least have learned where you sold the grain, we'd have
gone to look for it ourselves. (8) At this stage, how our
spirits shifted back and forth from one moment to another! "All is well: the sun set with no clouds in the sky, a
clear day is coming up, the wind is blowing our way. *Now*
he will come." 18. Meanwhile famine looms over us, and
keeps putting off what it has long been planning, while
leaving room for the constant calculation how many days
remain till death.[98] (2) "*Has* he made progress?" You certainly remember, when the winds began to turn round and
the waves started rolling out to sea, what weeping and

[98] Cf. nn. 49 and 91.

[QUINTILIAN]

3   ratio, quanti planctus fuerint.[78] "Retinebitur, stabit, labo-
rabit." At, si diis placet, legatus noster tum maxime bene
navigabat.

4   Nos in hac fortuna, in tam gravi casu, in eiusmodi cogi-
tationibus sumus; tu sinus maris circuis, et per omnis cur-
5 vatorum litorum ambitus terram legis. Sic fit ut te iuvet
diu navigare: nullus amoenus praetermittitur portus, nulla
celebris civitas invisitata transitur. Mentior?[79] Etiam ad
6 esurientis adplicas. Dein, si quam tu maris[80] iniuriam queraris,[81] non feram te morantem; quomodo satis accusabo
vendentem? Spiritus nostros transcribis, salutem nostram
exponis; quae diu inaestimabilis fuit, innocentiam publicam vendis. Frumentum non naufragio perdidimus, non
7 latrocinio: lucro perîmus! Tempestas quoque aliquam
navem in meum litus impingeret, nec[82] ex classe numerosa
omnes fluctus exhausisset. Perît frumentum quia classis
8 venit in portum! Ita nos alienae civitati[83] legatum misimus,
9 et vilia ac devota capita vicinorum deliciis morimur. Nobis
nihil iam residui spiritus superest, nos in conspectu mortis
stamus, nos legatum frumentumque nostrum ore aperto

---

[78] *plene distinxi*   [79] *interrog. dist. Håk.*
[80] tu maris *Bur. (firm. Håk.[2] 102)*: timoris (-res P) *codd.*
[81] -rar- *L. Greco ap. Str.[4]*: -rerer- V E: -rer- *cett.*
[82] nec *Sch.*: et *codd.*
[83] -i ⁵ (*cf. 12.3.2*): -is *codd.*

---

[99] As the winds started to blow in the opposite direction to
what was supposed to be the envoy's route home, people would
anxiously ask if the man was still managing to advance (AS).

[100] Because the envoy was not sailing home but in the opposite direction, going back to buy the second load of grain.

wailing there was.[99] (3) "He'll be delayed, he'll be stuck, he'll be in trouble." But, heaven help us, that was when our envoy was having a fair voyage.[100]

(4) *We* are in this plight, in such a grave situation, turning over thoughts like this; *you* are circling the inlets of the sea, hugging the shore along all the twists and turns of the coast. (5) That is how you get to enjoy such a long voyage: no pleasant port is neglected, no famous city is passed unvisited. Am I not telling the truth? You even put in where people are starving![101] (6) Further: if you were complaining of being harmed by the sea,[102] I should not tolerate you delaying; how then shall I accuse you with sufficient vehemence for *selling*? You are making over our lives to others, putting our safety up for sale; you are selling the innocence of the public, which had long been beyond price.[103] We lost the grain not by shipwreck, not by piracy: we perished for profit! (7) Even a storm would drive *some* ship on to my shore: the tossing sea would not have cost us *all* the ships of that great fleet. The grain was lost because the fleet made harbor! (8) So, it seems, the envoy we sent was accredited to another city, and now we die, valueless and doomed, to keep our neighbors pampered. (9) Our breath is quite gone, we stand in full view of death, open-mouthed[104] we await our envoy and our

---

[101] At city C: he was not afraid that the starving people would take the grain from him (12.22.5–6). Compare the different fate of city A, where no one would put in (12.17.7).

[102] Cf. 12.5.4.

[103] His delay caused the people to lose their long-prized reputation for innocence, and act so criminally.

[104] Cf. 12.17.3.

expectamus; classis nostra vecturam facit et vicinarum ci-
vitatum copias reconducit. Paene a conspectu nostro vela
conversa sunt: quantulo minus quam congesti[84] frumenti
10 pulverem vidimus! Tantum iam temporis transiit ex quo
pecuniam contulimus, legatum creavimus. Iam dinumera-
tis temporibus, quae secundi venti breviora fecerunt, cotidie spero—et sane prope est. At legatus meus ad emendum modo proficiscitur. 19. Tibi ergo tot civium mortis
imputo, tibi stragem populi, tibi liberum[85] parentumque
miserrimas poenas, tibi quicquid passi sumus, tibi—quod
gravius est—quicquid fecimus.

2   Et scilicet speras ut tantam sceleris invidiam ab animis
nostris duplae pecuniae strepitus avertat? Nescis quam
3 multa vendideris. "Duplo vendidi." Ita infelicitas mea
cocionanti[86] tibi lenocinata est? "Quod fame perire cives
meos patior, quod, ut vestram civitatem servem, meam
everto, quod a tam vicinis litoribus classem torqueo, quod
ad diem redire non possum,[87] quod pretium constituitis,
quid[88] occultum datis? Duplum? Patrocinio meo quantu-
4 lum lucror!"[89] At nos inepti ac vesani de fame querebamur,

---

[84] congesti ς: comesti (-edis- E) *codd.*: convecti *Hâk.*
[85] -rum B β (*cf. Leu. 428*): -rorum V $\gamma^* \delta$
[86] cociona- *Dess.[1] 73 (cf. ad 12.21.6)*: conciona- B V δ: negotia-
$\gamma^* \beta$ [87] V β^* *hic habent* quod prope civium constitit
discrimen, *e seq.* quod pretium constituitis (*quae om.* V) *nimirum
ortum (Reitz.[2] 14)*   [88] quod V Φ [89] *sic dist. Str.[4]*

---

[105] Sarcastic.   [106] Cf. 12.19.3.
[107] In city B, on the way back.
[108] Such as the lives of those who starved to death, and the
innocence of those who committed cannibalism.

grain. Our ships are plying as freight-carriers—they are under contract for the provisioning of neighboring cities.[105] Their course was altered almost within our sight:[106] how very close we were to seeing the dust rising from the grain heaped up in the holds! (10) It is so long since that we raised the money, named the envoy. Now, reckoning up the time, which fair winds have made shorter, I feel hope each day: and surely he is near—but my envoy is only just setting out to buy.[107] 19. So it is you I blame for the deaths of so many of my fellow citizens, you for the decimation of our people, you for the appalling sufferings meted out to children and parents, you for all we underwent, you—what is more serious—for all we *did*.

(2) And no doubt you hope that we shall be diverted from all the odium of your crime by the fuss you are making about the double price. You don't know how many things you sold![108] (3) "I sold at twice the price." So my misfortune worked in your favor as you haggled?[109]— "Because I allow my fellow citizens to die of hunger, because, to save your city, I ruin my own, because I diverted my fleet away from shore when it was so near,[110] because I am now unable to return on the day appointed:[111] what is your price for all this, what bribe will you slip me? Double? Not much to help pay for my defense counsel!" (4) Yet there we were, foolish creatures and out of our

---

[109] What follows is the alleged negotiation in city C: the envoy used the sufferings of his fellow citizens (for which the grain was intended) to sell at a higher price.   [110] Cf. 12.18.9.

[111] The envoy *was* actually able to return on the day appointed: he wants the buyer (in city C) to believe that he will not be able to do so, in order to ask for a higher price.

[QUINTILIAN]

gravis nobis inopia, intolerabilis et misera accersita mors
videbatur. Non agimus gratias industriae legati? Res pu-
5 blica nostra locupletior perit. Sacrosanctus mercator opor-
tunum, opinor, invenit mercis exactum. Miror hercules, si
tam bene negotium gesseras, quomodo nobis pecuniam
6 non retuleris. "Duplo vendidi."[90] Decepisti vicinam civi-
7 tatem, circumscripsisti; itaque queritur? "Duplo vendidi."
Hoc enim unum supererat, ut devectum tantidem ven-
8 deres! "Habita est itineris ratio, habita usurarum." Ego
vero malo quod tam magno vendidisti; apparet enim te
nihil coactum.
9   Sed si semel ponis hastam salutis, si redemptores vitae
admittis, et nos admone: melius vendis. Nos quicquid in
domibus habemus, quicquid in templis, quicquid civitas
10 suum vocat, congerere parati sumus. Frumentum pecunia
remetimur,[91] libertatem nostram addicimus, fines publicos tradimus. Omnia licet eadem vicina civitas polliceatur,
plus non potest. 20. Prosit mihi quod apud negotiatores

90 B ACD *hic corrupte iterant 12.19.3–5 ita infelicitas*—invenit (*vd. Håk., Str.*[4])   91 -im- *Reitz.*[2] 12: -iam- *codd.*

112 We kept complaining about hunger, as suicide seemed a
worse option (cf. 12.15.6).
113 He is inviolable *qua* ambassador (cf. *Decl. min.* 366), yet
he is betraying the city's trust by acting as an avid—and dishon-
est—merchant.   114 You deceived city C to our advantage
(cf. 12.10.3). But they are not complaining: thanks to you, they
have avoided hunger—unlike us (AS).
115 Sc., as you paid for it. You shouldn't have been selling at
all, though a lower price would have made it even worse.
116 The legate claims that he was not profiteering, but just

minds, lamenting our hunger; lack of food seemed to us a heavy burden, but suicide[112] an unbearable and sorry recourse. Aren't we grateful to our zealous envoy?—our state is perishing, but wealthier! (5) Our sacrosanct[113] merchant, I suppose, found a good moment to dispose of his cargo. If you bargained so well, I am really surprised you didn't bring us the money back. (6) "I sold at twice the price." You deceived our neighbors, you conned them: are they complaining?[114] (7) "I sold at twice the price." All that was lacking was for you to sell your load at the *same* price![115] (8) "The cost of the voyage was reckoned in, and the interest too."[116] In fact I *prefer* you to have sold for such a high price:[117] it is clear you were not acting under duress.

(9) But if you once conduct an auction in salvation, if you once open the door to contractors in life,[118] let us know too: you will make a better sale.[119] We are ready to get together everything we have in our houses, everything in the temples, everything the city calls its own. (10) We pay money for grain—weight for weight—, we knock down our freedom, we hand over public estates. Our neighbor[120] may promise all the same things, but it cannot promise more. 20. Let me benefit from the consideration

covering his costs. The speaker replies that this is an argument *against* him: it shows he was not—as he says he was—under duress (cf. 12.20.3, 12.21.6), for in that case he could *not* have got such a high price.   [117] For it helps my argument.

[118] Sc., admit them to the negotiation. Cf. 12.3.2.

[119] = we will give you a better price than city C. The speaker proceeds to describe the auction, with his own city bidding against the other.   [120] City C.

solet: in antecessus[92] dedi. Triplum, quadruplum, quantum poposceris accipe, et illa pecunia frumentum licet[93]
2 vicinis adferas. Si nobis nihil de commeatu nostro partiris, nos vicinae civitati vendemus;[94] liceat servire, ubi frumentum est. Non exigua res est: pro vita, pro sepultura, pro innocentia licemur. Non potest hic commeatus tam care emi quam expectari.

3 "Sed nisi vendidissem" inquit "fame laboranti civitati, timui ne raperet." Et ita utique occupare voluisti, ut nobis
4 iniuriam tu potissimum faceres? Multum mehercules vos fallit opinio, iudices, si ullam causam ita evidentem deferri posse in forum putatis, cui nulla ne mendacii quidem velamenta contingant. Opinione sua defenditur, et, quae res
5 minime coargui potest, utitur se teste! Ne nos periremus, non timuisti; ne repetiti commeatus post diem nostrae mortis applicarentur, non timuisti. Nostris certe malis quamquam nihil poterat accedere[95] inopinatum, tamen inter metus tempestatium et ancipites incerti maris casus, confiteor, ne frumentum salva classe perderemus non ti-
6 muimus. Non dico: "Ut maxima vis parata sit, ut more immanis latrocinii turba raptorum litus premat, vel repugna vel fuge vel roga, incensurum naves depressu-

[92] -um *Reitz.²* 12, sed vd. *Str.⁴*
[93] licet <et> *Wint.⁷ 155*
[94] *an* vende (*Reitz.²* 14), nos? [95] -ced- *scripsi (cf. 5.1.1, 6.1.6, 7.1.1, 13.1.3, 14.1.1, al.)*: -cid- *codd.*

[121] Cf. 12.6.2.
[122] The cost of waiting being cannibalism.
[123] If he had let them seize the cargo, *they* would have been responsible for his country's troubles. As it is, *he* is (DAR).

that normally holds in trading: I paid a deposit.[121] Triple, quadruple, take as much as you ask: with that money you may bring grain to our neighbors. (2) If you share with us nothing of cargo that belongs to us, we'll sell ourselves to the city next door; we are content to be slaves, where there is grain. It is no small matter: we are bidding for life, for burial, for innocence. These provisions cannot cost so much to buy as it costs to wait for them.[122]

(3) "But," he says, "if I had not sold the grain to a city suffering from famine, I was afraid they'd take it from me." So then you wanted to forestall this, in order that *you* in particular could do *us* an injury?[123] (4) You are very much mistaken, judges, if you think that any case, even as clear cut as this one, can be presented in court without at least *some* veil of lies being attached to it. This man defends himself by appeal to his own view of the situation, using himself (something that admits of no refutation) as his own witness! (5) So you weren't afraid that we might perish; you weren't afraid that the second supply[124] of provisions might arrive after we were all dead. Though, to be sure, nothing could be added to our suffering that we did not expect, yet amid the fears of storms and the uncertainties of the treacherous sea, I confess, we were not afraid we might lose our grain with our fleet intact. (6) I don't say: "Granted that a huge force is deployed there, granted that a crowd of looters hems you in on the shore like a huge band of brigands, fight back or flee or beg, threaten you

---

[124] The second cargo he bought at city B, after selling the first one at C.

rumque minitare."⁹⁶ Potius quam totum frumentum utique populo pereat,⁹⁷ partire vel gratis, dum nobis aliquid,
quo respiremus, adferas. Illud quo certe nihil asperius
7 accideret, rapi, patere. Faciat fortuna quod voluerit: legatus a praecepto non recedat. 21. Refer saltem nobis⁹⁸ iniuriam nostram, mitte nuntios; ira famem differemus, rapie-
mus furentes arma et se in obsidionem civitatis inimicae
2 sine dilectu populus effundet. Vastabo interim fines: hoc
est, per aliena prata pascar; si qua in villis deprehendero
pecora, diripiam. Bellum me alet. Citius ad frumentum
3 perveniemus quam tu cum frumento redibis. Adiuvabunt
pugnantem iusta sacramenta. Si contigerit aequum fortunae iudicium, non meos tantum commeatus recipiam; si
4 minus, certe dabitur bene mori. Liceat et manum conserere, in acie⁹⁹ confligere: condant se postea licet muris, in
longius obsidio eat, interim certe hostium potius cadaveribus vivemus.
5   Sed nulla vis fuit, nulla exterior iniuria; tuum certe
commeatum nemo rapuit. Iure miseri sumus et ex stipu-
6 latu legati nostri perimus. Vendidit quantum voluit quanti
voluit, et, ut hoc ad nostras accederet moras, fortasse diu

---

⁹⁶ *verba personata hic finit Wint.*⁹
⁹⁷ minitare—pereat *dist. Best 160–61*
⁹⁸ r. saltem n. V (saltem *imperativum subsequitur 6.9.4,
7.12.3, 8.18.6, 10.4.5*): r. n. salutem B E δ: r. n. saltem *cett.*
⁹⁹ -e ς (*def. Sh. B.*⁴ *205, Pas.*¹ *571*): -em *codd.*

---

¹²⁵ He is *not* advising the use of force, which would risk loss
of the grain. What he *does* advise is negotiation aimed at saving
at least part of the grain for city A.
¹²⁶ I.e., think of our anger before our hunger.

DECLAMATION 12

will burn the ships or scuttle them."[125] Rather than see the
whole cargo of grain lost to our people in any case, give
some of it away, so long as you bring us something to en-
able us to go on drawing breath. Or—the worst possible
eventuality—let yourself be robbed. (7) Fortune may do
what it will: the envoy must not disobey instructions. 21.
At least tell us the injury we have been done, send messages; in our anger we shall put off feeling hungry,[126] in
our rage we shall snatch up arms, and the people will pour
out to besiege an enemy city without waiting to be re-
cruited. (2) Meanwhile, I shall lay their lands waste: that
is, I shall look for food in someone else's pastures; if I come
upon any cattle in the farms, I shall rustle them. War will
feed me. We shall arrive at grain quicker than you will
come back with grain.[127] (3) In my fight I shall be aided
by the justice of our cause. If fortune's judgment is fair, I
shall get not just my share of provisions; if not, at least I
shall be granted a good death.[128] (4) Let me even join
battle, clash in the field: they may proceed to hide themselves behind their walls, the siege may drag on, but at
least we shall in the meantime be able to live off the enemy's bodies rather than our own.

(5) But in fact there was no violence, no injury from
without; no one, for sure, *seized* your grain. No, we are
wretched quite legally, and perish as the result of what our
envoy stipulated. (6) He sold as much as he wished at the
price he wished—and, to add to the delay for us, he per-

[127] If the neighbors rob your cargo, it will be faster for us to
take it back by force of arms than for you to go and buy another
cargo and bring that to us.
[128] At least, better than dying of starvation.

61

cocionatus[100] est. Omnis cum fide persoluta pecunia est. Hoc qui colligo? Qui quanti voluit[101] vendit, iudices, po-
7 test non vendere. Nam, per fidem, si rapere alienum frumentum et possunt et volunt, quid ita duplam pecuniam solvunt? Nam quomodo in magna inopia quicquid emi potest vile est, ita, cum possis habere gratuitum, duplo carum est.
8 Sed mihi credite: color iste patrocinii est et diu in saturo otio cogitata defensio. Non potest similis usquam[102] fames fuisse. 22. Nos grave huius anni sidus adflavit, nostrum hoc fatum fuit, quos non tantum sata sed etiam empta fallunt, qui nostra pecunia, nostra classe, nostro legato, nostro vento, felicissimo cursu, commeatum tamen
2 perdidimus. Nos a frumento longius sumus; ad illam civitatem potuit frequenter accedere negotiator, saepius adplicari onusta classis. Itaque non misere legatos, nullus illis commeatus longius petendus fuit: quod felicissima annona, affluentibus copiis, fortunatis opibus contingit,[103]
3 nihil emerunt nisi devectum. Quare nulla causa istius, quem fingis, metus fuit, nulla utique vis. Forum legisti, et, quia adhuc supererat tempus, obiter negotiatus es.
4 "Rapturos putavi." Quid dicis, scelerate? Et, cum hoc

100 coc- *Salm. 346 (cf. ad 12.19.3)*: conc- *vel* cont- *codd.*
101 vult V β*   102 umq- B, *sed vd. Reitz.*[2] *16.1*
103 -ing- E: -ig- *cett.*

129 It feels doubly expensive to buy something you could take for nothing.   130 I.e., city C was not in as hard a plight as we were in, and would not have gone so far as to wish to seize the grain: you chose to sell it there because you knew it was a favorable market (12.22.2–3).

haps took a long time over his haggling. All the money was duly paid over. How do I deduce all that? When someone sells at the price he wanted, judges, he is free not to sell. (7) For, believe me, if they are both able and willing to steal grain belonging to others, why then do they pay double the price? For as in a great shortage everything that can be bought is felt to be cheap, so when you might have it free, it is twice as costly.[129]

(8) But trust me, this is only a rhetorical ploy to color your defense, a plea mulled over in well-fed leisure. There can nowhere else have been a famine like ours.[130] 22. *We* have been blighted by the baleful star that presides over this year, this was *our* destiny. We are being failed by what we bought as well as what we sowed. Despite our money, our fleet, our envoy, our own wind, and a most prosperous voyage—we have lost our supplies. (2) We are further[131] away from sources of grain, whereas a trader could have reached that city many times over, a laden fleet might often have put in there. That is why they did not send envoys—they did not have to look for food from afar: as happens when the grain supply is at a peak, when the stores are brim-full, when wealth abounds, they bought only imported goods. (3) Therefore you had no reason for the fear you pretend you felt, and certainly there was no force. You chose your market and, because you still had time to spare, you did some business on the side.

(4) "I thought they would take it from me." What are you saying, you villain? You feared that, yet you put in

---

[131] Sc., than city C, which is also meant in what follows.

5 timeres, adplicabas? Onustus viator apud latrones hospi-
taris, commeatum publicum in scopulos annonae impin-
gis, et plenae frumento classis ancoras ad famem ducis?
6 Non praecides[104] medium mare, non velut inhospitales
Syrtis aut voracem Charybdim praetervehens[105] tota in
fugam vela torquebis? Nusquam est periculosius legatio-
7 nis tuae naufragium. Tu, ut cogi posses,[106] tu, ut auferri
frumentum posset, effecisti. Tantum habituri sumus
8 quantum reliquerit pudor esurientium. Quid te duplo
frumentum iactas vendidisse? Potuerunt nihil solvere;
quod[107] refers, alienum beneficium est.
9   Alterum confingitur hoc loco mendacium: 23. "Tempestate" inquit "appulsus sum." Ita plane: infelix navigator
es, et cuius votis aurae non respondeant. Nescimus te
duplo melius navigasse quam speraveramus, nescimus singulis commeatibus bina itinera confecta, nescimus in una
2 legatione ventos quater secundos? Sat erat verbo negare
quod verbo ponitur: remove hanc spem eludendae mendacio civitatis! Quo damno probas tempestatem, quid
3 amisisti? Frumentum certe totum venit in portum, nec

104 -des ς (vind. Wint.[7] 155): -dis codd.
105 -hens Plas. 16 (firm. Håk.[2] 103–4): -heris codd.
106 -es E (def. Str.[4]): -et cett.
107 quod π: quid cett.: <quic>quid Dess.[2]

---

132 If city C was as hungry as the envoy claims, that was all the
more reason for him to steer clear of it: they might have taken all
his grain away without even paying for it.
133 See n. 26.
134 Since he accomplished twice the distance in the given
time, he had twice as good a voyage (DAR).

there? (5) Are you, a traveler heavy-laden, prepared to lodge with thieves, to wreck the public supplies on the rocks of a grain-shortage, and to moor a fleet full of grain in a famine-port? (6) Won't you take a short cut over the open sea? Won't you go about and take to flight, under full sail, as though you were sailing past the inhospitable Syrtes and greedy Charybdis? Nowhere else is your embassy in more danger of shipwreck.[132] (7) *You* brought it about that you might be subject to compulsion, *you* brought it about that the grain might be taken away. What we are going to get is only as much as hungry men will have been decent enough to leave us. (8) Why do you boast of selling grain at double the price? They might have paid nothing; what you are bringing is a kindness we owe to others.

(9) Now another lie is being made up. 23. He says: "I was driven to land by a storm."[133] Yes, of course: you are a hapless sailor, not the kind whose prayers are answered by the winds. Don't we know that you had a voyage twice as good we had hoped,[134] don't we know that you made two journeys for each cargo,[135] don't we know that on one mission the winds favored you four times over?[136] (2) Words can suffice to deny what words assert: away with this hope of deceiving the city with a lie! What is the damage you adduce to prove a storm? What have you lost? (3) Certainly the whole cargo of grain came into port, and

---

[135] Journey 1: A to B to C; Journey 2: C to B to A.
[136] Carrying you from A to B, from B to C, from C back to B, from B to A.

laborasse,[108] tamquam nimium onustas, naves simulaveris: duplum adferre poterant. Non vexata armamenta turbatosque funes aut scissos velorum sinus quereris; classis statim exiit et, quod magnum integrae signum est, cito

4 redît. Porro tempestas in unum agebat angulum: nihil potuerunt obliquata vela deflectere? Non potes ultra pro-

5 cedere: citra applica.[109] Effuge raptores, effuge non dimissuros. Si aliud fieri non potest, cum tempestate decide

6 naufragio,[110] in desertum litus impinge. Quid devitata procella prodest, quid subducta nubium[111] minis[112] classis? In portu naufragium fecimus, et frumentum ad ancoras perdidimus.

7 "Ego vero" inquit "attuli, et quidem duplum." O nos felices! Rumpamus saturitate praecordia, pascamur in

8 praeteritum, et famem cruditate pensemus! Frumentum attulisti. Quid, quod medicina mortuorum sera est? Quid, quod nemo aquas infundet in cinerem? Quid, quod extincto populo etiam novendialis tarde venit? Quid, quod iam ego frumentum non desidero? Naufrago tabulam abs-

---

108 -asse *Håk.[3] 133*: -asti *codd.*: -asti. ⟨neque⟩ *Sh. B.[2] 206*

109 porro—applica *dist. Str.[4]*

110 *distinxi* (*cf. 12.12.6, Juv. 12.33–34, ThlL V.1.167.13–19*): *post* decide *vulg.*

111 -ium *Håk. necnon Watt[2] 28*: -ibus *codd.*

112 (nubibus) invitis *Scheff. 452* (*et vd. Bur.[1]*)

---

137 I.e., the people of city C (cf. 12.20.6, 12.22.4).

138 Figurative (proverbial) = We were ruined "in a quite gratuitous and absurd way" (Polyb. 6.44.8). See Tosi (2017[2], 365–66) (AS).

you cannot pretend the ships got into trouble because they were over-loaded: they were capable of carrying twice as much. You don't complain of damage to the rigging, tangled ropes or torn sails; the ships went off with no delay, and (a convincing proof of their soundness) they came back fast. (4) Suppose then the storm jostled them together into a single constricted inlet: could the sails not have been set aslant to change course? Suppose you can go no further: then land short of your goal. (5) Steer clear of robbers, steer clear of those who will not let you go.[137] If nothing else is possible, compromise with the tempest by wrecking your fleet, beach it on an uninhabited stretch of coast. (6) What good comes of having avoided the hurricane, or having saved the fleet from threatening stormclouds? We were wrecked in port,[138] losing the grain when we were at anchor.

(7) "But," he says, "I did bring it, and twice the amount at that." How lucky we are! Let us burst our vitals with overeating, let us feed to make up for lost time, and let us pay for hunger with indigestion. (8) Yes, you have brought grain. But what of the following?—First: medicine comes too late for the dead. Second: no one will throw water at the spent ashes of a fire. Third: when a people has been wiped out, even the ninth-day ceremonies come too late.[139] Fourth: I don't feel the need for grain any more. First you took the plank away from a shipwrecked sailor,

[139] Because there is nobody left to perform them. Those funeral rites in fact took place eight days after death ("*ninth* day" implies inclusive calculation): but hunger kills in seven days (nn. 49, 91), so even (*etiam*) a single day after that is too late for anyone to survive (AS).

9   tulisti, mortuo adplicas navem. Duplum est? Infunde in
sepulcra et admetire tumulis! Ibi sunt, qui mandaverunt.
10   Quid aliud effecisti adferendo frumentum quam ut nos,
quod adhuc fecimus, paeniteret? Nunc me magis pudet,
nunc cibos meos obiurgo: potui heri non comedisse. 24. O
nefas, in quo me scelere commeatus deprehendit![113] Si-
cine paria fecimus: adhuc nihil habuimus, sed nunc licet
reponamus? Quis autem umquam pensabit[114] necessaria
2   supervacuis? Duplum attulisti: sed illis qui perierunt nihil,
sed non possumus iam non fecisse quod fecimus, sed plerumque sera pro nullis sunt, et temporum ista momentis
3   aut pretiosa fiunt aut vilia. Vis scire quantum inter hoc
tempus et illud intersit? Tempta igitur forum tuum: totum
hoc non potes dimidio vendere.
4   Superest adhuc unum patrocinium, in quo spes omnis
profligatae causae consistat: "Ad diem veni." Stare hoc[115]
certe, iudices, immo[116] ferri,[117] non potest: exundat altius
5   dolor. Pudorem publicum quamvis proiectum et iam olim
sepultum hucusque protrahis? Cur non expectavimus, cur
famem non ad constitutum distulimus, cur ad tantum
6   nefas accessimus? In hac lance publica causa, iudices,
pendet: aut iste tarde fecit aut nos cito. Hoc videlicet ex-

113 -dit ℭ: -det (-deret H) *codd.*
114 -avit *Hâk.*
115 state hic (hec A) Φ
116 immo *Wint.⁷ 155*: nam *codd.*: iam *Sh. B.⁴ 205*
117 *dist. Str. ap. Wint.⁷ 155*

140 Cf. 12.9.2.
141 City and legate.
142 Because there are so few people left alive to buy.

now you bring a ship alongside a body floating in the sea. (9) Is there twice as much of it? Pour it into the tombs and measure it out to the graves! The people who gave you your instructions are *there* now. (10) In bringing grain what more have you achieved than to make us repent what we have done up to now? I feel more shame *now*,[140] I am upbraiding my food *now*: I could have avoided eating— yesterday. 24. Horror of horrors! In the commission of what crime did the arrival of the grain surprise me! Is this the way we[141] are quits?—hitherto we had nothing, but now we can put some by! Yet who will ever compensate for necessities by superfluities? (2) You have brought twice the quantity, for sure: yet to those who perished you brought nothing; yet we cannot undo now what we did in the past; yet too late is mostly the same as nothing, for circumstances can make things like this either valuable or worthless. (3) Do you want to measure the difference between then and now? Try the market for yourself: you cannot sell all this grain, not even at half the price.[142]

(4) There remains one line of defense to support the hopes of a case long ago scuppered: "I came on the day." This plea certainly cannot stand, judges—indeed, it cannot be *borne*: our pain wells up from too deep a source. (5) Are you even now dragging back to the surface the communal feeling of shame that we banished and long ago buried? Why did we not wait, why did we not put off our hunger till the appointed day, why did we embark on such a wicked course? (6) This is the nub of the state's case, judges: either this man was too slow or we were too hasty.

[QUINTILIAN]

spectasti,[118] et, ne captiosum esset officio tuo maturius
redisse, ex industria tempus trivisti. Non tempestas in
causa fuit, non vis ulla vicinae civitatis; una ratione mora-
7 tus es: nondum erat tempus. Adeone nobis miseriae publicae exciderunt, adeo insperato frumento obstipuimus, ut
haec audienda sint? Ultimum omnis memoriae reum una
8 vox innocentem facit? Populatorem eversoremque civitatis nisi ad supremum[119] damnabo, absolvatur; publicus
reus redît.

25. Illum—respondet—diem dedimus. Tu tamen, si
interpellatus tempestatibus serius venisses, excusares
mare et ambiguos flatus, et tibi bonam causam habere
2 videreris cum diceres: "Ante non potui." Et nos hoc cogi-
tavimus, his casibus ampliavimus tempus. Nos illum tibi
diem dedimus, sed quid illud?[120] Citius emisti quam spe-
ravimus, supra votum nostrum navigasti, ad proximum
3 litus mature classis adplicata est. Ego tibi possum satis
irasci? Felicitatem nostram perdidisti! Ergo, quantum in
te, tempus consumptum est, dies[121] excessit; peius pati
4 nihil possumus, sed pessima diu patimur. Imputas nobis

---

[118] sp- *Sch.*   [119] supr- ⟨supplicium⟩ (*immo* ⟨suppl-⟩ supr-)
Håk.[2] *104, sed vd. Str.*[4]   [120] quid illud? *Wint.*[7] *155* (quid
attinet? *Håk.*[2] *105*): q; ad illud B: quia ad il- V: quia il- Φ*
[121] -em *Reitz.*[2] *53, sed vd. Helm*[1] *377–78*

---

[143] Ironic: it is suggested that the envoy took care not to return
till the set day. The implication is that the citizens are at fault:
they did not delay their cannibalism till then.

[144] I.e., to face the people—who are ready to stone him (cf.
12.12.3).

[145] = we the citizen body.

70

No doubt you foresaw this, and wasted time on purpose so that it might not prejudice you that you came earlier than you were in duty bound to come.[143] It was not because of a storm, not because of any force applied by a neighboring city; you delayed for one reason alone: it was not yet time. (7) Have we so far forgotten the misfortunes we endured, have our wits been so dulled by grain we never expected to eat, that we have to listen to these pleas? Does a single phrase make an innocent of someone guilty beyond anyone in human memory? (8) If I do not get the ravager and destroyer of the city condemned to death, let him be acquitted: he has come back to plead his case before the *whole* citizen body.[144]

25. That was the day we[145] fixed, he replies. But if you had come late because the weather had held you up, you would have used sea and fickle winds as your excuse, and would have been thought to have a good case if you said: "I couldn't have come earlier." (2) We too thought of that, and allowed more time for such contingencies. Yes, we did give you that date: but what of it?[146] You made your purchase sooner than we expected, you sailed faster than we prayed, the fleet put in to the nearest shore[147] ahead of time. (3) Can I be sufficiently angry with you? You threw away the advantage given us by our good fortune. So far as you were concerned, then, the time *was* used up, it *did* exceed the days assigned. We can suffer nothing worse; but we go on suffering the worst for too long.[148] (4) You

---

[146] In fact, you did *not* have bad weather, and you could have got back much earlier (direct from city B).

[147] City B.   [148] What we were suffering was too much even before the time set for your mission expired.

propitios ventos et secundum mare et civitatis opulentae
liberalitatem, quae tantum frumenti vendidit, quantum
duobus populis satis esset?[122] Quantumlibet velocitate tua
glorieris, computa, si placet, quando primum conterminos
portus onusta classe deprehenderis:[123] quam tarde a vicina
civitate venisti!

5   At etiam, si dis placet, animo defenditur, et quam causam vexandae civitatis habuerit quaerit. Istud ego interrogare debueram. Non ubique, iudices, morandum est:
alioquin, si quid requirere vellem, multa occurrissent.
6   Solent enim[124] negotiatores praeter haec aperta pretia privatum aliquid ac proprium stipulari, utique cum alienam
rem vendunt. Potest fieri ut primo lucrari voluerit pretium, serius deinde subvenerit reddendae rationis dicen-
daeque causae cogitatio. Veniit fortasse frumentum lucro,
7   redemptum[125] est patrocinio. Potest fieri ut aliquam gratiam speraverit a civitate servata, occulta quaedam in civitate sua odia, quae plerumque ex inanibus causis obori-
untur, habuerit. 26. Multa succurrunt, sed si qua est,
iudices, dicenti[126] fides, ego nihil invidiosius reputo quam
quod civitatem suam sine causa perdidit.

[122] sic dist. Reitz.[2] 53   [123] dep- V: condep- B: comp- Φ
[124] enim M[2] E: in B: hi vel hii cett.
[125] -tum M: -to cett.
[126] -nti ς: -ndi codd.

[149] City C, then city A. The result of the calculation is shown
in quam tarde . . . ; the dates of arrival at C and then A are too far
apart because he delayed in C: see 12.15.7–8 on the "culpable
delay" as opposed to the journeys.
[150] In this case, to the city.

take credit with us, then, for the favoring winds, the calm sea, the generosity of a wealthy city—which sold you enough grain for two peoples? However much you may take pride in your speed, please work out when it was that you first got to two neighboring ports[149] with a laden fleet: how slowly you came from the city next door!

(5) But—ye gods—he also argues from motive, and enquires what reason he could have had for plaguing his city. *I* ought to have asked him that. But one cannot pause over every detail: if one could, many other topics for questioning would have occurred to me. (6) In fact, traders normally have some private and personal condition to make, over and above the stated price, especially when they are selling something that belongs to others.[150] It may be that he at first intended to make a profit on the sale, but that later it occurred to him that he would have to account for his mission and argue his case: maybe the grain was sold[151] to his own gain, and bought back[152] for the purposes of his own defense. (7) It may be that he hoped for some favor from the city he had saved,[153] or that he had some secret feuds[154] in his own city, of the kind that generally spring up for flimsy reasons. 26. Many possibilities present themselves; but if you believe what I say, judges, I think nothing more odious than that he destroyed his own city for *no* good cause.

---

[151] At city C.

[152] At city B: the double amount of grain would help him defend himself on his return home.

[153] City C. Cf. 12.6.5.   [154] And so starved the whole city to get at his personal enemies.

2   Quaecumque ratio, quodcumque propositum fuit, audi quae passi sumus postquam redire potuisti. Transeo tormenta nostrae inopiae, maciem corporis, vulsos terra destrictosque ramis cibos, quod aris altaria non imposuimus, quod populus corporibus suis vias stravit, quod mendicus
3 quem rogaret non habuit. Non obiciam tibi famem. O tristis recordatio, o tormentis omnibus conscientia gravior, rumpe ferreum pectus, et ardentia scelera viventisque intus epulas excute! Luctantur intra viscera animae, et
4 uterum funeribus gravidum in os agunt. Credibiles fabulas fecimus, felices miserias, scelera innocentia. Omnes quascumque clades fama vulgavit, solacia hinc petant: hinc audient occisos sine sanguine, sepultos sine ignibus
5 ⟨homines hominibus⟩127 cibos. Si quis mentitus est Cyclopas, Laestrygonas, Sphingas aut inguinibus virginis latratum Siciliae litus et quaecumque miser didici domi committens,128 [quaere]129 hinc argumentum, hinc fidem
6 accipiant. Quaedam plane falsa sunt: sol in ortus non occidit, nec ad humanorum viscerum epulas diem vertit; vidit nos vulneribus130 pastos et ad eviscerata corpora inluxit.

127 *suppl. Plas. 78.5*
128 committens *Håk.*: comites *codd.*   129 quaere B, *del. Håk. (firm. Watt.³ 55)*: quaero *vel* quero V Φ
130 fun- *Bur., sed vd. Str.⁴*

155 Taking up the division of misfortunes of 12.15.7.
156 It is not the famine I shall cast in your teeth but our crimes, which your delay has caused (DAR).
157 Cf. n. 40.
158 Because starved to death.

(2) Whatever motive you had, whatever you were aiming at, listen to what we endured after you *could* have come back.[155] I pass over how we were tormented by lack of food, over bodies wasted away, food torn from the earth or stripped from boughs; I do not mention that we had nothing to offer on the altars, that the people paved the streets with their bodies, that a beggar had no one to solicit. I shall not bring the *famine*[156] as a charge against you. (3) O melancholy memory, o conscience worse than any torture, break our ironclad breasts, and release the burning crimes and the banquets that live inside! Souls are struggling in our guts, and bringing up to the mouth a stomach pregnant with bodies.[157] (4) We have made myths believable, misfortune happy, crimes innocent. Every catastrophe that has been noised abroad by rumor may derive comfort from here: from here they will learn of ⟨men⟩, killed without blood,[158] buried without fire, to serve as food ⟨for men⟩. (5) Anyone who has fabricated tales of Cyclopes, Laestrygonians, Sphinxes, or of the shores of Sicily resounding with barking from the loins of a virgin,[159] and all the crimes I was unfortunate enough to learn from my own experience—by committing them—, may receive confirmation, and a chance of being believed, from *here*. (6) Some stories are quite untrue: the sun did not set in the east, or reverse the day at the sight of men feasting on human entrails;[160] it *did* see us nourished on mutilated bodies, and rose to shine on eviscerated corpses.

---

[159] Scylla. All these myths involve monsters who ate human flesh: compare Juv. 15.13–23.

[160] As it did in the myth of Thyestes: cf., e.g., Sen. *Thy.* 776–79, 1035–36; see also 4.16.4.

[QUINTILIAN]

Publice monstra commissa sunt, et inexpiabile nefas uno
ore civitas fecit.

7   Poenis nostris iam ne fames quidem satis est. Hoc non
immanes[131] ferae faciunt, et quamvis sensu careant muta
animalia, pleraque tamen innocentibus cibis vescuntur,
utique quae[132] consuerunt[133] 27. inter homines.[134] Etiam
si qua alienis membris imprimunt dentem, mutuo tamen
laniatu abstinent, nec est ulla supra terras adeo rabiosa
2 belua, cui non imago sua sancta sit. Nos, quibus divina
providentia mitiores cibos concessit, quibus sociare populos, mutuo gaudere comitatu, sidera oculis animisque
cernere datum est, busta nos[135] fecimus: nigros sanie[136]
dentes pallidis cadaveribus impressimus, et inter horrorem ac famem, restrictis labris, morsus[137] abrupimus.[138]
Cadavera rogis devoluta sunt, et ad funera tamquam ad
3 naves concurrimus. Deficit aliquis extremo iam spiritu
pendens; tamen durat, quia prius moriturum alterum
putat. Invicem expectant, et, si[139] spei figuratione tardius
4 cadit,[140] morsibus pugnant.[141] Non in omnibus mortes ex-
pectantur; pater liberos esurit, et oppressa decimo mense

---

131 imman- *Watt*[2] 29: omn- *codd.*
132 utique quae ς (*et vd. Håk.*[3] *133–34*): uti quaeque *codd.*
133 mans- *Håk.*[3] *133–34, sed vd. Str.*[4]
134 *hic dist. Håk.*[3] *133: ante* inter *vulg.*
135 busta nos *Håk.*[3] *133:* ius annos *vel* vis annos *fere codd.*
136 sanie *Håk.*[2] *105:* fame *codd.*
137 -sa *Reitz.*[2] *44, sed vd. Str.*[4]
138 -ump- B V γ
139 si ⟨quis⟩ *Håk., sed vd. Str.*[4]
140 -dit π: -det *cett.*
141 -ant *B. Asc.*[1] *lxxxviii v.:* -at *codd.*

Monstrous deeds were done by a whole people:[161] a city committed an inexpiable horror with a single mouth.

(7) At this stage, not even starvation is sufficient punishment for us. Wild beasts do *not* do what we did: dumb animals, even if they lack reason, generally feed off innocent food—especially those that have learned to do so 27. while dwelling among men.[162] Even if some of them leave the marks of their teeth on the bodies of other kinds of animal, they do abstain from tearing each other apart: there is no beast on earth so rabid that it fails to respect its own likeness.[163] (2) *We*, whom divine providence has granted softer food, who have been granted the ability to bring peoples together in alliance, to take pleasure in each other's company, to see and comprehend the heavenly bodies,[164] *we* have made ourselves into tombs: we have sunk teeth black with gore into pale cadavers, drawing back our lips and breaking off collops, poised between horror and hunger. Corpses have been rolled down off pyres, and we have flocked to funerals as if to ships.[165] (3) A man may be failing, his life now hanging by a thread; but he persists in living, for he thinks another will die before him. They wait for each other, and if the other drops slower than he had hoped, they fight it out with bites. (4) Nor is death awaited in every case; a father feels hunger for his children, and a mother, with her tenth month heavy

---

[161] See also 12.8.6 and cf. Juv. 15.31.

[162] Tacitly contrasting men who feed tame animals on innocent food with the citizens who ate each other.

[163] Cf. Juv. 15.159–64.   [164] Cf. Juv. 15.142–58.

[165] Sc., the ships that should have brought grain to the starving city.

mater sibi parit: redit in uterum laceratus infans. Cludunt
domos ne quis funus eripiat: solae sunt divitiae mortium.
5 Velut infaustae aves supra expirantes[142] stamus. Secreta
miseri petunt, in solitudinem fugiunt, et, ubi nulla spes
vitae superest, mortis suas abscondunt; iam morituri ad
feras confugiunt!

28. Dehisce, terra, et hanc noxiam civitatem, si hoc
saltem fas est, haustu aliquo ad inferos conde! Caelestes
auras contaminato spiritu polluimus, et sideribus ac diei
graves invidiam saeculo facimus. Nullas iam spero fruges,
2 propitios deos non mereor. Quomodo me a scelere meo
divellerem, in quas ultimas terras, quae inhospitalia maria
conderem? Mea sine ‹fine› conscientia:[143] urunt animum
intus scelerum faces, et, quotiens facta reputavi, flagella
mentis sonant; ultrices video furias, et, in quamcumque
3 me partem converti, occurrunt umbrae meorum. Habitat
nescioquae in pectore meo poena, et, ne morte saltem hos
metus effugiam, occupant gravia apud inferos supplicia,
volucris rota et fugacibus cibis elusus senex (adeo ne apud
inferos quidem ulla poena est fame maior—et ille haec
4 patitur, qui hominem apposuit epulandum).[144] Nobis im-

---

142 exp- ς: asp- B V δ: sp- γ β
143 mea sine ‹fine› con-: *Håk.*[2] 106 (*firm. Str.*[4]): meum sine
con- B V Φ*
144 adeo—epulandum *sic fere dist. Str.*[4]

---

166 Womb and stomach here identified.
167 They go off to die in secret; cf. 12.13.7.
168 Sc., rather than fleeing from them.
169 Cf. 12.15.6.
170 The punishment of Ixion (Verg. *G.* 3.38–39).

upon her, gives birth to feed herself: the child returns mutilated to the womb.[166] They bar the doors of houses in case anyone should snatch a body: only the dead constitute riches. (5) We stand like birds of ill omen over the dying. The wretched people look for privacy, they flee into the wilderness, and when no hope of life remains they conceal their own deaths;[167] now people about to die seek refuge with wild animals![168]

28. Gape, earth, and gulp down this guilty city—if this at least is allowed—into the shades below! We have polluted the breezes of heaven with our tainted breath; a burden on stars and the light of day, we bring odium upon our time. I can hope now for no crops, I merit no favoring gods. (2) How could I divorce myself from my crime, to what far-flung lands, what unfriendly seas could I flee to hide myself? My guilty conscience knows no ⟨bounds⟩: the torches of my crimes burn my soul within me, and, as often as I think over my actions, the whiplash of my mind rings out; I see the avenging furies: wherever I turn, I am confronted by the shades of my loved ones. (3) A penalty of a kind dwells in my breast: to prevent me escaping these horrors even by death,[169] I am taken over by the dire punishments of the underworld—the whirling wheel[170] and the old man taunted by food that ever escapes his grasp[171] (so true is it that even in the underworld there is no torment worse than hunger—and the sufferer is one who served up a human being at a feast!).[172] (4) The rock hangs

---

[171] Tantalus (Verg. *Aen.* 6.603–7).

[172] Tantalus served up his own son Pelops to the gods, to test their omniscience.

minet saxum, nobis stridunt ferreae turres, nostris causis
urna iam stetit, nobis vivax ipsum crescit iecur (quia illic
quoque viscera tantum aves laniant).[145] Excipiunt nos in
proximo litore inhumatae nostrorum animae.

5   Miserum me, verane haec sunt an mens aspicit? Laceros video manes et truncas partibus suis umbras. Quid hoc
est? Non de sepulcris insurgunt, non aliquo terrarum
hiatu[146] procedunt umbrae nostrorum: de populo exeunt!
6 Illuc ite, illi taedas intendite, illum anguibus petite et tam
longae morae exigite rationem. Vobis dicat: "Duplum attuli," vobis dicat: "Ad diem veni!" Ego, si huius poenam
videro, possum reddere rationem quod vixi.

[145] quia—laniant *sic dist. Str.*[4]
[146] hiatu 𝕾 (*vind. Str.*[4]): haustu (*sc. e 12.28.1*) *codd.*

over *us*,[173] the iron towers[174] screech for *us*, the urn is now in place to decide *our* cases,[175] *our* liver, tenacious of life, goes on growing of its own accord[176] (in fact, there too[177] birds rip up only entrails). The souls of our unburied[178] relations are there to welcome us on the shore nearby.[179]

(5) Ah me—is this all true, or a mere illusion of the mind? I see spirits of the deceased torn in pieces, and shades lacking parts of themselves. What is this? The shades of our dead are not rising from graves, not issuing through some cleft in the ground: they are coming out of the people![180] (6) Go to *him*,[181] brandish your torches at *him*, set your snakes upon *him*, and demand recompense for so long a delay. Let him tell *you*: "I brought twice as much," let him tell *you*: "I came in time for the day!" As for me, if I see *him* pay the penalty, I can justify my survival.

---

[173] The list of the damned is traditionally completed by Sisyphus, sentenced to *roll* a boulder up to a hill endlessly (Verg. *Aen.* 6.616); a *hanging* rock was part of the punishment of Ixion and Pirithous in Verg. *Aen.* 6.601–3. These punishments are here conflated.   [174] Those of the iron city of Rhadamanthus (Verg. *Aen.* 6.554–58).   [175] The urn from which Minos would draw the fate of each soul at the time of judgment (Verg. *Aen.* 6.431–33).   [176] Like the liver of Tityus, which was endlessly eaten by two vultures (Verg. *Aen.* 6.595–600).

[177] Even the birds that torment damned souls in Hades, like birds on earth, content themselves with innards (cf. previous note)—whereas we men have been eating the lot.

[178] Because eaten.   [179] Cf. the description of Palinurus in Verg. *Aen.* 6.374–75.   [180] I.e., out of the stomachs of the living.   [181] The envoy.

DECLAMATION 13

INTRODUCTION

Rich Man and Poor Man are neighbors in the country: Rich Man has flowers in his field; Poor Man keeps bees in his. Rich Man complains that the bees are ruining his flowers and requires Poor Man to remove them; when the neighbor does not do so, Rich Man sprinkles his flowers with poison, which results in the death of all the bees. Poor Man accuses him of malicious damage.

This speech envisages a realistic situation, well grounded in the Roman legal culture. Compensation to the owner of property unlawfully damaged was granted by the *lex Aquilia de damno* (third century BC); under this law, in particular, whoever unlawfully killed a slave or a farm animal belonging to another had to pay the owner the value of the damaged property.[1] To be compensated for his loss, therefore, Poor Man must prove (7.4–6): (1) that Rich Man did actually cause him a loss; (2) that the loss was caused maliciously.[2]

The second point is easily proved: Rich Man does not deny that he sprinkled his flowers with poison intending

[1] Cf. Gai. *Dig.* 9.2.2.pr.; see Zullo (2016, 324–26), with further references on the *lex Aquilia*; for its relevance to *DM* 13, see Krapinger (2005, 15–20) and esp. Mantovani (2006–7, 328–36).

[2] Cf. Desanti (2015, 177–80, 188–94).

to kill the bees (cf., e.g., 14.7–8);[3] nor can this action be considered lawful just because it took place on Rich Man's property (10.5–8).

Whether the loss of bees amounts to loss of property is a more complex question. Roman jurists agree that a wild animal should be considered private property as long as the owner keeps it under his custody; domesticated animals, like some birds, can be considered property even if not kept locked up, as long as the owner maintains his ability to bring them back into his custody.[4] What of animals that have to be left free to move far away from their owner's custody in order to carry out their functions, such as bees? Can their owner claim them to be his property (and request compensation in case of damage) even if he does not maintain custody on them? We are informed of a debate among Roman jurists on this topic, which the author of our declamation appears to be aware of: the arguments in favor of Poor Man's claim seem to exploit the position of the second-century AD jurist Celsus, while Rich Man's reported defense is grounded on the opinion of the first-century AD jurist Proculus.[5]

The speaker exploits Virgilian tones and images throughout the declamation.[6] Poor Man is presented as living a

---

[3] See Corbino (2009, 514–24) on the legal implications of Rich Man's confession.

[4] Cf. Mantovani (2006–7, 329–30); Desanti (2015, 180–86).

[5] The relevant arguments are quoted in *Coll. leg. Rom. Mos.* 12.7.10; cf. Mantovani (2006–7, 331–78); Berti (2015, 41–43).

[6] See Becker (1904, 42–51); Tabacco (1977–78, 200–208); Berti (2015, 35–44) (with further bibliography); Van den Berg (2016, 163–67).

peaceful life like the old man of Corycus (2.1–5); his small field is portrayed as a *locus amoenus* (3.4–5); and the description of activities and behavior of the bees is widely inspired by the fourth book of the *Georgics*.

The author displays a wider legal expertise: besides the *lex Aquilia* and its particular applications,[7] we find references to the *lex Cornelia de sicariis* on the administering of poison (6.6–9),[8] allusions to issues connected to transhumance (11.2) and grazing of livestock (12.2),[9] and even reflection on the concept of causality (12.4–6).[10] Less adequate is the author's understanding of the physiology of bees and the production of honey. He portrays the leader of bees as a king rather than a queen (9.6, 17.8);[11] two allusions to the gathering of morning dew in the work of the bees (4.2, 5.5) suggest that he follows the traditional view of bees as collectors of honey falling from the sky on

[7] E.g., 10.5, on the case of domesticated animals injured while on someone else's property (Krapinger [2005, 115n244]); 11.2, on robberies of persons and seizures of herds crossing one's land (ibid., 121n272); 14.5, on administering poison directly or letting the victim drink it (ibid., 135n336), with an allusion also to the killing of a man who crossed a sports field while javelins were being thrown (not punishable: ibid., 135–36n339). See Desanti (2015, 194–97).

[8] Krapinger (2005, 97n152).

[9] Krapinger (2005, 121n272, 126n299); Zullo (2016).

[10] Krapinger (2005, 127n302).

[11] Like all Roman authors (e.g., Verg. *G.* 4.210–12), who ignore Greek sources on queen bees (e.g., Arist. *Hist. an.* 5.553a.17–32); see now Berrens (2018, 231–38).

flowers and certain trees;[12] nor does he understand how bees come into existence: he seems to believe that the older bees make their progeny out of honey (16.3–4).[13]

The speech can be analyzed as follows:[14]

> PROEM 1.1–6
> NARRATION 2.1–6.9
> ARGUMENTATION
>   *Propositio causae* and *Partitio* 7.1–6
>   *Refutatio/Confirmatio* 8.1–14.8
> EPILOGUE 15.1–19.4

The connections between the arguments exploited in our speech and the opinions of the jurist Celsus, as well as a possible allusion to this case in a passage from Celsus preserved in the *Digest*,[15] may suggest a dating to the (very) early second century AD—and this hypothesis can be confirmed on linguistic and prosodic grounds.[16] In the late fourth century, Jerome ascribes to Quintilian both this speech in general[17] and a tag from it (2.3).[18] Later on, in

12 Krapinger (2005, 94n134).

13 See Berrens (2018, 146–59, esp. 157–58).

14 Krapinger (2005, 25–28).

15 4.4, *Volui relinquere avitos lares*; cf. Cels. *Dig.* 6.1.38, *Finge pauperem, qui, si reddere id cogatur, laribus sepulchris avitis carendum habeat*, and Mantovani (2006–7, 374–78).

16 See General Introduction, §4.

17 Cf. *Ep. ad Praes.* 1 (*PL* 30, col. 183a = Morin [1913, 54–55, ll. 13–15]), *puto te Quintiliani controversiae recordari in qua pauper causatur, dolens ob interitum apum, flores ab impotentissimo divite venenatos.*

18 Cf. *Quaest. Hebr. in Gen.* pr. (p. 1, 20–22 de Lagarde = *CCSL* 72, p. 1), *me vero procul ab urbibus, foro, litibus, turbis*

twelfth-century France, *DM* 13 inspired two poems of
uncertain authorship: the *Apes pauperis* (106 rhymed hex-
ameters)[19] and the *Causa inter pauperem et divitem de
apibus* (121 elegiac couplets).[20] A reply to the pseudo-
Quintilianic speech was composed in the sixteenth century
by Thomas More's daughter, Margaret, but it is no longer
extant;[21] another one is included in Patarol's *Antilogies*.[22]

---

*remotum, sic quoque (ut Quintilianus ait) latentem invenit in-
vidia*; with no mention of "Quintilian," also *Vit. Malch.* 6.1 Mo-
rales (*SC* 508, p. 196), *Sic quoque me latentem invenit invidia*.

[19] Republished with some notes by Krapinger (2007a, 193–
201).

[20] Ed. Boutemy (1949, 292–97). See Kauntze (2014, 46–47).

[21] See Bernstein (2013, 152–53).

[22] (1743, 352–70).

13

Apes pauperis

DAMNI PER INIURIAM DATI SIT ACTIO. Pauper et dives in agro vicini erant iunctis hortulis. Habebat dives in horto flores, pauper apes. Questus est dives flores suos decerpi ab apibus pauperis. Denuntiavit ut transferret. Illo non transferente flores suos veneno sparsit. Apes pauperis omnes perierunt. Reus est dives damni iniuria dati.

1. Credo ego, iudices, plerosque mirari quod homo tenuis et, iam[1] ante quam quod habebam perdidi, pauper, ausus sim iudicio lacessere divitem utique[2] vicinum eumque notae impotentiae, expertae crudelitatis, in tantis fortunae

[1] et iam *Gron.*: et AE: etiam *cett.*
[2] undi- *Sch. coll. 13.3.2*

13

The poor man's bees

CAUSING MALICIOUS DAMAGE[1] IS TO BE ACTIONABLE. A poor man and a rich man were neighbors in the country, and their gardens adjoined each other. The rich man had flowers in his garden, the poor man kept bees in his. The rich man complained that his flowers were being browsed on by the poor man's bees. He gave him notice to move them. When the poor man failed to do so, the rich man sprinkled poison over his flowers. The poor man's bees all died. The rich man is accused of causing malicious damage.

(Speech of the poor man)

1. I can well believe, judges, that very many people are surprised that I, a man of slender means, poor even before I lost all I did own, have dared to challenge a rich man at law: particularly as he is a neighbor, and one well known for his ungovernable character—a man of proven cruelty,

---

[1] *Damnum* in the succeeding speech often means (and is translated) "loss," looked at from the victim's point of view. On the legal proceedings against malicious damage, see Introduction to the present declamation.

viribus perniciosum inimicum etiam si venena non habeat.
Neque hoc ipse[3] periculum ignoro, expertus non levi do-
cumento quanti steterit mihi, quod semel imperata non
feci. Sed neque illud, iudices, damnum tolerabile est pauperi, cum tam parvis etiam divites moveantur, et mihi,
quamquam prope nihil iam relictum est quod perderem,
si tamen ista impune sustinenda sint, solacium erit iram
potius quam contemptum pati. Nec sane vitae causa iam
superest, si ad ceteras humilitatis nostrae contumelias hoc
quoque accedat, ut, si habemus aliquid, migrandum sit, si
perdidimus, tacendum. Unum oro, ne cui minor dignitate
vestra videatur causa litis meae. Ante omnia enim non debetis expectare uti[4] pauper magna perdiderim. Sed quantulum est quod abstulerit mihi dives, minus est quod reliquit. Et tamen quis indignatur apes formula vindicari,
cum venenis etiam flosculi vindicentur? Quod tamen, iudices, quamquam eversus et ab omni spe tuendae paupertatis exclusus, aequiore animo [omnia][5] tolerarem, si cuius
mihi conscius culpae etiamsi iniustam poenam, meritam
tamen iram tulissem. Sed circumspicienti omnia nihil mihi
obici potest a divite, nisi quod vicinus sum.

2. Est mihi paternus, iudices, agellus, sane angustus et
pauper, non vitibus consitus, non frumentis ferax, non pascuis laetus; ieiunae modo glebae atque humilis thymi, et
non late pauperi casae circumiecta possessio. Verum mihi

---

[3] h. i. B: i. h. V Φ   [4] uti *Obr.* (ut ⌐): ubi B V Φ*
[5] *delevi post Håk., et om.* π AE β (*ortum est nimirum e super.*
omni *vel infer.* omnia)

---

[2] Sc., if I lose my case.   [3] Rich Man will be angry at being accused, whereas before he merely despised Poor Man.

with such resources that he would be a deadly enemy even if he had no poisons. I am myself well aware of this danger: I have learned by bitter experience what it cost me to have disobeyed his orders on a single occasion. (2) But for a poor man, judges, that loss is not to be borne—even the *rich* are moved by such trivial things. There is now virtually nothing left for me to lose; but if I am to have to tolerate this treatment without any redress,[2] it will be a comfort to bear the brunt of his anger rather than his scorn.[3] (3) Certainly I have no reason now to go on living, if to the rest of the insults to my humble status is added the consideration that if I have something left, I must move away, and if I have lost everything, I must keep silent. (4) One thing I do ask: let no one think the reason for my suit too trivial for your honors to consider. For above all, you should not expect my loss to have been a big one: I am a poor man. But however little the rich man may have taken away from me, what he has left me is still less. (5) On the other hand, who can feel indignant that bees are being avenged by legal process, when even flowers are avenged by poison? (6) Yet even though, judges, I have been ruined, and shut off from all hope of defending my poverty, I should take this more calmly if I were conscious of some blame attaching to me, and had had to bear an unjust penalty, indeed, but wrath that I deserved. But when I look around at it all, the rich man can accuse me of nothing—except of being his neighbor.

2. Judges, I have a smallholding left me by my father, tiny indeed and poor, not planted with vines, not fertile in grain, not rich in pasture, just scanty grassland and humble thyme: and a small enclosure round my little cottage. But my holding was very dear to me precisely because

vel hoc fuit gratissima, quod non fuit digna quam dives
2 concupisceret. In hoc ego[6] vitae meae secreto, remotus a
tumultu civitatis, ignobile aevum agere procul ab ambitu
et omni maioris fortunae cupiditate constitui et, dum
3 molesta lege naturae transiret aetas, vitam fallere. Hoc
mihi parvulum terrae et humilis tugurii rusticum culmen
aequitas animi regna fecerat, satisque divitiarum erat nihil
amplius velle. Quid prodest? Sic quoque me latentem
4 invenit invidia. Nec ab initio, iudices, vicinus divitis fui;
pares circa me habitavere domini, et frequentibus villis
concors vicinia parvos limites coluit. Quod cives pasce-
5 bat, nunc divitis unius[7] hortus. Postquam proximos quos-
que revellendo terminos ager locupletis latius inundavit,
⟨postquam⟩[8] aequatae solo villae et excisa pagorum[9] sacra
et cum coniugibus parvisque liberis respectantes patrium
larem migraverunt veteres coloni et latae solitudinis indis-
creta unitas facta est, [postquam][10] ad apes meas divitis
fundus accessit.
6   Namque ego, iudices, dum fortius[11] opus permisit aetas, terram manibus subegi et difficultatem labore per-
domui, et invito solo nonnihil tamen fecunditatis expressi.
7 Cito labitur dies, et proclivis in pronum fertur aetas;
abiere vires, census meus, defectaque[12] labore senectus,
magna pars mortis, nihil mihi reliquit nisi diligentiam.
3. Circumspicienti quod conveniret opus invalidae senec-

---

[6] ergo V A   [7] unius M E: hunus B: unus B[2] cett.
[8] add. Reitz.[2] 78   [9] pagorum Leh.: pacor B V: patria Φ
[10] del. Reitz.[2] 78   [11] -ior Sch., sed fortius opus opponitur
13.3.1 quod—curae   [12] -taq- ⌐: -toq- codd.

---

[4] This sentence is quoted twice by Jerome: see Introduction
to the present declamation, n. 18.

it was not worth enough to excite a rich man's greed. (2) Living my life in this secluded retreat, remote from the bustle of the city, I resolved to pass an obscure existence far from ambition and all desire for a greater fortune, letting life slip away unnoticed while by the irksome law of nature time went by. (3) This scrap of land, and the rustic roof of my humble hut, my peace of mind had made into a kingdom, and it was wealth enough to wish for nothing more. To what avail? Though I hid away like this, envy found me out.[4] (4) At the start, judges, I was not a neighbor of the rich man. Round me there lived proprietors who were on my level: it was a harmonious district, with many small farms dotted about. What used to feed a citizen body in the past[5] has now became the garden of a single rich man. (5) My wealthy neighbor's land advanced further and further like a flood, uprooting all the boundary stones it came across. Farmhouses were leveled with the ground, village shrines were demolished; and the old husbandmen moved away, with their wives and little children, looking back at their family hearths. In the end there was one broad expanse, unenclosed and uninhabited—and the rich man's estate reached my bees.

(6) The fact is, judges, that so long as my age allowed me to do harder work, I worked the soil with my own hands, and mastered its problems by my exertions. The soil was recalcitrant, but I squeezed some fertility out of it. (7) Time slips swiftly away, and life goes downhill. Physical strength, my only asset, disappeared. My advanced years, worn down by toil, nearer death than life, left me nothing except my assidulity. 3. When I looked around for some activity to suit my feeble old age, I thought of being

[5] Cf. 13.11.1.

tutis curae, succurrebat sequi pecora, fetuque placidi gregis paupertatem tueri: sed ex omni parte circumiectus divitis ager vix tenuem ad gressus[13] meos semitam dabat.

2 "Quid agimus?" inquam. "Undique vallo divitiarum clusi sumus. Hinc hortuli locupletis, hinc arva, inde vineta, hinc saltus; nullus terra[14] datur exitus. Quaeramus animal quod

3 volet. Nam quid apibus invenit natura praestantius? Par-

4 cae, fideles, laboriosae. O animal simile pauperibus!" Et sane dabat occasionem mihi oportunitas hortuli mei. Est namque positus ad ortus solis hiberni et[15] apricus, omnibus ventis invius;[16] fusus ex proximo fonte rivus trepidantibus inter radiantes calculos aquis utrimque ripa virente

5 praeterfluit. Satis consiti floris[17] et viridis quamvis paucarum arborum coma nascentibus populis prima sedes, unde ego frequenter consertum novae iuventutis agmen

6 ramo gravescente suscepi. Nec me tanta capiebat voluptas quod fluentia ceris mella conderem, quod ad sustinendas paupertatis impensas deferrem in urbem quod divites emerent, quam quod adversus omnia lassae taedia aetatis

7 habebam senex quod agerem. Iuvabat aut lenta vimina vernis fetibus texere vel, ne[18] aestivus ardor aut hiberna vis gravidam penetraret alvum, hiantis rimas tenaci linire fimo, aut fessis apibus ultro praebere mella aut fugiens

8 examen aere terrere aut bella sedare pulveris iactu; tum,

[13] egr- E (*cf. §2* nullus—exitus)
[14] -ra *Gron.*: -rae *codd.*
[15] *om.* Φ (*et del.* B[pc])   [16] invius *Ruardi 34–35* (*vd. ad rem Kr.[1]*): medius *codd.* : vetitus *Wint.[9]*
[17] -ris *Bur.* (*cf. ThlL VI.1.928.59–68*): -res *codd.*
[18] vel ne π (*def. Håk.[2] 106*): vel B V: ne Φ

[6] Cf. Columella 9.9.2.   [7] Cf. 13.13.4 and 8, 13.19.2.

a herdsman, supporting my poverty with the offspring of peace-loving flocks. But the rich man's estate was all around, leaving scarcely a narrow path for me to get through. (2) "What's the point?", I said to myself, "I am fenced in everywhere by a palisade of wealth. Over here are the rich man's kitchen gardens, over there his plow-land, here his vineyards, there his woods. There is no way out on foot. Let's look for an animal that flies!" (3) Now, what has nature invented that is superior to bees? They are frugal, loyal, hardworking: an animal, in fact, just like poor men! (4) And my garden was happily placed for my purposes. It faces the rising sun in winter, a sunny spot, inaccessible to any wind. A stream passes by that takes its rise from a nearby spring; its water hurries along amid glistening pebbles, and both its banks are verdant. (5) A sufficiency of sown flowers, and green foliage—though only of a few trees—, are there to provide a first settlement for the growing population. Hence I could often welcome a new generation of bees swarming on a branch that drooped under their weight.[6] (6) It gave me pleasure to store the honey that poured from the waxen combs, and to take it to the city for the rich to buy,[7] so that I could defray the expenses of my poverty; but it pleased me even more that I now had something to do to counter all the tedium of my weary old age. (7) It was a joy to weave pli-able shoots for the spring brood, or, for fear the summer heat or winter frost penetrate the pregnant[8] hive, to smear gaping cracks with sticky dung, or give a present of honey to sick bees, or frighten a departing swarm by clashing brass, or calm down wars by throwing dust;[9] (8) or again—

---

[8] = full.   [9] Cf. Columella 9.9.6–7 on wars among the bees; see also 13.9.6.

ne quid periculi saltem singulis esset, avidas longe fugare
volucres et arcere parva aditu[19] animalia, reclusas interim
scrutari apium domos, ne per vacuas alvos foeda pestis
insidiosas texeret plagas.

4. Dederam laboribus meis iustam senex missionem;
habebam quae pro me opus facerent. Quo non penetras,
livor improbe, quidve scabrae malignitati clausum est?
2 Invidit pauperi dives! Cum evocasset me subito trepidum
totoque fortunae suae strepitu circumstetisset, "Quid?
Tu" inquit "non potes imperare apibus tuis intra privatum volent, ne hortorum meorum floribus insidant, ne in
3 meo rorem legant? Remove, transfer!" Impotentissime ty-
ranne, quo? Numquid tam latum possideo agellum, ut illum apes transvolare non possint? Neque tamen tantum
inerat pectori meo robur, ut non perturbarer denuntia-
4 tione notae impotentiae. Volui[20] relinquere avitos lares et
conscios natalium parietes et ipsam nutriculam casam,
iamque pauperem focum et fumosa tecta et consitas meis
manibus arbusculas destinatus exul ⟨deserere⟩[21] decreveram. Volui, iudices, decedere, volui: sed nullum potui
invenire agellum, in quo non mihi vicinus dives esset.
5 Nec tamen licuit diu quaerere. Forte serenus pura luce

---

19 aditu *Reitz.*[2] 58–59: dictu *codd.*
20 *del. (nihil infra supplens) Russ.*[1] 45
21 *add. Wint.*[7] *156:* decreveram B V γ δ: omittere dec- β

---

10 I.e., he would protect the individual bees (from bird at-
tacks, diseases, or other dangers) as well as the whole hive (threatened by inclement weather, bee wars, etc.).
11 Anticipation (prolepsis): some harmful creature may infest
the hives, which *as a result* are left empty of bees. Cf. 13.5.3.

so as to avert danger even[10] from individuals—to scare away greedy birds and stop insects getting in; and from time to time to open up the bees' homes and inspect them, to stop some foul pest weaving its treacherous nets across the deserted[11] spaces of the hives.

4. I had granted my labors a well-deserved discharge, for I was an old man now: I had those who would do the work for me. But, wicked envy, where do you not penetrate? What is closed to your filthy malevolence? A rich man envied a poor man! (2) All of a sudden, he summoned me trembling to his presence, surrounding me with all the hubbub of his wealthy household. "Can you then," he said, "not instruct your bees to fly within your own property without settling on the flowers in my garden, or gathering dew[12] on my land? Get rid of them, move them!" (3) Lawless tyrant, where to? Do I own so broad a plot that bees cannot fly right across it? But I hadn't the strength of mind not to be upset by a formal notice given me by someone notorious for his unbridled behavior. (4) I wanted to leave my ancestral home,[13] the walls that had seen my birth, the very hut where I was brought up: resigned to exile, I had now determined <to abandon> the poverty-stricken hearth, the smoky roof, the saplings planted by my own hands. I wanted to go, judges, I wanted to: but I could find no plot where I would not have the rich man for a neighbor.

(5) However, I was not permitted to search for long. It happened that one day it had dawned bright and clear, and

[12] Cf. 13.5.5; Introduction to the present declamation.

[13] Cf. Cels. *Dig.* 6.1.38; Introduction to the present declamation.

fulserat dies, et hilaris matutini solis tepor ad cotidiana
6 opera laetius solito agmen effuderat. Quin ipse spectator
operis (praecipua namque haec mihi voluptas erat) pro-
cesseram, sperans fore ut viderem quemadmodum aliae
libratae[22] pinnis onera conferrent, aliae deposita sarcina
in novas prorumperent praedas et, quamquam angusto
festinaretur aditu, turba tamen exeuntium non obstaret
7 intrantibus; aliae militaribus castris pellerent vulgus igna-
vum, aliae longum permensae iter fatigatae anhelitum
traherent, haec ad aestivum solem porrectas panderet pinnas. 5. Miserum me, ignoscite modo gemitibus meis: non
flosculos perdidi, nec caduca folia proximo lapsura vento;
[apes circumvolarent][23] suffugium[24] tenuitatis meae, solacium senectutis amisi. Numquam me alias pauperem pu-
2 tavi. Triste me excepit[25] silentium et inanis alvei inchoata
tantum opera et rudes cerae. Vos, iudices, aestimate quatenus recipiatis hunc adfectum meum: libenter bibissem,
si invenissem, venenum.

3   Hoc mihi damnum:[26] non brumae glacialis penetrabilis
rigor, non suppressi longa siti flores indixerunt[27] ieiunam
miseris famem, non aviditas iniusta domini nihil mellis
reservavit;[28] non aequalis[29] fessas morbus invasit, non
damnatis sedibus suis avias fuga petiere silvas; apes pau-
4 per miser in opere perdidi! Paravit homo nefarius ante

---

[22] -a *Russ.*[3]   [23] *haec esse interpolata et sic (e codd. varie
corruptis) reficienda ostendit Reitz.*[2] *17–18. de gloss. ad* q. *aliae
(13.4.6) agi suspicor*   [24] eff- B AE δ
    [25] -pit V AE δ: -pit expectatque (-tat B) *cett.*
    [26] *dist. Scheff. 452* (damnum = apes—perdidi, *infra*)
    [27] -dix- V (*cf. Bur. et ThlL VII.1.1158.39–44*): -dux- B Φ
    [28] -vantis M D β   [29] aliquis *Watt*[2] *30, sed vd. Str. ap. Kr.*[1]

the pleasant warmth of the morning sun had sent the troops out on their daily round more cheerfully than usual. (6) I had come out myself to watch them at work (this was one of my special pleasures), hoping that I should see how some of the bees hovered while taking on freight, others set down their burdens and shot away to gather plunder elsewhere—those going out not getting in the way of those coming in, despite the bustle in the narrow entrance; (7) how some turned the lazy crowd of drones out of their quarters, others, tired after a long journey, got back their breath, and one spread its wings to the heat of the summer sun. 5. Ah me! Just forgive my groans! I did not lose flowers, or evanescent petals[14] that would float to the ground the next time the wind got up. No, I lost the refuge of my poverty, the comfort of my old age. I have never thought myself poor at any other time. (2) A baleful silence greeted me; the hive was empty, the work in it no more than begun, the waxen combs still shapeless. Judges, you may decide for yourselves how to react to what I felt: I should gladly have drunk the poison if I had found it.

(3) *This* was my loss.[15] It was not that the penetrating frost of icy winter or the withering of my flowers by prolonged drought inflicted starvation on my poor bees; no owner out of criminal greed had failed to keep back honey for them; no epidemic had attacked the creatures when they were exhausted, they had not repudiated their home and made for the trackless woods. Wretched pauper: I lost my bees in midwork! (4) That wicked man, to begin with,

14 Cf. 13.19.4.
15 Looking forward to "I lost my bees in midwork!" below.

omnia tantum veneni, quod posset et divitis hortis satis
esse, et linivit flores maleficis sucis et in venenum mella
convertit. Sparsit omnibus floribus mortem, et quanto
5 plura interim corrupit quam quae apes abstulissent! Illae
studio cotidiani operis excitatae, ut primum aurora lucem
vocavit, in adsueta miserae pascua volant, ut, ante quam
noctis umorem radii solis ebiberent, matutinos legere[30]
rores et caelestis aquas ad horreum ferre possent, nec sibi
sed operi biberent. 6. Hic triste spectaculum et tantum
non ipsi, qui fecerat, miserandum. Illa ad primum feralis
suci haustum insolito consternata gustu fugit, sed fugisse
nihil prodest. Illa longiores expetitura pastus in altum tol-
2 litur vitamque in aura relinquit. Haec primo statim flos-
culo immoritur. Illa rigescentibus morte pedibus exani-
3 mis, sicut[31] haeserat, pendet. Alia defecta nisu volandi
adhuc per terram languide repit. Si quas tamen usque ad
sedem suam distulit mors lentior, sicut aegrae[32] solent sub
ipsis pendere portis, in globum nexas et mutuo amplexas
4 mors sola divisit. Quis figurare possit, quis dicere, quam
multas mali formas, quam varia leti genera fecerint tot
mortes! Semel ut[33] ipse tristem finiam expositionem, di-
5 cendum est: omnes perdidi. Celebre illud alvearium et
domino suo notius ad nihilum recidit.

[30] -re *Wint.[7] 156*: -rent *codd.*
[31] -ubi *Wint.[9]*
[32] -ri B V
[33] -el ut *B. Asc.[2]*: -el, ut *male Gr.-Mer.*

[16] Cf. 13.4.2; Introduction to the present declamation.

prepared enough poison to treat the gardens even of a rich man. He smeared the flowers with evil juices, and changed the honey into poison. He scattered death on all the flowers—and spoiled in the process so many more than the bees would have carried away! (5) They awakened out of eagerness for their daily work, as soon as dawn summoned the light, and flew off (poor things) to their usual pastures, so that, before the sun's rays drank up the damp of night, they could cull the morning dews and carry off the sky-born liquid to their storehouses, drinking not for themselves but for their work.[16] 6. Here was a sad sight, one to win pity, almost, from the very man who had brought it about. One bee, at the first draft of the deadly juice, flees, dismayed by the unusual taste: but flight is of no use. Another soars upward in search of food further away, and leaves its life on the breeze. (2) Another dies on the very first blossom. Another, its feet stiffening in death, hangs lifeless as it had clung. (3) Another, worn out by the effort of flying, creeps feebly along on the ground. But if to some death came more slowly and only when they reached their hive, they hung under the doors as sick bees are wont to do; huddled in a mass and embracing each other, they were parted only by death.[17] (4) Who could imagine, who could tell, how many forms of suffering, what different types of end were represented where so many died! But to finish this sad narrative once for all, let *this* be said: I lost them all. (5) That famous hive, better known than its owner, was reduced to nothing.

[17] "The individualized deaths are largely dependent on Ovid's tale [*Met.* 6.290–96] of the death of Niobe's children" (Van den Berg [2016, 168]).

6   Audete nunc lacessere divitem, quibus vitae causa
superest, exerite libertatem fortibus verbis, si quid offen-
derit: et[34] quod difficillimum fuit iam expertus est—vene-
7 num.[35] Quodsi mihi fortuna vel ingenii vires vel suas dedisset, crimen istud non privatam taxationem[36] formulae
merebatur. Venenum leges habere, emere, nosse denique
vetant, inevitabilem pestem occulta fraude grassantem.
Male haeret ibi innocentia, ubi in potestate est secretum
8 scelus.[37] [Velut][38] Venenum, et quidem praesentaneum,
inventum, compositum, datum est. Quantulum interest,
9 quis biberit! Homo dedit; et homini dari potest. Non adeo
desunt odiorum causae ut iam rara simultas sit, et, ut videatur aliquis nihil magis quam malos[39] odisse, libebit
aliquando longius manum porrigere et indulgere animis.
Credite mihi, iudices: difficilius est venenum invenire
quam inimicum.

    7. Sed me conscia mediocritatis infirmitas intra meas
tantummodo continet querelas. Nam damnum—id est, iudices, gravissimum pauper[40] vulnus—accepi.[41] Quod mihi

---

[34] id A, *sed hic* et = etiam (*B. Asc.[1] xci v.*)

[35] et—venenum *dist. Håk.[2] 107*   [36] taxat- 5: act- M E:
exact- A: extat- *cett.*: aestimat- *Reitz.[2] 63 (sed vd. Håk.)*

[37] *gravius dist. Obr.*   [38] *del. Gron. (corrob. Håk.[2] 107)*

[39] alios *Håk.[3] 134–35, sed vd. Mant.[1] 380.1 (coll. Quint. 11.1.42)*

[40] -ri *Sch. (plane facilius)*

[41] nam—accepi *dist. Gron.*

---

18 Poor Man himself does not: cf. 13.1.3.

19 I.e., show you are free by speaking out strongly even against
a rich man. Cf. 7.12.6.   20 Poison is the most difficult means
to commit a crime, as it needs to be procured, made up, and
administered in secrecy: cf. 13.6.8–9, and, e.g., 2.11.1, 2.12.2.

(6) Venture now to challenge the rich man, you who still have a reason to go on living,[18] assert your liberty with strong words,[19] if he gives offense: he has already tried out even what was the most difficult thing—poison.[20] (7) Yet, if fortune had bestowed on me either strength of intellect or its own power, this crime would not be meriting the assessment of damages in a *private* suit.[21] The laws[22] forbid possessing, buying, even having knowledge of poison—a plague that cannot be escaped, for it wreaks its havoc by hidden deceit. Innocence can hardly hold firm where secrecy in crime is within one's power. (8) Poison, and an instantaneous one at that, has been found, made up, administered. How little difference it makes who drank it! A man administered it; it can be administered to a man too. (9) There is not such a dearth of reasons to hate that feuding is uncommon nowadays: so even if a person seems to go no further than hating the wicked, sooner or later he will take delight in going one better and giving in to his feelings. Believe me, judges: it is harder to find a poison than to find an enemy.

7. But I am weak, and awareness of my limited powers restricts me to my own complaints only.[23] For I have, judges, sustained a loss—that is, being a poor man, I have received a most serious wound. I need to take more time

---

[21] I would have charged Rich Man with the more serious crime of poisoning, if only Fortuna had given me the talent needed to win the case—or at least had she helped me with her power to change things suddenly for the better.

[22] Specifically, the *lex Cornelia de sicariis et veneficis*.

[23] He is too weak to bring a public prosecution for poison: cf. 13.6.7.

diutius deflendum apud vos quam probandum est: nam
coarguendi[42] quidem criminibus quis labor est adversus
2 confitentem? Habent divites hoc quoque contra nos con-
tumeliosum, quod non tanti videmur ut negent. Porro qui
confessum defendit non absolutionem sceleris petit, sed
3 licentiam. Longius ista, quam finivi,[43] quaestio pervenit;[44]
non de praeterito tantum litigamus: hoc agitur, ut, etiam
si quid forte reparavero,[45] iterum diviti liceat occidere.
4 In duas enim, quantum animadvertere potui, quaes-
tiones dividit causam: an damnum sit, et an iniuria datum.
5 Negat esse damnum, quod animal liberum et volucre et
vagum et extra imperia positum perdiderim.[46] Negat iniuria datum, quod in privato suo, quod eas, quae sibi noce-
rent, extinxerit, postremo, quod sparso tantum per flores
6 veneno ipsae apes ultro ad mortem venerint. Ut nihil esset
quod his possem respondere: aequum erat inter vicinos sic
agi? Sed excutiam singula, nec prius meis argumentis nitar
quam diversa reppulero, quoniam quidem quaeritur an
damnum sit perdere quod lucrum est habere.

[42] -di M (*vind. Håk.*): -dis A: -dum *cett.*
[43] finivi *Dim.*: timui *codd.*
[44] -tinet *Gron., sed cf. Dim.*
[45] rep- ⟂: praep- *codd.*
[46] -im *Sh. B.² 207–8*: -it *codd.*

[24] This trial is intended not only to compensate Poor Man for
the loss he has suffered (as he has just stated: 13.7.1) but also to
prevent future loss, should he manage to restore his hives. Cf.
13.10.6.
[25] The arguments exploited by the two parties in what follows
are grounded on an actual dispute among Roman jurists: see
Introduction to the present declamation.

bewailing it to you than proving it: why go to the trouble of convicting by charges when your opponent confesses? (2) Rich men have this further means of insulting us: they don't think us worth a denial. Further, anyone who defends admitted guilt is not asking for acquittal from the crime, but for license to commit it. (3) What is at stake goes further than my statement of it just now.[24] We are not just going to law about the past; what is at issue is this: even if I make good my loss to some degree, the rich man may kill a second time.

(4) So far as I could make out, he is dividing the case into two questions: "Is it a loss?" and "Was it caused maliciously?"[25] (5) He says it is *not* a loss, because I have been bereft of an animal that is free, winged, roving, beyond the reach of orders. He says the loss was not caused maliciously, because he destroyed them on his private land, because they were bees that were harming him, and lastly because the poison was merely spread on the flowers and the bees came to their deaths of their own free will. (6) Even if there were no other answer to this, was it right[26] for there to be such dealings between neighbors? But I will discuss the points one by one, not relying on my own arguments before I have rejected those of the other side. For the question at issue is this:[27] is it a loss to be deprived of what it is profitable to possess?

[26] A brief mention of the general principle of *aequitas*, before going on to "technical" arguments.

[27] The first part of the division (13.7.4), phrased in a prejudicial way.

8. "Liberum est animal."[47] Puta non dico[48] fetus meis
manibus exceptos et in tutam conditos sedem, ex[49] reser-
vatis ad supplementa generis favis examen vernaculum,[50]
‹iam›[51] (quoniam quidem tyrannorum iura defendis) na-
2   tos in privato meo. Puta me vel inanis arboris trunco vel
cavis inventos petris domum favos retulisse; multa nihilo-
minus, quae libera fuerant, transeunt in ius occupantium,
sicut venatio et aucupatio. Nam, ut cetera animalia hominum causa finxerit providentia, quod omnibus[52] nascitur
3   industriae praemium est. Quid autem non liberum natura
genuit? Taceo de servis, quos bellorum iniquitas in prae-
dam victoribus dedit, isdem legibus, eadem forma, eadem
necessitate natos; ex eodem caelo spiritum trahunt, nec
4   natura illis[53] sed fortuna dominum dedit. Cur infrenatis
equis victor[54] insidet,[55] cur iniusto cotidie iugo boum colla
deterimus, cur in usum vestium saepe pecori lanae detra-
huntur? Taceo de sanguine et epulis per mortem paratis.
Si omnia, quae libera generantur, naturae reddemus,[56]

47 *verba personata agn. Reitz.*[2] *77.6 post Bur.*
48 p. n. d. *paratactice dictum, vd. Str.*[17] *994*
49 ex *Str.*[17] *994*: et *codd.*: et ‹ex› *Sch.*
50 sedem—vernaculum *dist. vulg., elucid. Wint. ap. Str.*[17]
994–95   51 *suppl. Str.*[17] *995*: ‹non dico› *Wint. ibid.*
52 homin- V   53 illis AE *(firm. Håk.*[2] *107)*: vilis *cett.*
54 vic- *codd. (def. Beck.*[2] *46)*: vec- *Gron.*: rec- *Bur.*
55 -dit V: -dis β: cur—insidet *post* natos (§3) *habent codd., huc
transp.* B[2]
56 redde- V: rede- B: reddi- B[2]: de- Φ

28 Literally, "tyrants," pejoratively; cf. 13.4.3.
29 My bees were born on my own land, and you as a *rich* man

8. "It is a free animal." Suppose I am not speaking about offspring taken out by my own hands and stored in a safe place—a homemade colony, bred from the combs I had reserved for the increase of the race—, ‹in sum› (you are yourself a supporter of the rights of owners,[28] aren't you?)[29] about offspring born on my private property. (2) Suppose, rather, that I found combs in the trunk of a hollow tree or in caves, and took them home with me; in much the same way, many things that were once free pass under the control of those who take possession of them, like the products of hunting or bird-catching. For granted that the other animals were made by providence for the sake of man, nevertheless what is born for the benefit of all is the reward of *industry*.[30] (3) But what was not in a state of freedom when nature brought it to birth? I pass over slaves, given as spoil to the victors by the injustice of war. They were *born* subject to the same laws, the same form, the same necessity, as other men; they draw breath from the same sky, and it was chance, not nature, that gave them a master. (4) Why does a man ride triumphantly on bridled horses, why do we every day chafe the necks of oxen with the unjust yoke, why are sheep often robbed of their fleeces to make our clothes?[31]—to say nothing of the bloody banquets furnished forth by death.[32] If we give back to nature everything that is born free, you rich men

are after all a defender of the rights of property owners—and so will agree that I *own* those bees.

[30] This is not the Golden Age. No doubt animals were created to serve man, but we can benefit from them only by working hard. See also 13.15.6.   [31] Sc., if all these animals were born *free*?

[32] Sc., of animals.

5 desinitis divites esse. Si vero haec condicio est, ut, quicquid ex his animalibus in usum hominis cessit, proprium
sit habentis, profecto quicquid iure possidetur, iniuria au-
fertur: ut[57] ⟨et⟩[58] volucres mutaque[59] [et][60] alia[61] quae per
rusticas villas quaeque ditibus cellis saginantur, in quibus
tamen domini ambigua[62] possessio est, et vaccae et ar-
menta et omne pecudum genus.[63]

9. "Sed illa impositus cohibet magister." Peiusne domino in his ius est, quibus custode non opus est? Nam si
hoc dicis,[64] nihil esse nostrum quod perire possit, ex nul-
2 lius animalis damno haec edi formula potest. Nam et er-
rare pecudes solent et fugere mancipia. Si hoc in ceteris
non obstat, vagari tu nolles ⟨apes⟩,[65] in opus exire et ad
cotidianum pensum[66] laboris assidui non detractare mili-
3 tiam? At[67] non ipsae domum sua sponte revolant finemque
laboris sui sole metiuntur, et omnis intra solitas domos
4 turba conditur, noctemque modesto silentio trahunt? Age
porro, ut non sit earum certa possessio dum volant, nempe
cum remearunt, cum cludi,[68] transferri, donari, venire
possunt, in potestate sunt. Quomodo autem potest sine
damno meo perire, quod cotidie meum est?

57 ut B²Φ: aut B V   58 addidi
59 mutaque scripsi (cf. ThlL VIII.1733.55–62; et alia muta Reitz.² 77): mutae codd. (def. Mant.¹ 382–84.3): multa Håk.
60 delevi   61 -a B²: -ae cett.
62 ⟨non⟩ am- Sch. (sed vd. Helm¹ 386, Mant.¹ 365–66.160, Corbino 517.28)   63 et vaccae—genus secl. Wint. ap. Kr.¹
64 -cis Håk.: -citis codd.
65 h.l. add. AE: ante vagari Håk.
66 pe- Gron. (cf. Colum. 3.10.7): ce- codd.
67 an ⌜   68 cum cl- Håk.: concl- codd.

110

cease to be rich. (5) But if it is the convention that any of these animals that have come to be used by man belongs to its possessor, surely whatever is legally owned is wrongfully taken away: including birds and other creatures that are fattened up in country villas and the cages of the rich—ambiguous as the owner's possession is, in their case—, as well as cows and draft animals and every type of cattle.[33]

9. "But a keeper is set over those animals to keep them in." Is an owner worse off in his rights over bees, which need no one to guard them? For if you say this, that nothing belongs to us that is capable of being lost, then this legal action cannot be brought in the case of the loss of any animal. (2) Cattle often stray, slaves often run away. If this is not an obstacle in the other cases, would you not want ‹bees› to rove abroad, to go out to work, to consent to a service that involves them in unending toil to complete their daily stint? (3) But don't they fly back home of their own free will, measuring the end of their working day by the going down of the sun, when the whole troop is packed away in the familiar hives and they spend the night in demure silence? (4) Look: right of possession over them may not be beyond dispute while they are on the wing; but when they have returned, when they can be shut in, moved, given away, sold, surely they are under control. Now, how can something that is mine every day[34] be lost without causing me loss?

[33] See Introduction to the present declamation.
[34] I.e., for part of every day (DAR).

[QUINTILIAN]

5   "At extra imperia positum est." Mirum hercules, si
negato commercio sermonis humani sunt in ceterorum
6 animalium forma. Tamen quam dominus dedit incolunt
sedem, lascivientem luxuria[69] fugam tinnitu compesci-
mus. Etiam, si diversis regibus coorta seditio ad bellum
inflammavit iras, exiguo pulvere vel unius poena ducis
7 residit[70] omnis tumor. Illa vero admiranda sedulitas, quod
operi totus insumitur dies, in dominorum reditus ablata
supplentur. Age, si obsequi possent, quid amplius impe-
rares?
8   Intellego his vanis ultra necessitatem esse responsum.
Si non sunt apes meae, ne id quidem, quod his efficitur,
meum est; atqui nulla umquam inveniri potuit impuden-
9 tia, quae fructus mellis in dubium vocaret. Hoc ergo fieri
potest,[71] ut quod nascitur meum sit, quod generat alienum? 10. Age, si mihi alvei furto abessent, utrum nulla
2 daretur actio? An viminis modo vilisque texti[72] pretium
formula taxarem,[73] et proinde agerem, quasi inanes perdi-
3 dissem? Nisi fallor, esset aestimatio et apum. An[74] tandem
quas subripere non liceret, liceat occidere? Non est damnum quod exutus sum, quod reditus perdidi, quod annuos

69 -a V (*vind. Håk.*[2] *107–8*): -ae AE: -am *cett.*: ‹in› -am *Dess.*[2]
70 -sidit *Lund.*[2]: -sedit *codd.*: -sidet *Gr.-Mer.*
71 potest γ β (*def. Wint.*[7] *157*): fortes B V δ: forte putas π:
forte potest M   72 -ti M[pc] γ β*: -it B V: -iit δ
73 taxarem *Wint.*[7] *157*: taxassem Φ: (formula)ta saxem B: -tas
axem V
74 apum an Φ: apuma in B: apumain V

35 Cf. 13.3.7–8.   36 See Introduction to the present declamation on the kings of bees; also 13.17.8.

112

(5) "But the animal is beyond the reach of orders." Heavens, is it any wonder that, being denied the ability to communicate with humans, bees are in the same state as other animals? (6) But they do live in a home that their owner has given them; when they flee the hive with exuberant indiscipline, we quell them with the clashing of brass.[35] What is more, if sedition arises between different kings[36] and stirs them to angry war, the whole flurry calms down if a little dust is applied, or a single leader is executed. (7) But what is astonishing is their persistence: the whole day is devoted to work, and what owners take away for their own profit[37] is made up again. Tell me, if they *could* obey orders, what more would you demand of them?

(8) I realize that I have given a longer answer to these flimsy arguments than was necessary. If the bees are not mine, neither is what they make. But no one could ever have been found shameless enough to call in doubt the right to possess honey. (9) Can it then be that the product[38] belongs to me, but the producer to someone else? 10. Look, if my hives had been stolen, would I not be allowed to bring an action? (2) In drawing up the formula, would I just assess the price of the withies and the worthless wickerwork, and proceed as though there was nothing inside when I lost them? Unless I am mistaken, a valuation would be put on the bees too. (3) Is it really permissible to kill animals which it would not be permissible to steal? Is it no loss that I have been stripped of my property, that my source of revenue has been taken away, that I have

37 Honey: cf. 13.15.5, 13.17.3.
38 Literally, "what comes into existence," i.e., the honey.

fructus, praesidia paupertatis, amisi? Non est damnum
id perdidisse, quod—ut proximo utar argumento—, si
4 habere voluero, emendum est? Quid ergo tibi opus est
maleficis sucis, cum liceret palam trucidare et plenas vel
cremare igni vel aquis immergere alvos? An est aliquod
animal, quod non liceat nisi venenis occidere?
5   "Ut damnum sit," inquit, "iure tamen feci in privato
meo." Per fidem vestram, iudices, succurrite exemplo;[75]
non sufficit his partibus unus rusticus pauper, obviam
publice eundum est et obiciendae adversus nascentem
6 licentiam consensu manus. Credite mihi, maior lite quaestio est. Hoc vobis hodie iudicandum est, ubi scelus facere
7 non liceat. Nam cur non hoc idem de homicidio respondeat, cur non de latrocinio? Non enim iure ista sed
modo differunt. Aperitur ingens facinori[76] via, et obluc-
tantia diu legum velut claustris scelera libera porta pro-
8 rumpunt.[77] Si in privatum iura non veniunt,[78] et[79] in mani-
festissima quoque noxa non de facto quaeritur, sed de
loco, non aequa portione cum sceleribus[80] terras divisi-
mus: ubi enim non iam divitum privatum est? 11. Parum
est proximos ⟨quosque⟩[81] aequare terminos et posses-
siones suas velut quasdam gentes fluminibus montibusque
distinguere; iam etiam devios saltus et silvas vasta solitu-

---

[75] dist. Gr.-Mer. (et vd. Hâk.[2] 108): post suc- vulg.

[76] facinori Scheff. 452–53 (cf. mox scelera synon. positum):
funeri codd.: facine- Sh. B.[4] 206 (in decll. nusquam obvium)

[77] gravius dist. Gr.-Mer.   [78] -iunt ⟂: -iant codd. (frustra
def. Kr.[1])   [79] et ⟨si⟩ Tab.[4] XXIII.1   [80] -ribus π (vind.
Reitz.[2] 76.5): -ris B V: -ratis Φ (def. Helm[1] 385)   [81] ⟨quosque⟩
supplevi (⟨quosque solo⟩ Wint.[7] 157): ⟨solo⟩ Bur. (at vd. OLD[2]
aequo §3.b): an ⟨usque⟩ (cf. Hor. Carm. 2.18.23–24)?

forfeited my annual returns, the support of my poverty? Is it no loss to have forfeited something that—to use the nearest argument to hand—I should have to buy if I wanted to acquire it? (4) Why then do you need baleful juices, when it was permissible to kill them openly and to burn or flood hives full of bees? Is there any creature which it would not be permitted to kill except by poison?

(5) "It may be a loss," he argues, "but I acted legally, for I was on my own property." I ask you, judges: give your aid in the fight against this precedent; a single poor countryman is not up to this role: we must attack with everyone helping us, and come together to oppose a license that is beginning to establish itself. (6) Believe me, the question goes beyond this particular case. Today you have to make a judgment: where is it not permissible to commit a crime? (7) Why, in fact, should he not make the same answer in a case of murder, or in a case of robbery with violence? These are different only in degree, not in the legal principle involved. This gives a wide opening to outrageous behavior: crimes that have long been struggling to break down—as it were—the barriers of the laws are now bursting forth with nothing to block their way. (8) If laws are not to extend to private property, and even in the most manifest crime the question concerns not the act but the place, we have not shared out the earth equally with crime:[39] where, after all, can you now find a place that is not the private property of the rich? 11. It is not enough for them to tear down ‹successive› boundary stones, and make rivers and mountains mark off their estates—as though they were different peoples. No, now they even

---

[39] I.e., we have given crime a larger share of the earth.

dine horridas occupant, totae aquae[82] intra paucorum
umbram latent, e finibus suis populus excluditur, nec ullus
procedentis finis est, nisi cum [et][83] in alterum divitem
2 inciderit. Adhuc tamen spolia transeuntium et abacti pecorum greges sub hoc titulo defendebantur; iam privati
veneni praescriptio[84] est?[85] Iterum ac saepius, iudices,
admoneo, considerate, dispicite:[86] aut nihil usquam contra
ius licet aut in privato omnia.
3   "At enim[87] adversus inferentem damnum iusta ultio
fuit." Dicam nunc quam iniqua sit invicem iniuriae com-
4 pensatio, quamque non solum legi adversa sed paci? Bar-
barorum mos est populorum, quos procul omni[88] iuris
humani societate summotos proxime beluis natura effera-
vit. Nos ideo magistratus legesque a maioribus nostris
accepimus, ne sui quisque doloris vindex[89] sit, et adsiduae
scelerum causae se reserant,[90] si ultio crimen imitabitur.[91]
5 Damnum accepisti?[92] Erat lex, forum, iudex—nisi si vos
6 iure vindicari pudet. At mehercule, si ad arma mittimur
et instituitur perniciosa nocendi contentio, et in vicem

    [82] totae aquae *Håk. (cf. Håk.[6] 23)*: tota qui B: totaque V (*def. Russ.[3]: "and all this"*): tot aquae Φ

    [83] *del. Wint.[9], et om.* V S

    [84] praes- *Sh. B.[4] 206*: trans- *codd. (frustra def. Reitz.[2] 76.5)*

    [85] *sic dist. Håk.*

    [86] -spici- *Håk.[2] 108*: -sci- *codd.*

    [87] at enim ⌐ (*sic 18^{ies} personatae obiectiones inducuntur in Decl. min.*): etenim *codd.*

    [88] -i π: -is *cett.*

    [89] vin- E (*def. Str.[17] 996*): iu- *cett.*

    [90] reser- *Str.[17] 996*: refell- *codd. (frustra def. Tab.[4] XXIV.1)*

    [91] -tatur *Wint.[7] 157, sed vd. H.-Sz. 661*

    [92] *sic dist. Håk.*

take over trackless moors and immense wastes of gloomy forest; whole waters[40] lie hidden in the shadow of a few; a people finds itself barred from its own territories, and there is no end to a rich man's advance except when he comes up against another one.[41] (2) Hitherto the robbery of persons crossing one's land and the seizure of their herds have been justified on this plea;[42] is there now a let-out clause for private poisoning?[43] Again and yet again I warn you, judges—consider, take a close look: either nothing is permitted anywhere if it is against the law, or everything is allowed on private land.

(3) "But, to be sure, it was fair to take revenge on someone causing loss." Do I have to tell you how *unfair* tit-for-tat compensation for injury is, how contrary to law—and to peace too? (4) It is the custom of barbarous peoples, removed by nature far from any share in men's legal systems and reduced almost to the level of wild beasts.[44] We have inherited magistrates and laws from our ancestors precisely so that each person should *not* be avenger of his own grievance: reasons to commit crimes will break out without cease, if vengeance imitates the action that provoked it. (5) Have you sustained a loss? There was the law, the forum, a judge—unless you rich men are ashamed to be vindicated in court. (6) Now surely, if we are sent away to take up arms, a damaging competition in mutual harm is set going, and anger takes

---

[40] I.e., whole rivers; cf. Sen. *Ep.* 89.20.   [41] Cf. 13.2.4.

[42] Sc., that they took place on private property: see Introduction to the present declamation.   [43] = is poisoning immune from prosecution if committed on private property?

[44] Cf. 3.4.2.

legis ira succedit, premetur quidem obnoxia infirmitas, et
paucorum dominio subiecta plebes triste servitium perfe-
ret; est tamen et[93] pauperibus interim dolor, et, ut facilius

7 nobis noceri potest, ita vobis latius. Postremo, placeas licet
tibi opum tuarum fiducia, dives, si mihi vivere[94] non expedit, pares sumus.

12. Quid ergo? Si quid tibi damni attulissent apes
meae, non mihi auferretur actio,[95] sed forsan aliqua dare-

2 tur et tibi. Nunc vero quid quereris? Credo, depopulatos
agros eversosque reditus;[96] non enim debet leve esse dam-

3 num, quod dives ferre non possit. "Decerpebant" inquit
"flores meos." Ecquid[97] intellegitis, iudices, quanto dolore
dignum sit quod ego perdidi, si etiam hoc damnum est?

4 "Flores auferebant."[98] Ita plane; alioquin tu illos in vetus-
tatem reservabas, et durarent adhuc, nisi ad hortum tuum

5 apes venissent. Cuius rei inveniri potest brevior aetas?
Namque dum immaturos exterior alligat cortex, nondum
dixeris florem. Paulatim deinde vividiore suco tumescit

6 uterus et albentis accipit rimas, necdum tamen flos est. At
cum se ruptis iam tunicis in patulum capita fuderunt et
velut fissa in orbem,[99] iam quae[100] tenerorum[101] videtur

---

93 et D β: nec *cett.*   94 vive- *Valla* Eleg. 5.92 (*cf. Char.*
401–2): vide- *codd.*   95 act- *Håk.*[2] 108–9: rat- *codd.*

96 -itus N: -it *cett.* (-it rursus $\pi \psi \delta \beta$)

97 ecq- ς: et q- *codd.*   98 -ferebant (*et* damnum—*hucusque sic dist.*) *Håk.*: -ferre (-ff- V) B V D: -ferri *cett.*

99 or- <exeunt> *Bur., sed vd. Angl. vers.*

100 iam quae *Dess.*[2]: iamque B V Φ*   101 tenerorum *scripsi*
(tenera eorum *Håk.*[2] 110): terrarum B V Φ*

---

45 A threat: If I am reduced to an intolerable life, I may kill or

the place of law, the weak and vulnerable will be oppressed: ordinary persons, subject to the dominion of the few, will find they have a bitter slavery to put up with. Yet even the poor do have their grievances at times, and while *we* can be harmed more easily, *you* can be harmed on a wider front. (7) In the end, rich man, however complacently you rely on your wealth, you and I are on a level if it is not in my interest to go on living.[45]

12. What then? If my bees had caused you some loss, I should not be denied the right to bring my suit, though perhaps a suit might be granted to you too. (2) As it is, what is your complaint? That your fields were ravaged and your revenues ruined?[46] Serious indeed must be the loss a rich man cannot bear! (3) "They were," he says, "culling my flowers." If this too counts as a loss, don't you realize, judges, how painful *my* loss is? (4) "They were taking away my flowers." Yes, indeed;[47] otherwise you would be keeping them till they grew old, and they would still be blooming now if my bees had not visited your garden. (5) Can anything be found that lives for so short a time? While they are still immature and bound up in their outer cover, you wouldn't call them flowers. Next, gradually, the bud swells as the sap becomes livelier, and white slits appear; but it is still not yet a flower. (6) Yet when the cases break open and the heads spread wide, as it were split to form a round, then what seems to be the maturity of delicate things is

otherwise harm you without fearing the consequences, however severe—and your riches will not be able to protect you.

[46] Alluding (ironically) to the *actio de pastu pecoris*, allowing the plaintiff to require compensation for damage caused by someone else's cattle grazing on his field.   [47] Ironic.

maturitas et innatus[102] occasus est: etiam[103] sine ventis
quoque soluta natura labitur gratia, nec quicquam est flos
7 nisi novus. Quare si dicerem: abstulere peritura et, quae
protinus humi iacuissent, in usus hominum conversa,
inauditus tandem[104] livor videretur etiam apibus invidere.
8 Nunc vero disserendum mihi est, quam momentosa sit
huius animalis rapina? Nescimus, qua pernicitate plerumque vix contactis floribus revolet discurratque per singulos
velox experimento, quam,[105] etiam ubi immorantur,[106]
9 libratis pendeant[107] alis? Quis umquam quod ferentem
apem viderat, ubi deesset, invenit? 13. Quantulum vero
est, quod ex his manu consitis floribus legant! Prata silvae-
que vel maturae fructibus vites et fraglantes thymo colles,
quantum coniectura suspicari potest, pabulum ministrant.
2 Non ‹ex›[108] omnibus floribus carpunt utilia operi suo, sed
in omnibus quaerunt. Praesens quidem illa protinus redditur merces, quod omnibus, quibus insedere, odorem
3 mellis inspirant et brevi contactu vim sui relinquunt. Hoc
tu damnum intellegis? Hoc veneno vindicas, quod mehercule inhumane etiam fumo prohibuisses?
4 An non te solus vicinus[109] colui? Non frugum mearum

---

102 inna- (*vel* ingeni-) *Dess.[1]* 90: igno- *codd.* (*def. Russ.[3]*:
"*unrecognized*")   103 et iam ⌐, *sed vd. ThlL* V.2.945.9ss.
104 tandem *scripsi*: tamen *codd.*   105 *dist. Wint.[9]*
106 -rantur β: -rabantur B V γ δ: -ratur π
107 -eat πM^pc
108 *add.* ⌐ (*vind. Wint.[7]* 158): ‹de› A
109 -lum -nus *Sh. B.[2]* 208, *Sh. B.[4]* 206: -lum -num *Str. ap. Kr.[1]*

---

48 Sc., the flowers (that were about to fall).
49 Ironic. Cf. Pasetti (2008c, 446).

also the decline that is inborn in them: even without a breath of wind, they fall apart by a natural process, and their loveliness slips away; a flower is only a flower when it is new. (7) So I would only need to say that they took away what was destined to perish, that what would very soon have been lying on the ground was turned to human use, and begrudging all that[48] even to bees would appear once and for all as an unheard piece of spite.

(8) All the same, need I now explain how weighty[49] is the thievery of this animal? Don't we know how quickly it usually flies away after barely touching the flowers, and hurries around the blooms in turn, swift to test them out; how, too, even when bees do stay for a while, they merely hover there, balancing on their wings? (9) And granted you've seen a bee carrying something off, have you ever found a gap where it was missing? 13. In any case, how small a part of what they cull comes from these *cultivated* flowers! Their food (so far as our guesswork can go) comes from meadows and woods, vines with ripened grapes, thyme-scented hills. (2) They don't take what they need for their product <from> all flowers, though they look for it in all. And they pay their dues at once, on the spot: everywhere they alight they breathe out the fragrance of honey, leaving some of their potency behind at a brief touch. (3) Do you regard this as damaging you? Do you avenge with *poison* what indeed you would have been heartless to prohibit with *smoke*?

(4) Am I not the only neighbor who has been civil to you?[50] Have I not sent you every spring the first pickings

---

[50] There is a sting in the words: he is the only neighbor *left*, because of Rich Man's greed (13.2.4–5, 13.4.4).

primitias omni vere misi? Non, si quis ceris novis candi-
dior incidit favus, tuis reservatus est mensis, cum parvis
mediocritate munusculis illa semper adiceretur commen-
datio: "Hoc tibi mittunt apes meae"? Puto, relata est mihi
gratia!

5   "Admonui," inquit, "et, ut transferres, denuntiavi."
6 Idcirco contumacem merito punisti?[110] Non enim video
quid aliud patrocinio tuo conferat haec denuntiatio
[supervacua],[111] si non licuit tibi facere quod queror,
iniusta, si licuit, ‹supervacua›;[112] ius[113] aut sine ista, aut
ne cum ista quidem valeat. Pudoris vero quod velamen-
7 tum est male audire culpa,[114] defendi superbia! An[115] tandem tuas pecudes quamvis diffusa stabula non capient,
tibi omne armentis mugiet nemus, tu gregibus arva sulca-
bis, et ad excolendos agros procedet ignota etiam vilicis
familia, tuis horreis populi annona pendebit, nec tamen
invidebimus, nec quisquam iam[116] grave putabit sibi istud
8 fortunae tuae pondus? Nos si paucas apes intra angustias
pauperis horti composuimus, quae tamen vobis mella faciunt, id prorsus indigne[117] ferendum est, et—quod numquam fando cognitum est—vicinus diviti pauper molestus
est? 14. Adeo parum est plurimum possidere, ut, cum
servis quoque vestris habere peculium liceat, invidiosum

---

110 *sic dist. Håk.*[2] *110*
111 *del. Wint.*[2] *48*
112 *h.l. suppl. Wint.*[3]*: post* iniusta *Wint.*[2] *48*
113 ius *Mant.*[2] (*unde* ius tuum *Wint.*[9]*, coll. sua adn. ad* Decl.
min. *294.2*): iusta *codd.*: *del. Wiles 69*
114 -am Φ   115 an ς: aut in B V: aut Φ
116 iam *Franc.*: tam *codd.*
117 -ne ς: -num *codd.*: -num ‹nec› *Sch.*

of my fruit? Have I not kept for your table any especially clear honey that fell into the new combs, always accompanying my gifts, small because of my humble means, with the greeting: "This is from my bees"? I've had my thank-you letter, I think![51]

(5) "I warned you," he says, "and gave you notice to move them." Does that mean you were justified in punishing me for contumaciousness? (6) I don't in fact see what new point this notice adds to the case for your defense. If it was not legal for you to do what I complain of, the notice you gave me was unjust; if it was legal, it was ‹superfluous›. Your case would hold good without the notification—or not even with it. What cover for shame is it to be in bad odor for wrongdoing, and then to defend yourself by arrogance! (7) Will your sheds then, extensive though they are, not be big enough for your beasts? Will every forest resound with their mooing? Will you plow your land with whole droves of oxen? Will a household of slaves, strangers even to the bailiff, go forth to tend the fields? Will the bread supply of a whole people depend on your granaries?—and shall we not envy you, even so? Will no one, at such a point, think your wealth is a heavy burden on him? (8) Then if *I* have housed a few bees in the narrow confines of a poor garden (and after all they make honey for *you* rich men),[52] is that so intolerable? Is a poor man a troublesome neighbor to a rich man? No one ever heard tell of such a thing. 14. Are you so dissatisfied to possess vast wealth that, though your slaves are allowed to have their little nest egg, you have to begrudge me anything

[51] Ironic.
[52] Cf. 13.3.6, 13.19.2.

[QUINTILIAN]

2   nobis putetis quicquid egestatis nomen excesserit? Tam
honestis[118] in hac, ut putamus, aequissima libertate legibus vivimus, ut nobis habere medellam non liceat, vobis
habere liceat venena?

3   Postremo quidem divitis patrocinio non putavi, iudices, respondendum, nisi rideri vestram maiestatem con-

4 tumeliosa defensione non ferrem. "Ultro enim" inquit "ad
mortem venerunt apes tuae." Ita plane; alioquin tu venenum floribus dederas. Impudentiaene, iudices, eius adsig-
nem, si hoc nihil[119] apud vos obtinuit,[120] an stultitiae, si

5 speravit? Si venenum homini dedisset, diceret ipsum la-
biis admovisse pocula; si percussorem posuisset[121] in saltu,
ipsum in insidias ultro venisse clamaret; si telum obiectas-

6 set[122] in tenebris, inlatum[123] sua culpa contenderet. Ego,
iudices, quid dico? Duo esse sola, quae omni in crimine

7 spectanda sint: animum et eventum. Quis animus divitis[124]
fuit, cum venenum sparsit? Ut apes perirent. Quis even-

8 tus? Perierunt. In summa, iudices, quis dubitat quin damnum ei sit imputandum, sine quo non accidisset?

    15. Intellego neque prudentiam vestram desiderare
plura de causa neque vestram fidem ac religionem egere

---

118 tam honestis *Håk.²* *111*: tantone his *codd.*

119 nihil *Håk.*: mihi *codd.*   120 -uit *Wint.²* *49*: -uerit *codd.*

121 potuisset B AC^{ac}D: posuit sed V   122 ob- ς: ab- *codd.*

123 ⟨non⟩ inl- AE, *sed hic* inferri (= *fere* incĭdere, *cf. ThlL*
VII.1.1378.46ss.) *ad victimam respicit*

124 -ti *Franc.*

---

53 Honey (see again 13.19.2).   54 Ironic.

55 If the bees hadn't come, Rich Man would (absurdly) just
have been poisoning his own flowers (DAR). Cf. 13.19.4.

that goes beyond what would be called neediness? (2) Do we live under such fair laws, in this—as we like to think it—completely just and free society, that people like me are not allowed to possess a remedy,[53] yet people like you are allowed to possess poison?

(3) I did not indeed think, judges, that there was any need to reply to the rich man's final line of argument: but I could not bear your authority to be mocked by such an insolent defense. (4) "Your bees," he says, "came to their deaths of their own accord." Yes, to be sure:[54] if they hadn't, you would have just given poison to the *flowers*.[55] Am I to call it his impudence, judges, if he made no impression on you with this argument, or his folly, if he hoped he would? (5) If he had given poison to a man, he'd say the victim moved the cup to his own lips. If he had stationed an assassin in a wood, he'd cry that the victim had been ambushed of his own volition. If he had thrown a spear in the darkness, he'd contend that if somebody had run into it, it was his own fault![56] (6) What can I say, judges? There are two things, and two only, that have to be considered in respect of every crime: motive and result. (7) What was the rich man's motive in sprinkling the poison? That the bees should die. What was the result? That they died. (8) To put it in a nutshell, judges: who can doubt that the damage is to be ascribed to the man but for whom it would not have taken place?

15. I am well aware that you[57] are too wise to require anything more to be said about the case, and too conscientious and too pious to need to be exhorted to judge accord-

---

[56] Sc., fault of the victim (with *suus = eius*).

[57] Judges.

2 exhortatione vere iudicandi. Quid moror igitur? Tenet me
   dolor et adsuetae voluptatis desiderium. Sunt quaedam in
3 hac causa, quae sarcire poena non possit. Maior forsitan
   materia videatur adfectus: sed[125] pauperes amare nisi paria[126] non possumus, et necessario nobis pretiosa, quae
   sola sunt. Animum meum extinctae unius horae momento
   tot animae movent, ‹movet›[127] quod perierint de me bene
4 meritae. Quin ipsum leti genus addit indignationem: veneno perierunt! Quis hoc ulla satis persequi[128] possit invi-
5 dia? Apes veneno! Haec illis gratia refertur quod fructibus
   nostris invigilant, quod cotidiana statione laboris adsidui
6 ne damno quidem summoventur? Namque[129] cetera animalia videtur mihi natura usibus nostris genuisse, haec
   etiam deliciis: cum eo quod in illis, quae vel scindendo solo
   vel maturando itineri comparamus, multus ante reditus
   insumitur labor, et cum perdomanda, cum alenda sint,
   nihil tamen possunt sine homine, et tantum coacta pro-
   sunt; apes ‹opus›[130] faciunt iniussae, ac[131] sine ullo ratio-
7 nis humanae ministerio totus fructus ultro venit. Adice

---

[125] sed *Wint.[7] 158*: si *codd.*
[126] parva *Bur., sed vd. Tab.[1] 102 et Tab.[2]*
[127] *lac. stat. Håk., explev. Sh. B.[4] 206 necnon Russ.[1] 45*
[128] pros- V Φ   [129] namque *scripsi*: nam et *codd. (sc. e
compendio male soluto)*: nam ut *Håk.[2] 112–13*: nempe *Wint.[9]*
[130] *add. Wint.[2] 49 (cf. 13.4.1)*
[131] ac H[2] *(def. Bur.)*: fac B V Φ* ·

---

58 I.e., not even a penalty.
59 Sc., the honey we take from them. Cf. 13.9.7, 13.17.3.
60 Cf. 13.8.2.
61 Literally, "considering that." For this rare meaning of *cum*

ing to the truth. (2) Why do I dwell on these things then? I am gripped by grief, and by my distress at the loss of a pleasure I had grown used to. There are certain things in this case that a penalty[58] could not mend. (3) My emotion may seem greater than the subject warrants: but we poor men can only love what is on our own level, and our sole possessions cannot but be precious to us. I am moved by the thought of so many lives snuffed out in a single hour, ‹I am moved› by the fact that they died despite deserving so well of me. (4) Indeed the manner of their end adds to the indignation I feel: they died by poison! Who could summon the bile to avenge that sufficiently? (5) Bees, by poison! Is this the reward for their concern for our income, for their refusal to abandon their daily duty of unending toil despite the losses they suffer?[59] (6) In fact, the other animals—I think—were created by nature for us to make use of them,[60] these for our pleasure as well: for indeed[61] the other animals, which we acquire for plowing or speed of travel, demand a great deal of trouble before there is any return—they have to be broken in, they have to be fed, still[62] they are capable of nothing without man, being only of use if they are coerced; *bees* do ‹their job› without being ordered, all the produce comes of its own accord without any contribution from human reason. (7) Add too

---

eo quod, expressing a condition connected or innate to something (Hand [1832, 166]), cf. Quint. 12.10.47 with Kühner-Stegmann (1976[5], II.2.272) (AS).

   [62] There is a play on *possunt/prosunt*: the other animals have to be tamed and maintained but cannot do anything without man; therefore, the good they do is done only under compulsion (DAR).

quod cetera aut satis incurrunt aut vitibus nocent, pri-
maque, ut fama est, hostiae causa pecudi fuit laesa fruges;
harum ita innoxius per prata silvasque discurrit labor, ut
tantum factum opus appareat.

16. Qua satis digna prosequar laude? Dicam animal
2 quodammodo parvum hominis exemplar? Hoc humana
excogitare non potuit sollertia. Etiam ratio nostra, quae
sub terris lucrum invenit, quae maria inquisitione sua sideribus immiscuit, hoc tamen efficere, consequi, imitari
non potuit. Venena potius invenimus.

3 Iam primum futurae laudabilis vitae digna principia:
non illas libido progenerat, domitrixque omnium animalium Venus, utque homines in excusationem sui fabulis
tradiderunt, etiam deorum potens,[132] has regnis suis ex-
4 cepit. Abest inimica virtutium voluptas castis sine labe
corporibus: solae omnium non edunt fetus sed faciunt.
Ipsae paulatim, sicut stipatae sunt,[133] per mella vivescunt,
5 et, ut oportet, animal laboriosum ex opere nascitur. Inde
ut adolevit iuventus, et ad similes labores aetas roborata
convaluit, relinquitur liber parentibus locus, et, ne coacta
in angustum multitudo nova turba laboret, quasi habita

---

[132] potens *Wiles 69 (firm. Håk.*[2] *104)*: poteris B: posteris V:
posteritas (pot- δ) Φ   [133] *dist. Wint.*[9]

---

63 Cf. Ov. *Fast.* 1.349–60.   64 *Hoc* = honey (here and
in the next sentence), arguably pointed to by the speaker in the
act (AS).   65 Referring to the ability of navigating by the
stars.   66 Cf. n. 64.

67 An attempt to explain the reproduction of bees—which was
a mystery throughout antiquity (see Introduction to the present

that the other animals trample on standing corn or harm vines: in fact, the first reason—as the story goes—for cattle to be used for sacrifices was the damage they had caused to crops;[63] *bees*, as they flit through meadows and woods, do their work so harmlessly that it can only be seen when it is already done.

16. With what praise shall I attend them that would come up to their deserts? Am I to say it is an animal representing in some sort a man in miniature? (2) Human wit has not been able to think up *this*.[64] Even our reason, which has found profit beneath the ground, which has involved sea and stars alike in its researches,[65] has not been able to effect, attain and replicate *this*:[66] we have chosen to invent poisons instead.

(3) First of all, the origins of bees match the praiseworthy life to follow. They are not generated by lust: Venus, mistress of all animals and—as men, to excuse themselves, have passed down in fable—with power even over the gods, has granted them exemption from her sway. (4) Their bodies are chaste and without stain, for pleasure, enemy of the virtues, is absent. Uniquely, they do not bring forth progeny, but make them.[67] They come gradually to life, crammed there as they are, throughout the honey: as is only right, a hardworking animal grows out of its product. (5) Then, when the young bees are older, and their mature strength has grown able to undergo similar labors, the place is left free for their elders:[68] lest the great numbers, forced into a narrow space, suffer from crowd-

declamation). The speaker believes that bees make their progeny out of honey: a theory with no parallels in surviving ancient texts.

[68] Literally, "parents."

verecundiae ratione cedit populus minor, suspensumque
proximis ramis examen humanas manus expectat; acceptas
6 cum fide colit sedes. Et, cum ingenia nostra, quae nos
scilicet ambitiosi nostri aestimatores proxima divinis credimus, ad percipiendas[134] disciplinas multo labore desu-
7 dent, nulla apes nisi artifex nascitur. Quid credas aliud
quam divinae partem mentis his animis[135] inesse?

17. Quid praecipuum referam?[136] Non, ut cetera animalia per pastus vaga, incertum quieti <locum >[137] capiunt,
cubile noctis arbitrio semper habitaturae: has tutae[138]
sedes continent; urbes tectis, turba populos imitantur.
2 Non, ut ferae volucres, [non][139] praesentis modo cibi me-
mores in diem vivunt; duraturus hiemi reponitur victus, et
3 repletis vere cellis tutus annus est. Etiam cum ad humanos
usus opera subducta sunt, reparare amissa contendunt et
labor damno incenditur, et numquam deficit animus ante
quam locus.
4 Quid, quod inter animalia, quae non verba coniungunt,
non vincla[140] rationis invicem nectunt,[141] tantus operis
consensus est, tanta difficillimae rei laboris concordia?
5 Non humano vitio in proprios[142] quaeque usus lucrum
ducit: in publicum vivitur, et communes opes congeruntur
in medium, nec fas[143] est delibare gustu prius quam plena

[134] perfici- B V, sed vd. Håk.[2] 113
[135] -malibus Beck.[2] 49, sed cf. 13.15.3 tot animae
[136] -am Russ.[3] (cf. 13.16.1): -as codd. (sc. e 13.16.7)
[137] suppl. et post capiunt dist. Wint. ap. Kr.[1]
[138] -urae et tutae Håk.[2] 113, has (vel apes) Wint. ap. Kr.[1]: -uras
et totis B V: -ura sed (sed et E) tutas Φ
[139] del. vDorp 42b (et om. A)
[140] vincla Gron.: verba (e super. sent.) codd.: [verba] rationes
Reitz.[2] 59

ing, the younger folk withdraw, as though out of conscious respect. Hanging on nearby boughs, the swarm awaits human hands, and once given a home it dwells there loyally. (6) *Our* intellects, which we fondly imagine to be close to divine (we are such biased judges of ourselves!), have to toil away at acquiring skills; but no bee is ever born that is not an artist. (7) What could you imagine being present in these souls if not a part of the divine mind?

17. What could I adduce as the key proof of this? The other animals which rove their feeding grounds find ‹a place› to sleep without planning beforehand, always ready to bed down where night dictates. But bees have safe lodgings: with their houses they mimic cities, with their numbers they mimic peoples. (2) They are not like wild birds, living for the day, and mindful only of the food immediately available. They lay up stocks that will last out the winter: once the cells are filled full in the spring, the whole year is secure. (3) Even when their produce has been taken away for men's purposes, they toil to fill the gaps and loss only stimulates labor: their zeal is unfailing as long as there is space to fill.

(4) What too of the cooperative effort, the coordinated labor in a task of such difficulty, seen in animals that have no words, no ties of reason to bind them together? (5) An individual bee does not devote its profits to its own use (that is the vice of *men*): they live for the general good, and pool the riches for all to share; they think it wrong to taste the honey until the storehouses are full and promise

---

141 nectunt *Reitz.*[2] 59: negant *codd.*

142 proprios AC[2]: proximos *cett.*

143 nec fas CD *β*: nefas *cett.*

6 horrea securos spondeant menses. Quis[144] porro tantus
ardor operis quaeve officiorum partitio, ut aliae congerant
onera, aliae accipiant, aliae liniant![145] Quae severitas in
7 castiganda inertia! Multa dictu visuque miranda: praevi-
dere tempestates nec dubio se caelo tradere[146] nec ultra
viciniam nubilo tendere. Iam[147] si levis[148] iniquior aura
rapuit, ad dirigendos in destinata cursus modico lapilli
8 pondere librare pinnas. Illa maiorum pectorum: motis[149]
pro rege castris procurrere et inire bella mortemque ho-
9 nestam pro duce oppetere. Adice quod, si quas aut aetas
longior aut morbus oppressit, efferuntur[150] prius corpora,
posteriorque operum quam funerum cura est.

18. Quid inligare cruribus flores? Quid ore fucos[151] in
2 publicum ferre? Me tamen ipsius operis praecipua admi-
ratio subit: non eas[152] temere nec fortuito[153] figuram et
sedes modo reponendis cibis quaesisse credas; rudis cera
3 componitur, accedit usibus inenarrabilis decor. Nam primum tenacibus vinculis fundamenta suspendunt, tum ab

144 qui B V, *sed vd. Kr.[1] et e.g. 13.19.3*
145 -nia- V (*cf. 13.3.7, 13.5.4*): -na- B Φ*
146 cred- *Franc. et Bur.* (*firm. Beck.[2] 49–50*), *fort. recte*
147 iam ⌐: nam *codd.*
148 -vis (*acc.*) B V: -ves Φ
149 mo- *Bur.*: vo- B: to- V Φ*
150 refe- B V δ   151 fu- V (*cf. Beck.[2] 50, ThlL VI.1.1461.39–
44*): su- B Φ   152 eas *Obr.* (*firm. Håk.[2] 113–14*): has π: est *cett.*
153 -to *Håk.[2] 113–14*: -tam B V Φ*

69 They seal with wax the cells in which they have stored their
loads of honey. Cf. Arist. *Hist. an.* 8(9).627a.10–11; below,
13.18.4.

months free of anxiety. (6) On top of that, how keen they are to work, how well they share out their duties—some bringing loads, others receiving them, others smearing them with wax![69] How sternly they punish laziness! (7) There are marvels aplenty to see and tell of: they foresee storms, and do not commit themselves to the sky when the weather is in doubt or leave their own neighborhood on a cloudy day. Again, if too boisterous a breeze has whisked the flimsy creatures away, they ballast their wings with a tiny pebble before setting course for their destination. (8) Or (something that calls for stouter hearts) they break camp for their king,[70] sally forth to war, and die heroically for their leader. (9) What is more, if a bee has succumbed to old age or disease, priority is given to carrying out the bodies: concern for work takes second place to concern for funeral rites.

18. What[71] then of the way they tie flowers[72] to their legs? What[73] of the way they carry off the glues in their mouths to add to the common store? (2) Yet personally I am astonished most of all by what they build. You shouldn't suppose they designed the shape of their homes at random or haphazardly, just to store their food:[74] the formless wax is structured, and to its practicality is added a beauty beyond description. (3) First they hang the foundations on tough cords; then the construction grows from the starting

[70] Cf. 13.9.6; see Introduction to the present declamation.

[71] Elliptical *quid . . . ?* + substantivized infinitive. Cf. Petron. 64.4, *Quid saltare? Quid deverbia?*; *OLD*[2] s.v. *quis*[1] §12.2 (AS).

[72] Referring to pollen and nectar that bees carry on their legs.

[73] See n. 71.   [74] They of course do it to store their food, but in the process they produce a kind of work of art.

exordio in omnem partem opus aequaliter crescit: nec
quicquam ex inchoatis ⟨tam⟩[154] parvum est quod[155] non
sua ⟨pro⟩[156] portione perfectum sit, nec iam[157] alia parte
opus esset. Ipsi enim sibi invicem anguli haerent, et ita
mutuo vinciuntur atque inligantur ut, quod voles, id me-
4 dium sit.[158] Gemina frons ceris imponitur, et, cum fora-
minibus tantum spatium detur quantum ad generanda
examina natura apum[159] capiat, his textis, ne universi mel-
5 lis effluat pondus, intersaepta onera cluduntur. Quis non
stupeat hoc fieri posse sine manibus, nulla interveniente
doctrina hanc artem nasci? Quid non divinum habent, nisi
quod moriuntur!

19. An vero auctorem vini Liberum colimus, primitiae
frugum Cereri referuntur, inventrix oleae Minerva honoratur,[160] mella genuisse minus est et ⟨in⟩[161] interpo-
nenda[162] gustus voluptate tantum effecisse, quantum ne
2 ipsa quidem rerum natura per se potuit? Ad plurima-
rum incursus valetudinum remedium, est praesentissima

---

154 *add. Wint.*[7] *158*

155 quod Φ (*vd. K.-S. II.2.298–99*): *om.* B V

156 *add. Wint.*[7] *158 ante* sua, *transposui*   157 crescit—
iam *dist. et* nec iam *coni. Str. ap. Kr.*[1]: iam ne B V: iam nec Φ

158 ipsi—sit *post* capiat (*§4*) *habent codd., huc transp.* Håk.

159 natura M, apum *Bur.*: (exanimi)na turam spem B: (exami)naturam spem V: (exami)na puram spem Φ

160 honoratur *Håk.* (*cf. ad rem Ov.* Met. 8.273–77): narrantur
B: -atur V Φ

161 *add. Wint.*[9]

162 *probum, cf. ThlL VII.1.2246.36ss.*

---

75 I.e., for the harmony of the structure to be kept (AS).

point equally in every direction: there is no part of what they begin, tiny ⟨as⟩ it may be, that is not perfect ⟨in⟩ itself, nor would there after that be need of anything more.[75] For the angles fit perfectly, and are bound so intimately together that any single cell you choose will count as the middle.[76] (4) The waxen cells are sealed on both sides:[77] as much space is provided for the holes as is required by the nature of the bees for the production of the swarms,[78] then these woven constructions are used to separate off and enclose the successive burdens,[79] so that the heavy bulk of all the honey does not run away. (5) Who would not be astounded that this can be effected without the help of hands, and that such skill can come about without instruction? Everything to do with bees is godlike—except that they die!

19. We worship Bacchus as the originator of wine; the first crops are attributed to Ceres; Minerva is honored as the inventor of the olive. Is it a lesser service to have engendered honey, and to have done as much ⟨in⟩ bringing pleasure for the palate as not even nature could have accomplished without assistance? (2) A remedy against the assaults of so many diseases,[80] ⟨honey⟩ is a highly effective

[76] Due to the overall symmetry of the hive, any single cell can be considered as its center.   [77] I.e., on both entrances. As explained below, the cells are first used to raise the larvae, then to store honey (and for this purpose they are sealed on both sides, to prevent honey from spilling; cf. n. 69).

[78] The cells are given the size required by the number of bees that the hive can naturally produce.

[79] Sc., the successive loads the bees bring in.

[80] Cf. 13.14.2.

\<mel\>[163] medicina—nam quod ad cibos quidem pertinet, divites viderint.

3   His animalibus aliquis insidiari potuit, et insidiari qua re[164] mella facerent? Haec pestiferis sucis, exquisita per fraudem morte, confecit et—quod sit indignissimum—, quo facilius deciperet, fortasse venena melle permiscuit? Quae tam inhumana crudelitas, quis tam inauditus livor!

4   Nihil est enim quod[165] utaris patrocinio tuo, dives, paucorum damno foliorum.[166] Doluisse te simulas? Dum meas apes occidere vis, flores tuos inutiles fecisti.

163 *suppl.* (*et dist. ante* est) *Str.*[17] 996–97
164 qua re *Franc.* (*firm. Håk.*[4] 156): quare *codd.*
165 quo *Russ.*[3] (*post* dives *gravius, ut vulg., distinguens*)
166 dives—foliorum *distinxi*

medicine—not to mention its role in the domain of food, for which the rich may vouch.[81]

(3) Was it against *these* creatures that someone was capable of laying a trap—and a trap that involved use of the very thing[82] they made into honey? Was it *them* he destroyed with noxious juices, after searching out a means of killing them by deceit? And, what would be most shocking of all, to make his trickery easier, did he perhaps mix the poison with honey? What inhuman cruelty, what unheard of spite! (4) Indeed, there is no way you can use in your defense the loss of a few petals,[83] rich man. Do you pretend that that caused you suffering? Well, you wanted to kill *my* bees: but in the process you made *your* flowers useless.[84]

---

[81] Rich people are the main consumers of honey: see 13.3.6, 13.13.4 and 8.

[82] Flowers.

[83] Cf. 13.5.1.

[84] For there are no bees left to make honey out of them (honey being mainly for the *rich*: cf. n. 81). Rich Man claimed to care for his flowers enough to feel pain, but in reality *he* damaged them, not the bees (AS).

DECLAMATION 14

INTRODUCTION

A prostitute has administered a hate poison to a poor client. As a result, the young man has stopped loving her, and he now accuses her of poisoning him. In *DM* 14 we have his speech; the speech on behalf of the girl follows in *DM* 15.

Poor Man blames the girl for manipulating his feelings. Throughout the speech, he portrays himself as in a Catullan state of mind: he hates the girl, but still loves her (e.g., 1.1–2.5); as a result he cannot turn his thoughts elsewhere (2.4), nor can he hope for any improvement for the rest of his life (9.2). The potion has made his feelings for the girl permanent, whereas otherwise they would have naturally faded away (9.5).

The girl is presented negatively. Her profession deprives her of all credibility (5.1), and she is an expert in the techniques required to make a man fall in love (5.2–4). Poor Man was her victim twice over: she captivated him in the first place (2.5), then rejected him. In short, she experimented on him, to see how much love and how much hatred a man can feel (3.4).

The legal issue is whether administering a nonlethal potion constitutes poisoning. The girl claims that only something that kills is poison (5.5, and in further detail *DM* 15); Poor Man counters this defense by arguing that the administering of any illegal substance should be considered as poisoning and has to be treated with extreme severity (5.6). This confrontation seems to reflect a development in the scope of the law punishing the crime of poisoning (the *lex Cornelia de sicariis et veneficis*), that took place in the imperial age: by the early third century AD, the crime of *veneficium* had come to cover the administering not just of poison but also of any dangerous drug, including love potions. Whether intention to kill has to be proved seems to be a moot point among Roman jurists.[1]

Poor Man, obviously, emphasizes the dangers of the potion used by the girl: although not lethal in itself, a hate potion is able to destroy families and set the whole human race warring (7.3–4). Nor can Poor Man be sure that the hate potion will not eventually kill him. With Lucretian undertones,[2] the speaker describes the potion acting on the victim's body: at first, it will affect only the organs where the passions the girl intended to remove are seated; but then, as its effect intensifies, all the other feelings will be destroyed, and the whole will be poisoned (7.1, 11.1–2).

The declamation can be analyzed as follows:[3]

> PROEM 1.1–2.4
> NARRATION 2.5–4.4
> ARGUMENTATION
>   *Propositio causae* 5.1
>   *Confirmatio* 5.1–7.4
>   *Refutatio* 7.5–9.8
> EPILOGUE 10.1–12.6

[1] Cf. Marcian. *Dig.* 48.8.3.1–2, and contrast Paul. *Sent.* 5.23.14. See Longo (2008, 21–22); Calboli (2010, 152–59); Pietrini (2012, 112–13).

[2] Longo (2008, 100–101nn71–72).

[3] Longo (2008, 35–36).

DM 14 and *DM* 15 are probably the work of different authors. They share many similarities in expression and argumentation, but neither of them counters facts and arguments adduced by the other party, even when the same fact is presented from opposite perspectives. Further, it is debatable whether *DM* 14 was in fact written before *DM* 15.[4] As seen above, both speeches are influenced by legal debate on *veneficium* in the third century AD; language, style, and prose rhythm accordingly point to a dating around the mid of that century.[5]

[4] See in detail Longo (2008, 40–44); also below, Introduction to *DM* 15.

[5] See General Introduction, §4.

14

Odii potio I

Meretrix amatori suo pauperi dedit odii potionem. Ado-
lescens desiit amare. Accusat illam veneficii.

1. Sentio, iudices, hanc quoque calamitatibus meis acces-
sisse novitatem, ut vobis nondum videar odisse, nec me
praeterit plurimum perire de nocentissimae potionis invidia, dum me putatis adhuc impatientia priore miserum.
Quaeso tamen vel hinc totam delati sceleris probationem
gravitas vestra prospiciat, quod dolori meo querelaeque
non creditur. Nec amo, qui accusare possum, nec odi, qui
amare mallem. Quid est aliud quod bibi quam venenum?

---

[1] The speaker means his situation is anyway novel, and this is
a further complication (DAR).

[2] This clarifies that a purpose of the speech is to show that he
does hate her; but he also loves her still: a Catullan mixture of
emotions, caused (it is argued) by the poison.

[3] The judges are right to think he is still in love, and that is *a*
proof that he has been "poisoned." But it is not the *entire* proof:

14

The hate potion I

A call girl gave her lover, a poor man, a hate potion. The young man stopped loving her. He accuses her of poisoning.

(Speech of the young man)

1. I am aware, judges, that a further novel element has been added to my calamities:[1] you don't yet[2] think that I feel hatred. Nor does it escape me that a large part of the reproach arising from a most harmful poison disappears, as long as you suppose that I am still made unhappy by the same uncontrolled passion as in the past. I ask, nevertheless, that your distinguished selves perceive that the entire proof of the crime I have brought to court consists precisely[3] in the fact that my grievance and my accusation are given no credence. (2) I do not love her, for I can bring this accusation,[4] and I do not hate her, for I should prefer to love her. What have I drunk, if not poison?

that would be a demonstration of the coexistence of hate and love, which is summarized in 14.1.2 and which the speech will proceed to enlarge upon.   [4] Cf. 15.1.1.

3   Licet igitur nocentissima feminarum rideat quod accuso, et in manifestissimi sceleris confessione per ludi-
brium malorum evadere temptet[1] meorum, ⟨non⟩ [sed
quod][2] hodie me torquet ac lacerat quod a taeterrimae[3]
mulieris caritate discessi, sed quod remedii mei patior
4   dolorem. Fidem[4] iustitiae, fidem severitatis humanae: ne[5]
meretrici prosit vel quod praevaricatione videor ex-
plicatus! Pro me forsitan fuerit ut amare desinerem; contra me inventum est ut invitus odissem.
    2. Hoc primum itaque, iudices,[6] a clementia publica
peto, ne, quod videtis tristem habitu dirumque conspectu,
verbis asperum, contentione terribilem, mores putetis.
Haec est illa sanitas mea, hoc odium,[7] in hanc[8] corporis
mentisque dierum noctiumque feritatem[9] ille modo laetus, ille, si creditis, nimium remissus amator excandui.
2   Miseremini, iudices, ne vobis venefica[10] sic imponat,[11]
tamquam hoc mei caritate commenta sit; suum animum,
suum tantum secuta fastidium est. Odii potionem contra
3   se nemo dabit homini, nisi quem oderit. Quaeso itaque

---

[1] -at β: om. B V, sed cf. 15.2.4
[2] ⟨non⟩ [sed quod] Helm[1] 382: non hoc est quod ς
[3] det- V E   [4] fi- ς: ei- B V Φ*
[5] dolorem—ne dist. Longo post vulg.
[6] id B V δ   [7] hoc odium Gron.: hic omnium codd.
[8] hanc Gron.: ac B: hac B[2] V Φ
[9] -tem B AE (hanc . . . -tem def. Longo): -te cett.
[10] -efica C[2] (firm. Håk.[2] 116): -ena codd.
[11] -ant B V E

---

[5] I.e., feeling love and hate at the same time.
[6] Sc., from my love for her.

(3) Therefore, although this most guilty of women laughs at my accusation, and while confessing to a patent crime tries to get herself off by making mock of my plight, what torments and tears me apart today is ⟨not⟩ that I have escaped from my affection for a most vile woman, but that I am having to endure the pain of the "cure" I was given.[5] (4) In the name of justice, in the name of the strictness that mankind demands: let it not benefit the girl, either, that I give the impression of having been freed[6] by collusion![7] It may perhaps have been for my own good that I should stop being in love: but that I should hate against my will is the result of a scheme to do me harm.

2. So my first request of the clemency of the public, judges, is that when you see me gloomy in manner and terrible to behold, biting in words, frightening in my forceful language, you should not think this is my real character. This is my "cure," this the hatred.[8] It is into this state of physical and mental ferocity, day and night, that I, the once happy and (if you can believe it) all too laid-back lover, have been inflamed. (2) For pity's sake, judges, do not let the poisoner trick you into thinking that she contrived this out of affection for me; she was only following her own inclination, her own disdain.[9] No one will administer a potion that induces hate of herself unless to a man she hates. (3) I ask you and beg you then, most respected

[7] The girl claims that the potion was intended to stop him loving her. He claims he is still in love; should he give the impression that he is not, that would be to concede her case—almost as if he were in collusion with her. In fact, he does still love her, but also hates her.   [8] Sc., the hatred she dosed me with.

[9] For me.

obtestorque vos, sanctissimi viri, ut calamitatis meae penitus velitis aestimare[12] mensuram: perdidi infelix quod
quandoque potui amare desinere, patior necessitatem rei,
quam breviter[13] utique voluissem.[14] Excogitatum[15] contra
animum futuramque rationem ne, quod relinqueretur,
4 meus esset adfectus. Iterum cum meretrice compositus
sum, rursus in se cogitationes meas, rursus retorsit oculos,
et hominem, quem ab incommoda caritate vel satietas vel
aetas vel fortunae suae fuit dimissura condicio, ad perpe-
tuam impatientiam viribus nimiae diversitatis implicuit.
Hoc solum insanabile genus amoris[16] est, ut odisse cogaris.
5 Festinas[17] ad complorationem praesentis doloris,
anime, festinas, et te[18] a prioribus malis recens abducit
indignitas; altius gemitus, altius querela repetenda est:
cum meretricis sit, quod amator odi, cuius putatis esse,
quod pauper adamavi?
6 Non quidem ego, iudices, ex illis umquam fui, quibus
nobiles[19] opes, adfluentes indulsit fortuna divitias, quorum felicitas capere possit in amore luxuriam. Habui tamen unde ad vitae necessitates concessa gaudia parca mediocritate sufficerent.[20] 3. Ideoque meretrice tantum, et,
quae certissima est in voluptate[21] frugalitas, una fui sem-
2 per[22] eademque contentus. At ista seria, gravis, quae nunc

12 aes- ς (*vd. Reitz.*[2] *63, Håk.*): exis- *codd.*
13 *probum, cf. Wint.*[7] *159*
14 vo- E P (*def. Sh. B.*[4] *207*): no- *cett.*
15 -um (*sc. est, velut 14.10.4*) *Håk.*: -ur *codd.*
16 amoris *Obr.*: mortis *codd.*: morbi *Gron.*
17 -nas *Reitz.*[2] *61*: -na *codd.*
18 -nas et te *Reitz.*[2] *61*: -na sedite (*vel* sed ite) B V δ: -na sed
te (ita E) M γ β   19 -litas *Bur.*   20 -em *Gron.*
21 -upt- M E H: -unt- *cett.*

gentlemen, to consent to take the true measure of my calamity: in my ill fortune I have lost the chance of falling out of love one day; I endure from necessity something which in a short time I should have wanted in any case. Against my wishes and to the prejudice of a future return to reason, it has been contrived that her being abandoned should not be the result of my own state of mind. (4) I am coupled with the girl all over again: she has drawn my thoughts, my eyes, back to herself, and has, to quite opposite effect,[10] entangled in perpetual obsession a man who would eventually have been freed from a disadvantageous affection by satiety, age or the state of his own finances.[11] This is the only type of love that is incurable: being forced to hate.

(5) My mind, you are hurrying on, yes, hurrying on, into lamenting your present pain, and the new outrage is distracting you from earlier troubles. Further back, further back are to be sought the origins of my groans and my accusation. Since it is this girl's fault that I am a lover who hates, whose fault do you suppose it is that I was a poor man who fell in love?[12]

(6) I was never, judges, one of those blessed by fortune with aristocratic wealth, a profusion of riches, one whose happy circumstances could find room for luxury in love. But I did have the means for legitimate pleasures to leave enough over for the necessities of life, so long as I was moderate and sparing. 3. Hence I was content just to have a mistress, and (the surest sign of thrift in the pursuit of

---

[10] Love has been changed to love/hate.
[11] Cf. 15.12.1.   [12] I.e., equally the girl's, as explained in the ensuing *narratio* (announced by: "Further back—accusation," above).

amari recusat, o quam voluit amari! Quibus artibus, qua
calliditate miseram simplicitatem meam sollicitavit primum, deinde tenuit, donec quantulamcumque substan-
tiam in huius sinus credulus iamiamque[23] securus amator

3 egererem! Iam frustra captavit videri miserari condicionem, in quam nos ipsa detraxit. Breviter totum nocentissimae mulieris accipite facinus: pauperem me fecit,
deinde ferre non potuit.[24]

4 Sive enim, iudices, pro[25] communium ⟨usu⟩,[26] quae ad
corrumpendas expugnandasque mentes excogitant ingenia meretricum, placuit experimentum, et in me tempta-
tum est quantum quis amare, quantum quis posset odisse,
seu mulier omnibus exposita mortalibus vanitatem fastidio
mei despectuque captavit, et[27] fama inde quaesita est, ut
a solis videretur amari debere divitibus, non eram[28] profecto quod[29] paulo ante;[30] patiebatur iam tunc noster

5 adfectus. Quod scortorum foribus haerebam, quod, si istis
creditis, pallore deformis, macie ⟨notabilis⟩[31] paupertatem in lupanarium obsequia transtuleram, inde venie-

22 fui (-it E) semper E δ: fuissem per *cett.*
23 iamque B¹ V DE   24 -ui B V
25 *om.* Φ: loco *Russ.*³   26 -nium ⟨usu⟩ *addidi post Wint.*⁷
159 (*cf. ad syntaxin Sant. 278.146*): -nibus *Leh.*
27 et *Obr.*: et ei π: ei *cett.*
28 -am *Reitz.*² 35: -at *codd.*
29 quod Φ (*cf. Hor. Sat. 1.6.60 et hic 14.8.9 esse aliud incipio*):
quid B V: qui πM
30 *dist. Reitz.*² 34–35
31 p. d. m. ⟨n.⟩ *Reitz.*² 35 *coll.* 15.3.7: pallor et indeformis
macie B V: pallor et deformis (indef- AD, inf- β*) macies *habent*
non h.l. sed post transtuleram π γ δ, *post* veniebant β

pleasure) always one and the same girl. (2) But this serious, high-minded woman, who now refuses to be loved, O
how much she *wanted* to be loved![13] How artfully and
cunningly she first won me over in my pitiful innocence,
then kept a grip on me, until—a credulous and by now
pretty trusting lover—I poured away into her lap such
little money as I possessed. (3) Then she sought—in
vain—to look as though she felt pity for the plight to which
she had herself reduced me.[14] Here, for your information,
is a summary of the complete criminal record of a most
guilty woman: she made me poor, then she could not tolerate my poverty.

(4) Perhaps, judges, instead of ‹using› the ordinary
devices that clever call girls employ to corrupt and con-
quer minds, it seemed to her a good idea to experiment: I
was used as a test case to see how much love, how much
hatred a man could feel. Or perhaps a woman who was
available to every mortal man tried to give herself airs by
treating me as a contemptible bore, seeking thus a reputation for having to be loved only by the rich.[15] Whatever
the case, I was definitely not what I had been shortly before; even then my feelings were in trouble.[16] (5) If I kept
hanging round prostitutes' doors, if (as these people[17]
have you believe), ghastly pale, ‹conspicuously› thin, I

---

[13] In the past.

[14] And consequently administered the drug.

[15] Cf. 15.7.8.

[16] Poor Man intimates that the call girl had initially administered him a *love* philter. His feelings—as well as his body (cf.
14.4.2)—were thus already upset when the girl turned to giving
him a *hate* potion.   [17] The girl and her advocate.

bant,[32] unde nunc quod excandesco, quod fremo. 4. Numquam hoc tantum meretrix scit, quemadmodum non
ametur.

2   Quod negari igitur, iudices, non potest, virus homine
firmius, mente constantius, quod immodico ardoris aestu
et exundante[33] impatientia possit etiam recusantis animi
dolorem compescere, diris utique carminibus et feralium
precationum terrore permixtum, lenitate vultus et blanda
porrigentis dissimulatione protectum iam perustis, iam
laborantibus visceribus infudit, et hominem solaciis potius
ac mollium remediorum ratione tractandum exasperavit
ira, dolore concussit,[34] magnaque miserum[35] commuta-
3   tione renovavit. An fecerit, iudices, ut amare desinerem,[36]
vos aestimabitis;[37] fecit ut[38] amare mallem. Explicitum me
putatis et ab incommodo hilariorem[39] dimissum? Nunc,
4   nunc me fateor debere sanari. Habet aliquod solacium,
quisquis in amore miser est: levior calamitas, cui blanditur
aliquid[40] de voluptate laetitia. Nunc infelix uror ac laceror,

---

32 -bat δ (*rectene?*)
33 exund- E: exsud- *cett.*
34 -cuss- *Reitz.*[2] 63 (*cf. 14.7.1*): -clus- *codd.*
35 -riarum *Wint.*[7] *159–60, fort. recte*
36 -inerem D O: -ierim A^sl: -iderem *cett.*
37 aes- V O (*vd. ad 14.2.3*): exaes- B: exis- *cett.*
38 *om.* B δ   39 -riorem πM A^slC: -riore *cett.*: -ri ore W
40 -qua (*vel mox* -titiae) *Håk., sed vd. Longo*

---

18 Sc., a potion administered by the call girl (see n. 16).
19 A mistress knows how to arouse both love and hate (cf.
nn. 16 and 18); see also 14.5.4.

had transferred my small means into dependence on brothels, that had the same cause[18] as my present blazing passion, my present cries of rage. 4. A mistress never knows only how *not* to be loved.[19]

(2) So, judges, what cannot be denied is this: into vitals already inflamed and suffering she poured a poison too powerful for a man, too strong for a mind to withstand, that by its extreme seething heat and irresistible onrush could subdue the distressed victim for all his attempts to decline the dose. For sure, it was blended with dread spells and terrifying imprecations addressed to the gods below,[20] but it was disguised by her gentle expression and the winning air of innocence with which she gave it me to drink. In this way she incensed with anger and shook with pain one who should rather have been comforted and put on a regimen of undemanding remedies, renewing his sufferings by means of a major reversal.[21] (3) It will be for you, judges, to consider whether her purpose was to stop me loving her;[22] she certainly made me prefer to be in love. Do you think I am set free, and discharged in a more cheerful frame of mind after this malaise? It is now, it is now—I insist—that I need curing. (4) Anyone who is unhappy in love has some consolation: calamity is easier to bear for someone who is soothed a little by the happiness that pleasure brings. *Now*[23] (what ill luck!) I am being

---

[20] Cf. 15.5.6.

[21] She first made him suffer by seducing him (14.3.2–3), then by driving him away with her potion.

[22] As is in fact her contention.

[23] Taking up 14.3.3.

nunc retinere mentem, nunc regere non possum. Crudelius est odisse meretricem.

5. Veneficii ago. Seposita paulisper, iudices, noxiae
potionis invidia, nonne vobis videtur implere sceleris fi-
2 dem, quod abstulit fidem condicio personae? Veneficium,
iudices, tota vita meretricis est. Parum se lenociniis, parum putant agere mendaciis, et, cum omnis ad expugnan-
das mentes cura conlata sit, ⟨non⟩[41] sufficit tamen ut de
sui caritate corpori credant: in hoc noctium dierumque
sollicitudo consumitur, quemadmodum de libidinibus fiat
adfectus, qua ratione transcurrentia cotidie desideria te-
neantur, ne cui prosit offensa, ne quem explicet pudor, ne
3 quem satietas aliquando dimittat. En quam putetis ignorare quibus vinciantur oculi,[42] quae per incommoda desideria flagrantes[43] mentes corrumpant[44] primum, deinde
consumant,[45] cum sciat quibus oscula, quibus artissimi
rumpantur amplexus, quae pro laetitia dolorem, pro blan-
ditiis gaudiisque tristitiam praecipiti velocitate substitu-
4 ant![46] Infinitum est, quantum ex hoc medicamento de-

[41] *suppl.* C[2]
[42] -ciantur *Reitz.*[2] 73, oculi *Gron.*: -catur oculis *codd.*
[43] -tesque B V: -tis β
[44] -ant *Gron.*: -at B V Φ*
[45] -ant *Gron.*: -at V Φ: commusat B
[46] -uant ⟨: -uunt *codd.*

[24] Sc., than to love her (painful as such a love may be).
[25] Looking forward to 14.5.5 (where *invidia* recurs).
[26] I.e., go on being loved.
[27] "No one" (here and below) = "no client."
[28] I.e., use it as an excuse to leave a girl.

burned and torn apart, *now* I cannot keep control of my mind, *now* I cannot rule it. It is more cruel to *hate* a mistress.[24]

5. I bring a charge of poisoning. Leaving aside[25] for a moment, judges, the stigma attaching to a harmful potion, do you not think that the crime is made entirely credible by the fact that the profession of the person accused has robbed her of credibility? (2) Poisoning, judges, is the whole way of life for women of the town. They think that wheedling and lies do not serve them well enough, and though they may have taken all possible trouble over conquering hearts, they are ⟨not⟩ happy to trust their *bodies* to ensure that they are loved.[26] What worries them night and day is how lust can be turned into affection, how the passing fancies of everyday can be tied down; they are concerned that no one[27] should take advantage of an offense,[28] that shame should let no one off the hook, that no one should sooner or later be set free by satiety. (3) Here is a woman for you to think ignorant[29] of what enslaves the eyes, what first corrupts and then consumes minds ablaze with inappropriate desires! No, she *knows* what breaks apart kisses and the closest embraces, what all of a sudden brings distress in place of happiness, sadness in place of caresses and joys.[30] (4) There is no limit to the extent to

[29] Ironic: of course she knows, as is clear from her accompanying knowledge of ways of breaking off relationships.

[30] The argument being that someone who knows how to prepare potions to erase passions knows also how to make love philters in order to catch and keep men.

[QUINTILIAN]

prehendi possit notitia peiorum: nemo[47] scit tantum remedia.[48]

5 Temptat, iudices, mulier impudentissima sceleris invidiam nomine potionis effugere, et venenum negat esse nisi tantum[49] quod occidit. Facinus est, iudices, evadere

6 nocentes, quia iam facinus plura[50] devitat. Quid refert, animo noceat aliquis an membris? Eodem scelere porrigitur omne quod non licet: unumquodque[51] ex his quod[52] datur, venenum est. 6. Excusatius mehercule[53] adhuc pro sexu tuo, pro condicione, mulier, esset[54] ut illa nosses gratia tui, desideriumque posses[55] ingerere nolentibus; excogitasti per quod maritos a coniugum caritate diducas,[56] per quod iuvenum mentes abiungas ab aliis fortasse meretricibus. Odii medicamentum numquam ideo tantum meretrix habuit, ut illo contra se uteretur.

2 Me quidem, iudices, si quis interroget, in comparatione veneficii, de quo queror, minus odisse debeas quod occidit, et si qua[57] ex ipsis quoque mortiferis mitiora sunt,

---

[47] ⟨amoris⟩ n. *Reitz.*[2] *73, sed vd. Helm*[1] *384*

[48] -ia *Wint.*[7] *160*: -ium *codd.*   [49] n. t. π *(firm. Beck.*[2] *82, Håk.*[2] *116.56)*: t. n. *cett.*   [50] peiora *Watt*[3] *55, sed vd. 3.9.7 et Longo*   [51] -odq- AE δ: -oq- *cett.*

[52] quoi *Håk., sed vd. B. Asc.*[1] *xcvii v.*

[53] -tius mehe- *Håk.*[2] *118–19*: -tione he- B: -tio mehe- V Φ

[54] -lier *Sch.*, esset *Obr. (comma interposuit Bur.)*: -lieris sed *codd.*   [55] -es ς: -et *codd.*   [56] diducas (edu- δ) Φ: ducat B: deducat V   [57] si qua Φ*: si quis B V

---

[31] Cf. 14.4.1. Knowledge of the kind of poison that quells passions can lead to knowledge of worse poisons, i.e., ones that arouse them.   [32] Cf. 14.11.1, 15.12.8.

which this kind of potion can lead to knowledge of worse: no one knows only *healing* drafts.[31]

(5) Judges, this most impudent woman is trying to escape the stigma of her crime by using the name of potion:[32] she asserts that something is poison only if it kills.[33] It is quite wrong, judges, for the guilty to escape conviction just because their crime ends up avoiding further consequences.[34] (6) What difference does it make whether you harm the mind or the body? Every illegal substance is proffered with the same degree of criminality: every single one of these things which is administered is a poison.[35] 6. Heavens, it would still be more excusable, in view of your sex, in view of your profession, woman, to possess such knowledge for your own sake, so as to be able to implant desire[36] in the unwilling. As it is, you have devised a way to stop husbands loving their wives, and maybe even to alienate young men's minds from other mistresses: a call girl never possessed a hate medicine just to use against herself.[37]

(2) If you ask me, judges, one ought, in comparison with the poisoning that is the subject of my accusation, to dislike less the kind that kills, and granted that even of the lethal type those are kinder which work immediately and

---

[33] See Introduction to the present declamation.

[34] I.e., in the present case: just because the girl's potion harms the *mind*, but does not bring the *body* to death (see also 14.5.6) (AS).   [35] I.e., administering any illegal substance amounts to administering poison. Contrast 15.5.2.

[36] Sc., for yourself.   [37] I.e., to make people hate her; as has just been said, the drug is also used to break up the relationships of others. Contrast 14.7.4; see also 15.6.8.

[QUINTILIAN]

quae statim tota velocitate grassantur et dolorem inter
exitum vitamque non detinent, ita crudelius quod sic ordi-
natur, ut corporis parcat invidiae et sit tantum animi ve-
3 nenum. Quid ais? Non est noxium virus, nisi quod occidit?
Quid ergo vocaremus illud, quo lumina sola raperentur,
quo pars aliqua membrorum debilitate languesceret?
4 Tu te veneficam negas, quae potes potione facere quantum offensae, quantum ira, quantum dolor? Amabit cui
permiseris, execrabitur ille quem iusseris; accipient a te
desideria nostra ortum, finem, modum. Sane et amor et
odium naturales videantur[58] affectus; veneficium sunt,
5 cum iubentur. Quid, quod non potest non habere vim
veneni, quod contra voluntatem homini datur? Video[59] cur
sibi medicina permittat corporum vitia membrorumque
morbos infusis medicaminibus expellere:[60] [et][61] sine animae spiritusque contagione, quaecumque extrinsecus ac-
cidunt, potione vincuntur. 7. Non potest ullus[62] adfectus
sedibus suis per virus expelli nisi totorum concussione
vitalium, et, cum anima constet ex sensibus, quaecumque[63] auferre temptaveris, illa statim prima nostri parte
potionibus enecta,[64] confectoque quod petebatur, reliqua
2 quoque viribus vicinae tabis expirant. Quaedam fortassis[65]

---

[58] -les -antur ς (*vind. Håk.*): -lis -atur *codd.*

[59] vide *Sch., sed cf. Longo*   [60] *colon pos. Obr.*

[61] *del. Sch.*   [62] ullus S O[pc]: illius B V A: ullius *cett.*

[63] quemc- B δ β   [64] potionibus *Sch.,* enecta *Wint.*[7] *160*
(*coll. 15.4.1 et 7*): prioribus retento *codd.*

[65] -tassis M E δ: -tis B V: -te *cett.*

---

[38] The call girl is addressed.   [39] Cf. 15.4.6.

[40] Implying that individual feelings have a physical abode in
specific organs.

158

instantaneously, allowing no interval of pain between life and death, the sort designed to avoid harming the body and to poison only the mind is all the more cruel. (3) What do you[38] say? Is a poison not harmful unless it kills? What then should we call one that merely robbed the victim of sight or caused weakness and disease in some limb?[39] (4) Do you say you are not a poisoner when you can use a potion to do as much as offenses can, as much as anger, as much as resentment? A man will love if you give him permission to love, curse if you order him to curse; our desires will take their beginning, their end, their degree from you. Granted, both love and hate may seem natural feelings: but they count as poisoning when they are ordered. (5) Besides, what of the fact that anything given to a man against his will cannot but count as poison? I can see why doctors allow themselves to drive away *bodily* impairments and diseases of limbs by the administration of drugs: everything befalling us from without is overcome by a potion without any effect on life and breath. 7. But no *emotion* can be driven from its seat by a poison without causing a complete shake-up of the vital organs:[40] as the soul is a complex of feelings, suppose you venture to remove anything, the first part[41] of us having been killed at once by the draft, and what was aimed at having thus been destroyed, the rest too expires by dint of the wasting nearby.[42] (2) Perhaps there are medications that

[41] = "what was aimed at," the feeling that was being targeted by the poisoner.

[42] As the soul (and life itself) is a complex of feelings, when one of them is removed through poison, all the others suffer and eventually die out, so undoing the overall individual. Cf. 14.11.1–2.

medicamina possunt aliud vocari quam venenum; dare
quod non licet, non est aliud quam veneficium.

3   Quantum, nefanda, de poenis humanis excogitare potuisti! Innocentius mehercules fuerat ut amaret aliquis
4 invitus. Potionem excogitasti, qua bella committere, qua
se totum humanum genus posset odisse. Potes[66] efficere
ut non ament liberos parentes, ut propinquitates,[67] ut
fraternitas, ut amicitia se[68] collidat. Odii potionem nemo
accipit, nisi contra hominem quem non debet odisse.

5   Temptat hoc loco nocentissima feminarum de scelere
suo facere beneficium: "Meretricem" inquit "adamaveras."[69] Differo paulisper, iudices, affectus huius excusationem. Dii deaeque, quantum in hoc contumeliae est,
6 quod sibi meretrix videtur adamata! Tu tibi cuiusquam
adfectus censoria gravitate pensitare,[70] tu tibi aestimare
permittis quam frequenter aliqui lupanar intret? Tu, cui
non licet excludere debilitates, fastidire sordes, exposita
ebrietatibus, addicta petulantiae, [et][71] quaeque novis-
sima vilitas est, noctibus populoque concessa, mores iuventutis emendas? Aequiore animo feram[72] ut meretrix
velit adamari.

      8. "Eras" inquit "et pauper." Volo, iudices, sic apud vos
paulisper agere, tamquam in hoc me adfectu propinqui

---

      66 -es β: -est *cett.*   67 -itas ς
      68 *om.* B V, *sed vd. Håk.*   69 adama- *Håk.*: ama- *codd.*
      70 pensitare *Wint.*[9] (-abis *Bur.*, -are vis *Dess.*[2]): praestabis
codd.: alii alia, locus dubius   71 *del. Håk. (cf. Håk.*[4] *156–57)*:
et quae no- ς   72 -am *Ellis 340*: -as *codd.*

---

      43 Cf. 15.6.7.
      44 In the present instance, he ought not hate his mistress.
      45 Looking forward to 14.8.1–2.   46 Sarcastic.

can be called something other than poison; but to give what is not legal can only be poisoning.

(3) How much, wicked woman, have you been capable of devising in the sphere of human pain! Heavens, it would have been less culpable to make someone love against his will. (4) You have devised a potion that might cause the whole human race to go to war and hate itself. You can bring it about that parents do not love children, that relations, brothers, friends clash.[43] No one takes a hate potion unless against someone he ought *not* to hate.[44]

(5) At this point this most wicked of women tries to make a good deed out of her crime. She says: "You had fallen in love with a call girl." For the moment, judges, I put off excusing this sentiment.[45] Gods and goddesses, what a matter for taking offense: a woman of the town thinks that someone has fallen in love with her![46] (6) So *you* take it upon yourself to weigh a man's feelings with a censor's gravity, *you* allow yourself to calculate how often someone enters a brothel? So *you*, who cannot refuse admission to cripples or draw the line at the filthy, who are exposed to sots, enslaved to the insolent, and—vilest of all—bound to give your favors to all and sundry, *you* presume to regulate the behavior of young men? I should rather tolerate a prostitute *wishing* to elicit love.[47]

8. "Moreover," she says, "you were poor." For a little while, judges, I want to plead before you as if my friends and relations[48] were criticizing me for feeling what I feel.[49]

---

[47] Whereas this one *complains* when she arouses love (cf. 14.7.5) (AS).

[48] Contrast 15.9.5.

[49] Thereby I will be explaining how I, a poor man, came to love a call girl.

2 amicique castigent. Non ego alicuius matrimonii corrup-
tor invigilo, nec efferas cupiditates per inlicitos duco complexus. Inventas credo meretrices, ut esset aliquid quod
3 liceret amare pauperibus. Nullam ego circa corpora ista
consistere impotentiam[73] puto; diliguntur immodice sola,
quae non licent. Ut in furorem caritas aliqua convalescat,
4 opus est difficultatibus. Brevis de concessis et[74] statim
satietati vicinus adfectus est. Non fovet, non nutrit ardorem concupiscendi, ubi frui licet, et quaecumque in
mentibus circa permissa coalescunt, non sunt desiderii
5 sed voluptatis.[75] Hoc ipsum tibi, mulier, obicio, quod nos
in fabulas sermonesque misisti; solus debet amare mere-
6 tricem, quem meretrix oderit. Pauperi dedit odii potionem; quid illam putatis dedisse divitibus? Si mehercules repente nobis contingerent opes, iterum nos in sui
caritatem alia potione revocaret, et ista[76] nunc seria, gravis, vellet impatientia priore retinere. Meretrix pauperem
amatorem propter se tantum non potest pati.
7   "Amanti" inquit "dedi." Hoc si remedium est, detur
scienti; prima pars sanitatis est ut libenter accipias.[77]

---

73 -pote- B. Asc.[1] xcviii r. (et vd. Håk.[3] 135): -patie- codd. (def.
Hömke 311.767)
    74 et ς: sed (si O) codd.
    75 -upt- ς: -unt- codd.
    76 ipsa Wint.[3]   77 -as Russ.[3]: -at codd.

    50 Compare the claim made by the woman in 15.2.3.
    51 Contrast 15.3.7.
    52 She will not seduce a man she hates, and this will spare him
the sufferings incurred by the speaker.
    53 Taking up 14.8.1.

(2) I do not spend sleepless nights breaking up marriages,[50] or satisfying unbridled desires in illicit embraces. My belief is that prostitutes were invented to allow the poor the chance of licit love. (3) I don't think there is any question of uncontrolled passion when it is a matter of *those* bodies; only bodies that are off limits become the object of immoderate affection. There have to be obstacles before a passing fancy can strengthen into a fit of madness. (4) Brief is the emotion felt in licit affairs, and all too soon it borders on satiety. A man does not cherish, he does not foster an ardent desire where satisfaction is allowed: whatever develops in the mind in connection with the permissible is a matter of pleasure, not of longing. (5) This is precisely what I have against you, woman: you have dispatched me into a world of tale-bearing and gossip;[51] the only man who should love a woman of the town is one whom she hates.[52] (6) She gave a *poor* man[53] a hate potion; what do you suppose she gave to the *wealthy*? If riches were suddenly to come my way, she would use another potion to summon me back to loving her: this woman, so serious and grave now, would want to tie me down in the same hopeless passion as before.[54] It is for her own sake only that a woman of the town cannot abide a poor lover.[55]

(7) "I gave it to a man who loved me," she says. If this is a cure, let it be given to someone who knows what he is in for; the first step toward being cured is to take your

---

[54] Cf. 14.3.2–3.

[55] The only reason she cannot abide a poor lover is her own financial interest. She is not concerned with what *he* feels about it all.

[QUINTILIAN]

8 Quin immo cur non potius datur amaturo? Quanto melius,
9 quanto providentius! Et minore bibentis dolore constabit
ut adhuc labentem adgrediaris animum, ut coalescentis[78]
ardoris impetus in parvis extinguatur elementis; eo tempore das potionem, quo pariter duos patiar adfectus: aliam
impatientiam paras, et accipio odium, qui[79] iam amorem
ferre non possum. Non desino, sed esse aliud incipio, nec
emendor in amore, sed transferor. 9. Illa vera[80] sunt remedia, quae fugatis morbis causisque languoris postea non
sentiuntur, et ea tantum innocenter dabuntur, quae potentiae suae qualitate consumpta desinunt, cum profuerunt.
2 Tu mihi dedisti quod semper exasperaret:[81] perpetua res
est odisse sine causa. Ducam licet uxorem, te tamen
odero; in peregrinas expeditiones patria dimittat, te tamen
3 cogitationes sermonesque respicient. Quid interest quemadmodum possederis animum meum, quemadmodum
mihi a te non liceat abire, discedere? Fecisti ut te ubique
persequar, ut meis fortassis manibus invadam, velim dare
venenum. Qui meretricem odisse non desinit, amator est,
sed infelix.
4   Misereris mei?[82] Quid ergo sanitate tam rigida? Paulatim potius ratione compesce, misceantur consilia blandi-

---

78 coal- *Håk.*[1] 319–20: cum adul- B: cum adhol- V: tum (*om.*
E δ, tamen β) adul- Φ
79 -i *Håk.*[1] 320: -ia *codd.*
80 -ra ς: -ro *codd.*
81 -peret M E β
82 est—mei *sic dist. Scheff. 453*: post est *plene dist. vulg.*

---

56 Sc., loving.
57 Cf. 14.3.4.

164

medicine willingly. (8) Why not give it, rather, to some *prospective* lover? How much better that would be, how much more foresighted! (9) It will indeed cost the drinker less pain if you attack a mind still uncertain, if the onset of a developing passion is extinguished in the early stages; instead, you give me the potion at a time when, as a consequence, I shall suffer two emotions at once: you are providing me with a second intolerable state, for I take hatred on board when I am no longer able to tolerate love. I do not stop,[56] but I start to be something else,[57] and I am not being cured in my love, but transformed. 9. *True* remedies are those that are not felt once the diseases and the causes of illness have been put to flight,[58] and those will only be given innocently which stop working after their special potency has been used up and they have done their good work. (2) But *you* gave me something that would embitter me for ever: to hate for no reason is a life sentence. Marry though I may, I shall still hate you. I may be sent by my country on foreign campaigns, but my thoughts and my conversation will always be of you. (3) What difference does it make how it is that you came to possess my mind, how it is that I am unable to go away and leave you? You have brought it about that I now pursue you everywhere, perhaps attack you with my hands, wish to give you poison. The man who never stops hating his mistress is her lover—but an unhappy one.

(4) You pity me?[59] Why then so stern a cure? Rather subdue me by reason, gradually, use a blend of advice and

[58] No "side effects."
[59] As you claim.

tiis,[83] severitas[84] temperetur. Alioquin non est quod abi-
gas, quod expellas; exasperant necessitates, et in amore
5 contentio semper accendit. Adiuvabit te interim libertas
ipsa, qua fruar, tempus, satietas et fortassis[85] amator
alius.[86] Admoneas[87] condicionis, sed inter oscula, inter
amplexus;[88] paupertatem non tamquam exprobres,[89] sed
6 tamquam miserearis, adlega. Quamquam quid opus, inde
si non[90] curer, ut desinam, si, quantum adfirmas, invi-
tum miseraris ac diligis? Amatoris unum[91] remedium est
7 amari. Si tamen necessariam putas emendationem, quam
multa sunt amantium remedia citra venenum! Exclude,
dimitte fastidio,[92] posce[93] quantum non possit praestare
8 paupertas. Fac ut me potius ipse castigem, ut erubescam,
ut aliquando desperem. Is tantum in amore sanatur, qui,
quod desinit, sibi debet.

10. Homo igitur, qui merito indignarer si hoc tantum
fecisset aliquis, ut diligi desinerem, quanto iustius queror,
factus cum iam sum alius infelix alia[94] patiens! Decipiunt

83 dist. Håk.: post -lia vulg.
84 seve- Gron.: ve- codd.: <comitate> seve- Sh. B.⁴ 207
85 -sis π (et vd. Wal.¹ 442): -ses B: -se cett.
86 dist. Håk.¹ 320–21
87 -neas Håk.¹ 320–21: -nens B V γ δ: -vens β
88 dist. Håk.¹ 320–21
89 exprobres B. Asc.¹ xcviii v.: exploraris codd.
90 inde si non Håk.³ 136: fide sine codd.
91 -ri (vel -ris) summum Håk.³ 135–36, sed vd. Beck.² 51–52
et Hömke 313.770
92 -dium M γ β: -di (imperat.) Sh. B.¹ 77 coll. 15.11.4
93 -sce Håk.² 119: -sset B V γ β: -sses δ
94 alius—alia non dist. Gr.-Mer.

blandishments, let severity be moderated. For the rest, there is no call to drive me out or expel me; imperatives only embitter, and in love a quarrel always inflames feelings.[60] (5) Meanwhile the very freedom I shall enjoy[61] will help you, together with time, satiety, and perhaps another lover. Remind me of my low status, yes, but while you are kissing and embracing me; bring up my poverty against me, but not as though you were chiding me, rather as though you felt pity for me.[62] (6) Yet in case I am *not* cured by those means, what need is there for me to stop[63] if, as you claim, you feel pity and affection for me when I don't want to be cured?[64] The one remedy for a lover is to be loved. (7) Anyway, if you think a cure is necessary, there are countless remedies for lovers that don't involve poison! Shut me out, send me away with disdain, ask for sums a poor man cannot afford. (8) Make me reprove *myself*, make me blush, make me, in the end, despair. He alone is cured of love who is himself responsible for his ceasing to love.

10. Well then, I should be justified in feeling indignant if someone had merely made me cease to be loved. How much more justly do I complain now that I have become a different kind of unhappy man, with different kinds of

[60] Cf. 15.10.4.

[61] The freedom of meeting with you, while you change my mind with your reasoned rejections: in the absence of a prohibition, my desire will not be exacerbated.

[62] Cf. 15.12.5–6.   [63] Sc., loving you.

[64] He might as well go on as he was, if she likes him enough to feel such pity and affection for him when he refuses to be cast off.

nos[95] rerum falluntque nomina: et ille, qui odit, de amore
2 miser est. Non refert animi quid nimium velis, et inter
sanitatem languoremque nihil interest, si utrumque ferre
non possis. Frustra mihi quisquam blanditur remedio,
cuius patior tormenta, cruciatus; aliud est ut amare desi-
3 nas, aliud ut oderis. Recessisse nunc me tantum putatis ab
amore meretricis? Ablatus est mihi ille hominis melior
adfectus, perdidi miser quicquid est unde gaudium, unde
4 venit vitae tota laetitia. Amor ille, per quem rerum naturae
sacra primordia totiusque mundi elementa creverunt, qui
tenet haec[96] figitque rixantia et de contrariis repugnan-
tibusque[97] seminibus molem perpetuae societatis anima-
5 vit, fugatus, eiectus.[98] Non habeo infelix adfectum, quo
quandoque possim ducere uxorem, amare liberos, ap-
petere amicitias, sperare convictus. Quisquis odii medicamentum biberit, unum fortasse oderit, sed amare
6 neminem potest. Dii immortales, quid ego hausi, quale
visceribus virus ingestum est? Non fuit illud unum venenum: bibi miser execrationis quicquid totius mortalitatis
ira contulerat, quo[99] erat omnium ferarum,[100] omnium
7 serpentium congesta rabies. Odii medicamentum quid
aliud est quam assiduus animi labor, perpetua tristitia?
En[101] homo ab omnibus gaudiis in contubernium doloris
adductus!

95 nos D (*vind. Wint.*[7] *160*): vos *cett.*   96 haec π: hunc B
V δ: nunc γ β   97 repugn- E (*def. Håk.*[2] *119–20*): de repugn- A:
depugn- *cett.*   98 -tus *Golz 81* (*firm. Håk.*[2] *119*): -tusque B
V CD β*: -tusque est π A: deiectusque E δ

99 quo *Reitz.*[2] *70* (*corrob. Longo*): quod *codd.*

100 ferarum *Beck.*[2] *83–84*: furorem B: furorum V ACD β: animalium ferorum (furor E) E δ: furor ferarum *Dess.*[2]

suffering! The names of things deceive and mislead us: even the man who hates is lovesick. (2) It makes no odds to the mind what it is that one wants excessively: there is no difference between health and illness, if both are intolerable. It is in vain for someone to try to fob me off with a remedy that causes me torments and agonies: it is one thing to stop loving, another to hate. (3) Do you think I have merely said goodbye to my love for a mistress? No, a man's better feelings have been taken away from me; I have, to my misfortune, lost every source of joy and all that makes life happy. (4) The love that caused the growth of the sacred beginnings of nature and the elements of the whole world, that holds them and keeps them in place despite their conflicts, and from opposed and warring seeds gave life to a mass eternally bound together in fellowship, has been put to flight, driven out. (5) In my unhappiness I do not have the feelings that might allow me one day to marry a wife, to love my children, to look for friendships, to hope for life in society. Anyone who has drunk a hate medicine may perhaps hate only one person, but he can love nobody. (6) Immortal gods, what have I drunk, what kind of poison has been poured into my guts? That was not a single poison: in my wretchedness I drank all the curses brought together by the anger of the entire human race, a draft in which the savagery of all wild animals, all serpents had been concentrated. (7) What else is a hate medicine but continual heartache, perpetual sorrow? Here before you is a man taken away from all joys to become the constant comrade of anguish!

---

101 en (*et ante sic dist.*) *Håk.*: et *codd.*

8   Fieri non potest ut virus tam impotens semel in viscera
receptum sidat[102] in unum tantummodo sensum, mande-
turque potioni quousque dominetur. 11. Ecce iam, mulier,
odi; quid tamen adhuc facere illud in vitalibus putas? Paulatim se necesse est per totum diffundat animum et,
quamvis primo statim haustu illud expugnet, in quod datur, brevi tempore in nominis sui potentiam omnes reli-
2   quos stringit adfectus. Medicamenti,[103] cui tantum contra
animum [primum][104] licet, prima fortassis vis erit odium,
exitus iste, ut venenum sit.

3   Respondere, iudices, illis libet, qui me paulo ante di-
cunt in amore fuisse miserabilem. Quanto crudeliora,
4   quanto graviora patior, qui dicor explicitus! Modestior,
cum amarem, et quietior; fuerit[105] sane pallor in facie, sed
5   ipsa quoque comis, optanda tristitia. Inveniebam conloquia merebarque sermones; nunc me omnes fugiunt,
aversantur,[106] oderunt. Tum frequenter a lupanari dedu-
cebat pudor, abigebat[107] occursus; nunc publice detinet[108]

---

[102] sidat *Vass. 115–16*: sit et *codd.*: saeviat *Reitz.*[2] *70.11* (*cf.
15.4.7*)   [103] -ti M ACD: -tum *cett.*: -to *Reitz.*[2] *70*

[104] *del. Bur.* (*et om.* V E)

[105] fuerit (*et ante dist.*) *Bur.*: fuerat *codd.*: fui; erat *Håk.*

[106] av- *ς*: adv- *codd.*

[107] -ige- *Gron.* (*cf. 15.2.6*): -icie- *codd.*   [108] publice *Sch.*,
detinet *Helm*[1] *383* (*vd. Håk.*[2] *120*): -ca -ent *codd.*

---

[65] Cf. 14.7.1. The poison will not affect only the targeted feeling (and the organ in which it resides), but will contaminate the
whole organism.

[66] = (in the present case) it makes the sentiment of love give
way to hatred.

(8) It is impossible for a poison so violent, once taken into the system, to settle in just one sense,[65] or for a potion to have a limit imposed to its power. 11. Look, woman, now I feel hatred. But what else do you think the potion is doing in my vital organs? It needs must spread gradually throughout the mind, and though at the first gulp it overcomes what it is administered to counter,[66] after a short time it binds fast all the remaining emotions to assert the potency of its name.[67] (2) The first effect of a drug with such power over the mind will perhaps be hatred, but the eventual outcome will be—to poison.

(3) I should like, judges, to reply to those who say that I was an object of pity not long ago when I was in love.[68] How much more cruel, how much more grievous what I now suffer, when I am said to have been cured! (4) I was more composed when I was in love, and more at peace with myself; my face may have been pale, but my very sadness was pleasant and something to be desired. (5) I found occasions to converse, and I was thought worth talking to. Now, instead, everyone runs away from me, shuns me, hates me. *Then* I was often led away from the brothel by shame, or scared off by some encounter. *Now* I am kept in the public eye by[69] my bringing a case, appearing in

[67] I.e., poison (not medication, as the girl maintains); cf. 15.12.8.   [68] They imply that he is better off now than when he was in love (DAR).

[69] When he was in love, the speaker was able to keep away from the brothel out of shame of being seen there; now he is exposed to public mockery (cf. 14.12.1) because of his crazy course of action against the prostitute. This is further proof that he was more in control of his feelings before the alleged cure.

quod queror, adsisto, convicior. 12. Pro miseranda condicio! Rideor ubique, narror, ostendor, ego sum tota civitate
meretricis inimicus; sic[109] patior miser illas lupanarium
2 insultationes, illa coponarum[110] maledicta, convicia. Non
possum satis tormentorum exprimere mensuram: odi, nec
umquam visus sum magis amasse.

3   Intellegitis, puto, iudices, hominem, qui tantos[111] ad
vos detuli[112] animi mentisque cruciatus, et pro vita queri.
Sic[113] patior[114] infelix quicquid est, per quod paulatim pro-
ficitur ad mortem; assidue mecum rixatur adfectus, et
4 brevi necesse est consumar, quo cotidie vincor. Quae putatis esse tormenta, quem dolorem, cum mens vetatur oculos sequi, cum a luminibus suis animus abducitur? Odio
5 quod non proficit, hoc superest, ut occidat. Me infelicem,
si venenum istud non habet mortem, si mihi inter hos
dolores longior vita ducenda est! Quas[115] ego post hoc
6 animi vices, quae tormenta[116] prospicio? Si meretricis impotentiae[117] omnia licent, hoc erit[118] remedium, ut amare
rursus incipiam.

[109] sic ς: si *codd.*

[110] coponarum *Watt³* 56 (*firm. Longo*): corporarium B^ac V:
-alium B^pc Φ

[111] -tos *Sch.* (*corrob. Str.⁷ 310–11*): -tum *codd.*

[112] -i *Håk.* (*vd. Longo et Håk.⁶ 34*): -it *codd.*

[113] sic *Håk.*: sed *codd.*

[114] patior *Reitz.² 71*: potio (pono E) *codd.*

[115] quas M A: qur B: cur *cett.*

[116] tormenta *Obr.*: commenta *codd.* (-taque π ψ β)

[117] -pote- ς: -patie- B V Φ* (*frustra def. Helm¹ 383*)

[118] sit *Sch.*

court, abusing.[70] 12. What a pitiable state of affairs! I am
laughed at everywhere, talked about, pointed at; all over
town I am the courtesan's enemy. And so I have to put up
with insults in brothels, curses and abuse in bars. (2) I
cannot fully convey the extent of my agony: I hate, and
seem never to have been more in love.

(3) You can understand, I think, judges, that I, who
have brought to your notice such distress of heart and
mind, am acting in defense of my very life. This is how it
is: I am (such is my misfortune) suffering from something,
whatever it is, that is leading little by little to death;[71] my
passion battles with me unceasingly, and I must soon be
consumed by what overcomes me each and every day. (4)
What do you imagine are the torments, what the pain,
when the mind is forbidden to follow the eyes, when the
understanding and the sight that belongs to it are sun-
dered?[72] All that remains for a hatred[73] that does not work
is to kill. (5) How unhappy I am if this poison is *not* lethal,
if I have to live on and on amid these sufferings! What
vicissitudes of the mind, what torments have I to look
forward to in the future? (6) If my uncontrollable mistress
can do everything, her remedy will have to be this: that I
should fall in love again.[74]

[70] I.e., to insult her, as a part of his accusation. Cf. 15.3.6, and
also 15.1.4.

[71] Cf. 14.7.1 and n. 42.

[72] His eyes are attracted by the call girl, his mind (under the
effect of the hate potion) makes him avert them.

[73] = a hate poison.

[74] = she should give me a *love* potion.

DECLAMATION 15

INTRODUCTION

This declamation, on the same theme as *DM* 14, is the speech of the girl's advocate. The speaker does not deny that the girl administered a potion to her poor lover, but he maintains throughout the speech that this was *beneficium* rather than *veneficium*—a good deed rather than a poisoning. The girl's only intention was to help Poor Man, by curing him of the madness into which he had fallen. Whether the potion was effective, and Poor Man cured, is still a matter of doubt.[1]

The speaker portrays the morals of the girl as irreproachable, despite the life she was forced to lead by her poverty (2.1–4).[2] She had intended to help Poor Man all along: she did not seduce him in the first place, but gave him her favors to help him, as she realized that he was too dependent on prostitutes (2.7). However, soon seeing that all she did for him only fed his passion, she had tried to drive him away by degrees: the potion was just the last of the measures she took to help him (e.g., 12.2).

---

[1] In fact, Poor Man seems to feel anger rather than hatred, and he may be still in love (1.3–5); overall, although with some uncertainty (13.5), the girl's advocate declares that Poor Man is now healed (e.g., 14.4): cf. Longo (2008, 151n7).

[2] On the girl's characterization, see most recently Strong (2016, 51–53).

On the basic legal issue, that is, whether administering a potion not intended to kill falls under the charge of poisoning,[3] the defense naturally advocates an interpretation more restrictive than the accuser: poisoning is something that kills, or at least hurts, the victim (4.4); a charge of poisoning requires something more harmful than what Poor Man suffered—and, crucially, requires the victim to be *dead* (4.1–7)! This does not apply here: the victim cannot display any sign of poisoning in his body; indeed, his health has actually improved (5.1). The case, therefore, should be put on the level of trivial brothel complaints and lovers' tiffs, not deserving to be heard in a criminal court (4.2). However, even admitting that the potion actually had some effect, Poor Man should rather be thankful to the girl: a potion like this could be the salvation of the human race, helping us all to hate our own vices (8.1). Further, Poor Man has no reason to complain: what he has lost is the worst kind of love, uncontrolled passion rather than affection, torment rather than pleasure (10.6–7).

The declamation can be analyzed as follows:[4]

PROEM 1.1–5
NARRATION 2.1–3.7
ARGUMENTATION
   Propositio causae (expanded with an *excessus* on the futility of this lawsuit) 4.1–3
   Refutatio 4.4–8.5
   Confirmatio 8.6–13.6
EPILOGUE 14.1–9

[3] Cf. Introduction to *DM*14.
[4] Longo (2008, 36–37).

Although the girl's defense logically presupposes Poor Man's accusation, it is not certain that *DM* 15 was in fact written after *DM* 14. The two speeches obviously have some topics in common, but *DM* 15 does not seem concerned to give a detailed refutation of *DM* 14. Sometimes the two pieces exploit different perspectives on the same facts; more often, the defense voices a reconstruction of the facts opposite to the one of the accusation. But neither of the two mentions the other side's arguments, and this makes it unlikely that both speeches are the work of the same author.[5] In any case, judging from the language and style, as well as from the legal arguments exploited in *DM* 14 and 15, a dating to the mid-third century AD may be suggested for both pieces.[6] It is possible that a passage of this speech[7] is alluded to in a grammatical text falsely ascribed to the late antique scholar Charisius.

[5] See in detail Longo (2008, 40–44); also above, Introduction to *DM* 14.

[6] See Introduction to *DM* 14, and General Introduction, §4.

[7] 10.2: see apparatus *ad loc.*

15

Odii potio II

Meretrix amatori suo pauperi dedit odii potionem. Accusat illam pauper veneficii.

1. Etsi, iudices, ita a natura comparatum est, ne sit ullus iustior dolor quam beneficii sui perdidisse rationem, nihilque gravius adficiat conscientiam bonorum quam quotienscumque nulla[1] merita ceciderunt, non efficiet tamen nefandum praesentis reatus indignumque discrimen ut misera puella non gratuletur sibi quod illam pauper accu-
2 sare iam potest. Timuerat infelix ne remedio suo sic repugnaret pauper, ut magis amaret, ne iuvenis in omni genere animi contentiosus ac pertinax potionem illam dolore coactae sanitatis expelleret. Bene quod et terribilis

---

[1] *probum, vd. Longo*

---

[1] Cf. 14.1.2. She is glad that Poor Man is accusing her, as it shows he is not now passionately in love. But, she goes on (cf. 14.1.3), perhaps that is a superficial view: has the potion not

15

The hate potion II

A call girl gave her lover, a poor man, a hate potion. The poor man accuses her of poisoning.

(Speech on behalf of the girl)

1. Even if, judges, nature's design is that there should be no more just motive for resentment than to have failed to gain recognition for a good deed, and that nothing should be more grievous for someone with a good conscience than any occasion on which his services have gone to waste, yet the unspeakable and unmerited peril of the present accusation will not stop a wretched girl from congratulating herself on the fact that the poor man is now capable of accusing her.[1] (2) She had—unlucky woman—been afraid that the poor man would rebel against his cure by loving more ardently, that a youth so headstrong and obstinate in every aspect of his character would reject the potion in his resentment at having health forced upon him. It's *good* that the poor man is frightening and menac-

worked after all, and is his suit the result of anger rather than hate?

et minax est pauper, quod poenam nostram, quod sanguinem petit! Non expectes ut statim gratias agat, qui sanatur
3 invitus. Nobis tamen, iudices, hodiernam pauperis mentem non prima fronte tractantibus miserrimus iuvenis
nondum videtur explicitus, et, si bene prioris ardoris impatientiam novi, quod cum[2] maxime facit, ira, non odium
4 est. Alioquin, si profecisset remedium et, a pristino furore
iam liber, animo intellectum sanitatis admitteret, omnem
adhuc puellae vitaret occursum, non sibi crederet ulti-
onem et ipsum quoque iudicii timeret adire complexum.[3]
5 Deprehensa est, puto, novissime potionis supervacua persuasio: amat, iudices, amat, qui queritur quod non ametur.[4]

2. Quid agam hoc, iudices, loco? Sub quo tempera-
mento defensionem periclitantis adgrediar? Timeo ne, si
coepero simplicissimae puellae laudare mores, referre
2 probitatem, amare rursus pauper incipiat. Sive enim, iudices, malignitas est persuasionis humanae formam va-
cantem vocare meretricem, seu miserae nominis id[5] imposuit aliquis amator, cui cum corporis bonis fortuna non
dederat unde severi matrimonii castitati[6] sufficeret, labo-
3 ravit necessitatium suarum custodire probitatem. Nullius
umquam per hanc matrimonii turbata concordia est,

    [2] *om.* Φ   [3] *probum, cf. OLD²* §3.c
    [4] -et *Vass. 116 (clausula in decll. 14–15 inaudita)*
    [5] mi- nominis id Vᵖᶜ (*ad* id nominis *cf. Liv. 7.26.12, Vell. 1.3.2,
ThlL VII.2.482.61ss.*): mi- nominis iūd. B: nominis mi- id Vᵃᶜ:
mi- nomen id Φ   [6] -ti A² : -te *cett.*

---

[2] Whereas Poor Man would hate her, if the potion had actually
"healed" him.   [3] Cf. 14.11.5.

ing, that he is seeking to punish us, to have our blood. You are not to expect someone cured against his will to express thanks on the spot. (3) But if, judges, we consider the poor man's present state of mind more than superficially, the wretched young man is *not* yet, it seems, healed: if I know the fury of his previous ardor, his present course of action is the result of anger, not of hate.[2] (4) Otherwise, if the remedy had worked and, free now from his old passion, he were ready to accept the idea of being healthy, he would have all the more reason to be avoiding any contact with the girl, would not have the confidence to pursue his revenge, and would be afraid even of a confrontation in court.[3] (5) Trust in the efficacy of the potion has, I think, been finally proved baseless: a man is in love, judges, yes in love, if he complains that he is not loved.[4]

2. What am I to do at this point, judges? What balance am I to strike in approaching the defense of the accused? I am afraid that, if I start praising the character of a straightforward girl and enlarging on her virtue, the poor man may fall in love with her all over again. (2) Indeed, judges, whether it is because the spite of human prejudice applies the term "courtesan" to any pretty woman with no attachment, or because some lover gave this name to a girl endowed by fortune with physical advantages but not the means needed for remaining chaste in a strict marriage, she has taken pains to behave herself even in the life she was forced to lead. (3) No one ever had his harmonious marriage upset because of her,[5] no father had cause to

---

[4] Cf., e.g., 14.1.2. The girl is suggesting that she cannot have given him a hate potion, because she does *not* hate him.

[5] Poor Man makes the same claim about himself in 14.8.2.

[QUINTILIAN]

nemo questus est pro filio pater, nemo exhaustas facultates
4 in avidissimos sinus paenitentiae dolore deflevit. Temptet
licet ingratissimus iuvenis invidiam miserae facere prioris
adfectus, non poterit[7] obicere meretrici et quod amarit et
quod amare desierit.

5 Ne quem igitur accusator hac prima fortunae suae
comploratione decipiat, tamquam meretricis caritate consumptus sit. Securi estote pro innocentia nostra: talis incidit, talis adamavit, nec habuit quod perderet in tam immo-
6 dico ardore nisi mentem. Vidistis enim notissimum tota
civitate miserum. Cum lupanari noctibus diebusque[8] de-
serviens et, quamvis indulgentissimae puellae simplicitate
frueretur, modo tamen maledictis opprobriisque vulgi,
modo crebra rivalium contentione pulsatus, abigi tamen
compescique non posset, movit[9] mitissimam puellam hic
7 infelicis adfectus. Laboranti primo[10] sui voluit facultate
succurrere: sed quicquid indulserat fovebat ardorem,
quaeque in hac impatientia[11] prona persuasio est, quia
nihil praestanti meretrix tam saepe contingeret, amator
sibi videbatur. 3. Postquam nihil miseratio, nihil proficie-
bat humanitas, temptavit asperitate discutere. Poposcit,

7 -rit π C[2]: - rat *cett.*
8 -busque γ (*ut 16.8.7 et semper in Latinit.*): -bus *cett.*
9 -vet B V
10 -mo ς: -ma *codd.*
11 in hanc patientiam B V

---

6 As he does in 14.3.1–4.
7 Presumably meant to be ambiguous—between "affection"
and "high price."
8 = the financial straits.

complain about his son, no one had in a fit of repentance
to bewail wealth drained away into her bottomless purse.
(4) The deeply ungrateful youth may try to discredit the
poor woman because of what he used to feel for her, but
he will not be able to lay the blame on the girl both for
having loved her and for having stopped loving her.[6]

(5) So the accuser should not deceive anyone by his
opening gambit of bewailing his finances, on the plea that
he was cleaned out by her being so dear.[7] You may rest
assured about our innocence: this is the state[8] he was in
when he came across her,[9] when he fell in love with her,
and all he had to lose by such an immoderate passion was
his reason. (6) After all, you have seen him, the most notorious unfortunate in the whole town. Night and day he
was in thrall to the brothel, and, despite the favors he
enjoyed from an exceedingly kind, naive girl,[10] he was
subject to the pressure sometimes of the curses and abuse
of the crowd, sometimes of repeated disputes with rivals.
But he would not be driven off and restrained; and so this
gentlest of girls was moved by the unhappy man's affection. (7) At the start she wanted to help him in his troubles
by giving her favors to him, but all she lavished on him just
fed his passion: he thought—this being a conviction that
comes easily to someone so desperately in love—that, just
because a call girl so often provided him with her services
free of charge, he was her lover. 3. After pity, after kindness proved of no avail, she tried to shake him off by being

[9] I.e., Poor Man ran into the girl by chance, and was not cunningly seduced by her (contrast 14.3.2).

[10] This seems to anticipate the girl's kind reaction described
in 15.2.7.

exclusit: non defuerunt misero preces.[12] Adhibita sunt ex
ipsa iuvenis condicione consilia, sed ista vincebat, et vires
amoris impedimenta perdebant,[13] donec intellegeret[14]
hominem, qui explicari ratione non poterat, necessitate
2 servandum. Puto, iudices, frustra male audit immodico
pauper ardore: meretrix magis amavit[15] hominem, a[16] quo
noluit amari.

3   Consumptis igitur optima[17] feminarum cunctis indul-
gentiae severitatisque consiliis, dum apud omnes de pauperis sui amore conqueritur, incidit <in>[18] remedium,
4 quo[19] iam dicebatur alius amator explicitus. Quae prima
igitur medicamenti pariter ac dantis integritas est, non
negatura[20] porrexit. Adiuvit deinde quod dederat, impera-
vit sibi ne quas admitteret amplius preces, ne querelis
5 adsistentis, ne lacrimis moveretur exclusi.[21] Vultis scire,
iudices, ubi sit medicamenti, quod obicitur, totus effec-
tus?[22] Quisquis odium dedit, omnia post hoc facit ne[23]
6 debeat[24] amari. Quanto, iuvenis, hoc melius! In forum
aliquando venisti, incipis agere serium, gravem, iam leges,

[12] poposcit—preces *dist. Sh. B.*[2] *210 (firm. Watt*[2] *31)*
[13] prod- *Sh. B.*[2] *210, sed vd. Håk.*
[14] -ret AC[2]: -rent (-rant DE) *cett.*
[15] amov- B V
[16] *om.* B V
[17] -a V δ: -ae *cett. (frustra def. Håk.*[2] *120–21)*
[18] *add. Franc. (firm. Reitz.*[2] *42.12; cf. ad 15.5.2)*
[19] quod B V β
[20] neca- β, *sed vd. Sch.*
[21] -si *Reitz.*[2] *42.12*: -sit *codd.*
[22] eff- *B. Asc.*[2] *(corrob. Håk.*[2] *121–22)*: adf- *codd.*
[23] ne *Håk.*[2] *121–22*: ut *codd.*
[24] (ut) desinat *Sch. (firm. Watt*[2] *31)*

tough. She made demands, she shut him out: but the wretched fellow was never short of entreaties.[11] Advice based on the young man's very circumstances[12] was brought to bear, yet he was more than a match for it: his overwhelming love made light of the obstacles in his way—until she came to realize that a man who could not be cured by reason had to be saved by compulsion. (2) I think, judges, that there is no point in abusing the young man for his excessive passion: the *call girl* loved that man the more, since she did not want him to be her lover any longer.[13]

(3) So when this best of women had done all she could think of, in the way of both indulgence and severity, and while she was moaning to everybody about the love professed by "her" poor man, she came ⟨across⟩ a remedy that had been (it was said) successful with another lover. (4) She gave it with no intention of denying having given it: the prime proof of the innocence of both the drug and the giver. She then reinforced what she had given, instructing herself not to listen to any more prayers, not to be moved by his complaints in her presence or his tears when he was shut out. (5) Would you like to know, judges, what makes the drug named in the charge completely effective? Whoever has administered a hate potion does everything afterward to make sure she does not deserve to be loved. (6) How much better off you are now, young man! You have come to the forum at long last, you are beginning to behave like a serious-minded and respect-

---

[11] Though he was short of money. [12] Sc., his poverty.

[13] She stopped pandering to the young man's passion because she did not want to go on bringing him to ruin—this being proof of the intensity and sincerity of her love (AS).

iam iura loqueris, conviciaris maledicisque meretricibus.
7 Hunc tu animum modo inter libidines ac scorta perdebas
macie notabilis, pallore deformis, solaque impatientiae
tuae fabula notus. Perieras, infelix, nisi bibisses venenum!

4. Veneficii agit. Credam mehercules, iudices, ad sub-
scriptionis huius immanitatem expectasse publicae severitatis aures quodnam[25] saeculo nefas nuntiaret hic gemitus,
quae prosiliret orbitas de novercalibus questura[26] com-
missis, quem pestiferis heredum[27] medicaminibus enec-
2 tum[28] tristis comploraret adfinitas. Non pudet ergo quod
vacatis lupanarium querelis et ad vos deferuntur amantium rixae? Videtis hunc[29] accusatoria fronte terribilem;
3 oscula poscit, destitutos queritur amplexus. Vultis vos
abire potius in vestra secreta, ibi gaudia querelasque mu-
tua[30] conversatione consumere? Non agnoscunt leges ac
iura miseros; hic audiuntur seriae calamitates. Non est
ultione dignus, de quo potest efficere meretrix ut queratur.
4 Ecquando[31] umquam, iudices, audistis de veneficio
vivum querentem? Facinus hoc semper ex mortibus acce-
5 pit invidiam. Si latrocinium probes, cruore, vulneribus; si
sacrilegium, spoliis numinum praedaque templorum;[32]

---

[25] -odn- ς: -odd- B V Φ*   [26] quest- ς (def. Reitz.[2] 83.6):
quaesit- vel quesit- codd.   [27] -dum Bur.: -dem codd.
[28] necdum B: nec tum V: evectum D β   [29] nu- B V E δ
[30] -tua Bur.: -tata codd.   [31] ecq- ς: et q- codd.
[32] si l.—templorum sic fere dist. Obr.

---

[14] Cf. 14.11.3–5.   [15] Contrast 14.8.5.   [16] = "poison,
as you—the prosecutor—term it." This alleged "poison" did not
harm Poor Man, but saved him!   [17] Judges.

able person, you are talking now of laws and legalities, you are abusing and cursing women of the town.[14] (7) This is the character that only recently you were ruining on sexual adventures and prostitutes, an object of derision for your meager frame, your looks spoiled by pallor, known to gossipers only for your unbridled passion.[15] You would have perished, unfortunate man, if you had not drunk—poison![16]

4. His accusation is of poisoning. Heavens, judges, I should suppose that so monstrous a charge made the ears of this grave court wonder what conceivable wickedness was signaled to the world by this cry for help, what orphan was going to spring forward to denounce the crimes of his stepmother, what grieving relative was going to bewail the victim of baleful drugs administered by heirs. (2) Are you[17] not then ashamed that you spend time listening to brothel complaints and that lovers' tiffs are paraded before you? This man you see before you inspires fear with his accusatorial frown; but he is claiming *kisses*, he is complaining of deserted *embraces*! (3) Won't the two of you withdraw instead to your private haunts, to talk over your joys and sorrows together in private? Laws and regulations do not take account of the unhappy; here we have serious disasters to listen to. A man does not deserve to win his case, if a woman of the town can make him come to court to accuse her.

(4) Judges, have you ever heard a live man complaining of being poisoned? That is a crime that has always been hated because of *deaths*. (5) Armed robbery is proved by blood and wounds, sacrilege by spoil taken from the gods and plunder from temples; similarly, in a case of poisoning,

ita, veneficium si arguas, oportet ostendas putre livoribus
6 cadaver, inter efferentium manus fluens tabe corpus. Ut
iam istud obicere possit et vita,[33] debet aliquid esse passa,
quod invidiam mortis imitetur. Veneficium voca quod caecitate grassatur, quod in aliqua deprehenditur debilitate
7 membrorum. Profer agedum corporis notas, in quae[34] se
noxiae potionis vagus fervor effuderit, ubi depastis, enectis[35] visceribus saevitura consederit. Aspicio par laboribus
corpus retinere sua ministeria, sufficientem animum seriis
actibus, accusatoria firmitate robustum. 5. Crede, iuvenis,
hominibus, qui te modo noveramus: nunc acrior ⟨es⟩,[36]
erectior; rediit[37] in sensus vigor, in membra sanguis, viribus velut novae iuventutis exultas.[38] Bibisse te medicamentum probare non posses, nisi meretrix fateretur.
2   Quodsi permittitis, iudices, ut, quicquid contra[39] con-
suetudinem datur, ad huius vocabuli[40] referatur infamiam,
⟨in⟩ veneficium[41] male audiendo vertetur[42] sanitas,[43] sta-
timque merebitur sceleris invidiam quicquid profuerit
3 invito. Illud tantum noxium virus vocavere[44] leges, quod

---

[33] dist. B. Asc.²: post possit vulg.

[34] quae scripsi (neut. pl., cf. 14.7.1 quaecumque . . . reliqua
. . . in simili contextu): quas codd., unde quas se ⟨partes⟩ Reitz.²
71.6

[35] depastis Gron., enectis Sch.: depasta senectus codd.

[36] h.l. add. Wint.⁷ 161: post erectior Håk.

[37] rediit Gron. (corrob. Bur.): resedit codd.

[38] -as Gr.-Mer.: -ans codd.   [39] ex contra B: extra Φ

[40] vocabuli Obr.: vulgi codd., unde ad ius vulgi r. infamiamve
Best 192   [41] ⟨in⟩ veneficium Håk.: beneficio (ve- O) B V E
HO: beneficium cett.   [42] vertetur Dess.² (firm. Helm¹ 374):
ut et B δ: ut ad V: vitetur M AD β: utetur CE

[43] -as δ: -atis cett.   [44] -care B V HJO^ac

you must present us with a cadaver livid and rotting, a pus-soaked body in the hands of those who carry the bier.[18] (6) For a *living* person to be able to bring this charge, he must have suffered something that resembles the horror of death. Give the name "poisoning" to something that does its evil work by causing blindness, that is detected by some impairment of the limbs.[19] (7) Come on, show us the marks on your body, show us into what regions the heat of the noxious potion spread in its wanderings, where it settled to have its cruel effect on organs eaten away and wrecked. What I in fact see before me is a body up to hard work, still able to carry out its normal functions, and a mind capable of serious actions, tough enough to bring a prosecution. 5. Young man, believe us, who knew you not so long ago: you ⟨are⟩ more lively now, more animated; the life has come back into your senses, the blood into your limbs. You luxuriate in your strength as though your youth had been renewed. You could not prove that you took a drug, were it not admitted by the call girl herself.[20]

(2) But if you concede, judges, that the giving of anything unusual is to be classified under this opprobrious name, a cure will turn ⟨into⟩ poisoning just by being badly spoken of, and whatever does good to someone against his wish will at once deserve to be stigmatized as a crime.[21] (3) The laws meant by a harmful poison only something

---

[18] Cf. 6.3.4.
[19] Cf. 14.6.3.
[20] Sc., that she gave it to you.
[21] Contrast 14.5.6, 14.7.2.

non admitteret interpretationis incertum. Iniquissimum est venenum videri, quod in potestate bibentis est an sit remedium.

4   Sentit, iudices, iuvenis crimen quod detulit nec nomine nec effectu scriptionem legis implere; itaque ex vocabulo mulieris quaerit invidiam. "Meretricem" inquit 5 "accuso." Nescis, mihi crede, iuvenis, sceleris quod detulisti qualem mihi debeas probationem. Rei[45] expecto mehercules ut sit ante omnia minax vultus, feralis habitus; horreant squalore crines, rigeat super nefandas cogitationes 6 efferata tristitia. Facinus, quod dicitur inquietare superos, sidera diris agitare carminibus, tumulos, busta scrutari et amputatis cadaveribus ipsas in scelus armare mortis,[46] fieri non potest ut auctorem suum non statim 7 primo prodat aspectu. Vides[47] veneficae non horridos vultus placidamque faciem; si cogitationes, si consilia pertractes, sola cura de forma, omnis in hoc conlata meditatio, ut sollicitet aspectu, sermone detineat. 6. Addo[48] subinde exactas mero noctes, ‹inter›[49] tua, mulier,[50] convivia perditas amantium rixas. Meretricis unum veneficium est, ne desinat amari.

---

[45] rei *Håk.*: rem B V Φ*
[46] mortis B[ac] V (-tes B[pc]): manus Φ*
[47] -etis *Wint.*[9]   [48] addo (*vel* adde) *Håk.*: audio *codd.*
[49] *supplevi*: ‹post› *Sch.*
[50] tua mulier *codd.*: tumultuosa *Gron.*

---

[22] The idea of the name applied to the girl is taken up only as late as 15.6.2.   [23] Cf. 14.4.2.   [24] Addressed to the accuser, unless we read *videtis* ("you—judges—see").

[25] The vocative clarifies the connection of the sentence with

admitting of no uncertainty of diagnosis. It is quite wrong for something to be regarded as a poison, when it is up to the person who drinks it to decide whether it constitutes a cure.

(4) The young man, judges, is well aware that the act he has brought to court does not strictly fall under the letter of the law either in its name or in its effect. That is why he seeks to arouse feeling by what he calls the woman. "I am accusing a woman of the town," he says.[22] (5) Believe me, young man, you do not realize what kind of proof you should be giving me for the crime you have brought to court. Heavens, I expect a defendant to be above all else menacing in face, grim in manner. I expect his hair to be dirty and unkempt, I expect a savage moroseness inflexibly fixed on wicked thoughts. (6) An act that is said to disquiet the gods above, to disturb the stars with dire spells, to delve into tombs and sepulchers, and after the mutilation of their corpses to arm even the dead for criminal purposes—such an act must needs betray its author at the very first glance.[23] (7) The woman you see[24] before you is a "poisoner" with a face that makes no one blench, and an air of tranquility; if you examine her thoughts and concerns, she is interested only in her looks: she thinks of nothing beyond attracting a man by her appearance and hanging on to him by her conversation. 6. I add the nights often passed in drinking, the desperate quarrels between lovers ⟨during⟩ *your* parties, woman.[25] For a courtesan, poisoning consists only in making sure she doesn't cease to be loved.

the context: the girl's interests include parties for her lovers—to boost their attachment to her.

2   Numquid inique, iudices, in tanti sceleris subscriptione deposco ne nominibus reos velitis aestimare, sed
3 moribus? Venefica tua quid prius umquam, quid simile commisit? Cuius per hanc expugnatus animus? Quis queritur iuvenis, quis senex, quis dives, quis pauper alius? In te ergo solo venefica, in te tantum aliud ista quam mere-
4 trix? Vultis integritatem puellae breviter probem? Hanc, quam nunc pauper detestatur, accusat, amare mallet.

5   Omnia, iudices, facinora, ni[51] fallor, causas vel de cupiditate vel de simultatibus trahunt. Quod odium de amatore meretrici, quae praeda de paupere?

6   "Odium" inquit "accepi." Ecquid,[52] iudices, satis eam[53] contra infamiam veneni vel solum medicamenti nomen absolvet?[54] Nec invenio cur debeat idem videri, quod po-
7 test non[55] idem vocari. Agedum, iuvenis, potionis imple[56] huius immanitatem, dic: "Odium accepi contra coniugem, contra liberos meos, ut a sacris avocarer adfectibus, ut
8 pignora sancta despicerem." Illud odium in meretrice facinus est, quo utitur in sui caritatem. Ita vel hoc solum sufficit excusationi, quod illa contra se tantum dedit.

---

51 nisi V Φ, *sed vd.* K.-S. *II.2.423*
52 ecq- ς: et q- *codd.*
53 eam *Håk.*[3] *137:* me *codd.*
54 -vet *Håk.*[3] *137:* -veret *codd.*
55 p. n. *Sh. B.*[2] *210:* n. p. *codd.*
56 -ple ς: -pie *codd.*

---

26 I.e., if it can be called a medicine, then there is no reason to regard it as poison (DAR).   27 Cf. 14.7.4.
28 Sc., and hatred for everybody else. If she gave him a potion to make him hate all his family and love only her, that would be

DECLAMATION 15

(2) When the charge specifies such a hideous crime, am I wrong, judges, to ask that you consent to judge defendants not by what they are called but by how they behave? (3) What has your poisoner ever done like this before? Whose mind has she reduced to subjection? What young man, what old man, what rich man, what other poor man finds anything to complain of in her? Is she then a poisoner in your case alone, is she anything other than a courtesan toward you alone? (4) Would you like me to prove the girl's blamelessness in a single sentence? This woman, whom the poor man now loathes and accuses, he would prefer to love.

(5) If I am not mistaken, judges, all crimes derive their motives from either greed or enmity. What hatred does a lover excite in a courtesan? What plunder can be taken from a poor man?

(6) "I was given hate to drink," he says. Judges, won't the mere word "medicine" clear her of the disgrace of administering poison? For I see no reason why something which can be given a different name should be regarded as the same thing.[26] (7) Come on, young man, tell us the whole enormity of this potion; say: "I was given a dose of hatred against my wife, against my children, to sunder me from my nearest and dearest, to make me count sacred ties as nothing."[27] (8) In the case of a courtesan, such a poison is criminal when she uses it to cause love for herself.[28] So the only excuse she needs is that she gave it to work against herself—and nobody else.[29]

disgraceful. That she has just made him hate her is a sufficient defense of her conduct (see below) (DAR).

[29] Cf. 14.6.1.

195

7. "Odium" inquit "accepi." Nunc te hic reposco, iuvenis, invidiam, quam fortunae nostrae paulo ante faciebas.
Dic: "Meretrix dedit, prostituta porrexit"—o quam timue-
2 ram ne adiceres[57] "amatorium sui!"[58] Consurge agedum,
iuvenis, et totis corporis animique viribus imple susceptae
accusationis horrorem. En[59] quod audiente tota civitate
3 proclames: "Miseremini mei, adiuvate, succurrite! Bibi
medicamentum crudele, saevum: desii pauper amare me-
4 retricem! Iam iam non inquietis noctibus vagus vilissimi
cuiusque perditos patior ictus, nec exclusus ante lupanarium fores posterum diem pervigil amator expecto. Possum navigare, colere terras, sufficio militiae, redditus mihi
est animus quo fierem maritus, quo senectuti liberisque
5 prospicerem." Quantum, dii deaeque, remedium ⟨hoc⟩[60]
condicioni[61] bibentis valuit! Fecerat te potione[62] ista[63]
felicem et[64] divitem puella.
6   Ita vel hoc non solum,[65] iudices, innocentissimae puellae pro defensione sufficeret, quod nihil fecit causa sua?
Amatorem dimisit, explicuit illa, quae captare dicitur ut

---

57 adi- *Reitz.*[2] 60: di- *codd.*
58 sui ς: sibi *codd.*
59 en *Wint.*[7] 161: est *codd.*
60 *supplevi*
61 -ni M γ β: -ne *cett.*
62 -tione *Longo*: -tio M ψ: -tu A: -tius *cett.*
63 -tam B   64 et *scripsi*: si *codd.*
65 non vel hoc s. *Reitz.*[2] 60

---

30 It would be an outrage if the girl used the potion for her
own benefit (15.6.8): so the speaker asserts that the girl is fright-
ened the prosecution might allege this (DAR).

7. "I was given hate to drink," he says. Here and now, young man, I insist that you repeat the slur that you were trying earlier to cast upon our station in life. Say: "A courtesan gave it, a prostitute proffered it"—O how I had feared you might continue "as a potion to make herself be loved."[30] (2) Come on, young man, get to your feet and use all your powers of mind and body to bring home the full horror of the accusation you have taken on. Here is something for you to proclaim for the whole city to hear: (3) "Pity me, help me, come to my aid! I drank a cruel and savage drug: I, a poor man, have stopped loving a courtesan. (4) *Now* I do not have to spend restless nights wandering the streets, putting up with the blows of every worthless desperado, nor do I have to play the sleepless lover denied admission, waiting at the doors of brothels for tomorrow to come. I can sail the seas, cultivate estates, qualify for military service. I have had restored to me a state of mind enabling me to marry, make provision for an old age and children." (5) Gods and goddesses, what a difference ⟨this⟩ remedy made to the circumstances of the man drinking it! By her potion, the girl had made you happy and prosperous.[31]

(6) Would it not be enough, then, to plead in defense of a completely innocent girl just that she did not act with any thought for her own advantage? She let her lover go, she gave him his freedom—the woman who (it is said)

---

[31] Happy, because finally free from his obsession (cf. 15.11.6, *felicem . . . sanitatem*); prosperous, because now able to work and earn money (15.7.4). Cf. Sen. *Ep.* 115.17, *felicem illum homines et divitem vocant.* Poor Man has already countered such claims in 14.11.3ff. (AS).

7 ametur, quae sollicitat, quae corrumpit adfectus. Ingrate,
quanta de te potuerat[66] gloria frui! Non quidem confers
pretia, non stipes, sed adsides, sequeris, haeres, praestas
8 comitatum, favorem, laudas ubique, miraris. Hinc ergo
causa[67] meretricibus quod illas[68] etiam pauperes ament,
quod facile contingant, quod laboribus exorentur adeun-
9 tium: faciet[69] hic amator ut divites ament.[70] In crimen
maximum captas transferre beneficium: ut aliquis amare
desinat, non nisi ab amante praestatur.

8. Quid ais, iuvenis? Ita <non>[71] bibisti potionem quae
finem cupiditatibus daret, premeret ardorem, desideria
restingueret? Abi, recede, dum puellae publico generis
humani nomine gratias agimus, quod hoc fieri posse mon-
2 stravit. Furor ille, qui, si credimus, numina quoque de-
tracta sideribus misit in terras, qui de sacris venerandisque
pigneribus monstra commentus est, ardor, qui miscuit
hominum ferarumque concubitus, ferrum, ignis, claustra
laxabat, per interiecta[72] late maria fugiebat, vetatur, perit.

---

[66] -tuerat (*vel* -terat) *Gron.*: -tuerit *codd.*: -tuit W *necnon Sch.*
[67] causa *Håk.*[3] 137: iam *codd.*   [68] *probum* = se (*Håk.*[3] 137)
[69] -et *Reitz.*[2] 60: -es *codd.*   [70] *gravius dist. Scheff.* 454
[71] *add. Wint.*[7] 161   [72] -eriecta ⟨: -errita (-eri- P¹) *codd.*

---

[32] As he does not recognize the advantages he received: cf.
15.7.4–5.   [33] Implying the elegiac imagery of "love slavery."
[34] Poor Man's loyalty would have drawn richer admirers to
her; so turning him away was against her interests. Contrast
14.3.4.   [35] I.e., it was only because she loved him that she
was willing to forego the benefits of his continued company.
[36] Contrast 14.10.4.   [37] As in the case of Pasiphae and
the bull, giving birth to the Minotaur.

seeks to be loved, who works on, who corrupts hearts. (7) Ungrateful man,[32] how much prestige she could have won thanks to you! You do not—it is true—pay what she charges, or give her douceurs; but you do sit by her, you attend her, you are always at her side, you give her companionship and support, you sing her praises everywhere you go, you admire her. (8) Yes, this is why courtesans allow even poor men to love them, why they are happy to grant them their favors, why they are won over by their labors[33] when they visit. A lover like this will cause rich men to love them.[34] (9) You are trying to make a capital crime out of a good deed: it is only someone who loves him who can cause a man to stop loving her.[35]

8. What *are* you saying, young man? After all, have you ⟨not⟩ drunk a potion capable of putting an end to your desires, suppressing your passion, extinguishing your longings? Go away, withdraw from the court, while we thank the girl in the name of the whole human race for showing us that such a thing can be! (2) The madness which, if we can believe it, drew deities down from the stars and landed them on earth, which made sacred and revered relationships spawn monsters;[36] the passion that brought together men and animals in sexual congress,[37] opened a way through iron,[38] fires,[39] locked doors, fled[40] over wide stretches of sea—this is banned and destroyed.

[38] A possible allusion to the myth of Danae, in the version of Ov. *Am.* 3.4.21–22.

[39] Probably referring to the myth of Aegina, who was raped by Zeus in the form of fire according to Ov. *Met.* 6.113, *ut . . . Asopida luserit ignis.*

[40] As in Zeus' abductions of Aegina and Europa.

3   Accipite quod magis debeatis stupere, mirari: remedium
amoris mulier invenit. Desinite nunc incestum timere,
mortales, nulla pietas horreat nefandae cupiditatis instinc-
tum. Quicquid non parentium irae,[73] castigationes, non
serii propinqui, non paupertas, non necessitas poterat effi-
4   cere,[74] haustus brevis, facilis, unus extorquet. O si quis
odium posset omnium bibere vitiorum! Felix profecto
mortalitas, si reliquos lapsus incommodosque mentis er-
5   rores fas esset infusa potione compescere. Facinus est
quod maximum remedium gratiam sui vocabulo perdit
auctoris. Miraremur hominem, qui illud contra meretricem dedisset.
6   Tibi tamen ultra omnes immodica cupiditate flagranti,
tibi praecipue succurrendum, iuvenis. Cuius homo condi-
7   cionis adamaveras! Divitiis opus est, ne simus in amore
miseri, et impotentissimi mali difficultates illi fortasse non
sentiant, quos contra fastidia ceterosque contemptus explicat felicitas magna perdendi.[75] 9. Felix profecto, qui
non ‹nisi›[76] facultates in lupanari effundit;[77] tu perdis
animum. Ille fastum opibus exorat,[78] tu lacrimis rogas,
pallore blandiris et, quod ad pessimum spectat eventum,
2   miserabilis sis oportet, ut amator esse videaris. Finge te
nullum[79] huius adfectus sentire cruciatum;[80] sed[81] amare

    [73] irae *Ellis 342 (corrob. Håk.)*: minae E: mirae *vel* -re *cett.*

    [74] eic- *Russ.[3] (cf. mox extorquet): an* exig-?

    [75] -rden- *Gr.-Mer. (firm. Håk.[2] 122)*: -reun- *codd.*

    [76] qui non ‹nisi› C[2]: quam B V: qui non (qui E δ) Φ: qui modo
Håk. (sed modo = tantum *in decll. 14–15 non invenitur)*

    [77] -und- *Wint.[9]*: -ud- *codd.*   [78] i. f. o. e. *(et ante sic dist.)*
Håk.[2] 122–23: ille est tu bibis uxor attu B V Φ*

    [79] -los A   [80] -tus B V A δ *(sc. ex* -tū s-, *vd. Håk.[2] 123)*
    [81] sed *Ellis 342*: id B V Φ*: sic *Sch.*

(3) Here is something that should astonish you more, amaze you more: a *woman* has found a cure for love. Now stop being afraid of incest, mortals, let no one who feels love for his family dread the promptings of wicked desire. All that angry and reproachful parents, pontificating relatives, poverty, necessity could not bring about is forcibly achieved by one short and simple draft. (4) O if only we could drink a poison to make us hate all vices! How happy would mortal men no doubt be, if it were possible by administering a potion to quell all the other failings and troublesome errors of the mind! (5) It is an outrage that a sovereign remedy loses favor because of the name given to its author.[41] We should admire a man who had given it to make a woman of the town hated.

(6) On the other hand you, young man, *you* especially needed help, for you blazed with immoderate desire more than anyone else. Think of the circumstances you were in when you fell in love! (7) One requires wealth to avoid being unhappy in love: the problems posed by the most irresistible of evils may perhaps not be felt by men who, fortunate enough to be able to waste money on a grand scale, are freed from disdain and every other kind of contempt. 9. Happy the man, surely, who pours away nothing <but> his substance in a brothel: *you* are losing your mind. He prevails over disdain with money, you entreat with tears, coax with the pallor of your face, and (a sign of the worst outcome) have to arouse pity in order to be regarded as a lover. (2) Suppose you feel none of the agony of this emotion; yet are you not, poor man, at least *ashamed* of

---

[41] Sc., *meretrix*. Cf. 15.5.4, *ex vocabulo mulieris*.

te, pauper, saltem non pudet? Homo, cui non vacaret
agere longa languoris, aegrumque non deceret totarum
noctium quies, excusari[82] non possis si totos[83] perdideris
3 dies. Cuius census ex manibus, ex laboribus substantia,
quem cotidie poscit ultro[84] rationem ‹cibus›[85] in dies dimensus,[86] amantium[87] pateris adversa[88] felicium:[89] oscula
tantum amplexusque meditaris et, unde tibi calamitatis
huius non potest nec venia contingere, de voluptate miser
4 es. Expectandum videlicet quando te famis, inopia casti-
get? Sed inter ista coepisti; quid iam facere potest ratio,
consilium? Odio sanandus[90] est, quem non explicat quod
pauper adamavit.
5   Nunc[91] tamen intellegere possumus te non sola fuisse
paupertate miserum;[92] non opes tantum tibi, non facultates defuerunt: non erant, quantum video, propinqui,
non amici. Alioquin illi te potius nostra potione sanassent,
vel, si ignorassent huius graminis vires,[93] vinculis nexibus-
6 que tenuissent. Quid? Blandis adfatibus[94] impotentissi-
7 mum eludis adfectum? Datum est remedium dolori qui

82 -ri V: -re (-rire S, *ut vid.*) *cett.*

83 totos *Str. ap. Longo*: tantum *codd.*

84 -ro *Bur.* (*elucid. Håk.*): -ra *codd.*

85 *h.l. add. Wint.*[9], *alii alibi*: (rat-) cibus (demensus) *Bur.*

86 dimensus *Håk.*[2] *124* (de- ⊊): demersus (di- B) *codd.*

87 amantium *scripsi*: -ia B: -iam A: amentia V (*ex* ama-, *ut vid.*)
δ β: -iam M ψ

88 -sa *Håk.*[2] *124* (*cf. mox* calamitatis): -sus *codd.*

89 *dist. Håk.*[2] *124*

90 -um B V

91 nunc *Bur.* (*firm. Håk.*[1] *322*): non *codd.*

92 s. f. p. m. *Håk.*[1] *321–22*: solam f. -atem iterum *codd.*

93 -res M[2] ψ (*def. Håk.*) -rus *cett.*

94 -fat- ⊊: -fect- *codd.*

being in love? A man with no freedom to be idle when ill, who, if sick, should not allow himself complete nights of repose, you could not be excused if you waste complete *days*. (3) Your money comes from your hands, your substance from your labor; your dole of daily ⟨bread⟩ relentlessly demands to be accounted for every day.[42] Yet you undergo the misfortunes[43] of *rich* lovers: you think of nothing but kisses and embraces, so that—to make it impossible for anyone even to be indulgent with you in this disaster—you are miserable because you search for pleasure. (4) Must you then wait until hunger and lack of means bring you to your senses? Yet you set out on this affair under those handicaps.[44] What can reason and good advice do now? A man must be cured by hate, if he is not brought to his senses by having fallen in love when he was poor.

(5) But, as it is, we can understand that you were not to be pitied only because you were poor; it was not only wealth, not only means that you lacked: you did not have, so far as I can see, relations or friends.[45] Otherwise *they* would have cured you with the potion we employed, or, if they had not known the powers of this herb, would have restrained you with shackles and bonds. (6) What? Are you trying to escape the clutches of an irresistible emotion just by sweet talk?[46] (7) A remedy has been administered for

---

[42] = you are urged to toil every day by your own daily need for food. For the personification of a need, cf. 15.10.2 (AS).
[43] Ironic, like "disaster" soon after.   [44] I.e., though you were hungry and poor.   [45] Contrast 14.8.1.   [46] Even your friends would have used stronger means than just sweet words (such as physical constraints, if not the potion itself) to treat your madness —or at least to prevent you from committing suicide (cf. 15.10.7).

saepe egit in laqueos, in praecipitia compulit, qui cruciatus laborantis animae vulneribus emisit. Quantum amori
in homine[95] liceat, illi magis sciunt, qui ‹non›[96] amantur.

10. Iunge nunc cum fortuna tua condicionem mulieris
adamatae. Incideras quidem, miser, in puellam minime
superbam minimeque difficilem; quaestum tamen non
2 possumus circumire meretricis.[97] Quam multa pro illis
exigit sexus, aetas! Poscit semper necessitas, petit corporum cultus, postulat[98] tristissima stationis impatientia.
3 Totos[99] infelix dies lupanarium foribus impendes,[100] ut
quando[101] prostituta pauperi vacet, et[102] contentione nu-
merantium dilatus, exclusus, otium meretricis expectas.
4 Negatur tibi complexus: indignatione persequeris; contingit:[103] iterum[104] felicitate corrumperis. Spem gaudia parant, adversa contentionem;[105] ex utraque fortuna deside-
5 ria coalescunt. Nobis crede, qui vidimus: quis tibi tunc[106]
fuit corporis habitus, quis pallor, quam miserabilis, quam
pudenda tristitia! Quotiens tu venenum bibere voluisti!
6   Non est igitur, iuvenis, quod tibi queraris illam mitissimam partem humanae mentis ablatam; non caritatem, sed

⁹⁵ -em γ β, sed vd. Longo 165.44   ⁹⁶ add. Håk.⁴ 157
⁹⁷ quaestum . . . -cis Håk.¹ 322: quasdam . . . -ces codd.
⁹⁸ postulat scripsi, quo perfecta synon. variatio fit (cf. [Char.]
Syn. Cic. p. 437, 32 Barwick-Kühnert Petit: poscit, postulat, exigit; an locus noster respicitur?): poscit codd.   ⁹⁹ ‹tu› totos
Wint.⁷ 161 et Russ.² ibid.   ¹⁰⁰ -des ϛ: -dit B V: -dis Φ
¹⁰¹ u. q. probum = fere si quando (vd. OLD² quando §4.a)
¹⁰² om. Φ, sed vd. Håk.² 125   ¹⁰³ -tigit B AD
¹⁰⁴ iterum (et ante dist.) Ed. Oxon. (cf. 15.2.7 tam saepe contingeret): verum codd. (cf. ad 7.11.3): vero Helm¹ 363, sed vd.
Lund.¹ 67–68   ¹⁰⁵ -tentionem Gron. (firm. Håk.² 125): -ditione
B V: -tritionem (-trict- S) Φ   ¹⁰⁶ tunc Obr.: uni codd.

a pain that has often driven men to hang themselves or hurl themselves over cliffs, or has released a troubled soul from its agonies by the infliction of fatal wounds. Those who are ⟨*not*⟩ loved[47] know better how much power love has over a man.

10. Now alongside your means put the circumstances of the woman you fell in love with. You had happened, poor man, on a girl far from proud and far from hard to deal with; but we cannot get around a courtesan's need for gain. (2) How much their sex and their youth requires them to ask! Their necessities are always making demands;[48] their bodily adornment has requirements; the dreadful boredom of standing around waiting[49] asserts its claims. (3) For whole days, unlucky man, you hang round brothel doors in hope, some time, of a prostitute with a moment to spare for a poor man: put off and excluded by the competition of paying customers, you wait for a tart's hour off. (4) Embraces are denied you: you pursue her with fury. You get them: you are spoiled all over again by your success. Joys make you hopeful, adversity makes you quarrelsome; either way your longings grow stronger.[50] (5) Believe us, we have seen you: to think of your appearance in those days, of your pallor, of your pitiful and shameful depression! How often you *wanted* to take poison!

(6) You have no reason then, young man, to complain that the gentlest part of the human mind has been taken away from you; what you have lost is not affection but

---

[47] And are therefore impelled to suicide (above).

[48] Of the client, whose bill will include money (cf. 14.3.2), cosmetics, clothes, jewelry, waiting time . . .

[49] For a client.   [50] Cf. 14.9.4.

[QUINTILIAN]

impatientiam, non voluptatem, sed tormenta, non amo-
7 rem, sed quod amaveras,[107] perdidisti. Amoris, si sapien-
tiae sequamur auctores, antiquissimum numen, et cui se
naturae debet aeternitas: sed ille[108] mitis et serius, honestis cupiditatibus et viribus sacrae caritatis exultans, ut
qui cuncta priscae noctis operta caligine diduxerit[109] primum, deinde miscuerit; hic vero, quo[110] perditis visceribus adhaeremus inquieti, audax,[111] lascivientis adhuc aetatis instinctu tumultuosus ac petulans, telis, funereis facibus
8 armatus. Praestat igitur ille mortalibus liberos ac duratura[112] coniugia pietate, hic incesta, libidines, adulteria,
meretrices. 11. Referam nunc fabulosas immodici furoris
prodigiosasque novitates, conceptum nescientibus oculis
ignoti hominis affectum,[113] formam[114] suis in se luminibus
ardentem, virgines[115] patrum[116] senectute flagrantes, mortalium ferarumque volutatus[117] usque in monstruosa fe-
2 cunditatis onera perlatos? Ex omnibus tamen, quae nobis
patientibus[118] extorquet affectus, hoc saevissimum patimur, quod[119] nemo vult in amore sanari.

---

107 adam- V H   108 numen *et* ille: *sc.* est
109 did- γ: ded- *cett.*
110 quo γ β (*adv., cf. H.-Sz. 208–9*): quod B V δ: cui π
111 audax *Hâk.*: aut ad B V δ: *om.* γ β   112 ac duratura
Helm¹ 363: accusatura B V δ: hac usitata ACD β*
113 affe- *Sh. B.² 211–12*: aspe- *vel* adspe- *codd.*
114 -am O: -as *cett.*
115 -nes π: -nem B: -num V γ δ: -nis β
116 patrum ς: -uum B V H: partum (-rv- O) *cett.*
117 volutatus *scripsi* (volutus *Beck.² 86–87*): vultus *codd.*: coi-
tus *Klotz¹*
118 pate- B V δ
119 quo B V δ

206

uncontrolled passion, not pleasure but torment, not love but the former object of your love.[51] (7) If we believe the philosophers, love is the oldest of divine powers, and the one the perpetual continuance of nature depends on.[52] But one love is gentle and serious, delighting in honest desires and in what holy chastity can do: for it first separated out and then mixed together[53] everything shrouded in the darkness of primeval night. The other love, to whom we restlessly cling with desperation in our hearts, is impudent, wild and wanton—goaded on as it is by a youthfulness still full of lust—, armed with arrows and funeral torches. (8) The one, then, offers to mortals children and marriages based on enduring affection, the other incests, lusts, adulteries, women of the town. 11. Shall I tell now of unbridled infatuation leading (as myth relates) to extraordinary and portentous results—love felt for an unknown before eyes are set on him,[54] a beauty burning with passion after turning his eyes upon himself,[55] virgins afire with love for their old fathers,[56] frenzied couplings of mortal men and animals carried to the length of fetuses monstrously[57] engendered? (2) Of all the things, however, that this emotion forces upon us when we are subject to it, the most cruel is that no one wishes to be cured when he is in love.

[51] I.e., the person you loved—and should not have loved.

[52] Cf. 14.10.4.

[53] For this cosmology, cf. Ar. *Av.* 693ff. (DAR).

[54] A recurring theme in love poetry, exploited, e.g., in Parth. 17.4 and parodied in Juv. 4.114.

[55] Narcissus.   [56] Myrrha.

[57] Cf. 15.8.2.

3   "Ego tamen" inquit "amare mallem." Hoc est ergo, propter quod opus odio fuit. Nihil agebant castigationes et[120] preces consilia perdebant. Odio debet amator expli-
4   cari, quem sanat adamata. Interrogare te hoc loco libet: numquid accusare posses, si, quod fecit medicamento puella, fecisset animo? Licuit te reposcere quantum nume-
5   rare non poteras, fastidire, contemnere. Iam indignaris quod te maluit remedio quam dolore sanari? Mulier, cui ad dimittendum amorem sufficiebat ut odisset, ipsa pro
6   te commenta est ut illam tu potius odisses. Finge te tamen aliqua remedii tui[121] sentire tormenta; adrogantissime miserorum, tu autem sperabas ardoris immodici feli-
7   cem statim sanitatem? Quid si queratur aeger abstinentiae dolore sanatus? Excussa sunt plerumque languentium vitia verberibus, redempta debilitate vita,[122] ignibus, vulneribus interdum profutura grassata sunt, et, quae fuissent mala sanitatis, in gratiam remediorum de maioris periculi comparatione redierunt. 12. Vix mehercule contingere potest ut hilares ab hac impatientia laetique discedant, quos pudor, quos satietas, quos paenitentiae ratio dimittit, nec sine aliquo morsu resilitur a malis quae voluptate

---

120 et *Håk. coll. 15.3.1*: nec *codd.*
121 -ia tua B V δ
122 -ta *Dess.[1] 98*: -tia *codd.*

---

58 Cf. 14.9.6.   59 I.e., a hate poison.
60 Cf. 15.3.1: Poor Man's prayers would frustrate both the girl's attempts to drive him away harshly and her patient efforts to bring him back to reason.
61 Perhaps alluding to the forceful manipulations performed by physicians to "reduce" joint dislocations.

(3) "But I should prefer to go on being in love," he says.[58] That is exactly why there was need for *hate*.[59] Her reproaches got nowhere, and his entreaties overcame her advice.[60] A lover has to be set free by hate, when the object of his passion is conducting the cure. (4) I want to ask you at this point: would you be able to prefer a charge if the girl had brought about by her attitude what she has brought about by a drug? She could have asked sums you were unable to pay, scorned you, despised you. (5) Are you now angry because she wanted you to be cured by a remedy rather than by pain? In order to relieve you of your love, that woman only needed to hate you; but she devised—herself, for *your* sake—a way of making you hate her instead. (6) Suppose however you do feel some pangs as a result of your cure; most arrogant of unhappy men, did you then expect to be happily cured of an immoderate passion in a moment? (7) What if a patient were to complain of being cured by a painful course of fasting? Often the troubles of the sick have been knocked out of them by blows,[61] lives have been saved at the cost of incapacitation, sometimes beneficial treatments have involved burning and wounds; in fact, things that would have been bad for a healthy man have proved acceptable remedies when compared with the danger of something worse. 12. Surely to heaven, people who are released by shame, by satiety, by considered remorse could hardly walk away from such a wild passion feeling happy and cheerful:[62] some pang is inevitable, when there is a rebound from evils which have maintained their grip by means of pleasure. It is a fuel for

[62] Contrast, e.g., 14.2.4.

tenuerunt. Iterum[123] materia amoris est desinere nec

2 queri. Opus fuit pari diversitate, viribus quantis adamasti, ut[124] resipisceres neque[125] frequenter in media sanitate subsisteres. Quale tibi remedium debuerit adhiberi,[126] vel ex hodierno senti, iuvenis, adfectu: pro homine, qui post odium queritur quod non amet, parum fuit si amare desi-

3 neret. Audi igitur, ingratissime, quatenus ad publicas au-

4 res secreta vestra proferre voluisti: "Dedi. Quid enim" inquit "facerem, quae remedia tam[127] multa perdideram? Ferre misera non poteram quod te iam coeperunt[128] om-

5 nes ridere meretrices. Repete agedum illarum conloquia noctium, quibus te frequenter alterius et fortasse divitis amatoris iniuria receptum inter oscula amplexusque mo-

6 nui: 'Quid, miser, cum fortuna, quid cum mea condicione rixaris? Parce necessitatibus meis: duo pauperes sumus.'

7 Sed et tu quotiens in sinus meos lacrimis fletuque resolu-tus exclamasti: 'Sentio furorem, sed imperare oculis, sed animum regere non possum! Quam libenter te, mulier, odissem!'"

8 Non est igitur, ingratissime mortalium, quod benefi-cium nostrum nomine potionis infames. 13. Remedium

---

[123] *probum* = iterati (*vd. Sh. B.⁴ 208, Longo*)
[124] ut *Håk.² 122.57*: ne *codd.*   [125] ne V Φ
[126] -ri M ψ: -re *cett.*   [127] tam *Obr.*: tua B V γ δ: *om.* β: iam *Bur.*   [128] -rant *Franc.*

---

63 I.e., without suffering (implying that one can cease to love once and for all only by going through sufferings).

64 Merely falling out of love was not enough: he needed to hate; hence the potion.

65 By your very accusation.

renewed love if you stop loving without complaining about it.[63] (2) There was need for something different but equally potent, for as much strength as you displayed when you fell in love, if you were to come to your senses without making frequent halts on the road back to health. What sort of remedy needed to be applied to you, young man, you cannot but feel even from your emotions today: for a man who after taking a hate potion complains that he does not love, it would not have been enough to stop loving.[64] (3) Listen then, most ungrateful man—given that you have shown your willingness[65] to reveal the secrets of the pair of you to a wide audience:[66] (4) "Yes, I gave you it," she says. "For what else was I to do after wasting so many remedies in the past? Ah me! I could not bear it that other courtesans had started laughing at you. (5) Come on, go back over our conversations on those nights when I entertained you—and stood up a second, perhaps even a rich lover. Kissing and embracing you, I warned you over and over again:[67] (6) 'Why, wretch, why do you quarrel with fortune, with my position in life? Try to understand *my* needs: we are both paupers.' (7) But *you* too—how often, weeping and wailing on my breast, did you cry out: 'I feel my madness, but I cannot command my eyes,[68] I cannot rule my mind! How willingly, woman, should I hate you!'"

(8) There is no call then for you, most ungrateful of mortals, to discredit the good deed we did you by the name you give to the potion.[69] 13. You drank a cure, but

---

[66] Cf. 14.11.5.

[67] Contrast 14.9.5.

[68] Cf. 1.6.7.

[69] I.e., "poison" rather than "remedy": cf. 14.5.5, 14.11.1.

bibisti, sed illud odium tuum est. Quid?[129] Quod furis,
conviciaris, exclamas, non est haustus illius adfectus;[130]
2 et[131] amator[132] talis fuisti. Aliud sunt, aliud illi, quos in
voluptates superfluentium facultatium mittit secura felici-
3 tas; improbius pauperes amant. Sic tumultuabaris admis-
sus, sic moras, sic impedimenta ferre non poteras; maledi-
cebas populo, conviciabaris intrantibus. Cuius umquam
felicius commutata fortuna est, si tunc omnes oderas, nunc
4 unam, pauper, odisti? Quin potius, iuvenis, admittis con-
silii rationem? Quid agis, infelix, cur redditam modo sani-
5 tatem rigore nimiae contentionis exasperas? Praedico,
testor: consumis odium; nondum totam mentem vis per-
fusa possedit, adhuc circa te duo maximi rixantur adfectus.
6 Adiuva potius, adiuva potionem. Contradic agedum quicquid est illud[133] quod tumultuatur, exaestuat, totumque
sanitas componat hominem. Tunc te sciemus amare de-
sisse, cum desieris odisse.

14. Et innocentiam quidem puellae satis, ut spero,
defendimus; magnitudo periculi advocet[134] preces. Consurge agedum, miserrima feminarum, reliquam defensio-
2 nis tuae partem tuere lacrimis. Accusator, quid speras,

129 del. Sh. B.[1] 77
130 eff- Watt[2] 32 (post Warr)   131 sed Φ
132 amator (et ante, non post, dist.) Håk.[2] 125–26: amor codd.
133 illud Obr.: aliud codd.   134 advocet Håk. (firm. Longo):
vocet B V Φ*: vocat (Franc.) <et> Russ.[3]

70 I.e., poor men need to strive harder than rich men to win a
lover.
71 To the brothel.
72 Sc., to finish its work.

the hatred you feel is your own. Why, that you rave, abuse, cry aloud, is not an emotion produced by that draft: you were exactly like that when you were in love. (2) It is different, yes, a different story with those who go smoothly along the road to pleasure, thanks to the happy freedom from worry that superabundant resources bring with them; poor men love more outrageously.[70] (3) Thus, when you were let in, you would cause a commotion; thus, you could not brook delays and obstacles. You used to curse all and sundry, abuse everyone who came in.[71] Whose fortunes have ever been more happily changed? Then you hated everybody, now, pauper, you hate just one woman. (4) Why, young man, don't you rather take on board the counsel of reason? What are you doing, unhappy man? Why are you endangering your health, only just restored, by being so obstinately and excessively contentious? (5) I proclaim and bear witness: you are still taking in the dose of hate; its force has not yet spread and got possession of your whole mind; two great emotions are still disputing over you. (6) Rather, help the potion, yes, help it.[72] Come on, stand up against all those tumultuous, seething emotions, and let health bring order to the whole man. We shall know you have stopped loving when you have stopped hating.[73]

14. Well, I have said enough—I hope—in defense of the girl's innocence; but let the gravity of the danger summon the aid of prayers. Come on, most wretched of women, get to your feet and let your tears plead the rest of your case. (2) What are you hoping, what are you wait-

---

[73] I.e., you will be cured once *both* emotions have disappeared.

quid expectas? Ad genua tua non mittimus [eam]:[135] toto licet infelicem terrore convenias, non exosculabitur ma-

3 nus; mortem, suprema denunties, te non rogabit. Frustra tibi aliquid de periculo nostro metuque promittis: nes-

4 cit[136] puella, non habet odii remedium. Sane tamen viribus potionis effectum sit, ut accusaveris innocentem: sufficit ultioni vidisse pallentem, satis est audisse gemitus. Memineris hanc esse quam tu nunc,[137] iuvenis, odisti.

5 Quid ais?[138] Etiamne perferes illud pronuntiationis anceps, illud humanae salutis incertum? Numerabis ergo sententias et, si damnaveris, exultabis, nefande, gaudebis?

6 Puto, non adamasti. An et sequeris dum carnifex trahit, intereris dum hos oculos occisura conteget[139] manus, dum haec amplexibus tuis nota cervix ad supremos nudatur ictus? Non exilies, non pectus oppones, non fidem hominum deorumque clamabis? Aspicies[140] percussam, super

7 palpitantia membra[141] consistes?[142] Potes hoc videre, potes hoc ferre? Sanatus es!

8   Quodsi quid tristius iudicii huius attulerit eventus, di turpiter[143] pereuntium beneficiorum semper ultores, di,

---

[135] del. Wint.[9] ut gloss.: -mus. iam (vel nam) Håk., sed vd. Watt[3] 56   [136] -it Gron. (firm. Håk.): -is codd.

[137] nunc Sh. B.[4] 208: om. B: non V Φ: non <diu> Håk.

[138] ais M (vd. Breij[1] 246–47.294, Sant.-Str. 128.166): agis cett.

[139] -teg- Reitz.[2] 55: -ting- codd.

[140] aspicies Bur.: accipies codd.

[141] super p. membra 5: nuper (numquid non V) p. merori ad codd.   [142] -stes Obr.: -stentes codd. (dein membra nudabis V): -stens 5

[143] di turpiter Sh. B.[1] 77–78 (cf. fere Sen. Ben. 3.1.1): di rapite δ*: diripite cett.

ing for, accuser? We are not casting her at your knees. You may bring to bear on the unlucky woman all the terror at your command, but she will not kiss your hands; you may threaten death, threaten the ultimate penalty,[74] but she will not beg for mercy. (3) It is in vain that you promise yourself some advantage from any fear of danger on our part: the girl does not know, does not possess any cure for hate. (4) But granted that the poison has had the power at least to make you accuse an innocent, it is revenge enough to have seen her so pale, enough to have heard her groans. Remember, young man: this is the woman you *now* hate.[75] (5) What do you say? Will you really endure the suspense over the sentence, the doubt whether a human being will come through safely? Will you then count up the votes, and, if you get her condemned, will you exult, wicked man, will you rejoice? You did not really fall in love with her, I think. (6) Will you actually follow behind at the moment when the executioner drags her off, will you be there when the hand that will kill her blindfolds these eyes, when this neck, so well known to your embrace, is bared for the final blows? Will you not spring forward, will you not put your body in the way, will you not appeal to men and gods for help? Will you gaze upon her after the fatal blow, will you stand over her quivering limbs? (7) Can you see this, can you bear it? You are cured!

(8) But if this trial turns out unfavorably, ye gods who never fail to avenge good deeds when they go shamefully

[74] Which she would face if convicted of poisoning.

[75] "Lover is asked to remember that he hates Meretrix *now*, i.e., that he once loved her" (Shackleton Bailey [1984–97, 208]).

quos iste crudelis in amplexibus puellae frequenter mae-
rore, lacrimis aut finem amoris rogavit aut mortem, date
9 nobis iustam de ingrato iuvene vindictam. Non impre-
camur debilitates,[144] naufragia, morbos:[145] pauper sit et
amet quamcumque meretricem et amare non desinat.

144 -tes δ: -ti V: -tis B γ* β
145 -bos δ: -bi B V γ* β

unappreciated, ye gods whom this cruel man, in the embrace of this girl, often begged with tears of grief either for an end to his love or for death, let us see an ungrateful young man punished as he deserves. (9) We do not invoke on him mutilations, shipwrecks, illnesses: may he be a poor man, and love any call girl at all, and never stop loving her.

DECLAMATION 16

INTRODUCTION

Two friends set out on a journey by sea that comes to a dramatic end: they are brought to a land ruled by a tyrant, who decides to imprison only one of them. The prisoner's mother,[1] learning that her son is in the tyrant's hands, weeps until she loses her sight.[2] The prisoner is allowed to leave temporarily to visit his mother, on condition that his friend be imprisoned instead of him[3] and be punished with death if he does not return on a day assigned. The son promises to respect the agreement and comes to his city; however, his mother tries to keep him there, appealing to the law by which a son shall not abandon a parent in distress.[4] The declamation is the speech of the son, who requests permission to return to rescue his friend.

The narrative framework of this case recalls the story of Damon and Phintias, the two friends who gave a similar proof of loyalty at the court of the tyrant Dionysius II of Syracuse (fourth century BC).[5] That story guides our

[1] No mention is made of his father, nor of the friend's parents.

[2] On this motif, cf. Introduction to *DM* 6, n. 2.

[3] For the pattern of a character replacing another one in distress, see Introduction to *DM* 6, n. 3.

[4] Cf. 5.7.4, 6.11.8; see also Introduction to *DM* 5, n. 2; Introduction to *DM* 6, n. 4.

[5] Cf. in particular the account given by Val. Max. 4.7.ext.1; full discussion in Santorelli (2014b, 181–91).

[QUINTILIAN]

speaker, first of all, in the presentation of the tyrant and
his schemes: a virtuoso in cruelty (10.5), he aims at testing
the friendship of the two young men, hence his decision
to imprison only one of them in the first place (leaving the
other free to leave, abandoning his friend: 3.4), and then
to let the prisoner go (in the hope that he may not return:
7.7). The literary model influences the speaker's arguments as well: he portrays the bond between the two
youths as an extraordinary friendship, leading to a constant competition in generosity (2.7), already known and
observed by the whole human race (e.g., 3.2, 7.4); even
the optimism of the son, who is certain that the tyrant will
not kill him on his return (4.1), may be due to the awareness of the happy ending of Damon and Phintias' story.

   Son feels obliged to help both his friend and his mother.
Inevitably, then, there is a conflict between the authority
of the ties of blood and the weight of the bond of friendship: the speaker maintains that even relatives are held
together by a bond of mutual friendship, a deeper and
more precious affection than the inherited bonds of kinship (2.4–6). In deciding this case, then, judges are invited
not to consider merely the "names" of the characters involved (Mother vs. Friend), but to assess: (1) which of
them can benefit more by the speaker's presence (1.3–4);
(2) who did more for the speaker himself while he was in
chains (8.1–9.5); and (3) who is currently in the more dangerous predicament (11.2–4).

   As for the law Mother is appealing to (children are not
to abandon parents in distress), the speaker maintains that
it is not relevant to this case: on one hand, the law applies
only when parents are left *all alone*, while this mother can

222

count on the support of friends and relatives (5.4, 11.3); on the other hand, the law was intended to apply to sons who deliberately abandon their parents in spite of their filial duties, while the speaker is forced to do so by a more compelling sense of piety (6.1–3).

This declamation has been transmitted in an incomplete form (see below). The surviving portion can be analyzed as follows:[6]

> PROEM 1.1–2.6
> NARRATION 2.7–3.7
> ARGUMENTATION
>   *Refutatio* 4.1–6.5
>   *Confirmatio* 7.1–11.4

The text of all the manuscripts ends abruptly at 11.4, in the middle of a sentence: the final part of the argumentation, and the whole epilogue of the speech, are lost. This must be due to the loss of a few pages in the course of the manuscript tradition: an especially tormented one for this piece, as the plentiful corruptions and lacunae that mar it throughout show.[7]

DM 16 is close in language and style to *DM* 10 and 7, and should probably be dated to the mid-second century AD.[8] A reply to Son's speech was composed by Patarol.[9]

---

[6] Santorelli (2014b, 197–202), with a slight change.
[7] See General Introduction, §6.
[8] See General Introduction, §4.
[9] (1743, 371–83).

16

Amici vades

Duo amici, ex quibus uni mater erat, peregre profecti ad
tyrannum appliciti sunt. Mater, cognito quod filius haberetur[1] a tyranno, flendo oculos amisit. Oblata est a iuveni-
bus tyranno condicio ut dimitteret alterum ad visendam
matrem ad diem praestitutam reversurum, ita ut, nisi oc-
currisset ad diem, de eo qui restiterat poena sumeretur.
Et iureiurando adstrictus est. Venit iuvenis in civitatem;
mater detinet ex lege qua parentes in calamitate deserere
non licebat.

1. Etsi,[2] iudices,[3] olim omnes videor humanorum pectorum adfectus in solam amicitiam contulisse, et patior invidiam hominis qui sibi non reliquerit ut amaret et matrem,

[1] ‹vinctus›*vel* ‹in vinclis› h. *Håk., sed cf. ThlL VI.3.2428.55ss.*
[2] etsi—olim Φ (*e coniect., ut vid.: Wint.*[8] *305–6*): *om.* B *et*
(omnes *tenus*) V
[3] iudices *Wint.*[8] *306*: sanctissimi viri Φ (*vd. super. adn.*)

16

The friends who stood surety

Two friends, one of whom had a mother,[1] went abroad, and put in[2] at a place ruled by a tyrant. The mother, learning that her son was in the tyrant's hands, wept till she lost her sight. The young men offered the tyrant an arrangement by which he should let one of them go to visit his mother, provided he returned on a day assigned; if he did not come in time, the one who had stayed behind would pay the penalty. And he[3] swore to keep the pact. The young man came to the city. His mother tries to keep him there, appealing to the law by which it was not permitted to abandon parents in distress.[4]

(Speech of the son)

1. Although, judges, I have for a long time given the impression that I have concentrated all the affection a man can feel upon friendship alone, and although I am being stigmatized as one who has left himself no room to show

---

[1] I.e., one still alive.   [2] 16.3.3 takes this to mean "cast up."
[3] The departing youth.
[4] Cf. Introduction to the present declamation, n. 4.

quotiens tamen universam pietatis meae conscientiam
intueor, in qua minimum est quod videor bonus amicus,
non possum non hanc primam electionis nostrae complorare fortunam, quod mihi necesse est aut amicum relin-
2 quere aut matrem. Facinus, severissimi viri, facinus fit
impatientissimis adfectibus meis, quod succurri non potest duobus. Excedit omnem querelae meae complorationem[4] quod me[5] tam diversis meorum conatibus adversa
3 conveniunt, ut videar[6] eligere. Quid[7] non darem, miser,
pro luce matris, qui ut illam viderem[8] amicum dedi!
Fidem vestram, iudices, ne inter maximas necessitates
pereat usus hominis, qui paratus est duobus impendi! Iam
hic est tota ratio clementiae, ne ibi me detineatis ubi non
4 prosum. Nec dissimulo, sanctissimi viri, perferre me cum
maxime tam incredibilis exempli fidem, ut non immerito
possim videri cum matre colludere. Ego videor excogitasse
istum colorem, et hoc, quod detineor, amicitiae vocatur
5 infirmitas. Miseremini, iudices, temptate me et dimittite.
An voluerim reverti, scire non potestis, nisi revertor.

    2. Illud, sanctissimi iudices, illud adfectus meos tor-

---

4 compara- *De Fel., sed vd. Sant.*
5 om. Φ, *sed vd. Håk.*[2] 127
6 verear *Bur., sed vd. Sant.*
7 quid M: quod *cett.*   8 vise- *Wint.*[9]

---

    5 I am accused of leaving my mother for my friend; this could
at least earn me the good reputation of being a loyal friend, yet
this is a minor merit in my eyes: what matters to me is the duty
to assist both.

    6 Whereas he has in fact a *single* option: going back to save his
friend's life (cf. n. 29).   7 Cf. 6.19.1 for the same argument.

love for his mother as well, nevertheless, whenever I consider the whole extent of the sense of duty I feel within me, the least part of which is my reputation as a good friend,[5] I cannot but complain first and foremost of the disastrous dilemma that compels me to abandon either my friend or my mother. (2) It is mortifying, most austere gentlemen, yes, mortifying for someone with such overmastering feelings as mine that *both* cannot be helped. Nothing is more deplorable, in the accusation I face, than that adversity confronts me with such different designs on the part of those dear to me that I seem to be making a choice.[6] (3) Unhappy me! What would I not give for my mother to recover her sight, after I gave my friend so that I could see her! I beg you, judges, to make sure that amid the direst of necessities the usefulness of a man prepared to sacrifice himself for *two* people does not go to waste. Here, in fact, is the whole reason why you should show clemency: do not detain me here, where I can be of no use.[7] (4) Nor will I try to conceal, most respected sirs, that I am at this very moment giving proof of an act of heroism so incredible that I quite deserve to be suspected of colluding with my mother.[8] It is thought that it is *I* who have contrived this ploy, and my failure to return is called a flaw in my character as a friend. (5) For pity's sake, judges, put me to the test, and let me go: you cannot know whether I was willing to go back unless I go back.

2. It is this, it is this that tortures my feelings and tears

[8] It is hardly credible that Son wants to leave his home to go back to the tyrant's prison; indeed, someone may suspect that he has staged the present trial in agreement with Mother, so as to avoid leaving.

quet ac lacerat, quod sim⁹ ingenti expectatione deceptus:
speraveram futurum ut hoc loco rem magnam faceret et
mater. Paraveram apud tyrannum hanc iactationem, ut me
crederet remissum, et genus ostentationis adamaveram, ut
2 mirarentur homines¹⁰ fidem etiam in orbitate. Quo vultis
hoc animo feram, quod, etiam ut revertar, amico meo
mater imposuit, et quantum ad hanc pertinet, maximum
iuvenem decepit, illum, qui meos crediderit adfectus?¹¹
3 Non possum, iudices, litis huius dissimulare facinus: innocentius fuerat ut ego nollem reverti.
4   Viderint, sanctissimi viri, qui¹² receptas nominum persuasiones velut aliquam servitutem caritatis attendunt.
Me si quis interroget, nullos affectus tantum nasci puto,
et, si quis omnia vera ratione respiciat, quicquid ⟨pa-
rentes,⟩¹³ liberos, fratres, propinquos invicem tenet, ami-
5 citia est. Homines igitur, quos cum maxime incredibilium
rerum loquitur invidia, sumus sine dubio non eiusdem
pars animae, non eiusdem pondus uteri; sed¹⁴ quanto
minus in causis, tanto plus in affectu¹⁵ est. Admirabilior
6 caritas, in quam coimus viribus nostris. Non pudet, iudices, hanc fateri persuasionem: minus debetur homini
qui aliquem ideo tantum amat, quia necesse est. Ita est,

⁹ sum *Håk., sed vd. Sant.*   ¹⁰ -nes Vᵃᶜ (*def. Håk.² 127*):
-nis B Vᵖᶜ Φ   ¹¹ imposuit—adfectus *dist. Wint.⁹*: meo se
credidit adfectui *coni. Håk.*   ¹² qui ⊊: sed *codd.* (*ante quod
lac. indic. Dess.¹ 89*), *at vd. Sant.*
        ¹³ *add. Sh. B.² 212*   ¹⁴ -ri sed V: -ris et B: -ri et Φ
        ¹⁵ eff- *Reitz.² 31, sed vd. Sant.*

⁹ Sc., by my mother.   ¹⁰ Sc., rather than my mother refusing to let me go.   ¹¹ Literally, "(kinship) names."

them to shreds, most respected judges: that I have been cheated of a lofty expectation. I had hoped that at this juncture my mother too would do something heroic. I had prepared myself to be boastful when I came before the tyrant, so as to make him believe I had been *sent* back:[9] I had fallen in love with a kind of showing off that would make men amazed at someone keeping good faith even when it meant losing her son. (2) How do you expect me to bear it that, even if I do return, my mother has deceived my friend—for, so far as she is concerned, she has let down a matchless youth, one who did not doubt the sincerity of my feelings? (3) I cannot, judges, conceal the outrageousness of this lawsuit: it would have been less objectionable if *I* were unwilling to return.[10]

(4) I take no heed, most revered sirs, of those who regard the accepted conception of ties of blood[11] as a kind of enslavement of affection. If you ask me, I think no feelings are merely born with a man: if one looks at everything in the right light, whatever holds <parents>, children, brothers, relations in a mutual bond is *friendship*.[12] (5) We, therefore, who are at this very moment on the lips of people jealous of our incredible deeds, are of course not part of the same soul, nor were we carried in the same womb; but the less binding force there is in our origins, the greater there is in the feeling. Affection is the more admirable when we enter on it together, of our own volition. (6) Judges, I am not ashamed to confess my firm belief: less is owed to a man who loves another only because he has to. That is how it is, judges, that is how it is:

---

[12] Affection is not just an automatic effect of a birth relationship: it needs *amicitia* to bolster it up (DAR).

iudices, ita est: a primis statim aetatibus[16] in eandem coire
vitam habet aliquem fraternitatis affectum.

7   Sic effectum est ut nos statim fama committeret, et tali
certamine coîmus ut, si quid accidisset,[17] uni deberet alter[18] exemplum. Inde est quod [et][19] pariter everti[20] con-
tempsimus[21] et, quasi facilius esset in terra fides,[22] placuit
sub incerta[23] pelagi cohaerere. 3. Nec tamen vanitate nec
discursu putetis extractos; magnas et inexplicabilis navi-
gandi fuisse causas vel hinc potestis aestimare, quod nos
non detinuit haec mater.

2   Utrumne igitur, iudices, sumere de nobis etiam nunc
voluit experimentum ipsa amicitia, et parum fortuna credidit[24] hominibus adhuc tantum feliciter amantibus, an
haec est magnae semper opinionis invidia, nec ulli umquam tam plena confessione laudantur, ut illos[25] non ipsa
3   quoque ad‹miratio[26] in discrimen vocet? *** tyranni›[27]
litoribus appulsi sumus. Homines, quorum omnis[28] casus

---

16 *probum, vd. Corb. 334*

17 *dist. Håk.: post* uni *vulg.*

18 *-er Sch.:* -eri (et -eri V DE) *codd.*

19 *delevi* (*et s.l. habet* B)

20 ev- *Helm¹ 359–60:* (pariter) rev- *codd.*

21 consens- *Baden 750, sed vd. Helm¹ 360*

22 in terra fides A (*nota* terra *vs.* pelagi): inter fides (-dos C²E)
cett. (*frustra def. Sant.¹ 229–30*)   23 -to ς, *sed vd. Håk.*

24 -edidit π (*vind. Reitz.² 33.1*): -edit *cett.*   25 -las B V δ

26 ad B δ: ab B²: a V H²: *om. cett.* (*vd. etiam infer. adn.*)

27 *lac. stat. Reitz.² 32–33, post quem* (ad‹miratores in d. vocare velint? tyranni *vel* iniusti regis›) *sic textum e.g. constitui:*
(ipsa q.) amicitia temptare velit (lito-) γ β (*om. cett.*), *plane e
coniect.* (*Reitz.² 32*)

28 -is π J: -i B V HO: -ia *cett.*

to fall together into the same manner of life right from the earliest years involves something like the attachment between brothers.

(7) So it came about that report made a pair of us[13] from the start, and we entered into the kind of competition in which, if anything went wrong, one of us owed the other a notable action. Hence the fact that we faced the danger of shipwreck with equal composure: as though loyalty were something too easy on dry land, we determined to confront the hazards of the deep side by side. 3. But you should not imagine we were drawn away from home by a foolish desire to travel hither and thither; our reasons for going to sea were compelling and unavoidable, as you can tell if only from the fact that a mother like this did not hold me back.

(2) Was it therefore, judges, that friendship herself even at this stage wanted to test us out, and fortune was unready to trust those who had till then only loved in favorable circumstances?[14] Or is this the disfavor always felt for those highly regarded, people being never so wholeheartedly praised that even their very ad‹mirers do not summon them into danger?[15] (3) *** on a tyrant's› shore we were cast up.[16] Being men whom report kept an eye

---

[13] With some implication of opposed rivalry (as, e.g., of a pair of gladiators).   [14] = Maybe our hardships were sent our way by Fortune as a test of our friendship. Cf. 16.7.3.

[15] They maliciously urge the virtuous into dangerous ways of giving further proof of their virtues (AS).

[16] In the lacuna there will have been mention of the tyrant ruling the land, and perhaps of the circumstances that brought the youths there.

fama custodiebat, ⟨eo⟩[29] consumimur[30] terrore, qui pa-
4 rentibus statim caecitas est. Hinc illud evenit, quod
⟨non⟩[31] sumus pariter alligati: sic magis adversus solutum
carcer inventus est. Pudet, iudices, fateri: iam in hoc victus, iam inferior recessi; ex duobus magis amator,[32] quem
tyrannus paratus[33] est ablegare.[34]

5   Quantum tibi, amice, debeo! Non potuit nos dividere
nisi mater. Tibi[35] primum caecitas nuntiata est, tuus hic
6 affectus fuit, quod credidit tyrannus. Quid ille non fecit!
Ut rex desideravit[36] vicarium corpus, amplexus est catenas; sponderi sibi voluit hominem rediturum per maria,
per matrem: repromisit de incertis tamquam de animo
7 suo. Quis hominum pro se tam multa fecisset? Praestitit,
inquam, amicus, praestitit rem quam videbatur ideo tyrannus indulsisse, ne fieret, et hominem, qui in rebus humanis hunc esse nolebat affectum, decipimus dum tempta-
mur.

29 *add. Wint.*[9] *coll. 5.21.5*   30 -mus B δ
31 *add. Håk. necnon Wint.*[3]   32 -ator V (*cf. OLD*[2] *§2*):
-atur B Φ: -at *Guil. Malm.* (*vd. Wint.*[6] *258*)   33 pactus (. . .
alligare) *Wint.*[7] *162*   34 ableg- *Sh. B.*[2] *213*: allig- *codd.*
35 ubi *Håk., sed vd. Sant.*[1] *232–33*   36 -vit V E: -verit *cett.*

17 The plural is generic: (in the world of declamation) all parents are at risk of losing their eyesight out of weeping once they
hear that their sons are in the sort of danger the two youths were
in. Cf. Introduction to *DM* 6, n. 2.

18 The youth not in prison was free from chains, yet he was
unable to go back home because he was bound by loyalty to his
friend. For a comparable paradox see 9.8.3.

19 I.e., when the tyrant decided to imprison me and let my
friend free: he had understood that my friend was the more trust-

on whatever befell us, we were overcome by the ⟨very⟩ terror which for parents results in immediate blindness.[17] (4) Our distress came about precisely because we were ⟨not⟩ both thrown into chains—for in this way prison was, as it turned out, more of a punishment for the one who was at liberty.[18] I am ashamed to confess it, judges: even then[19] I came off the loser, yes, the inferior: for he is the more devoted out of two friends, whom a tyrant is ready to let *go*.

(5) How much I owe you, my friend! Only my mother could divide us. It was to you that her blindness was first reported,[20] it was your emotional response on that occasion that made the tyrant believe it. (6) My friend left *nothing* undone! When the king asked for someone to take my place, he welcomed the chains. The tyrant wanted a guarantee that the other man would come back, despite the sea, despite a mother: my friend in turn gave promises on matters yet uncertain as if it were his own intentions that were in question. (7) Who of all men would have done so much for his *own* sake?[21] My friend, I say, guaranteed, yes guaranteed, something that the tyrant seemed to have intended to concede just in order that it should *not* happen:[22] and so, by passing the test we were subjected to, we disappointed the expectations of someone who refused to believe that an affection like ours exists in this world.

worthy of the two of us—the one who would actually stay around out of loyalty (although free of chains).

[20] Because he was *not* imprisoned, unlike his friend—the woman's son.   [21] Cf. 6.5.6.

[22] I.e., so as to prove that our friendship was not as strong as we claimed.

4. Ego non invenio cur horreat mater arcem, quid sibi
velit quasi destinatas operire cervices. Non odit me tyran-
2 nus, cuius non interest an alium occidat. Miserere, mater,
si quis est magnorum meritorum pudor, querere, quod
unum decet te,[37] impatientius ex duobus[38] amari[39] semper
3 absentem. Cui tu fortunae,[40] quibus necessitatibus inicis
manum! Me ad amicum meum admitterent alterius catenae[41] tyranni, nunc mihi portas <hostis>[42] aperiret, sub-
4 sidio navigium pirata praestaret. Si mehercules ante morerer, ire deberes, mater, ad diem. Misera, non intellegis
quanto te magis [plus][43] obligaverit amicus? Plus debes
homini qui me tibi remisit, ex quo pati non potes ut revertar.
5 Libet mehercules, iudices, libet misereri hominum,
qui me laudant revertentem. Amicus mihi credidit ut redi-
6 rem. Ita nunc ego facio rem magnam, ego sum ille bonus

37 decet *Håk.*[2] *128,* te *scripsi*: de (d B) caecitate *codd.*
38 duobus *Håk.*: nobis *codd.*
39 -ri B[2]: -ris B V Φ
40 -ae *Obr.*: -as *codd.*
41 -ae *Dess.*[1] *75–76*: -a et *codd.*
42 *supplevi*
43 *del. Reitz.*[2] *79* (*et om.* πM E): pius *Gron.*

23 = the tyrant (always based in a citadel in declamation).
24 She has no reason to think the tyrant would kill me: he has
shown that his aim was only to test our friendship.
25 Out of two persons equally dear to us, we are normally
fonder of the absent one. Mother has reason to regret this, as it
means that Son currently loves his absent friend more dearly than
her.
26 Explained in the next sentence. Another tyrant would un-

4. I see no reason why my mother should dread the citadel:[23] I do not see what she means by trying to protect my neck as though it were destined for the ax.[24] The tyrant does not hate *me*: killing someone else would make no difference to him. (2) Take pity, mother, if great services win any respect; complain—the only fitting course for you—that of two people the absent one is always loved the more passionately.[25] (3) What fortune, what extreme circumstances you are trying to resist![26] The chains of a different tyrant would admit me to my friend's cell, now <an enemy> would open the gates to me,[27] a pirate would provide a boat to help me. (4) Heavens, if I were to die in the meantime, mother, *you* ought to go to meet the deadline. Unhappy woman, do you not see under how much greater an obligation my friend has put *you*? You have come to owe more to the man who sent me back to you, ever since you have found it intolerable that I should go back.[28]

(5) Heavens, judges, I am inclined to pity, yes pity, people who praise me for returning. My friend trusted me to come back.[29] (6) So am *I* doing such a big thing now,

derstand the gravity of this situation and allow me to return to my friend's cell (in *this* tyrant's prison); even war enemies or pirates would be equally understanding. You instead, Mother, are trying to stop me—thus behaving more cruelly than the cruelest characters of declamation. Cf., e.g., 9.12.7.

[27] Sc., to release me—although a prisoner of war—and let me go to my friend.

[28] Mother has spent more time with Son than she might have expected, during the time since she has started holding him back. In doing so, she has increased her debt to Friend, who had made Son's visit possible (AS).

[29] So I had no choice, and mine is *not* an act of heroism.

235

amicus, ille mirabilis,[44] ille narrandus? Si qua dicenti[45]
fides est, facinus mihi videtur quod scio me non esse periturum.

7   Sentit, iudices, et ipsa mater rem se facere turpissi-
mam, si necessitate detinear; itaque mulier, quae adhuc
de affectu cuncta fecerat, ad legem subito convertitur. 5.
Pessima, iudices, causa matris est, in qua plurimum lex
potest. LIBERI PARENTES IN CALAMITATE NE DESERANT.

2   Facinus est, iudices, hoc dici homini reverso. Ita nunc
ego contemno matrem, ego despicio caecitatis obsequia,
homo qui omnium calamitatium mearum ambitum in hoc
consumpsi, ut redirem, qui inter supremas sollicitudines
non pro me rogavi? Mihi quisquam contumaciam supplicia liberorum, mihi neglectae pietatis minatur invidiam?

3   Bone Iuppiter, quanti mihi constitit ut[46] malus filius viderer! Imputem tibi necesse est, mater, quod meum amicum
propter te reliqui, ad quem facinus est non reverti.

4   Nondum, iudices, necessitates meas, nondum amici
merita refero; interim contendo tunc esse[47] tantum legis
huius usum, cum in calamitate soli sunt parentes. ⟨∗∗∗⟩[48]

---

44 mir- C[2] E: miser- *cett.*   45 -ti *Gron.* (*firm. Sant.*): -tis
codd.   46 -tit ut *Reitz.[2] 51*: -tui B: -tui ut V: -tit ne Φ
47 tunc esse ς: tu necesse B V Φ*
48 *lac. stat. Wint.[7] 162*

---

30 Sc., by appeal to ties of blood (cf. 16.2.4).
31 And not emotional reasons, as it ought to be.
32 Sc., to help his mother.
33 This claim is not made in the subsequent text: what *does*
follow is the argument for necessity, which the speaker has just
said he will defer. The text exploiting the argument here an-

am *I* the good friend, the object of wonder, the topic of storytelling? If anyone will believe what I say, it seems outrageous to me that I know I shall not perish.

(7) Judges, even my mother herself feels she is doing something altogether shameful, if I am kept from going by necessity;[30] and that is why, though up to now she had proceeded entirely by appealing to emotion, she now suddenly changes tack and appeals to the law. 5. A mother's case is very weak, judges, if the law[31] is the strongest point in it. CHILDREN ARE NOT TO ABANDON THEIR PARENTS IN DISTRESS. It is outrageous, judges, for this to be said to a man who has returned.[32] (2) Am *I* really now undervaluing my mother, am *I* slighting the attentions owed to a blind person—I, who used up all the sympathy my calamities aroused precisely in order to come back, I, who amid extreme anxieties asked nothing for myself? Does anyone dare threaten *me* with punishments appropriate to contumacious children, threaten *me* with the stigma of neglecting my filial duty? (3) By Jupiter, look how much it has cost me—all to be thought to be a bad son! I cannot but charge to *your* account, mother, my having left my friend for your sake, a friend it is a crime to fail to go back to.

(4) Judges, I am not yet talking of the compulsions that weigh on me, not yet of my friend's services. For the moment, my claim is that this law is not to be used except where parents are all alone in their distress.[33] ⟨∗∗∗⟩

nounced (Mother was not alone, therefore the law does not apply to her case) must have been lost in a significant lacuna—or, perhaps (AS), the point was planned but remained for some reason undeveloped.

[QUINTILIAN]

5 Magnam partem mortalium fortuna dimisit a legibus, nec
ulla iura tam tristia sunt ut ea in adversis patiantur homines. Ego, cum te[49] necessitas rapit, sic habeo queri,[50] quasi
6 relinquar?[51] Excusatae sunt parentibus liberorum calamitates, et, si quem lex ista deprehenderit in alterius fato,[52]
7 transeat necesse est tamquam orbitatem. Quid enim, si me
detinente matre pater a[53] latere revocaret, [et][54] si bella
8 militem poscerent, si legatum patria dimitteret?[55] Vel, uti
ad propriam descendam necessitatis meae complorationem, si me damnatum poena constringeret, videlicet ef-
fringeres carcerem, mater, iniceres carnifici manum et
perituri filii iugulum auctoritate iuris operires?

6. Dii deaeque, quam longe est lex, quae detinet[56]
hominem, qui paene[57] non venit! Nescis, quantum intellego, mater, quantam invidiam debeant facere liberis
2 parentes, a quibus relinquuntur. Mater, quae se deseri
queritur, illud exclamet: "Filium meum civitas peregrina
sollicitat; ut amoenos nesciocuius[58] recessus orbis petat,
debilitati meae subtrahit umeros." "Iuvenis meus abduci-

---

[49] te Wint.[7] 162: me codd.

[50] h. q. probum, cf. Wint.[7] 162   [51] sic dist. Håk.

[52] -to scripsi post Wint.[9] (fat<o occupat>um), mox dist. Leh.:
-ctum M A P^{ac}: -tum cett.

[53] pater Gron., a π (cf. Håk.[2] 128): altero B V: alter e Φ*

[54] del. Wint.[7] 163   [55] quid—dimitteret sic dist. Wint.[7] 163

[56] de- Sh. B.[4] 208–9: re- codd.

[57] paene π D: penae C H P[2]: pene cett.: poenae ς

[58] -oquos Franc., sed vd. Håk.

---

[34] If you are removed by necessity, ought I to complain of
being deserted? No! (DAR).   [35] Alluding to the law.

238

(5) A large proportion of mankind is exempted from the laws by fortune: no regulations are so harsh that those in adversity have to obey them. When necessity is sweeping *you* away, am *I* to complain of being abandoned?[34] (6) The calamities[35] of *children* are excused by their parents: if this law comes upon a child engaged[36] in someone else's fate, it should pass over him as though he were an orphan. (7) Indeed, what if a[37] father called his son back[38] from his mother's side when she wanted to stop him leaving her? What if wars demanded his presence as a soldier? What if his country sent him away as an ambassador? (8) Or, to come down to my own deplorable plight, if I had been condemned and were subject to an unavoidable penalty, I suppose, mother, you would break into the prison, lay hands on the executioner, and shield the throat of your doomed son by appealing to the authority of the law?

6. Gods and goddesses, how far from applicable here is the law that holds back a man who almost did not come at all![39] To my mind, mother, you have no idea in what lurid colors parents should paint their children when they are abandoned by them. (2) Let *this* be the cry of a mother who complains she is being deserted: "A foreign city is seducing my son: it is in order to make for a pleasant corner somewhere in the world that he is withdrawing his shoulders[40] from supporting me in my enfeebled state"; or

---

[36] Sc., at a time when his parents need him (AS).

[37] Generalizing: the speaker's father does not seem to be alive.

[38] I.e., called him away, exerting his paternal authority over him.   [39] Sc., who only just managed to come—thanks to exceptional circumstances (AS).

[40] Cf. 1.6.9, 5.22.4.

tur amore meretricis, et ab officiis caecitatis[59] vitiis abstra-
hitur oculorum." Eiusmodi gemitu filium necesse est per-
3 sequaris, ut, quod detineor, obiter et poena sit. Non facit
ista lex ad liberos qui misericordia detinentur. Ut turpe
sit quod recedo, in eo tantum est ad quem revertor, et
ut facinus sit relicta mater, non faciunt nisi causae re-
linquendi. Homo qui ad tyrannum revertor, si malo animo
4 relinquo matrem, dignus sum qui detinear. Non est itaque
quod subinde nominis vestri beneficia, mater, opponas,
non est quod vilitati tuae fieri putes,[60] si credimus esse in
5 rebus humanis et alterum affectum. Amicitia est,[61] quam
mihi videtur natura excogitasse ut coire invicem possit
totum hominum genus, quae ideo nondum circa se tenet
omnes admirationes, quia tota non contigit,[62] quae iam[63]
pervenerat ad incredibilium fidem, nisi illam[64] vos impe-
diretis; amicitia, plurium[65] corporum unus animus, vica-
riae manus, fortior quam matris affectus.

7. Rogo, quid refert[66] quid vocetur ille, qui sic amat?
Quid interest ex quibus magna merita descendant? Vultis
scire quid de hoc affectu sentiat mater? Et amicum meum
2 putat malle ne revertar. Finge me sepositis[67] paulisper

59 caeci- *Sch.* (*firm. Håk.*[2] *128–29*): civi- *codd.*
60 putes *Gron.*: potest *codd.*   61 -ia est *Dess.*[2] (*cf. Reitz.*[2]
61): -iae si *codd.; ante* amicitia *plene dist. Håk.*   62 -ig- *Håk.*[2]
129: -ing- *codd.*   63 iam *Gr.-Mer.* (*firm. Reitz.*[2] 61.3): tam B
V δ: tamen γ β   64 -am M ACD β (*def. Sant.*): -a *cett.*
65 -ium E (*def. Sant.*): -imorum δ: -imum *cett.*
66 -rt ς: -rent *codd.*   67 sepo- *Wint.*[3]: po- *codd.*

41 I.e., you, Mother, and other parents like you.
42 I.e., friend or blood relative (picking up 16.6.4).

240

"My young son is being lured away by love for a prostitute: he is removed from tending on my blindness by the vicious lusts of his own eyes." That is the sort of complaint you should bring against a son, if my being kept back is to be a punishment as well. (3) This law, however, is not applicable to sons who are detained by pity. Only the person to whom I return can make my departure shameful: for only the motives for leaving a mother can make leaving her a crime. If returning to the tyrant means for me abandoning my mother maliciously, then and then only do I deserve to be prevented from going. (4) So there is no reason for you, mother, to keep confronting me with the benefits implied by the name of parent, no reason for you to think you are being personally slighted if we believe there is another emotion too that holds sway in the affairs of men. (5) I mean friendship, which seems to me to have been contrived by nature so that the whole human race might draw close together; which does not yet command everyone's admiration only because it has not been manifested at its full potential; which by now would have made people believe in miracles, if you[41] were not getting in its way— friendship, one mind in more than one body, hands that stand in for others, a feeling stronger than a mother's.

7. I ask: what difference does it make what one calls a man who loves like this?[42] What difference does it make who the source of great services is? Yet do you want to know what my *mother* feels about this affection? She thinks that even my friend would rather I did not go back to him.[43] (2) Now, imagine that, leaving aside for a mo-

---

[43] Mother disregards the claims of friendship, and so assumes that Friend would be thinking like her.

meritis, quibus obligatus sum, hoc tantum dicere: "Amicus
alligatus est." Ire volo, mater, ut redeam,[68] ut consoler, ut[69]
dominum rogem,[70] ut, si tyrannus exegerit, vicarium cor-
3 pus opponam. Quid detines, quid moraris? Hoc est tempus propter quod coîmus. Nescias an diligat, cuius non
habet experimenta nisi sola felicitas, et, si vitae praestes
4 omnia secunda, amicus otiosa res est. Dicturum me putas:
"Hoc expectat alligatus"? Expectat totum immo genus
hominum, et nos in hanc fidem persuasiones[71] receperunt,
5 ut, si hoc faciam, nemo miretur. Vis scire, mater, quem
affectum, quam reverentiam in calamitatibus amico praestare debeamus? Nullam legem timuit,[72] ne relinqueretur.
6   Differo interim causam amicitiae; agere paulisper om-
7 nium libet. Et[73] tyrannus mihi credidit; volo reverti. Nulli
umquam, mater, plus commisit fides, neminem magis ob-
ligaverunt expectationes. Credidit mihi homo, cui res fa-
vorabilis contingit si decipitur, qui sibi excogitasse con-
8 tra omnes amicos videtur ut illi imponeremus. Non est
quod mihi supplicia, quod omnem mortis[74] apparatum,
mater, opponas; facinus est id tantum hominibus bene
credi,[75] quod expedit, et actum est de rebus humanis, si

---

68 -am *coni.* (*nec voluit*) *Wint.*[7] *163*: -at *codd.*

69 -ler ut ⊆: -letur *codd.*

70 rog- ⊆: reg- *codd.*

71 -nes *Håk.*[2] *130*: -nis *codd.*

72 -la lege t. *Håk., sed vd. ad Angl. vers.*: *an* -la me lege (*Sh. B.*[4] *209*) detinuit (*Watt*[3] *57*)?

73 *del. Håk.*

74 -nem mor- ⊆: -ne mar- B: -nem ar- (mar- δ) *cett.*

75 -di *Sch.*: -dere *codd.*

ment the services by which I am bound to him, I say merely this: "My friend is in chains." I want to go, mother, to return to him, to comfort him, to beg the despot to relent, to give myself in exchange if the tyrant so demands. (3) Why are you holding me back, why delaying me? This is the sort of crisis we anticipated when we became friends. You cannot know if a man loves you if you only have experience of him while your luck lasts;[44] and if life is granted only prosperity, a friend is a superfluity. (4) Do you think I shall go on to say: "The prisoner is expecting this"? No, the whole human race is expecting it, and public opinion has put such faith in us that no one will be surprised if I do this. (5) Do you wish to know, mother, what affection, what reverence we should give to a friend in distress? *He* never feared that any law might cause him to be abandoned.[45]

(6) For the moment I do not plead the cause of friendship; I want for a short time to plead the cause of all men. (7) Even the tyrant trusted me; I want to return. Mother, no one has ever had so much asked of him by good faith, no one has been more bound by what is expected of him. I was trusted by a man who is very happy to be deceived, who apparently planned that our letting him down would strike a blow against *all* friends. (8) No need, mother, to try to deter me with the prospect of execution, with all the preparations for death. It would be criminal, were people to be trusted only about what suits them: all is up with human relations,[46] if faith is kept just for expediency's

---

[44] Cf. 16.3.2.   [45] So I *must* go back to him. *Nullam legem timuit, ne . . . = Non timuit ne ulla lege . . .* , with proleptic accusative (AS).   [46] Cf. 11.6.2.

sola servatur utilitatium fides. Infinitum est quantum mihi
crediderit tyrannus, si me occiderit reversum.

8. Intellegit, iudices, et ipsa mater quantae reverentiae
locum amicus optineat, quae incipit contendere adfectu.
Nisi fallor igitur, cum ego sim materia litis, hoc primum
aestimare debetis, uter[76] in mea calamitate plus fecerit.
2 Ante omnia permitte mihi de hoc adfectus tui genere,
mater, queri. Quid tibi tam rabido, tam praecipiti dolore
voluisti, quid adversis tuis praestare faciem et in oculos
tuos accipere nuntium? Non reliquisti tibi ut redimeres.
3 Sine dubio adiecisti ad matris adfectus: oculos in media
orbitate fudisti; sed illud non laxat catenas, non explicat
corpus. Quid mihi prodest iste, qui se citra filium consumpsit, adfectus? Plus fecisset mater, quae isset ad tyrannum.
4 Alligatus sum; tu nunc sic flebis, tamquam solvar in lectulo, tamquam in tuis manibus expirem? In quibusdam
calamitatibus desperatio non est summus affectus, et quisquis orbitatem statim credit, festinat ad impatientiae secu-
5 ritatem. Dissimules licet, mater tantae pro me impatientiae, tam incredibilis adfectus: amicus rem difficiliorem
fecit, quod servavit oculos suos ut alligaretur.

---

[76] uter ⊊: ut *codd.*

---

[47] By killing me, the tyrant would prove that he had been
planning my execution when he let me leave. If that was the case,
he was *not* testing our friendship (hoping to be deceived: 16.7.7),
but risking the loss of a person under sentence of death: an even
greater act of faith in my reliability.   [48] She has not understood it until now (16.7.1), hence Son's need to explain it to her
(16.7.1–5).   [49] What happened to *me* needs to be assessed.
    [50] Judges.   [51] I.e., blinded her.
    [52] Son speaks as though *he* were still in the tyrant's prison.

sake. The trust the tyrant put in me will prove to have been limitless, if he kills me on my return.[47]

8. Even my mother, judges, now understands how worthy of respect my friend's position is,[48] for she is beginning to compete with him in affection. So unless I am mistaken, since *I* am the specimen in the case,[49] you[50] must first of all assess which of the two has done more for me in my calamitous plight. (2) Before all else, permit me, mother, to complain about the way *you* reacted. What did you hope to gain from so crazy, so headlong a grief? Why did you choose to take your adversities full in the face, letting the news affect your eyes? You did not leave yourself the chance of ransoming me. (3) There is no question that you went beyond the emotions appropriate to a mother: you poured away your eyes while your bereavement was as yet uncertain. But that does nothing to loosen chains, nothing to free limbs. What use to me is this emotion, that fed on itself[51] without helping your son? A mother who had gone to meet the tyrant would have done more good. (4) I am in chains.[52] Will you weep just as if I were fading fast in my bed, expiring in your arms? In some calamities despair is not the greatest mark of affection: someone who believes in a bereavement straightaway is just hurrying toward freedom from strong feeling.[53] (5) You may pretend otherwise, mother, excessively grieved and incredibly moved though you are on my behalf, but my friend did something more difficult:[54] he preserved his sight—so that he might be put in chains.

[53] I.e., has found a short route toward not feeling anything.
[54] Sc., than what you did. When I was imprisoned, *you* surrendered to pain and lost your sight, thus needing to *be assisted*; *he* held on, so as to be able to *assist* me.

245

6   Dii deaeque, quantum ille praestitit, qui[77] vidit[78] poenam meam nec recessit! Ille, ille terribilem carcerem facit,
7   qui inde procedit. Iam non corpori[79] nexus haerebat, nec
aliud quam resederant pondere catenae; consumpti longo
squalore vultus, concretae noctibus diebusque super ora
lacrimae.

9. Miseremini, iudices, ne perdat auctoritatem meri-
tum, quod ultra expectationem est. Ponite sub oculis[80]
alligatos, quorum alterum amicus redemerit, alterum ma-
2   ter: rogo, uter plus fecerit? Bone Iuppiter, quam avide,
quam fortiter vincla nostra tractavit! Quibus ille precibus
3   exegit ut sibi crederetur! "Accipe" inquit "has manus, haec
membra, si fieri potest ut amicum matri remittamus. In
totum explebo, si videtur, vicaria poena locum recedentis,
vel, si vis utique tibi dimissa membra restitui, spondeo
4   quemcumque iusseris aperto iugulo diem." Fidem deorum hominumque, quid non factum est ut amicum meum
paeniteret? Ingestum est misero illud carceris tenebra-
rumque secretum, gravioribus vinculis opus esse carnifex
5   dixit ad bonum amicum. Accedere ad illud cubile iussi
sunt homines nocentes, et subinde dictum est: "Vide tamen, amice, si tanti est." Una vox, unus miseri gemitus:
"Urite, lacerate, distrahite: ille tamen revertetur."

---

[77] qui δ: qui me B V: qui mihi γ β, *unde* mihi qui *Håk.[4]*
157–58   [78] vi- *Guil. Malm.* (*cf. Wint.[6] 258*): invi- *codd.*
[79] -i *Sant.[1] 234*: -is *codd.*   [80] -lis π²M AE δ (*vind. Sant.[1]*
234–35): -los *cett.* (*def. Corb. 334*)

---

[55] I.e., to others who see him.
[56] Because of my wasted frame, they were not tight around
me; cf. 6.4.1 and 9.4.3.

(6) Gods and goddesses, what a service *he* did: he *saw* the manner of my punishment, yet did not recoil from it! It is the released prisoner, yes, he who makes imprisonment something fearful.[55] (7) The bonds no longer clung to my body, and the chains no more than lay heavy upon me;[56] my face was disfigured by long-accumulated dirt, my cheeks were encrusted with tears poured over them night and day.

9. For pity's sake, judges, do not let a good deed lose its authority just because it exceeds all expectation. Imagine two chained prisoners, one ransomed by his friend, the other by his mother. I ask you, which of the two ransomers did more?[57] (2) By Jupiter, how greedily, how bravely he handled my bonds! What prayers he used in asking to be trusted! (3) "Take," he said,[58] "these hands, these limbs, if it is possible for us to send my friend back to his mother. If you wish, I will fill his place in every respect while he is away, by taking over his penalty; or, if you insist on getting back the body you are letting out of your hands, I offer my throat as a guarantee for any day you specify." (4) By gods and men, what was left undone to make my friend think better of his decision? On the poor fellow was inflicted the notorious confinement of a murky dungeon—the warder saying that a good friend needed heavier chains. (5) Felons were told off to come to his bunk, with the constant admonition: "But make sure it's worth it, mate!" Yet the wretched man had only one thing to say, one groan to utter: "Burn me, rend me, tear me limb from limb! All the same, he will come back."

---

[57] Answer: the former, as he is not expected to do for a friend as much as a parent should do for a son.   [58] To the tyrant.

6   Miserere, mater, magna res agitur: amicum meum reliqui contendentem cum tyranno. Excuso me vobis, humani
generis adfectus, et tibi ante omnia, mater, excuso, quod
7   hoc fieri passus sum. Ulla ergo in rebus humanis necessitas
tanti fuit, ut illum amicum meum in carcerem ipse dedu-
cerem, ut squalorem meum, meas catenas in membra fes-
tinantis exuerem, ut tam abrupti commeatus diem contra
8   tot incerta promitterem? Testor te, misera conscientia, et
si quod nos in illa necessitate numen aspexit, quantum
simus rixati circa catenas, quam omnia fecerim, ut ille
potius veniret ad matrem. 10. Fateor, iudices: unius cogitationis pudore victus[81] sum, quod tam magni beneficii
difficultatem ab amico non accipere adfectus videbatur
hominis qui non credidisset.

2   Miserere, mater, ne me solutum putes: amicum alligavi. Hae sunt catenae quae tenent[82] membra, quae per
maria, per infinita terrarum spatia restringunt; hic[83] non
potest carcer effringi. Invideo tyranno: scit alligare [ami-
3   cos],[84] scit tenere dimissum. Iterum ac subinde procla-
mem necesse est: ego amicum meum alligavi et, ut te viderem, poenam meam altero homine implevi. Scio quo hoc
amicus praestiterit animo, sed ego rem feci hominis non
4   reversuri. Interrogo hoc loco impatientiam tuam, mater,

---

[81] evi- *Bur.* (*corrob. Beck.*[2] 55)   [82] -nent *Bur.*[1] *coll. 5.16.5*:
-gunt *codd.*   [83] hic *Sch.*: sic *codd.*
[84] del. *Wint.*[7] 163 (*et om.* V)

---

[59] Sc., whether I would be so loyal as to come back or not.
[60] I.e., the feeling that he owes so much to his friend.
[61] = I am still (metaphorically) in prison, and I cannot get out
of it by forgetting my friend.

(6) Take pity, mother, a great deed is afoot: I have left my friend disputing with the tyrant.[59] I ask you to excuse me, men of feeling, and you above all, mother, for allowing this to happen. (7) Was then any constraint in the world so compelling that I had in person to escort my friend to prison; that I had to transfer my filth, my chains to his limbs—while he hurried to take them over; that in the face of so many uncertainties I had to guarantee a day for the end of so short a leave of absence? (8) I appeal to you, my wretched conscience, and to any deity which looked upon us in that crisis: how we bickered over the chains, how I did all I could, to make sure *he* went to my mother rather than me! 10. I confess it, judges: I was overcome by a single shaming consideration, that not to allow a friend to do me so signal and difficult a service looked like the reaction of a man who did not believe him.

(2) Take pity, mother, do not think I am free: I have put my friend in prison. *These*[60] are chains that tie down a man's limbs, that exercise their constraint beyond seas, beyond vast stretches of land; *this* is a prison that cannot be broken open.[61] I envy the tyrant: even after letting someone go, he knows how to keep him in chains, he knows how to maintain a hold on him. (3) Time and again I must cry: It is I who put my friend in chains, for in order to see you I took my punishment—in the person of another man. I know what my friend's motives were in granting this, but *I* acted like a man who intended not to return.[62] (4) At this point I ask you, mother, yes I ask you,

[62] If I hadn't been really tempted to escape for good, I wouldn't have accepted the offer.

[QUINTILIAN]

interrogo: quid faceres, si nos ad te videndam deduxisset[85] alligatos aliqui satelles,[86] si barbarus aliqui? Fruereris

5 osculis,[87] fruereris amplexibus.[88] Non est quod te ista tamquam levior, tamquam expeditior condicio decipiat. Quid putas esse, quod me dimisit solutum ire quo vellem? Crudelis artifex non reliquit nobis ut imponeremus.

11. Supervacuo igitur hoc vos in matris causa movet, quod caeca est. Hoc, quod nobis invidiam facit vulneribus oculorum, nolite detinendi putare causas: idem videns faceret, nec plus est quod non potest caecitas ferre quam mater. Ut aliqua filio carere non possit, non umquam[89]

2 calamitas facit. Quodsi, iudices, in persona mea nec adfectu nec meritis inferior est amicus, quid aliud iustitia

3 vestra debet attendere quam uter plus patiatur? Iam satiavit dolorem mater, egessit aestus, effudit impetum; iam non desiderant oculi, cum cadunt. Adice quod hanc qualemcumque fortunam inter amicos tenet, inter propinquos; habet omnia ministeria sua debilitas, suas compara-

85 deduxisset V^{uc} γ β (*def. Sant.*[1] *235*): duxisset B: deduxissent V^{pc} δ

86 -les π ψ β (*def. Sant.*[1] *235*): -lites *cett.*

87 osc- β* (*def. vDorp 42b, Sant.*): oc- V AC δ: *om.* (*cum inseq.* fruereris) B DE

88 *sic dist. Håk.*: *interrog. vulg.*

89 non umq- *Leh.*: numq- E: non numq- *cett.*

---

63 You would have to be satisfied with kissing and hugging me, for I could do nothing to help you. Equally now, under a different kind of constraint.

64 I.e., I am "bound" by my conscience as tightly as if I were chained in the hands of a henchman.

overwhelmed by grief as you are: What would you do if some henchman, some brutish foreigner had brought me in chains to see you? You would have to make the most of kissing me, you would have to make the most of embracing me.[63] (5) You should not be deceived into thinking my present condition easier to bear or less constraining.[64] What do you think it amounts to that he let me free to go where I wished? That virtuoso in cruelty left us no chance of cheating him.[65]

11. In view of all this, it is beside the point for you to be moved by this element in my mother's case, that she is blind. She may be making me an object of hatred by displaying her wounded eyes, but you should not think they are the reason for her trying to keep me at home: she would do the same if she were still sighted, for what is intolerable to a blind person is no more than what is intolerable to a mother. It is never calamity that makes a woman incapable of doing without her son.[66] (2) But if, judges, in my case my friend is inferior[67] neither in affection nor in the services he has rendered, what else have you to consider in your concern for justice than this: which of the two is suffering the more? (3) My mother has by now sated her grief: she has voided her seething feelings, poured out the onrush of her emotion. Eyes no longer feel a loss when they fail. And there is more: however harsh her lot, she can face it among friends and relatives. In her physical handicap she has available all the attention she

---

[65] Again, because Son's conscience would not allow him to stay at home.

[66] Sc., but maternal affection.

[67] To my mother.

4 tiones.[90] Vis scire quanto intolerabilius sit quod patitur
amicus? Excaecavit te quod ego sic tenebar.[91] Accipere
cibos quos carnifex, quos tortor apponit[92] ⟨∗∗∗⟩

[90] cooper- ς, *sed vd. Sant.*
[91] *hic deficit* V, *duobus fere verbis post* tenebar *erasis*
[92] -onit Φ: -endebat B: -onebat *Håk.* (*sed vd.* Wint.[7] *163–64,
qui* -onat *coni.*)

needs, all the necessary provision. (4) Do you[68] want to know how much less tolerable is my friend's suffering?— That *I* was imprisoned like that was what blinded you. To have to accept food that an executioner, that a torturer serves up ⟨∗∗∗⟩

[68] Mother.

DECLAMATION 17

INTRODUCTION

A father tries three times to disown his son, but the judges reject his application in each case.[1] After the third hearing, Father finds Son in a secluded part of the house, preparing a drug; when he asks what it is, Son declares that he is making poison to take his own life. Father orders him to prove it by drinking the brew, but Son pours it away. Father accuses him of (intended) parricide; the declamation is the defense speech by Son.

The case combines three familiar motifs from the fictional world of declamation: disownment, poisoning, and parricide.[2] Our speech, however, does not linger on any of them. Son's main purpose is to persuade the judges that he was actually going to take his own life by poison; to this end, he will have to: (1) establish his own (good) character;

[1] The threefold repetition of such a hearing is not likely to have been admitted by actual court procedure; but the triplication of an event is a well-established narrative pattern in both literature and folklore: cf. Pasetti (2011, 89–90n1).

[2] On disownment, see Introduction to *DM* 9, Pasetti (2011, 90–91n2), and Krapinger[-Stramaglia] (2015, 35–39); on poisoning, see Introduction to *DM* 14, and below, n. 6; on parricide, see Krapinger[-Stramaglia] (2015, 43–48), and especially Lentano (2015a).

(2) describe his relationship with Father, especially after the three previous disownment trials; and (3) clarify why he did not drink the poison when he was ordered to do so by Father.

Son is naturally portrayed as an innocent youth who did not deserve to be disowned (as three trials have already proved: 8.2), let alone suspected of parricide. Proof of this is the very incident that triggered the current trial: Son had withdrawn to a secluded part of the house to die without creating disturbance, as an innocent person would do (4.2); unlike someone preparing poison for others, he did not take any precautions to avoid being caught (4.3, 15.6); even when Father asked him what he was preparing, nothing but his truthfulness could force him to admit that it was poison (5.3, 15.5).

The motive for Son's plan to kill himself is argued to be Father's hatred of him. The speaker portrays Father's animosity as increased by each of the unsuccessful disownment hearings (3.1–3, 8.4–9.4); conversely, Son's existence is increasingly unbearable, owing to the hostility of his whole household (10.4, 14.2–7), hence the decision to put an end to his sufferings (14.8).

Why, then, did Son first resist Father's attempts to disown him, and then disobey his order to drink the poison? In both cases, Son was prompted by the need to assert his innocence: had he moved out of the house, it would have looked as though he was admitting the grievances Father had brought to the court (3.4); had he drunk the poison as he was ordered (and as he was planning to do, before the interruption), he would have looked like a poisoner caught in the act (12.3–4). That is why Son went on living, yet

wishing to die. But the option of suicide is not ruled out
for the future (20.3–5): this will fulfill Father's wishes, and
so prove that *he* is the real parricide (6.6–7).

The declamation can be analyzed as follows:[3]

> PROEM 1.1–2.7
> NARRATION 3.1–5.5
> ARGUMENTATION
>> *Propositio causae* (expanded with an *excessus*
>> on Father's schemes) 6.1–4
>> *Confirmatio* (opened by a further *propositio*
>> *causae*)/*Refutatio* 6.5–19.8
> EPILOGUE 19.9–20.5

The motif of spilled poison must have been popular in
antiquity: in Latin, the same theme is included in the El-
der Seneca's collection, and a similar case appears in one
of the *Minor Declamations*,[4] while a Greek version is mentioned in a short anonymous treatise;[5] an allusion to it may
be detected also in Juvenal's *Satires*.[6]

This speech is close in language to *DM* 2, another piece
featuring a Son accused by his father of planning parricide
by poison; but it is unlikely that the two speeches were
written by the same author.[7] Also, the author of our speech

---

[3] Cf. Pasetti (2011, 37–40).

[4] Sen. *Controv.* 7.3; [Quint.] *Decl. min.* 377. Cf. Winterbottom (1984, 578).

[5] *Problemata anonyma in status*: *RG* VIII.411.13–15 Walz.

[6] Juv. 7.166–70, cf. Stramaglia (2017[2], 200); in general, on
declamations featuring poisoning, see Pasetti (2015).

[7] Cf. [Krapinger-]Stramaglia (2015, 62–63 and n. 188).

might have known *DM* 4, in which another son claims to be ready to commit suicide.[8] *DM* 17 is probably to be dated to the early or the mid-third century AD.[9] A reply to Son's speech was composed by Patarol.[10]

[8] Compare 17.9.3 with 4.15.6 and 4.16.5; see General Introduction, §4, with n. 117.

[9] See General Introduction, §4.

[10] (1743, 384–402).

17

Venenum effusum

Filium ter abdicare voluit pater, ⟨ter⟩[1] victus. Invenit quodam tempore in secreta domus parte medicamentum te-
rentem.[2] Interrogavit quid esset, cui parasset. Ille dixit
venenum et se mori ⟨velle⟩.[3] Iussit pater bibere. Ille effudit medicamentum. Accusatur a patre parricidii.

1. ⟨Iactatus,[4] iudices,[5]⟩ lassatusque[6] per diversos miserae
mentis aestus et[7] eundem dolorem, dum me ab utroque
animi genere semper, quod impulerit, abduxit,[8] et inter[9]
pertinaciam desperationemque neutram[10] mihi licet[11]
perferre patientia,[12] hoc primum a notissima clementia

---

[1] add. Håk. (cf. Sen. Controv. 7.3.th.)   [2] ten- B V β, sed
cf. 17.5.3, 17.17.5   [3] add. C²E (def. Håk.² 130)   [4] lac.
stat. et uno hoc verbo explev. Reitz.² 53: ⟨vexatus⟩ Håk.² 131
      [5] supplevi e M (infra)   [6] -tusque V: om. B: -tus γ δ: me
-tus (Elass- S) β: licet iudices inveniam M (sc. e coniect., cf. Wint.⁸
306)   [7] sed Best 161–62   [8] -cit Reitz.² 53: -cat codd.
      [9] inter Reitz.² 53: in codd.   [10] -rum Gr.-Mer.

17

The spilled poison

A father three times sought to disown his son, but ‹three times› lost his case. One day he found him in a secluded part of the house pounding up ingredients for a drug. He asked what it was and for whom he had prepared it. The son said that it was poison and that he ‹wished› to die. His father ordered him to drink the drug. He poured it away. He is accused by his father of parricide.

(Speech of the son)

1. ‹I am tossed about, judges,› and exhausted by surges of emotion: they are different in kind, yet the pain they cause me in my wretched heart is the same. What brought each frame of mind upon me always removes me from it, and I cannot, poised as I am between obduracy and desperation,[1] go on enduring either. So I ask this first of your well

---

[1] The determination to live (to clear his name), and the hopelessness that makes him wish to die.

---

11 -eat B C²
12 -am V γ, *sed vd. Håk.*² 131

[QUINTILIAN]

vestra peto, ne miremini quod inter tam varia tristissima-
que fata[13] consilio diductus sum; nec pro malis meis quicquam melius invenire potui, quam ut morerer, nec pro
2 innocentia, quam ut viverem. Novo igitur, iudices, inaudi-
toque genere discriminis utriusque animi reus, qua satis
calamitates meas comploratione,[14] quo deflebo gemitu?
Filium mori volentem paene occidit quod intervenerat
3 pater. Vidistis[15] adhuc illa secreti nostri contentione rixan-
tem: quidquid[16] citra suprema, citra exitum est, contumaciam vocat, ⟨quasi⟩ quartam[17] absolutionem aspicit vitam.
4 Quis[18] post hoc quaerat ac dubitet, quo me affectu iusserit
virus haurire? Qui parricidium vocat quod non biberim,
permissurus fuit si bibere voluissem.

5   Quaeso itaque, iudices, delationis hodiernae penitus
velitis perspicere causas. Obicere putatis parricidium pa-
6 trem? Pro se negat![19] Uritur sine dubio, torquetur; vitam
ex hoc tamen non potest ferre, quod mori filium iussit nec
coegit, et scit facinus fuisse in imperio, si innocentia[20] est
7 quod recusavi. Suae quod crudelitatis est, vel ab invidia se

---

13 fata C[2]: facta *cett.*   14 -plora- ⟨ (*def. Håk.*[2] *131–32*):
-para- *codd.*   15 -dist- B[2] V (*cf. Håk.*[2] *132.60*): -dit- B: -det- Φ
    16 quidquid γ β: quid *cett.*: quod *Reitz.*[2] 53
    17 ⟨quasi⟩ *Wint.*[7] *164*, quartam *Bur.*: quantum *codd.*: tam-
quam *Håk.*[2] *132*: quasi *Pas.*   18 quis C[2]E: qui *cett.*
    19 -gat M (*vind. Håk.*[2] *133*): -cat B V δ: -catur γ β
    20 -ae *Håk., haud male* (*cf. mox* suae . . . crudelitatis)

---

2 Earlier in this trial, in his prosecution speech—which is
taken to precede Son's defense plea, in accordance with customary procedure (AS).
3 Sc., when Father found me mixing the poison.

known clemency: do not be surprised that I am torn in my mind between such diverse and desolating destinies. I have been able to discover nothing to mend my ills better than to die, nothing to defend my innocence better than to live. (2) I am thus faced with a new and unheard of type of legal peril: I am thought guilty whatever I choose. With what complaints, what groans shall I sufficiently bewail my disastrous plight? A son wanted to die: it almost killed him that his father came upon the scene. (3) You have seen him[2] still as disputatious as he was when we were arguing in private:[3] anything short of the final step, anything short of death, he dubs contumacy; he regards my survival ⟨as⟩ a fourth acquittal.[4] (4) After this, who could inquire, who could doubt in what spirit he ordered me to drink the poison? The man who calls it parricide that I did not drink it is the same who would have raised no objection if I had been willing to drink.

(5) I request you, then, judges, to look closely at the reasons for today's accusation. Do you think that my father is accusing me of parricide? Not at all: he is *denying* it[5] on his own account! (6) No doubt he is burning, he is on the rack; but what really makes him unable to tolerate my survival is that he told his son to commit suicide without being able to force him to do it; and he knows that it was a crime to have given such an order,[6] if it shows my innocence that I disobeyed it. (7) It is typical of his cruelty

---

[4] I.e., another (fourth) decision by the judges in favor of the son and against the father.

[5] I.e., denying that in fact he had tried to kill his son.

[6] Father fears he will be charged with attempted murder for ordering Son to drink poison (cf. 17.17.7, 17.18.1, 17.19.7).

criminibus meis defendit, excusat, et, ne vocem illam tamquam peractum facinus oderitis, substituit pro malo patre
miserum. 2. Hic est, iudices, deprehensae impietatis aestus: nemo umquam volet innocentem filium videri, quem
voluerit occidere.

2   Illud quoque, iudices, a gravitate publica peto, ne quis
me mori voluisse non credat.[21] Contumaciter adhuc, prioris constantiae meae more, defendor; alia est mihi ratio,
3   cum vici. Fortior sum reus quam absolutus, et[22] tunc tantum par esse non possum calamitatibus meis, cum me
4   constare coepit nihil aliud esse quam miserum. Bene quod
rursus vocavit in forum, iussit integritatis agere causam!
Fecit ut mihi videar perdidisse mortem: si paenitet patrem
quod me bibere iussit venenum, ego ferre non possum
quod effudi.

5   Licet igitur immitissimus senex confundere publicos
conetur adfectus querelarum fronte mutata, non sumus
novi vobis accusator et reus, nec nos modo pietatis eversae
recens adseruit immanitas; parricidam me olim vocat.
6   Ita est enim, iudices, ita est: iam pridem omnium[23] nefan-

---

[21] *dist. Sch.*   [22] et *Håk.*[2] 133–34: sed *codd.*
[23] omnium *Reitz.*[2] 59: hominum *codd.*

---

[7] = when he betrays his true feelings.   [8] In each successive court case concerning his disownment, and then in the present case for parricide.   [9] He is braver in court than after his
victory in each successive case: despite his show of courage in
public, he has never ceased to wish to die.   [10] *After* he has
been acquitted, it comes over him anew how wretched he is.

[11] See n. 6.   [12] If my father was in fact liable to a charge
for murder for ordering me to drink poison, then I can only regret
that I did *not* drink it (AS).

that he is trying to defend and excuse himself even from odium by accusing me: in case you hate him for saying what he said as though that was in itself an accomplished crime, he makes himself out to be not an evil father but an unhappy one. 2. This is, judges, the tumultuous emotion felt by an impious man when he is caught out:[7] no one will ever wish his son to be thought innocent if he has resolved to kill him.

(2) This too I ask, judges, of the weight that you bring to your public role: let no one doubt that I wished to die. Hitherto[8] I have been defending myself obstinately, with my old strength of mind; it is a different matter when I have won.[9] (3) I am braver when I am on trial than when I have been acquitted: I only fail to face up to my calamities when it becomes clear that I am wretched, and nothing else but wretched.[10] (4) It is good that he has called me back to court and bidden me speak in defense of my integrity!—For he has caused me to feel that I have missed a good chance to die: if my father regrets[11] that he ordered me to drink poison, *I* cannot bear the thought that I poured it away.[12]

(5) Although, then, this heartless old man is trying to confuse the feelings of the public by changing the outward appearance of his complaints against me,[13] we are by no means unfamiliar to you in the role of accuser and defendant. It is not just recently that a brutal overthrow of family feelings has asserted a claim on me: he has been calling me a parricide for a long time now. (6) Yes, that is the case, judges, that is the case: I have long been accused of every

---

[13] By portraying himself as a victim (cf. 17.1.7).

dorum solis nominibus accusor;[24] sic mihi illa prima patris

7 maledixit asperitas. Hic est ille, quem desinere iam ius-
seratis, qui semper ad vos recurrit et vincitur. Fallitur,
quisquis illam[25] de moribus senis lassitudinem vel patientiam sperat: patri, qui abdicare non potuit, minus obest[26]
filius nocens quam absolutus.

3. O pertinacissimum accusatorum genus, victi parentes! Dum auctoritatem nominis vestri fortius imperiosis
adseritis adfectibus, et, ne pudorem paenitentiamque
fateamini, contumacia vindicatis errorem, calamitatibus

2 meis accessit ut ter absolverer. Namque ut erat in supervacuo odio mei senex prima lite[27] deprensus, ferre non
potuit quod reddebar invito, et, quia a iudicibus non impe-
traverat ut abdicaret, apud se tenuit, ne desineret hoc

3 velle. Credidit tamen[28] aliquid profecturum querelarum
errore repetito, et speravit iuxta contentionem suam ut

4 lassesceret aliquando pro me iusta miseratio. Quid facerem igitur, quo verterem iam fatigatam innocentiam?
Nec exire me decebat ex domo, ne viderer quicquid vos

---

[24] -sor *Sch. (firm. Håk.[2] 134)*: -satur *codd.*
[25] ul- *Håk., sed cf. Wint. ap. Pas.*
[26] obest *Sh. B.[2] 214*: est *codd.*
[27] lite *Obr. (firm. Håk.[2] 135, Fairw.[2] 183)*: luce *codd.*
[28] tandem *Fairw.[1] 260, sed vd. Pas.*

---

[14] Father accuses Son only with the wording (*nomina*) of his allegations—no proofs.

[15] I.e., most old men might lack persistence, but not this one.

[16] Father is determined to have Son convicted not so much because he considers him guilty as because he could not tolerate being defeated again.

possible wickedness, though in words that lack all substance.[14] Such is the abuse my pitiless father has leveled at me from the very start. (7) Here is the man whom you had already ordered to desist, who always keeps coming back to you—only to be defeated. It is quite mistaken to expect to find here an old man's typical attitude of sloth and resignation.[15] For a father who has failed to have his son disowned, a guilty son is less troublesome than one who has been acquitted.[16]

3. You parents who have lost a case are the most obstinate of accusers! You forcibly press the claims of your relationship[17] with emotionally charged commands, and to avoid confessing your shame and remorse you seek to justify error with contumacy. As a result, my misfortunes have only been added to by my three acquittals. (2) For when as early as the first trial the old man had been shown to hate me beyond reason, he could not tolerate my being restored to him against his wishes. Because he had not obtained my disownment from the judges, he kept me by him to make sure he did not stop wanting to get rid of me.[18] (3) But he believed that he would make some progress if he repeated his mistaken complaints, hoping that, in the face of his vehemence, the sympathy I had rightly excited would one day grow feebler. (4) What then was I to do? Where was I to turn now that I had grown tired of protesting my innocence? It was hardly appropriate to move out of the house: it would look as if I was admitting

[17] Literally, "of your name (sc., parents)."
[18] Cf. 17.3.5.

non credideratis agnoscere, nec expectare poteram, cum
mihi rursus aliam seriem malorum minaretur, quod me
iam coeperat pater contentione, qua vobis irascebatur,
5 odisse. Tandem infelix miseritus mei, miseritus patris,
cum de praeteritis prospicerem iurgia tam longa quam
vitam, captavi—fateor—omni eum[29] occursu,[30] quem mihi videbar exasperare praesentia, exonerare,[31] dum morior, et tamquam novissimi[32] ambitus genus excogitavi ut
me in honorem sui reverentiamque pereuntem sic odisse
6 desineret, quomodo parcere solet ira cedenti. Non habet
alium quam mortis exitum filius, qui nec reconciliari potest nec abdicari.

4. Erat in domo nostra locus, in quem secedebam semper reus, in quem revertebar absolutus, querelis meis la-
2 crimisque iam conscius [in quem se ferant].[33] In hunc, non
tamquam custodiae patris imponerem[34] (nam quid posset[35] inveniri, quo non me captantis aliquid deprehendere
cura sequeretur?), sed sicut solent qui mori[36] volunt pudore, non ira, ab omnibus, quae videbantur avocatura, se-
cessi. Nam nec placuerat exitus genus querulum, tumul-
3 tuosum aut quod faceret invidiam. Sed quid mihi tecum
est, integritatis nimia simplicitas? Non putat se posse

---

[29] omni eum *Wint.*[7] *164*: hominem B: -nis V: omnem Φ

[30] -su *Wint.*[7] *164*: -sum *codd.*   [31] exoner- *Obr.* (*corrob.*
Wint.[7] *164*): exor- *codd.*   [32] -mum *Reitz.*[2] *79, sed vd. Helm*[1]
388   [33] *secl. Reitz.*[2] *83*   [34] -rem E δ: -re *cett.*

[35] -set *Reitz.*[2] *83*: -sit *codd.*

[36] mori M: immori B V Φ*: iam mori *Sch.*

---

[19] Judges.

everything you[19] had refused to believe. Nor could I stay put when my father was threatening me with yet another round of troubles: he had already begun to hate me, as virulently as he was enraged with you. (5) In the end, out of pity for myself, out of pity for my father, foreseeing by what had taken place that our wrangling would last as long as my life, I aimed (I admit it) to relieve of all chance of meeting me one whom my presence seemed only to rile— by dying. I thought up a quite new (so to speak) method of influencing him: if I died out of honor and respect for him, he would stop hating me—anger generally spares those who give way. (6) A son has no way out except death, when he can be neither reconciled nor disowned.

4. In our house there was a spot to which I used to retreat every time I was tried, and to which I used to return after each acquittal: a spot already privy to my complaints and tears. (2) To it I now withdrew, not to elude the strict watch of my father (where indeed could I find a place to which he did not follow me, in his anxiety to catch me out in some misdemeanor?), but as men do when they wish to die out of a sense of honor, not out of anger, away from any possible source of distraction. Indeed I had also decided against a demise that would provoke sighs, disturbance or disapproval. (3) Now what am I to do about you, you excessive naïveté of my innocent conscience?[20] Any-

---

[20] I hadn't publicized my plans for suicide (17.4.2), true, but I didn't believe I might be misunderstood—i.e., be thought to be preparing murder instead—being a straightforward man (cf. below). Here, as often in declamation, a speaker "dissociates himself" from a psychological or physical feature of his own: see Stramaglia (2018b, 65n293); and in general Pasetti (2016).

4 deprehendi, quisquis venenum parat ipse poturus. Totus
oculis animoque conversus haerebam miser in opere moriendi, nec dissimulo, cum quadam cunctatione, cum
mora, sicuti bonae conscientiae lenta mors <est>,[37] nec
praecipiti per suprema trepidatione festinant quos hoc
5 solum, quod sui miserentur,[38] occidit. Abiit per tacitas
conquestiones mens in obitus contemplatione posita, et
hausurus potionem, qua renuntiarem rebus humanis, totam apud se reputabat[39] animus innocentiam suam, cum
pater secretum, quod per impatientiam pereuntis imple-
veram, quantum credo, lacrimis meis gemituque perduc-
6 tus, intravit. Non potest videri, iudices, suspicatus aliquid
de parricidio: quid tererem, cui pararem, nesciebat qui
interrogavit.

5. Nuntio vobis, sanctissimi viri, nihil a morientibus
2 fingi: nihil vita laborante simplicius. Ad subitum interven-
tum patris non tamquam deprehensus obstipui, facinus
me tacente non pallor, non est confessa trepidatio, nec,
sicut accidere nocentibus solet, illa obvia semper erran-
tium patrociniorum verba variavi, cum me repente in-
3 terrogatione subita avocavit, abduxit.[40] Quaesivit quid tererem, cui pararem; sed ego sine cunctatione, sine tarditate
respondi [et][41] me mori velle, eadem<que> veritate [et][42]

---

[37] add. 𝔖 (nisi mora: sic est bo- supra legamus)
[38] -ntur πM (vind. Håk.): -nt cett. (peiore clausula)
[39] -puta- B E (vind. Håk.[2] 135): -pete- (-peta- A) cett.
[40] gravius dist. Wint.[9]   [41] del. Gron.
[42] -<que> addidi, [et] Gron. (migratam videl. coniunctionis
notam prave legit scriba; cf. ad 13.15.6)

---

[21] Cf. 4.7.2.   [22] Cf. 17.16.5.

one who prepares a poison he means to drink himself does not imagine he can be caught out. (4) My eyes, my mind completely concentrated, I was absorbed (ah me!) in the business of dying, and—I am not trying to conceal it—not without some hesitation, some delay: slow ⟨is⟩ the death of a man with a good conscience, so those who are prompted to die just by pity for themselves do *not* hurry with precipitate confusion through their last moments.[21] (5) As they dwelt on death, my thoughts went off into a series of unspoken complaints, and, before I drained the draft with which I was to bid farewell to human affairs, my mind was going over all its innocence, when my father entered the hiding place which I had filled with the uncontrolled moans of a dying man—indeed, I believe he was brought there by my tears and groans. (6) Judges, he cannot seem to have had any suspicion of parricide. He did not know what I was pounding, for whom I was getting it ready: those were the questions he *asked*.

5. Highly respected sirs, I tell you with all solemnity that the dying make nothing up: nothing is more truthful than a life at its last gasp. (2) When my father suddenly burst in, I did not go into shock, like someone caught in the act; I said nothing: no pallor, no confusion made confession of wrongdoing. When he abruptly diverted my attention, distracting[22] me with sudden questioning, I did not, as the guilty usually do, offer the contradictory explanations that always come to the lips of those who try to defend themselves when they are in the wrong. (3) He asked what I was pounding, whom I meant it for; for my part, I replied with no delay or hesitancy that *I* wished to die, ⟨and⟩ with equal truthfulness admitted that it was

4   confessus sum venenum esse quod terebatur. Date,
iudices, patrem, qui filium mori nolit:[43] et credit. Quis
habeat, iudices, dicenti[44] fidem? Venenum filii, quod in-
venerat pater, non[45] ille potius effudit; stetit quin immo
intrepidus, adrogans iuxta orbitatem quam videbat, et
mihi mortem quam promiseram, quam minabar, ingessit.

5   "Bibe" inquit. Quis post hoc, iudices, expectat ut continuo
pareo iubenti? Ita demum mihi non est aliud relictum,
si patri paravi.[46]

    6. Audite nunc, dii pariter atque homines, quid post
tres abdicationes et querelas totiens iudicum gravitate
percussas[47] velut attonitus, amens nuntiet saeculo pater:
parricida saevus, parricida crudelis non bibi[48] venenum![49]
Hoc est totum facinus meum: vivo, respondeo, non fugio

2   iudicem, non cedo criminibus. Iam non miror quid sit,
circa quod impatientia deceptae crudelitatis exaestuet;
‹est›[50] plus quam orbitatis gaudium, quod[51] modo perdidit senex: speraverat ut occidere me posset meo veneno.

3   Sed quatenus invenisse se putat quod crederetis, ut[52] con-
tentionibus subinde damnatis auctoritatem de novo do-

4   lore circumdaret, inusitata commentus est. Quae sola mihi
superest ratio vivendi, facinus ea simplicitate, ea fide de-
nego, qua confessus sum de veneno.

  [43] *dist. Sch.* (*et vd. Sh. B.*[4] 209)   [44] -nti C^2: -ndi *cett.*
  [45] pater non Φ: paternum B V: pater num (*omisso mox* ille) π
  [46] -ravi ſ (*def. Håk.*): -rui *codd.*
  [47] -sus *Reitz.*[2] 54
  [48] -it *Gron., sed vd. Plas.* 55.1
  [49] pater—venenum *dist. Eng.* 44.2 *post alios*
  [50] -et ‹est› *addidi*: p. q. o. gaudium ‹est› *Wint.*[7] *164* (‹erat›
Håk.): *tradita frustra def. Helm*[1] *379*   [51] *del. Gron.*
  [52] ut Φ (*def. Pas.*): et B V: et, ‹ut› *Reitz.*[2] 55

poison I was working on. (4) Imagine a father, judges, who does not want his son to die: he believes him too. Who would credit such[23] a story?—a father found poison in his son's possession, but *he* didn't pour it away rather than his son. No, he stood there unshaken and arrogant, the loss of his son before him in full view, and thrust upon me the death which I had promised, which I was threatening. (5) "Drink," he said. After such an order, judges, who expects me to obey straight away? I only had no other choice,[24] if it was for my father I had mixed the potion.

6. Hear now, gods and men alike, what, after three attempts to disown me and three peremptory rejections by wise judges, my father is announcing to the whole world, like someone stunned and out of his mind with astonishment: I, the savage parricide, the cruel parricide, did not drink the poison! This is the sum of my crime: I am alive, I answer back, I am not afraid to face the judge, I do not give in to the charges. (2) I am not surprised at this point that he is seething, in his distress at the foiling of his cruelty. What the old man has now lost <is> *more* than the pleasure of bereavement: he had hoped that he could kill me with my own poison. (3) But he thinks he has found something you *would* believe:[25] since his efforts have repeatedly been repelled, he has thought up a novel device to buttress his authority by raising a new grievance. (4) This is my only reason to go on living:[26] I deny the charge with the frankness and the sincerity with which I confessed to the poison.

---

[23] Looking forward.   [24] Sc., but to drink it.

[25] I.e., the charge of parricide.

[26] He still wishes to die, but the need to defend himself against this new charge is a reason for not dying yet.

中文

5   Parricidii agis. Abstulisti quidem mihi partem,[53] ut
6 exclamarem hoc loco: "Fieri non potest." Scio quantum
defensioni meae difficultatis adiecerit, quod iam pridem
in domo nostra humanorum pignorum ratio non constat;
sed pronuntiatum liquet utri ex nobis facilior sit impietas,
7 uter iuxta alterius languorem suprema confecerit.[54] Tu
unicum cotidie proturbare conaris e domo, velles inopiam
meam, velles aspicere squalorem; ego osculor illas expel-
lentis manus, ego abicientis genua teneo, et ad patrem, qui
me tam notabiliter odit, non habeo cur velim redire, si non
amorem.[55]

    7. Praevaleret nominis tui fortassis auctoritas, si con-
tentio nostra coepisset a veneno. Consumpsisti quicquid
est, quod parentes ab omnium scelerum suspicione defendit. Non habet pater unde parricidium de filio credat,
2 nisi quem posset occidere. Me quidem, pater, de[56] infelicis
huius persuasionis simplicitate[57] si quis interroget, nec a
te parricidium fieri posse credo—nisi meo veneno.[58] Facinus tamen in omnibus incredibile pignoribus nullis dif-
3 ficilius quam liberis puto. Vos adhuc in suprema nostra

[53] ‹hanc› p. *Wint.*[7] *164–65 (q.v.), sed cf. Pas.*
[54] conf- *Obr.* (*cf. 17.5.4, 17.12.7*): non f- *codd.*
[55] -orem *Wint. ap. Pas.*: -or *codd.*: -o *Gron.*
[56] de *Pas.*: et B V: *om.* Φ   [57] -te *Sch.*: -tem *codd.*
[58] credo—veneno *sic fere dist. Gr.-Mer.*: credo n. m. -no, *Håk.*

[27] In such a dysfunctional household, parricide is *not* out of
the question—though only on Father's part.
[28] The pathetic state in which Father had found Son in his
private place.
[29] I.e., the name—and the role—of father.

274

(5) You accuse me of parricide. You have certainly deprived me of my chance to exclaim right now: "It is impossible." (6) I know how much harder it has made my defense that in our house human relations have long since failed to add up;[27] but it has been made perfectly clear which of us finds lack of natural affection easier, which of us in the face of the other's sickness[28] tried to finish him off. (7) *You* every day contemplate ejecting your only son from his home; you would like to see me poor, you would like to see me shabby. *I* kiss those hands of yours, even as you drive me out, I cling to your knees, even as you cast me off; and I have no other motive for wishing to return to a father who so blatantly hates me—except love.

7. Perhaps the authority of your name[29] would be thought decisive if our dispute had begun with the matter of the poison. As it is, you have used up everything that defends parents from suspicion of any crime.[30] A father has no reason to believe his son capable of parricide unless he is the kind of son *he* could himself kill.[31] (2) If anyone, father, asked me to state frankly a painful conviction of mine: I don't believe even you could commit parricide[32]— except with my own poison.[33] But a crime that is impossible to credit of any family member is especially difficult[34] for *sons* to commit. (3) In the case of you fathers, your

[30] Son argues that Father has forfeited his authority by his previous attempts to disown him.   [31] By an act of *patria potestas*, for extreme misdemeanors. It is implied that this son is not in that class.   [32] = kill me.   [33] This qualification shows he *does* believe him capable of parricide.

[34] There is some slippage between "difficult to believe of a son" and "difficult for a son to commit" (see previous note).

[QUINTILIAN]

praecipitat auctoritas, qui filium occidere vocatis plerumque gravitatem, sicut abdicationem emendationis,[59] sicut
reliqua supplicia nostra rationis fronte protegitis, cunc-
tosque praerigidae mentis adfectus vocabulo molliore le-
4 nitis. Nos nec felices facinus istud possumus concipere
nec miseri. Non perveniunt ad nefas istud nec necessi-
5 tates, omnis citra desperationem dolor, ira languescit. Et
quanto, dii deaeque, difficilius, si paretur sine conscio,
sine ministro, totumque facinus et animum filii poscat et
manus! Memento, cuius obicias immanitatis horrorem;
patrem occidere velle hinc[60] tantum accipit[61] vires, ut
mori possis deprehensus.
6 "Ut sciatis" inquit "verum esse quod obicio, et abdicare
volui." Non potest, pater, efficere pertinacia querendi
7 genus probationis. Tu, cum dicis: "Filius me voluit occidere," videris tibi facere prioribus iudicibus invidiam,
exclamare: "Vos faciles, vos misericordes, hunc mihi red-
ditis?" 8. Sed iniquissimum est ut abdicatio, quae nec in
sui valuit effectum, fidem maiori crimini praestet. Non
sum reus inexplorati pudoris, nec ante acta vitae meae sub

[59] -cationem -dationis (*sc.* fronte) *Wint.*[3]: -cationis -dationem
codd.
[60] horrorem—hinc *sic dist. Håk. post Håk.*[2] *135–36*
[61] -it *Håk.*[2] *135–36*: -is *codd.*

---

35 As it so often did in the past (a customary topic for *exempla*:
e.g., Val. Max. 5.7; Sen. *Controv.* 10.3.8) (AS).
36 I.e., to commit suicide and thereby escape the frightful
punishment reserved to convicted parricides, the *poena cullei*
(see 17.9.3, 2.14.4) (AS).
37 I.e., even before accusing him now (DAR).

supreme authority still hurries[35] you into making an end of us. You commonly call killing a son an act of severity, just as you hide disownment behind a façade of "improvement" and the other dire punishments you inflict on us behind a façade of "reason": all the passions of an unbending mind you seek to soften by employing a milder word. (4) We, on the other hand, cannot conceive of doing something so terrible, whether our lot is happy or unhappy. Not even dire necessities suffice to bring us to such an appalling deed; every sense of grievance, every feeling of anger weakens before so desperate an act is reached. (5) And, gods and goddesses, how much more difficult the deed if it is planned without an accomplice, without a helper, if the whole crime requires not just the son's intention but his hands too! Bear in mind the horror of the monstrous act you are charging me with; wishing to kill one's father may draw strength from one source only: being able to die if you are caught in the act.[36]

(6) "You can tell my charge is true," he says, "from the fact that I also[37] wanted to disown him." Father, persistence in accusation does not count as proof. (7) When you say: "My son wanted to kill me," it looks as though you are casting aspersions on the earlier judges, to be shouting: "Are you,[38] then, in your soft-heartedness, in your clemency, giving a boy like *this* back to me?" 8. But it is completely unfair that a disowning that did not even come into effect should make a graver charge more credible. I am not a defendant whose modesty has previously gone unexamined: my past record is not being discussed for the first

[38] I.e., the earlier judges after they have refused to allow the *abdicatio*.

2   hodierna primum lite tractantur. Felicior innocentia est citra suspiciones, certior post reatum, et quantum infamiae praestant obiecta dum nutant,[62] tantundem auctori-

3   tatis absoluta restituunt. An scilicet superatus est gratia pater, et apud senes, [et][63] apud parentes auctoritate praevalui? Viderint qui calamitatibus suis sic blandiuntur, ut sibi adfuisse credant misericordiam, favorem; filius a patre

4   delatus numquam poterit superior esse nisi causa. Sane tamen feramus ut prima abdicatione non egesseris totum dolorem, multa tibi de criminibus meis verecundia querendi, multa paternae pietatis abstulerit infirmitas; quid

5   non implet repetita delatio? Reversus es in forum iam ad iudices iratos. Quanto terrore cuncta perculit[64] pudor ille iam victi et redeuntis in damnatam conluctationem! Acrior

6   semper ex verecundia dolor. Sed et iudicum cura quanto malignior circa redditum reum! Quam multis placet illa de dissimilitudine pronuntiationis auctoritas, ut[65] severior videtur diversa sententia!

    9. Tertia vero abdicatio, dii immortales, quem adparatum, quem movit ambitum! Ego miror quod mihi licuit

---

    [62] dum nutant (-tunt B[ac]) *codd.*: damnato (*deinde* absoluto) *Gron., sed vd. Scheff. 455 et Pas.*   [63] *del. Pas.* (*et om.* W)
    [64] -cu- *Gron.*: -tu- *codd.*   [65] ut B V (*H.-Sz. 589, 631*): et Φ

---

    [39] Unlike Son in the present case.

    [40] Sc., after being acquitted.   [41] At the second trial the judges were shocked (and inclined to sympathize, it is implied) to see Father—an old man and a parent, like them (cf. 17.8.3)—fighting on in spite of his previous defeat.

    [42] Father's irritation was made keener by his earlier failure to secure the disownment.

time at today's hearing. (2) Innocence is more fortunate if
it does not come under suspicion, but it is more surely
founded after a court case: accusations do harm to one's
reputation when they are still in the balance, but once they
have been refuted they provide correspondingly greater
authority. (3) Was, I wonder, my father defeated because
I was favored? Did I prevail before a panel of old men, of
fathers, thanks to any authority I commanded? Welcome
to their opinion are those who[39] tone down[40] the troubles
they have gone through under the illusion that it was pity
and favor that stood by them: a son brought to court by his
father will never be able to win unless his *case* is superior.
(4) Let us grant that, at the first attempt to disown me, you
did not give vent to all your grievances, that you were
robbed of much of what you had against me by your bash-
fulness in complaining of me, by the weakness arising
from your paternal affection; but what gaps does a second
accusation not fill? (5) You came back to the court to find
the judges already incensed. How great was the terror,
how universal the shock at the shaming sight of a man,
already defeated, coming back to a conflict where judgment had previously gone against him![41] Disgrace always
leads to more bitter resentment.[42] (6) But also, how much
less sympathetic are careful judges when they are dealing
with someone sent for trial a second time! How many take
pleasure in winning prestige by coming to a different verdict, how much more rigorous is thought to be a sentence
opposite to a previous one!

9. But as for the third disownment, ye gods, what preparations, what intrigues it put in motion! I am surprised

[QUINTILIAN]

audiri, quod me non statim primus querelarum tumul-
2 tus oppressit. Quid post ista novi, pater, obici potest? Inter leges, inter iura consenui, non habeo in moribus meis
3 quod non melius[66] iudices sciant. Scilicet capit natura rerum ut futurus parricida non praemiserit notas, nullis ante
sit maximi sceleris immanitas tumultuata flagitiis, et quandoque culleo, serpentibus expianda feritas sub placida
4 mente primam pertulerit aetatem? Aliud est miserorum
genus quod clementia, quod succurrendi favore dimitti-
tur: absolverunt me qui sciebant non profuturum mihi
quod non abdicarer.
5 Proclames igitur licet: "Subinde detuli, saepe questus
sum, ter abdicare volui!", hoc tamen res ista debet efficere,
ut tibi non oporteat credi, quicquid aliud obieceris. Non
enim sequitur, pater, ut me tuis criminibus accuses, quod
6 nocentem tuis moribus probes.[67] Filium parricidam non
facit severitas vestra, non saevitia, non terror; ad tam
grande facinus non ira opus est, sed moribus, non dolore,
sed mente. Nocentes[68] iniuriae levius exasperant, levius
offendunt;[69] innocentis fili ultio est mori.

---

[66] <me> (*abl.*) mel- *Watt*[3] 57   [67] *dist. Håk.*[2] 136: *post*
filium *vulg.*   [68] nocentes *Russ.*[3]: omnes *codd.*
[69] offend- *Sch.* (*firm. Håk.*[2] 136–37): oder- *codd.*

---

[43] Ironic.   [44] A possible reminiscence of the *Mathema-
ticus*: cf., e.g., 4.15.6 and 4.16.5.   [45] Cf. 1.6.1–2.
[46] Cf. n. 36.   [47] The unsympathetic judges (cf. 17.8.3)
acquitted me at the third trial only because they knew that I
would thus incur new torments—such as the present lawsuit.
[48] Accuse me of parricide though you may, the fact that you
are yourself a parricide (i.e., you wished to kill your son) does not
mean that *I* am.

that I managed to get a hearing, that I was not over-whelmed at once by the first storm of his accusations. (2) Father, what new charge can be brought after all that? I have grown old amid talk of laws and rights; there is nothing in my behavior that the judges do not know better than I myself. (3) Is then nature[43] supposed to allow for the possibility that a future parricide[44] did not show preliminary indications, that the enormity of the ultimate crime did not break forth in earlier outrageous acts,[45] that the barbarity one day to be punished by the sack and the serpents[46] passed its early years behind the cover of a quiet mind? (4) Different, however, is the kind of wretch who is acquitted by clement judges, by sympathetic helpers; *I* was acquitted by judges who knew it would be of no avail to me to escape disownment.[47]

(5) So you may cry: "I often brought him to court, I frequently complained of his behavior, three times I wished to disown him!" But this ought rather to ensure that you are *not* believed if you bring any other charges. You may be accusing me of your own crimes, father, but it does not follow that you can prove me guilty by your own behavior.[48] (6) The rigor of fathers like you, your cruelty, the terror you inspire, does not make a parricide of your son; to commit so great a crime one needs not anger but the right character, not a grievance but the right cast of mind. The guilty are provoked less, caused less offense, by wrongs done to them; an *innocent* son takes revenge by suicide.[49]

---

[49] Guilty persons are less upset by being wronged; an innocent person, like Son here, is so upset that he wants to commit suicide: that is *his* "revenge."

10. Quodsi manifestum est nihil tunc in moribus meis fuisse, quod posset esse suspectum, aestimemus unde
2 postea traxerim parricidii causas. Vos hoc loco libet[70] interrogare, iudices: quis magis debet innocentiam amare? Vici patrem: omni nunc sollicitudine, omni labore custodiam[71] illam gratiam, illum ambitum meum, quo remuneror advocatos, quo persolvo iudicibus, illud propter quod audeo domum reverti, propter quod non timeo casus, non
3 subita [pro patre],[72] non maligna fata. Fidem non capit ut me tres absolutiones et innocentem probaverint et effecerint parricidam.

4 Praeterea, pater, quam infirmum me, quam trepidum reddit ipsa victoria! An scilicet ignoro quod me reversum circumstat[73] totius domus maligna cura, quod vivo inter homines, quibus apud te gratiam parat si de nobis aliqua
5 mentiantur,[74] fingant? Videlicet hoc nos in facinus praecipitat, impellit, quod aliquid speramus de testamento tuo. Quid? Ego non sentio quod, sim licet remissus[75] in
6 domum, a caritate tamen exclusus, abiectus sum? Rogo, qua fiducia facinus paro totiens delatus et paterna conquestione praedictus?[76] Quod vis patrocinium sperem pro parricidio meo? Defendi non possem, si bibisses tu vene-

---

[70] hoc l. l. *huc transp.* C[2] (*et vd. Klotz*[2] *102.12*): *post* innocentiam *habent cett.*

[71] -dio iam *Sch.*

[72] *secl. Pas. utpote gloss.* (= subita *patris causam fulcientia*)

[73] -stat *Plas. 40* (*firm. Håk.*): -sistat *codd.*

[74] mentian- AD β (*def. Helm*[1] *366*): nuncien- B V: nuntian- CE δ: nuntient *Reitz.*[2] *40*

[75] s. l. r. *Obr.*: simili scelere missus *codd.*

[76] -dictus (*vel* petitus) ς (*cf. 4.2.5, 4.17.3, 17.12.3*): -ditus *codd.*

10. Now, if it is quite obvious that there was at that time nothing in my behavior that could arouse suspicion, let us consider where I can have acquired motives for parricide later. (2) At this point, judges, I should like to ask you: who has better reason to love innocence than I? I have defeated my father. Henceforth I shall always be anxious, always strive, to guard that favor, that credit, with which I reward my advocates and pay my debt to my judges:[50] everything that gives me the courage to return home, that lets me forget all fear of chance events, of sudden, of malign strokes of fate. (3) It is past belief that three attempts to disown me proved me innocent—and also made a parricide of me.

(4) What is more, father, how weak, how fearful the very fact of my victory over you makes me! I am perfectly well aware that, on my return, I am surrounded by a household whose every service to me is ill-meant,[51] that I live among people who can win favor with you for any lies, any fictions they may tell of me. (5) But of course[52] what hurries me on, what impels me to precipitate action, is the hope of benefiting from your will.—Do you think I am unaware that even though I have been taken back into the house I am shut out, cast out of your affection? (6) I ask you, how confidently can I arrange a crime when I have been so often taken to court and signaled in advance by my father's complaints? What defense do you expect me to hope for if I committed parricide? Indeed, I would have

[50] He owed it to his advocates and judges to behave well in the future.
[51] Cf. 17.11.1.
[52] Sarcastic.

[QUINTILIAN]

7   num. Finge me parricidii voluntatem, finge habere causas:
    unde occasionem, unde fiduciam? Ego nec mori possum,
    nisi ut deprehendar.

        11. Venenum paro qui ministrum, qui non invenio con-
    scium? Despicior a libertis,[77] contemnor a servulis: evitant
    sermonem meum, conloquia fugiunt, et caritatem tui
2   simulant odio mei. An videlicet spero posse fieri ut ipse
    porrigam? Est enim mihi ad convictus tuos facilis acces-
    sus. Venenum mehercule putabis quicquid dederint hae
3   manus! Et virus praesentaneum paro, quod statim, quod
    subito corripiat? At[78] quemadmodum mihi supersit ulla
4   defensio? An lentum et quod tarda peste consumat? Sci-
    licet ut non statim exclames, ut te meum virus bibisse non
5   credas.[79] Rogo, cui paravi venenum, quod dare non pos-
    sum nisi mihi?

6   "At"[80] inquit "parricidii[81] argumentum est et hoc ip-
    sum, quod habuisti venenum." Omnibus, iudices, quibus
    ad scelerum conatus adiuvatur deteriorum cotidie fe-
    cunda mortalitas, non hanc solam potentiam natura con-
    cessit, in quam malis mentibus et nocentium ducuntur

---

77 -rtis *Gron.*: -ris *codd.*
78 at AC: ut B V δ: ad D: ac E: et P: est S
79 *sic dist. Gr.-Mer.*: *interrog. vulg.*
80 at *scripsi*: ita *codd.*
81 -dii *Dess.*²: -dae C: -da *cett.*

---

53 Even supposing you took poison voluntarily to commit suicide, I would be suspected of having murdered you—and would
have a hard time defending myself. A fortiori, if I *really* meant to
murder you, how could I ever get away with it?
54 Cf. 17.10.4.

284

none to offer if *you* had drunk the poison.[53] (7) Imagine for a moment that I wish to kill you, imagine that I have motives to do it: how could I find the opportunity, the confidence to act? I cannot even commit suicide without being detected!

11. Am I preparing a poison when I can find no helper, no accomplice? The freedmen look askance at me, the meanest slaves scorn me. They avoid talking to me, flee from any conversation: they simulate affection for you by showing dislike of me.[54] (2) Maybe I hope I can hand you the poison myself? After all, I have easy access to your table. But—heavens!—you will think anything these hands offer you is poison! (3) Suppose the potion I am brewing to be instantaneous, the kind that strikes down the victim at once and all of a sudden. But what hope would remain for me to explain myself away afterward? (4) Or suppose it is not quick to act, the kind to eat away with a slow wasting. No doubt so that you do not cry out at once, so that you do not believe it was my poison you had drunk.[55] (5) I ask: for whom have I mixed a poison that I can only give to myself?

(6) "But," he says, "what proves parricide is also the very fact that you possessed poison." Judges, to everything that helps humankind—fertile in conceiving schemes that grow worse and worse every day—to execute their nefarious plans, nature has not given merely the potentiality to which they are led by evil minds and a disposition to harm

---

[55] Ironic: as though the use of slow poison was specially designed to make it possible for the victim to be aware of what was happening to him and who the poisoner was.

[QUINTILIAN]

ingeniis, sed illis usus ex animo est, totumque, quod fa-
7 ciunt, de conscientia possidentis accipiunt. Quid enim, si
latronem gladio tantum probes? Sic munimus et somnos.
Excute peregrinantium sinus: haerent tela sollicitis. Non
vetant ista leges parare, prospicere, nec instrumenta
8 prohibent, sed aestimant usus. Finge me velut in media
prosperitate vitae proclamare: "Venenum paravi, ad quod
incerti casus, ad quod languor, dolor, ad quod confugeret
improvisa debilitas." 12. Miramini quod hoc fecerim,
homo qui circa me fortunam, qui discrimina humana las-
savi? Cui nescio quid adhuc paret totiens victa delatio?
Debuit habere in sua potestate mortem, quem iam pater
poterat occidere.
2   "Non est" inquit "credibile ut mori volueris absolutus,
qui reus noluisti." Poteram quidem dicere: pater, vixi, dum
spero fas esse ut incipias aliquando misereri, ut te squalor
meus frangat, mitigent lacrimae, pallor exoret; sed ignosce
innocentiae: tunc me decuit pertinax, rigida[82] defensio.
3 Vixi, ne me videretur expulisse de saeculo profundorum

---

[82] -nax et r. γ β, *sed vd. Pas.*

---

[56] I.e., things like this can help as well as harm; cf. Quint.
2.16.6.
[57] Even in prosperity anyone might take such precautions (not
just a criminal).
[58] The present charge of parricide, which was still in the future when Son procured the poison, and any other future charge
Father may have in store for him.
[59] By *patria potestas*. Cf. n. 31.
[60] The scruffy clothes he wore (as defendants in court usually
did, to arouse sympathy) at the three trials. See also 17.14.6.

others;[56] the use made of them is dependent on the intention of the user: it is the conscience of the possessor that gives them their full effect. (7) What if you were to judge a man to be a brigand just because he owned a sword? That is how we guard ourselves even while we sleep. Search the pockets of travelers: their anxiety makes them keep their weapons close at hand. The laws do not stop us providing ourselves with such things and procuring them; they do not prohibit the implements themselves: it is their use they judge. (8) Imagine that—as it were—amid a life of prosperity I declare:[57] "I have procured poison to have recourse to at critical moments, in weakness and pain, in sudden illness." 12. Do you wonder, then, that I did this after I had worn out upon myself fortune and the perils of human life? And who knows what trouble may still be in store for me from an accusation so often foiled?[58] A son whom his father might already have killed[59] needed to have death under his own control.

(2) "It is impossible to believe," he says, "that you wanted to die after being acquitted, considering that you did not when you were on trial." I might well have replied: "Father, I went on living in the hope that you might perhaps one day begin to pity me: that my shabby appearance[60] might break your resolve, my tears placate you, my pale face win you over." But pardon my innocence:[61] at that point an obstinate, unbending defense was appropriate. (3) I went on living so that it would not look as if I had been driven from life by fear at having been caught out in

---

[61] = the way I behaved because I was conscious of my innocence (see below).

scelerum deprehensa trepidatio, ne super cadaver meum
proclamare posses: "Certe merito timui, merito praedixi;[83]
venenum qui <bibit>,[84] vivendi non habebat audaciam,"
ne supremis meis conviciareris, ne quid posses obicere
4 iam non negaturo. Verum tibi de impatientia mea faten-
dum est: eadem mente nolui mori, cum abdicares, qua
non bibi, cum iuberes.

5 Sed fruere iterum, fruere saepius confessione tam misera, et, quia oculos spectaculo non licuit implere, satien-
tur aures: volui mori. Adice, si videtur, hanc malis nostris
contumeliam, ut interroges quare:[85] abdicare me subinde
6 voluisti! Quid ais, rerum natura, pietas? Ita iustiores
causas <haec non>[86] habet impatientia quam corporum
7 damna, quam facultatium tristis eversio? In suprema praecipitat me pater. Ita non haec una vox complectitur omnes
calamitates? Non videmini nunc vobis universos audire
8 miseros? Possimus fortassis aliorum accidentium sperare
9 finem; non habent proximorum odia regressum. Quaecumque nexus accepere naturae, et[87] quae sanguine vis-
ceribusque constricta sunt, non laxantur diducta, sed

---

83 *dist. Gron.*
84 *h.l. add. (dein dist.) Håk.*[2] *137: ante* ven- *Gron.*
85 *dist. Gr.-Mer.:* nihil *vulg.*
86 *supplevi:* ita <non> i. c. <haec> habet *Sch.*
87 *explicativum, dein* quae = quaecumque (*H.-Sz.* 563)

---

62 I.e., to await the trial and its possible consequences (cf.
n. 36).
63 I.e., my failure to act on my wish to die.
64 Of my dead body.
65 Sc., when you caught me brewing the poison.

the midst of bottomless crimes; so that you would not be able to declaim over my corpse: "I was quite right to be afraid, quite right to foretell what would happen. He ⟨drank⟩ poison: that shows he did not have the nerve to go on living";[62] so that you would not jeer at my funeral; so that you could not make new accusations when I was no longer in a position to deny them. (4) I must tell you the truth about my failure to go through with my resolution:[63] I did not want to commit suicide when you disowned me in just the same spirit as I did not drink the poison when you ordered me to.

(5) But enjoy for a second time, enjoy again and again the confession that brings me such pain. Since your eyes did not have the chance to gloat over the spectacle,[64] let your *ears* be satisfied by these words: I *did* want to die.[65] Add, if you like, to my misfortunes by asking me the insulting question: "Why?"—Because you always wanted to disown me! (6) What have nature and the ties of affection to say? Does ⟨not my present⟩ inability to endure life have more legitimate causes than some bodily injury, than some financial disaster? (7) It is my *father* who is hurrying me to death. Doesn't this one sentence sum up all my calamities? Do you[66] not hear in these words the voice of all wretched men? (8) We may perhaps hope for an end to other misfortunes; from hatred between relations, there is no turning back.[67] (9) All bonds laid down by nature, drawn closer by blood and the deepest instincts, are not just loosened if there is a split: they perish altogether. For

---

[66] Judges.

[67] As explained in what follows.

pereunt, et quae[88] de primo tenore nascendi vix in contra-
rium victa deflectunt diuque[89] pravitatis suae rigore du-
rata, mox in pristinum cursum remissa non redeunt, sed
quo totum pondus omnesque vires inclinata traxerunt,
vigore, quo sibi permissa crevissent, in ipsius vitii robur
adolescunt. 13. In hoc est tota difficultas, ut incipiat non
amare filium pater. Hoc cum frontem confessionis accipit,
reliqua praecipiti furore decurrunt, et redituris caritatibus
obstat quicquid obstiterat [ab][90] odiis. Semel sibi parentes
2 liberique mutantur, semel auferuntur. Felices qui habent
in conscientia sua quod debeant emendare, corrigere! Illa
demum potest ira desinere, quae coaluit ex vitiis libero-
3 rum. Ego quid facio, cui non luxuria, non est mutanda
petulantia, cuius abdicatio non de meis, sed de patris
moribus venit? Frustra mihi exhortationes, frustra blan-
4 dientur vana solacia. Hominis, quem pater odisse non desinit, unus exitus est, ut se oderit.
5   Et quantulum habet de toto dolore nostro ille, quo ve-
nitur ad iudicem, dies! Ego, cum dico: pater me odit, illud
exclamo: omnes sine me sunt festi dies, omnis laetitia sine

88 -nt et quae M (*def. Wint.[7] 165*): -nte quae B V: -nt atque π:
-nt quae Φ
89 diu *Sh. B.[2] 215*
90 *del. Gr.-Mer.* (*et cf. Pas.*)

68 Cf. 17.12.9.
69 Explained below: once at loggerheads, fathers and sons are
difficult to reconcile. All the same, peace may still be made if the
break was caused by some misconduct of the sons (17.13.2). Since
I haven't done anything wrong, there is nothing *I* can amend

when those bonds are deflected from their natural course and have, though only with difficulty, been overcome and turned in a contrary direction, they grow hard with the rigidity of their own depravity, and subsequently refuse to return into their former track even if one tries to make them do so. Instead they take the aberrant direction given them by their whole weight and all their strength; with the same vigor with which they would have grown strong if left to themselves, they grow to the maturity of vice itself. 13. This is where the whole difficulty arises: a father must begin not to love his son. But when this feeling reaches the point of being openly acknowledged, everything else follows in an avalanche of madness; whatever had stood in the way of hatred now stands in the way of a return to affection.[68] It is once for all that parents and children change in each others' eyes, once for all that they part company. (2) Happy are they who have on their consciences something they need to correct and put right.[69] A father's anger *can* cease, at long last, when it was his children's vices that fostered it. (3) But what can *I* do, when I have no spendthrift habits or insolent behavior that I could change, when my disownment is the result not of my character but of my father's? Exhortations and vain comforting alike will flatter me to no effect. (4) When a man's father does not stop hating him, his only way out is to hate himself.

(5) And how little of all my grief is the result of a day in court! When *I* say: "My father hates me," what I really mean is: Every day is a holiday for him if I am not there, all his joy lies in being without his son. He does not talk to

(17.13.3): so I have no means of appeasing my father, and I am just left with hatred for myself (17.13.4).

filio; non adloquitur maestum, non adsidet ille languenti.
Gratissimus, quisquis de nobis tristius aliquid attulerit,
6 quisquis maledixerit, conviciatus fuerit absenti. Ego si hoc
possum ferre, merui. Alia sunt adversa, quae de conti-
nuatione sui patientiam parant, quae durant adsiduitate
firmantque mentem; quod te pater oderit, cotidie novum
7 est. Minus fortassis urant invicem simultates, et mutuis
detestationibus invisa respirent; odium is tantum filius
perferre poterit, qui et ipse oderit patrem.

14. Vos nunc, iudices, universos quin immo mortales
infelicissimus iuvenis interrogo: quid me facere vultis?
Explicuit nos sine dubio de criminibus exitus, quod absolutus sum; tamen non hoc effecit, ne mori velim, sed ut
2 mihi liceat et vivere. Victus sum enim mehercules, victus
sum, iudices, absolutionibus meis, et, quae certissima est
animae laborantis infirmitas, misera felicitate defeci.
3 Quem mihi vultum domum reverso, quem suadetis animum? Non decet gaudium me, non ⟨maeror⟩:[91] exas-
pero hilaritate, offendo tristitia. Capto sermonem: invisus
sum, tamquam adroganter insultem; doloris causa dicor,
si propius aspiciar,[92] videor,[93] si recedo, contemnere.
4 Quousque vincemus? Nesciunt prorsus abdicationibus

---

[91] me non ⟨maeror⟩ *scripsi*: meum *codd.*: me *Gron.*: ⟨non
decet maeror⟩ *post* hil- ⟨: gaudium ⟨me, non decet⟩ maeror
Wint.[7] *165–66*

[92] -ior *Wint.*[7] *166, sed vd. Eng. 72*

[93] sermonem—videor *sic fere dist. Obr.*

me when I am sad, or sit at my bedside when I am ill. If someone has brought bad news of me, or spoken ill of me or abused me in my absence, he gives him the warmest of welcomes. (6) If I can put up with this, I have deserved it. There are other adversities that become endurable by long continuance, that harden and strengthen the mind by their constant presence. To be hated by your father is a new cross to bear each day. (7) It may be that a mutual animosity tortures less, that where each hates the other their hostility finds some relief. The only son who can bear his father hating him is one who returns him hate for hate.

14. As the most unfortunate of young men, I ask you now, judges, or rather I ask every human being: what do you expect me to do? True, my escape from the charges against me, my acquittals, have given me relief. But that has not made me stop wanting to die: rather, it has also made me able to go on living.[70] (2) In fact (by heaven!) I have been defeated, yes, defeated, judges, by my acquittals, for I have collapsed—the absolutely unmistakable malady of a soul in trouble—under the weight of my hapless good fortune. (3) How do you suggest I should look, how feel, when I return home? Joy does not suit me, but neither does <sorrow>: if I am cheerful, I annoy; if I am gloomy, I give offense. If I try to make conversation, I am met with hostility, as if I were being arrogant and triumphal. I am said to cause pain if I am seen too close by; if I keep out of the way, I am thought to be showing disdain. (4) How much longer shall I have to go on—winning? Sons

---

[70] As well as wanting to die: these are two different, equally unwelcome results of his victories. What follows explains the unwelcomeness of the second.

mederi, qui non statim cedunt, qui conscientiae suae ri-
5 gore nituntur. Non vincitur pater, non sum absolutus: cum
domum veni, nemo me diligit, nemo reveretur. Iam ad
nos de penatibus illis non pertinent nisi secreta, nisi late-
6 brae. Non exuo, non depono sordes, et mihi cotidie senex
tamquam accusaturus occurrit. Attendo quid faciam, quid
loquar, qualis aspiciar, et, quod malignissimum est solli-
7 citudinis genus, me ipse custodio. Satiasti me, vita, satiasti,
et, cum felicibus quoque veniat ex nimia prosperitatis con-
tinuatione fastidium, quod taedium paras lassitudine mi-
seriarum![94] Consumpta est in lacrimis, in precibus aetas,
8 exacti sordibus dies, anxietate noctes. Quid mihi contra
tam indigna, tam gravia promittit integritas? Abdicari debet, quem nocentem pater odit, mori, quem innocentem.
   15. "Sed, ut credamus" inquit "voluisse te mori, cur
2 potissimum veneno?" Possis quidem, pater, hanc de omni
supremorum genere litem facere morientibus, et, quia rerum natura varias fatorum vias indulsit animae, in nullo
non exitu simili ratione reprehendas[95] quicquid electum
est. Sic super strictum nudatumque mucronem procla-
3 mares: "Cur non veneno?" Sed nihil est delicatius exitu,

[94] -riar- *B. Asc.*[1] *cxii v. (firm. Pas.)*: -ror- *codd.*
[95] re- ς: de- *codd.*

---

[71] I.e., who, conscious of their innocence, are not prepared to
admit the offenses they are charged with.
[72] Explained below (17.14.5–8).
[73] After each acquittal.
[74] Appropriate to one being accused (n. 60)—and Father
looks to be about to accuse him again.

who do not give in at once, who rely on their unshakable consciences,[71] are quite unable to cope with attempts to disown them.[72] (5) My father is *not* defeated, I am *not* acquitted: every time I come back home,[73] no one shows affection, no one shows respect. In that house I have nowhere to call my own except nooks and crannies. (6) I do not take off, I do not lay aside, my mourning clothes:[74] for every day, if the old man encounters me, he looks as if he is on the point of bringing a new accusation. I have to watch out what I do, what I say, what I look like; in fact (the most malign kind of concern), I have to be my own jailer. (7) I have had enough of you, life, yes, enough. If even happy people can find that good fortune is tedious when it is drawn out too long, how oppressive is a life that tires one out with miseries! My existence is taken up by tears, by prayers; my days are passed in mourning clothes, my nights in anxious thoughts. (8) What can my blamelessness promise me to counter such cruel, such overwhelming ills? A son hated by his father has to be disowned if he is guilty; he has to die if he is innocent.[75]

15. "But," he says, "even if we believe that you wanted to die, why by poison particularly?" (2) Father, when people wish to die you could dispute with them on those lines about *every* means available to them: since nature in her bounty has provided the human soul with different routes to approach its destiny, you could raise the same objection to any and every method that has been selected. So, in the presence of a sword drawn and bare, you would exclaim: "Why not use poison?" (3) In fact, nothing requires more

[75] As his life will be made unbearable by the hatred of his father and the whole household: cf. 17.10.4, 17.14.2–7.

quem non supplicia, non metus, sed collecta de calamita-
4 tibus commendat infirmitas. Mihi tamen praecipue cum
hoc mortis instrumento propria concordia est: non spargit
cruorem, nec trucem cadaveris relinquit aspectum; placida est, quieta est. Ingratissime senex, ego et hoc sic mo-
riendo prospexeram, ne me occidisse alius videretur.

5   Te nunc adprehendo, te interrogo, pater: ita parricida
sum ego, qui venenum adfero in domum tuam imparatum,
rude, terendum, cui tam multa restant, ante quam dari
possit? Ita parricida sum, qui iuxta te quaero secretum, qui
de potione tibi incerta, quam nemo detulit, tam[96] simpli-
6 citer, tam facile respondi? Secedo in medios penates, nullos ab introitu praepono custodes, non evito transitus, non
excludo venturos. Rogo, utrum haec omnia sunt occidere
7 volentis an mori? Venenum, quod tibi pararetur, inve-
nisses absconsum, reconditum; multum circa illud palloris
attoniti, concisa verba, trepida suspiria et me negantem.
Parricida deprehensus effudisset venenum, ne fateretur.

    16. "Cur ergo," inquit, "si tibi paraveras, non bibisti?"
2 Breviter, pater, et secundum naturam condicionis huma-

---

96 tam π: quam *cett.*

---

76 E.g., Father; contrast 17.10.6 (with reversed roles).

77 A pointed allusion to the poison scene, when Father *invenit*
and *interrogavit* Son (cf. 17.th.). Now the tables are turned and
Father is under interrogation.   78 Son could have just spilled
the drug he was preparing, without admitting what it was; in that
case, Father would have had no means of knowing that it was
poison. So Son's frankness is another proof of his innocence.

79 I.e., he would have poured it away at once, before being
ordered to drink it.

fastidious choice than a departure prompted not by judicial punishment or fear, but by a sickness of mind deriving from an accumulation of calamities. (4) On the other hand, *I* have a special affinity with this means of death: it does not spill blood, it does not leave the body looking grim. It is a peaceful, a tranquil death. You most ungrateful old man! By dying like this, I had also made sure that no one else[76] would be thought to have killed me.

(5) It is now my turn to seize *you*, to question *you*, father:[77] am I a parricide if I bring poison into your house unprepared, raw, needing to be pounded up, in a state where much remains to be done before it can be administered? Am I a parricide, if I look for privacy in a room near yours, if I gave such a frank, such a ready answer about a potion which you could not identify[78] and of which no one had informed you? (6) I withdraw into the heart of the house, set no guards to prevent entry, do not worry about people who might pass by or shut out anyone who might come in. I ask you: are all of these the actions of someone wishing to kill, or of someone wishing to die? (7) If the poison was intended for you, you would have come upon it hidden, out of the way; in that scenario you would have found the extreme pallor of one startled out of his wits, broken words, anxious sighs—and me denying everything. A parricide caught in the act would have poured away the poison in order not to have to confess what it was.[79]

16. "Well, if you had got it ready for yourself," he says, "why didn't you drink it?" (2) My reply is brief, father, and consistent with human nature: all the unhappy have under

nae respondeo nihil aliud esse in potestate miserorum, quam ut mori velint. Ego cum dico: "Mori volo," non hoc dico: "Moriturus sum"; de animo meo respondeo, non

3 promitto de fato. Miraris quod, quamvis iam teneam venenum, multum tamen adhuc casibus incertisque superest? Accepere[97] perfossis plerumque[98] visceribus vitam tamen ab ipsa desperatione redeuntem; strictos circa colla laqueos aut nexus aut ipsius corporis ruina decepit; rotatos per abrupta mollis[99] iactus explicuit. Tam consentaneum

4 est ne moriatur qui velit, quam quod morimur inviti. Sed malo, sicut coepi, simplici tecum ratione consistere. Nihil aeque, pater, impetu constat, quam mori velle, nec quicquam res humanae impatientius habent pereuntis adfectu.

5 Hunc si retinere velis,[100] sufficit ut moreris, et rationem quoque homini mortis eripiet, si quis abstulerit ardorem. Frangit animum quisquis intervenit; abducit, avocat quisquis adloquitur. Ambiuntur[101] cuncta moriendi spatia pro

6 vita. Ideo nos mehercules crediderim ‹in›[102] eiusmodi exitum eligere secretum. Minimum est quod confundat hominem infirmitate morientem, et exiguis causis opus est

---

97 -cep- ς: -cip- *codd.*

98 -riq- *Gron.*

99 mollis V: molis B Φ*

100 velis *Gron.*: vales A: velles *cett.*

101 -nt *Gron., sed vd. OLD² §3.b*

102 *add. Bur.*: ‹ad› *Wint.*⁷ 166, *sed vd. omnino Tos. 57*

---

80 Sc., about what will in fact happen.

81 In an attempt at suicide, some people have jumped off a cliff, but too gently: so they rolled down the cliff (and survived), instead of falling headlong from it (AS).

their control is their *wish* to die. When I say: "I want to die," I do not mean: "I am going to die." My reply expresses my intention: I make no promises on behalf of destiny.[80] (3) Are you surprised that, even though the poison is already in my hand, much is still left over to chance and uncertainty? Well, often enough men, after having their vitals pierced, have nevertheless found life returning to them, though hope itself had been abandoned. Nooses drawn tight around the neck have been frustrated by the knot failing or by the very way the body dropped. Some people have rolled right down a cliff, saved by their feeble spring.[81] Not dying when one wishes to is as natural as dying when we do not wish to. (4) But I should rather rest my case with you upon a straightforward argument, as I started to.[82] Nothing, father, is so much a matter of impulse as the desire to die, and there is nothing in the world more fickle than the feelings of a dying man. (5) If you want to keep him alive, all you have to do is delay him: if you remove his eagerness to die, you will also take away his reason to die. Anyone who comes on the scene breaks his resolve; anyone speaking to him distracts and diverts him. All delays in dying are eagerly sought out to save one's life. (6) That is why, indeed, I incline to think we seek privacy ⟨for⟩ a death of this kind. It needs only the slightest thing to throw into confusion a man dying out of weakness;[83] it takes but flimsy reasons to make a wretched man

[82] At 17.16.1, after which the argument has been somewhat diverted.

[83] Cf. 17.17.2–3 (suicide through depression, despair, etc.); also 17.19.10.

7 ut displiceat obitus quem misero suasit integritas. Quid,
si interveniat aliquis qui gaudeat, qui vindicari se putet,
si testis adhibeat oculos, quibus invidendum sit? Statim
mehercules adrogans vita simulabitur,[103] statim contumax
dolor cum deprehensa morte dissentiet.

17. Nescis quantum mihi haesitationis paraveris cum
interrogares,[104] dum respondere cogis rationemque[105]
2 reddere, iterum litigare, defendi. Me vero tunc pariter
omnes tenuistis, adfectus: indignatio, pietas, reverentia,
dolor. Ego propter patrem mori possum, coram patre non
3 possum. Adice nunc quod et dixisti: "Bibe." Si mehercules
saucium palpitantemque iussisses adigere ferrum, preme-
rem clausis vulneribus animam; ‹si›[106] stringere aptatos
ad colla nexus, conarer abrupto desilire laqueo; si non
iniceres manum ad praecipitia properanti, flecterem in
plana cursum. Merito prorsus, anime,[107] secretum solitu-
4 dinemque captaveras. Intervenit pater, actum est; perit
ille susceptae mortis ardor et utroque nos resolvit adfectu:

103 sti- *Sh. B.*[2] *215, sed vd. 17.19.3 et Wint. ap. Pas.*
104 -gares *Hamm.*[2] *524:* -ges *codd.:* (dum) -gas *Sch., sed cf.
17.18.5 et Håk.*[2] *138.64*   105 rationem *Str. ap. Pas.,* -que (*cf.
ad 17.5.3*) *adscripsi:* (cogis)setis quem et B V: sed (h)is (is *om.*
CD; sedis A β) quem et Φ: et aliquam ‹ration›em *Watt*[2] *32*
106 *add.* ς   107 -me V: -mae B: -ma Φ

84 Such a person is wretched enough to wish to kill himself,
though he is not doing so out of guilt.   85 The third element
generalizes the other two: we would grudge the spectacle both to
the man who takes pleasure in it and to the man who thinks he is
getting his revenge.   86 *Amour propre.*
87 The victim's continuing resentment against the other man

think twice about a death urged on him by his own inno-cence.[84] (7) What if he is interrupted by someone glad to see him die, someone who thinks he is getting his revenge, if a witness brings eyes to the act which must be grudged the sight of it?[85] At once, make no doubt, he will out of conceit[86] pretend to wish to go on living; at once, his ob-stinate resentment will be at odds with the death in which he has been caught out.[87]

17. You have no idea how much you disconcerted me when you questioned me, as you forced me to answer and give an explanation, to be litigant and defendant yet again. (2) At that moment you all gripped me simultaneously, you emotions: indignation, affection, respect, resentment. I can die because of my father, but I cannot die in his pres-ence. (3) What is more, you also[88] said "Drink!" If—I swear it—you had found me wounded and gasping for breath, and told me to drive the sword home, I should have bound up the gashes to hold back my departing soul. <If> you had ordered me to tighten a rope already in place round my neck, I should have tried to break the noose and jump to the ground. If you did not catch hold of me when I was hurrying to the edge of a cliff, I should have run back to level ground. You had been quite right, my mind, to seek out a secret and solitary place. (4) My father ap-pears—all is up; the old impulse to die as I had planned vanishes, and he frees me from my emotional conflict:[89] I

will make him think better of dying, after his enemy has come upon him in the act.

[88] Sc., as well as asking what I was doing (17.5.2–3) (DAR).

[89] The emotions are pro and contra dying; when Father says "Die," the problem is solved: Son can only live.

5   mori non debeo, si vetuerit, non potero, si iusserit. "Bibe"
inquit. Nondum quidem potioni virus aptatum est, sed me
ideo deprehendisti, quia adhuc terebatur. Multa tamen
mihi, pater, ante facienda sunt: volo prius convocare servulos, contrahere libertos, complorare, conqueri, man-

6   dare, defendi. "Bibe." Mihi vero tunc adiecisse visus es:

7   "Teneris, haeres: eamus ad iudicem!" "Bibe." Sic hoc iu-
bes, tamquam negem venenum. Interrogare vos velut in
illa secreti nostri praesentia libet: quem mihi post hanc
vocem animum datis? Dicit hoc accusator, dicit hoc victus,

8   dicit secreto, dicit sic, ut possit negare, si bibero. "Bibe."
Ego quidem volo, et hoc cum maxime paro: sed totum

9   hunc animum, senex, tua aviditate mutasti. "Bibe." Quid
restat quam ut recusantis ora diducas, ut infundas per
oppositas manus? Mihi vero tunc excidit quid vellem,[108]
quid pararem. 18. Vidi truces loquentis oculos, vultus par-
ricidali ardore suffusos. Iuberi mihi videbar ut biberem

2   tuum venenum. Nescisti, pater, pertinaciam meam servare, nescisti. Filium propter te mori volentem deprehen-

3   disti; vis occidere? Veta. Invade poculum, ne hauriam;
bibam. Exclama: "Temerari, quid facis? Iam desino irasci,
iam revertor in gratiam!";[109] properabo ut hoc secum aures

---

[108] vellem *Håk. necnon Wint.*[3]: velim *codd.*

[109] *tota verba* temerari—gratiam *recte tribuit patri B. Asc.*[1]
cxiv v.

---

[90] Explained by Patarol (1743, 400n4): If I had denied it was
poison, you would have ordered me to drink to establish if I was
telling the truth; now, however, *I* am informing you that I am
pounding poison: so you have no reason to make me drink it, unless you actually want my death. Cf. also 17.5.4.   [91] Judges.

must not die, if he forbids it; I shall not be able to, if he orders me to. (5) "Drink," he said. The poison had not yet been mixed into the drink: you caught me, in fact, just because the pounding was still in progress. Well, there is still much to do, father, before I die: I wish first to summon the slaves, assemble the freedmen, make complaint, lament, give my last instructions, justify myself. (6) "Drink." To me at that moment it was as if you added: "You're caught, you cannot escape: off we go to the judge!" (7) "Drink." You bid me do that as if I were denying it to be poison.[90] Let me question you,[91] as though we were there in private on that occasion. What do you think I felt like after hearing that word? It is my accuser speaking, my defeated accuser, in secret, and in such a manner that he can deny it if I drink. (8) "Drink." I certainly want to drink, and that is what I am planning to do this very minute; but this whole intention of mine you changed, old man, by your eagerness. (9) "Drink." What is left but for you to part my reluctant lips, to pour the potion down my throat even though I push the cup away? For sure, that was when I forgot what I meant to do, what I was preparing to do. 18. As you spoke I could see your grim eyes, your face flushed with the burning desire to kill: I thought I was being ordered to drink poison *you* had mixed. (2) You did not know, father, how to keep my obstinacy going, you really did not know. You have caught in the act a son who wanted to die because of you; do you want to kill him? Then forbid him. (3) Grab at the cup, to make sure I do not drain it: I will drink. Cry: "Reckless boy, what are you up to? Now I am ceasing to be angry, now I am becoming reconciled with you," and I will make haste, so that my ears may carry

4 ferant, ut impatientia tua fruantur oculi. Tibi imputes quod me retorsisti, quod ablata sunt sacramenta pereundi;

5 innocenti facilius est mori, si rogetur ut vivat. Fidem deorum, in quam me contumaciam, pater, in quem tunc impulisti contentionis ardorem, cum diceres "Bibe!" Nec vivere mihi libuit nec mori, ereptus sum miser animo meo, et[110] improvisa voce percussus[111] steti sine affectu, sine cogita-

6 tione[112] attonitus, amens, et me paene aliter occidi. Nihil est profecto improvisorum dolore torrentius, et fractae malorum contentione mentes ad inexpectata caligant. Non querelas post hoc invenio, non verba, non lacrimas.

7 Ad nullius rei conatum sufficit mori alterius animo et suo veneno.

19. Licet igitur nova me reatus mole convenias, non paenitet tamen flexisse,[113] non paenitet, illum spiritum

2 rigoremque pereundi: tamquam parricida moriebar. Pater, qui queritur quod non bibi, iam nunc diceret: "Deprehensus erat, negare non poterat." Essem nunc ter abdicatus, et me contenderet ad iudices meos redire non

3 ausum. Bene quod sic effudi, tamquam rursus vita placuisset; venenum, quod videretur deprehensum, nemo

---

110 del. *Franc.*

111 -uls- D

112 cogitati- *Wal.[1] 442* (*firm. Håk.[2] 138–39*): negati- π O: negotiati- (*vel* -oci-) *cett.*

113 flex- *Gron.*: fix-B V δ: fr≡x- C: finx- *cett.*

---

92 I.e., into death.

93 To die.

94 I.e., by shock.   95 Because by living on he has a chance to refute those accusations.

these words away with them,[92] so that my eyes may gloat over your anguish. (4) Count it as your fault that you changed my mind, that my solemn resolve to die was snatched from me: it is easier for an innocent son to die if he is asked to live. (5) By heaven, into what contumacy, what fierce contentiousness did you drive me, father, when you said: "Drink!" In a state where I wished neither to live nor to die, ah me, I had my resolve[93] taken away from me: struck by that unexpected word, I stood there with no feelings, dumbfounded and with no thought in my head, quite beside myself—so that I almost killed myself by another means.[94] (6) Nothing, to be sure, sweeps one away more irresistibly than the pain arising from the unforeseen: minds shattered by the struggle against misfortune black out in face of the unexpected. After this I could find no complaints, no words, no tears. (7) To die by one's own poison but at another's will makes all effort impossible.

19. Even if, therefore, you are confronting me with a fresh heap of accusations, I am not sorry—no, I am not—that I went back on my unflinching resolve to die:[95] as it was, I was dying a parricide. (2) My father, who accuses me for refusing to drink, by this time would be saying: "He had been caught in the act, he could not deny it." I would now be the thrice-disowned son,[96] and he would be asserting that I had not had the courage to come back to face my judges. (3) It was well indeed that I poured away the drink, as if I had opted for life again; when poison[97] looked to have been caught in the act, no one would be believed

---

[96] The previous charges would now be believed.
[97] I.e., an attempt to poison someone else.

4 ideo bibisse crederetur, quia sibi paraverat. Dic nunc:
   "Non fui passurus, si bibere voluisses." Deinde hoc sic
5 probas, ut me hodieque coneris occidere?[114] Non eras passurus. Quando, per fidem, inicis manus? Potuit eadem,
6 potuit peragi brevitate, qua iusseras. Non eras passurus.
   Deinde non timuisti ne mihi animum pereundi vel hoc
7 faceret, quod putabam me iuberi? Facinus est, si morior,
   ut postea quaeratur an volueris occidere. Tu licet invidiam
   vocis illius alterius mentis simulatione defendas, occisuri
   tamen fuit ipsum experimentum, nec interest rigoris quae-
8 dam patiaris an temptes. Numquam movebit patrem filius
   hoc, quod moritur, quem non movit hoc, quod paratus est
   mori.
9   Quid nunc faciam, iudices, pertinacissimo rigori? In
10 quod me componam patientiae genus? Videtis hominem,
   quem nullus animi mei status mutat, quem constantia
   nostra, quem offendit infirmitas. Vivere volo: proturbat,
11 expellit. Mori conor: interpellat, exagitat. Iam fortassis
   aliquid, si nobis hodieque clementia vestra succurrerit,
   paravit, invenit. Quis[115] finis, quis exitus incredibilium ma-

---

114 *et hic et infra post* iuberi (§6) *interrog. dist. Håk.*
115 qui B V, *sed vd. Pas.*

---

98 Drinking it would have been a sign of guilt; see also 17.15.7
and n. 79.   99 You are trying to kill me today (on the parricide charge), just as you did when you told me to take poison.
100 Sc., so you claim (17.19.4).
101 To stop me killing myself (DAR).
102 So saying "Drink" was a dangerous game, if you did not
mean it.
103 Sc., *only* afterward, when I can no longer contradict your
claim that you were just testing my intentions.

to have drunk it because he had mixed it for himself.[98] (4) *Now* go ahead and say: "If you had been willing to drink, I should not have allowed it." So is this the way you prove the point—by trying to kill me today too?[99] (5) You would not have allowed it.[100] So when do you lay a restraining hand on me?[101] The act could have been done, it could indeed, as quickly as you gave the order. (6) You would not have allowed it. Then were you not afraid that the very fact that I thought I was being given an order would make me resolve to die?[102] (7) It is criminal, if I die, for the question to be raised *afterward*[103] whether you wished to kill me. Even if you defend the hateful thing you said by pretending you spoke with a different intention, the very experiment was the action of one meaning to kill: as regards severity, it makes no difference whether you allow an act or attempt it. (8) The fact that a son is dying will never move a father, if he was not moved by his readiness to die.[104]

(9) What am I to do now, judges, in the face of this unbending severity? For what kind of endurance am I supposed to make myself ready? (10) You see a man unaffected by any state of my mind, who is offended by my constancy, by my weakness. I wish to live: he throws me out, he expels me. I try to die: he interrupts me, he harasses me. (11) Perhaps, if your clemency comes to my aid today too,[105] he has still got something up his sleeve. What

---

[104] A father unmoved by his son's intention to commit suicide will not be moved by his actually dying (DAR). The implication is that this is a father who is ruthless enough to order his son to poison himself and to watch him dying.

[105] As in the three trials I have already won against my father.

lorum? De filio absoluto fecit ut mori mallet, de moriente
ut vivere.[116]

20. Vos vero, sanctissimi viri, quo iam ambitu, quibus
possim[117] convenire precibus? Ille vester infelix, ille vester
absolutus flere vetitus est: non habet gratiam suam totiens
genua complecti, et ad fatigatam misericordiam novi dis-
2 criminis pondus attulimus. O mors semper imparata[118]
miseris, negata cupientibus, quando succurres? Me in-
3 felicem, perdidi venenum! Sed quatenus aliquid, pater,
expectationi tuae repromisi, nolo desperes. Fruere quin
immo ante suprema, ante exitum meum hac voce: "Vi-
4 cisti." Nescio quidem quod rursus eligam obitus genus, an
placeat reparare virus infelix, sed praedico, testor: quaecumque sederit ratio[119] leti, miserere, ne iubeas, miserere,
ne cogas. Facilius me occident[120] gemitus tui, lacrimae
5 tuae. Et, ne mihi putes[121] illam secreti nostri excidisse vocem: venenum quidem te iubente bibere non potui, quandoque tamen hoc occidet, quod bibere iussisti.

[116] -e *Obr.*: -et *codd.*
[117] -sim (*ex* -em, *ut vid.*) M: -sem *cett.*
[118] -par- ς (*def. Pas.*): -per- B V: -p- Φ
[119] ratio *Sch.* (*corrob. Håk.*[2] *139*): traditio *codd.*
[120] -dent *Håk.*[2] *139*: -deret B: -derent V Φ
[121] -es ς: -etis *codd.*

end, what outcome for evils beyond belief? He has made an acquitted son prefer to die, a dying son prefer to live.

20. But as for you, most revered sirs, how can I win your support, how pray to you? That unlucky man you know so well, that man you acquitted, has been forbidden to weep.[106] It wins no favor to embrace your knees so often: it is to a wearied pity that I have brought the burden of a fresh dispute. (2) O death ever unavailable to the wretched, ever denied to those who long for it, when will you come to my aid? Unlucky me, I have wasted my poison! (3) But since, father, I have raised your hopes a little, I do not want you to despair. Indeed, before I die, before my end, enjoy these words: "You have won." (4) I do not know what kind of death to choose on a second occasion—am I to make up another dose of the potion that was not successful before? But I declare in all solemnity: whatever means of death I decide upon, pity me enough not to give me orders, pity me enough not to apply pressure. I shall more easily be killed by your groans, by your tears. (5) And, in case you imagine that I have forgotten the word you used at our secret meeting: I may not have been able to drink poison when you ordered me to, but one day or other I shall be killed by your having ordered me to drink it.

---

[106] Because he has now wearied the judges with his laments, this being his fourth lawsuit. See below and, e.g., Sen. *Controv.* 7.3.2 (on the same theme) (AS).

DECLAMATION 18

INTRODUCTION

A handsome youth is talked of as having an incestuous affair with his own mother; Father tortures him to death in a secluded part of their house, without witnesses, then refuses to disclose to Mother what he has learned from the interrogation. She accuses him of ill-treatment.[1] This piece is the accusation speech by Mother's advocate, while *DM* 19 presents Father's defense.

A gloomy variation of the conflict between Fathers and Sons,[2] this speech brings to the fore the thorny topic of incest, a taboo often featuring in mythology and literature.[3] The speaker does not play down the enormity of the allegation made against his client, but uses it against Father: his ultimate aim is to show that Father tortured Son in haste when he did not have the slightest proof of his incest with Mother (11.1–6),[4] that he killed him just to conceal that his interrogation had failed to extort any con-

[1] On this charge, see Introduction to *DM* 8.
[2] Breij (2015, 26–40).
[3] See Breij (2015, 40–59).
[4] In fact, the only point that Father can mention in his own defense is that Son was handsome (repeatedly in 9.1–10.4): contrast on this *DM* 19.

fession (14.3–4), and that his current silence is a desperate attempt to avoid admitting all this (16.1–6).[5]

Since the only motive for Father's initiative was a rumor, the speaker dwells at length on the factors that could have fostered gossip about the incest: all mothers love their sons as if they have fallen in love with them (10.8), and only someone who does not himself feel paternal love (like Father: 3.5–6) could mistake such affection for an illicit passion (4.1). Mother, additionally, had always been forced to love Son more fondly than normal, because she had to compensate by her affection for Father's harshness (3.5–6).[6] Knowing all this, and being aware of the chastity that Mother had always shown in her life (3.2), Father should have *protected* his family from such an infamous allegation (5.4–6.1, 11.1–4); instead, he believed the rumor so promptly that one might suspect that he had started it himself (4.1–3, 8.2–4; cf. 1.1).

In view of the seriousness of the allegation, the speaker does not absolutely deny Father's right to resort to torture; but he should have admitted to the interrogation either Mother (13.6) or a domestic council (12.11), if not the whole city, which was gossiping about Son (12.8–9):[7] by the secrecy of the interrogation and his present silence, Father only means to cover up the wickedness of his crime (14.5).

The speech may be analyzed as follows:[8]

> PROEM 1.1–2.6
> NARRATION 3.1–5.1

---

[5] See with further details Breij (2015, 78–82).
[6] A recurring motif: cf., e.g., 10.3.1–6, 10.4.1–3.
[7] See also Introduction to *DM* 19.
[8] Cf. Breij (2015, 89–92).

DECLAMATION 18

ARGUMENTATION
    Propositio causae (expanded to include an
       excessus on the inadequacy of this lawsuit)
       5.2–3
    Refutatio 5.4–10.7
    Confirmatio 10.8–15.6
EPILOGUE 15.7–17.5

The subject of *DM* 18 and 19 must have been well
known in the schools of rhetoric of the first century AD:
Tacitus and Quintilian mention it,[9] and close resemblances
may be detected also in the *Minor Declamation* 328.[10]
However, these sources seems to refer to the matter only
from Father's perspective (presented in *DM* 19), while
there is no trace of a speech from Mother's side, which
may therefore be a conscious innovation.[11] Both *DM* 18
and *DM* 19 were probably composed sometime in the
early third century AD; all evidence suggests that the two
speeches are the work of two different authors, each of
whom apparently worked without knowing, or without taking into consideration, the other side's arguments.[12]

[9] Cf. Tac. *Dial.* 35.5, and especially Quint. 9.2.79–80; see Breij
(2015, 41–42, 77–78).
[10] Winterbottom (1984, 502); Breij (2015, 86–87).
[11] Breij (2015, 78).
[12] See General Introduction, §4 with n. 119.

18

Infamis in matrem I

MALAE TRACTATIONIS SIT ACTIO. Speciosum filium, infamem, tamquam incestum cum matre committeret, pater in secreta parte domus torsit et occidit in tormentis. Interrogat illum mater, quid ex filio compererit; nolentem dicere malae tractationis accusat.

1. Etsi, iudices, callidissimus parricida facinus suum sic ordinavit, ut vobis matrem faceret invisam, sive dissimularet misera mortem filii sui, sive quereretur, tantaque monstrorum novitate circumdatam eo perduxit, ut sibi videatur infamaturus iterum vel patientiam nostram vel dolorem, matri tamen, ⟨in⟩[1] cuius calamitatibus vel[2] mini-

1 *add.* ⟨⟩
2 vel *Håk.* (*H.-Sz.* 502 *(c)*): ne *codd., del. Gron.:* nunc *Watt[3]* 57–58

---

[1] Father: "parricide" can be used of anyone causing—or even attempting—the murder of a close relative.
[2] If she did not show sorrow for Son's death, Father would

The son suspected of incest with his mother I

ILL-TREATMENT IS TO BE ACTIONABLE. A handsome son was being talked of as committing incest with his mother. His father tortured him in a remote part of the house and killed him in the process. The mother asks him what he learned from his son. He refuses to say, and she accuses him of ill-treatment.

(Speech of the mother's advocate)

1. Although, judges, this most cunning parricide[1] has so arranged his crime as to make the mother hated in your eyes whether she (poor wretch) took no notice of her son's death or lodged a complaint,[2] and has brought her, surrounded by such a novel set of awful circumstances, to a point where he thinks he can cast aspersions for a second time[3] on either our[4] acquiescence or our resentment, nevertheless this mother, ⟨among⟩ whose calamities the

have claimed that she was just trying to conceal her amour; if she did, he would have used it as proof of her incestuous love.

[3] It is hinted that Father initiated the original rumor (cf. 18.4.2–3, 18.8.2–4).

[4] = of Mother and her party (involved for further pathos, as, e.g., in 18.16.3).

mum sibi vindicat orbitas locum, ideo ad vos fugiendum
2 fuit, ut sciretis non illi praestari quod tacet maritus. Laudo,
iudices, laudo miseram, quod interrogare noluit domi,
3 quod nihil fecit et ipsa secreto. Hic coram civitate, coram
liberis ac parentibus et, licet dissimulare parricida videatur, coram rumore, mater inquirit quid tormentis unici
quaesierit, quid morte compererit.[3] Respondeat saltim
4 reus, fateatur ⟨vel⟩[4] iratus.[5] Cur iam peracta[6] crudelitate
modestiae fronte substitit?[7] Nec uxori potest videri parcere, de qua scire voluit an esset incesta, nec filio, quem,
tamquam sciret, occidit.

5   Ante omnia igitur, iudices, mulier infelicissimi pudoris
hoc ab adfectibus publicis petit, ne vobis accusare videatur: ream se incesti, ream parricidii putat, exhibet populo
conscientiam suam et adversus quemcumque sermonem,
quodcumque secretum marito famaeque praestat interro-
6 gandi potestatem. Vellet innocentiam suis probare visceribus, vellet in eculeos, in ignes hanc miseram praecipitare
pietatem. 2. Ignoscite, iudices, impatientiae, quae contra

      ³ -perit B V S
      ⁴ *add. Wint.*⁷ *166–67*
      ⁵ (-tur) invitus *Breij*¹ *coll. 18.16.1. gravius distinxi, nempe*
respondeat eqs. spectant ad superiora (inquirit *eqs.*)
      ⁶ iam *Sch.*, (in) peracta Φ: inperata B: imp- V
      ⁷ *sic dist. Breij*¹

     ⁵ Judges.
     ⁶ I.e., that the two are not conniving (see also 18.14.7).
     ⁷ Unlike Father with Son.
     ⁸ Until now, he has *not* answered Mother's questions.
     ⁹ Without, that is, going on to reveal what he learned from the

loss of her son perhaps claims the smallest place, has been forced to have recourse to you,[5] in order that you might learn that her husband's silence is not a present from him to her.[6] (2) I commend, yes, judges, I commend the poor woman for not wanting to question him at home,[7] for not—like him!—doing anything in secret. (3) It is here, in the presence of the city, in the presence of children and parents, and—though the parricide seems to want to forget this—in the presence of rumor, that the mother puts her questions: what he sought to find out by torturing his only son, what he learned by his death. Let him answer at least now, when he is on trial,[8] let him set the record straight, angry ⟨though he may be⟩. (4) Why, now that his cruel action is complete, has he put on a show of restraint and cut himself off short?[9] For he cannot be thought to be sparing the feelings either of his wife, about whom he was willing to learn whether she was guilty of incest, or of his son, whom he killed as though he already knew.

(5) Before anything else then, judges, a woman of such ill-starred chastity asks this of a sympathetic public, that you should not think of her as an accuser: she regards *herself* as being on trial for incest, on trial for parricide; she is putting her good conscience on display before the people, and giving her husband and public opinion the chance to question her so as to counter any gossip, any secret talk. (6) She would be glad to prove her innocence at the expense of her own vital organs, to hurl this unhappy maternal affection of hers upon the racks, upon the fires. 2. Forgive, judges, her lack of self-restraint, which seethes

---

torture. As the speaker proceeds to say, Father can hardly be keeping silent to spare the feelings of Wife or Son.

callidissimam dissimulationem libertate doloris exaestuat;
incestum probaretur silentio patris, si taceret et mater.

2   Equidem, iudices, tam contrarios adfectus senis satis
admirari, satis stupere non possum: in rumore tam suspicax, post tormenta ‹tam›[8] patiens, modo ad fabulas vulga-
resque sermones pronus ac facilis, in orbitate, in parrici-
3   dio, ‹in›[9] reatus quoque dolore conticuit. Quo repente
conversus est, in quam modestiam desperationemque de-
fecit? Torsit tamquam dicturum, tacet tamquam dixerit.
4   Fidem igitur vestram, iudices, ne cui praestet magnae severitatis auctoritatem non posse defendi, neve ideo suspicari nefanda malitis,[10] quia se silentio parricida tutatur.[11]
5   Parcere nunc illum cuiquam tacendo creditis? Loqui se
cum maxime putat, et, si bene artes et profundae[12] mentis
consilia perspicio, respondere sibi videtur plus[13] quam
6   mater interrogat. Fallitur, quisquis hunc esse credit inexplicabilis doloris aestum et inter silentii confessionisque
causas miserum pudorem! Alium exitum non habet quam
ut respondere nolle videatur, quisquis filium occidit et
probare non potest propter quod debuerit[14] occidi.

       3. Coniungat quantum volet nocentissimus senex cum

---

8 add. Håk.[2] 139–40
9 add. Håk.[2] 140.65
10 -da malitis C[2]: -dam (-da E) alius codd.
11 tuta- Sch.: mira- codd. (frustra def. Håk.[2] 140, Breij[1])
12 -da Håk. coll. 2.14.1
13 prius Bur., sed cf. 19.14.9
14 deb- M γ* β (def. Håk.[2] 140–41): erub- cett.

---

10 Cf. 19.1.5 on Father's amazement.
11 I.e., incest.

with the frankness of grief in face of a most cunning pretense of ignorance; the father's silence would prove incest
if the mother kept silent too.

(2) For my part, judges, I cannot express wonder
enough, amazement enough[10] at the old man's inconsistency of attitude: during the rumor so suspicious, after the
torture ⟨so⟩ forbearing; not so long ago easily swayed by
rumor and common gossip, he has, despite losing his son,
despite killing, ⟨despite⟩ the distress, too, of being put on
trial, he has fallen silent. (3) What is this sudden turn he
has taken, what is this restraint and hopelessness he has
succumbed to? He tortured his son as though he was likely
to talk, he keeps quiet as though he did talk. (4) I ask you
then, judges, not to let inability to mount a defense give a
man a reputation for strict morality, nor to choose to suspect unspeakable acts[11] just because a parricide shields
himself by keeping silent. (5) Do you really suppose that
he is covering up for someone by his present silence? He
thinks it is precisely now that he is speaking,[12] and, if I see
aright into his devious mind and the plans buried deep in
his heart, he imagines he is answering more than the
mother is asking. (6) If anyone supposes this to be a surge
of an inescapable pain, an unhappy shame torn between
reasons to be silent and reasons to confess, that is a mistake! Anyone who has killed his son and cannot prove why
he had to be killed has no recourse, except to appear unwilling to reply.

3. Let the nefarious old man connect his silence with

[12] Because his silence can be construed as an accusation.

rumore populi silentium suum, et relatura[15] ordinem tris‐
tissimae sortis conlata malignitate cludat ora, compescat
adfectus.[16] Securi tamen estote, mortales, fas est, fas est
innocentissimae matri velut in templis, velut apud ipsos
2 proclamare superos: "Amavi filium meum!" Matrona, iu‐
dices, cuius puellares annos, primam rudemque coniugii
mentem nulla libidinum respersit infamia, cui impudens
rumor, suspicax maritus nihil umquam potuit obicere nisi
filium, quae pudicitiae prima fiducia est, edidit partum
quem maritus agnosceret. Non timuit ne stupra furtivos‐
que concubitus parvuli vultus aut crescentis infantiae[17]
3 similitudo detegeret. Natum de te[18] continuo, si quid ipsi
creditis, impatientius complexa quam reliqui[19] parentes,
non in nutrices nec in ministeria seposuit: suis aluit ube‐
4 ribus, suo fovit amplexu. Numquid et hos annos, parricida,
numquid et pueritiam miseri iuvenis infamas? Actum est
de sacrorum nominum fide, si, ut videatur innocens mater,
5 aetas tantum filii facit. Accendebat hanc erga unicum op‐
timae matris impatientiam rigidus pater, asper maritus,
nec[20] sibi videbatur parum implere quem pro duobus

15 -ra Φ (def. Sh. B.² 216, Wint. ap. Breij¹): -re B V: -rae π
(vind. Håk.² 141–42)   16 adfe- Reitz.² 45–46 post affe- Sch.
(cf. ad rem 18.4.8, 19.5.7): adie- B: abie- V: aditus Φ: audi- ς
17 -anti- C² β: -ami- cett.   18 se ς, sed cf. Bur.
19 -quae C²E, sed cf. Breij¹
20 nec Wint.⁷ 167: et codd.

13 I.e., give the impression by his silence that Son was guilty,
thus confirming the rumors.   14 = over and above the mal‐
ice of the people who fostered the rumor.
15 = Father may be silent, but Mother must speak out.

322

the popular rumor[13] as much as he likes: let him, contributing his own share of the malice,[14] close the mouth that would have told the story of the melancholy sequence of events, let him restrain his feelings. But[15] rest assured, mortals: it is right, it is right for a totally innocent mother to cry as if in a temple, as if in the very presence of the gods: "I loved my son." (2) Here we have a lady, judges, whose girlhood and character before marriage were stained by no scandalous talk of sexual liaisons. Shameless rumor, a suspicious husband could never bring anything against her—except her son. She produced—and this is the first guarantee of her chastity—a child whom her husband could acknowledge. She was not worried that the face of the babe or any similarity[16] of the growing child would lead to the detection of illicit sex or secretive beddings. (3) The child you begot she straightway took into her arms—more eagerly, if you believe her, than other parents. She did not banish him for wet nurses and servants to bring up; she fed him at her own breast, cherished him in her own embrace. (4) Surely, parricide, you do not cast aspersions on *these* years too, or on the *boyhood* of the poor youth? All is over with trust within a family[17] if it is only the *age*[18] of her son that lets a mother be thought innocent. (5) The sternness of the father, the hardheartedness of the husband, just fired up this excellent mother's passionate love for her only son: she did not feel she was giving him too little affection even when she was having to supply it on behalf of the two

---

[16] Of course, to someone other than her husband. Cf. Fr. 4.

[17] Literally, "with faith in the sacred names" (of mother and son).

[18] I.e., an age too young to arouse suspicions of an affair.

[QUINTILIAN]

conferebat adfectum. Rarus hic namque ad oscula, diffici-
lis amplexibus et qui unicum aspiceret animo, quo quandoque posset occidere, fecit ut notabilior esset caritas
6 matris. Omnis igitur miserae sermo cum filio, omnis in
publicum pariter egressus. Gaudebat etiam quod laudan-
dus occursibus, quod omni frequentia coetuque conspi-
cuus, populo iam ipse fateretur quod plus amaretur a
matre. 4. Miseremini, iudices, ne nefandas suspiciones
maritum ex ullius²¹ traxisse credatis indiciis: suum rigorem, suum tantum secutus est animum. Filium si non
ames, videatur tibi mater adamasse.²²

2 Questurum²³ nunc me, iudices, putatis de licentia sermonis humani? Ego vero iuxta hunc patrem non accuso
3 rumorem. Quae materia fabulae tam impudentis, qui fuerit auctor, iste probavit qui credidit. Facillimum fuit ut
loqueretur populus de incesto, de quo mirabatur patrem
suspicari.

4 Haec sunt, iudices, quae mater fecit secure, simpliciter, palam, coram marito, coram civitate. Referat nunc
5 suum iste secretum. Iuvenem, quae integritatis prima
simplicitas est, nihil timentem in partem domus, qua nulla
proclamatio, nullus poterat gemitus audiri, rapuit, abduxit.

---

21 ill- Φ*
22 *sic dist. Gr.-Mer.*: *interrog. vulg., sed cf. Håk.² 142*
23 quest- C² (*vind. Reitz.² 83.6*): qu(a)esit- *codd.*

---

19 Contrast Father's version in 19.2.5; see also 19.4.7.
20 Cf. 18.17.2.
21 A man with no notion of parental love may mistake maternal affection for incestuous passion.
22 Cf. n. 3.

324

of them.[19] For *he* rarely kissed the child, and hugged him only with reluctance. He was a man able to look at his only son with the feelings that would one day make him able to kill him:[20] and this only made the fondness of the mother the more obvious. (6) So the unhappy woman talked to no one but her son; she never went out in public without him. She was overjoyed, too, that her son, the object of praise by those who met him, the cynosure of all eyes in every crowd and every gathering, already proclaimed to all and sundry that it was his mother who loved him more. 4. For pity's sake, judges, do not believe that the husband based his wicked suspicions on anyone's evidence: all he was doing was following the lead of his own harshness, his own cast of mind. If a man happens not to love his son, he may well think the mother has fallen in love with him.[21]

(2) Do you imagine, judges, that I shall now go on to complain of the license of men's gossip? In fact, with this father before me, I do not accuse rumor. (3) *He* proved what the foundation of this shameless fiction was, and who started it—when he believed it.[22] It was all too easy for people to talk of a case of incest when they saw with amazement that the father suspected it.

(4) This,[23] judges, is what the mother did, serenely, straightforwardly, openly, in front of her husband, in front of the city. Let *him* now tell us his secret. (5) He snatched up the young man, who was quite unafraid (a naïveté which is the prime sign of innocence), and whisked him off to a part of the house from which no cries, no groans could be heard. There he put an end to him with lashes,

[23] Summarizing the narrative of her previous life (18.3.2–6).

Ibi verberibus, ignibus, omni crudelitatis arte consumpsit.

6 Quis umquam, iudices, peius de innocentia temporum, de sacris meruit adfectibus? Torsit filium ut probaretur incestum; occidit ut crederetur.

7 Ponite nunc ante oculos, iudices, duorum parentum confessionem. Mater exclamat: "Filium amavi!"; pater dicit: "Occidi." Nefas est ut[24] utrumque putetis innocentem.

8 Iam quidem, nocentissime senex, grande deprehensae feritatis indicium[25] est quod, cum filium occideris, ut interrogeris expectas: non erumpis ab illo secreto tuo terribilis in publicum, et homo filii cruore perfusus non proclamas, non deos hominesque testaris, non occidis et matrem?

9 Scilicet modestia te scelerum tuorum cum[26] maxime decet, et ideo tibi relinquis unde sis quietae patientiae: 5. miser parcis uxori, coniugales deos et lectuli iura revereris. O quam non habet nec quod mentiatur!

2 Malae tractationis agimus. Placet ergo, iudices, ut illa voce, qua matrimoniorum conquerimur iniurias, ⟨illo⟩[27] gemitu, quo corporum contumelias, damna cultus[28] et negatos in publicum deflemus egressus, orbitates ac liberorum suprema plangantur? Quid tamen facere vultis

3 miserum dolorem, si non habet aliam sexus hic legem, si intra iuris huius angustias omnis nuptiarum querela

---

24 ut β (def. Breij¹): om. cett.
25 iud- B V γ β
26 quam Φ
27 add. Wint. ap. Breij¹
28 -na cu- Gr.-Mer.: -na, cu- vulg., sed vd. Håk.² 142

---

24 Cf. the theme: "The mother asks him what he learned."
25 Ironical.

with fire, with every refinement of cruelty. (6) Who, judges, ever deserved less well of the innocence of our age, of sacred relationships? He tortured his son to have incest proved; he killed him to have it believed.

(7) Now take a close look, judges, at the assertions of the two parents. The mother cries: "I loved my son!"; the father says: "I killed him." It would be wicked for you to think both of them innocent. (8) Now, you most guilty old man, it is a signal proof of your barbarity being laid bare that, after killing your son, you wait to be questioned.[24] Don't you storm out of that secluded place into the open air, terrible to behold? Drenched as you are in your son's blood, don't you shriek aloud, don't you call gods and men to witness, don't you kill the mother too? (9) Obviously[25] some restraint in your wickedness is in order at this very point, and that is why you are allowing yourself room to be quiet and forbearing: 5. wretched though you are, you are sparing your wife, you are showing respect for the gods of marriage and the rights of the bed.—The fact is, he doesn't even have a lie to tell!

(2) We are bringing a case for ill-treatment.[26] Are you happy then, judges, that bereavement and the death of children should be lamented in the same terms with which we complain of slights within marriage, with ⟨the same⟩ groans with which we bewail physical maltreatment, deprivation of finery and denial of permission to go out in public?[27] (3) But what do you want unhappy grief to do, if this sex has no other law to turn to, if every complaint of married women has to confine itself within the narrow

---

[26] Cf. 19.5.1.   [27] Cf. 8.6.1–4, 10.9.2–3; also, e.g., Cyr. *RG* VIII.389.25–27 Walz.

[QUINTILIAN]

constricta est? Mater, quae de morte filii maritum malae tractationis accusat, non vindicat, sed probare contenta est quod non debuerit occidi.

4   Omittamus paulisper, iudices, orbitatis tristissimae dolorem, et in parricidio malae tractationis reddamus aliunde causas. Ita non iuste quereretur uxor, si diceret: "Adulterium de me facile suspicatus es, cito credidisti"?

5   Matronalis pudor tutelam non ex sua tantum innocentia habet, infirmitas huius sexus non potest totam probitatis[29] existimationem debere tantum moribus suis: omnis in feminas venit maritorum praedicatione reverentia, omnes

6   sermones originem de vestris pectoribus accipiunt. Tristior vultus, querela, fastidium, fatum est coniugii:[30] de pudore pronuntiat, mittit in ora populi, mittit in fabulas. Hoc proxima ministeria narrant, hoc exteri putant.[31]

7   Nemo peiore exemplo temere de uxore credit, quam cui omnes credituri sunt.

8   Sane faciat vos pronos ad suspiciones nimia caritas, ex[32] impatientia diligendi plerumque descendat ut credas facile quod timeas, furtiva stupra raptosque concubitus obiciat vel falso maritus: fas est, fieri solet; parcius tamen, si iam sit et mater, si in fidem castitatis uxoria fecunditate profecerit. Quid, si sit iam iuvene quoque filio severa, iam nurum nepotesque prospiciat? 6. Miseremini temporum,

---

29 pr- ⊊ (corrob. Håk.[2] 143): impr- codd.
30 -gi (dat.) Håk., sed cf. Kr.-Str. 136–37.63
31 imp- Wint.[7] 167 vel rep- Wint.[9], sed cf. e.g. 19.14.10
32 ex Dess.[2] : et codd.: et ⟨ex⟩ man. alia in C, sed vd. Breij[1]

---

28 Husbands'.   29 I.e., the husband.
30 Literally, "you" (plur.).

bounds of *this* statute? A mother who, when her son has died, accuses her husband of ill-treatment is not seeking revenge: she is content merely to prove that that son should not have been killed.

(4) For a short time, judges, let us pass over the grief caused by a most painful loss, and, though this is a case of parricide, let us look elsewhere for reasons for a charge of ill-treatment. Would then the wife not be justified in lodging a complaint if she said: "You suspected too readily that I had committed adultery, you were too quick to believe"? (5) A married woman does not look for support of her virtue only to her own innocence, the weakness of this sex cannot owe a reputation for integrity merely to a woman's own behavior: all respect for women is the result of praise from their husbands, all gossip derives from *your*[28] hearts. (6) A rather black look, a word of complaint, an expression of disgust seals a wife's fate: it pronounces a verdict on her chastity, it casts her upon the lips of the people, it makes her the subject of tales. This is what the in-house servants talk about, this is what outsiders think. (7) No hasty believer in a story about a wife sets a worse example than the man whom everybody is going to believe.[29]

(8) True, excessive affection may make a man[30] over-ready to feel suspicion, passionate love may cause you to be quick to believe what you fear, a husband may even bring a mistaken charge of secret liaisons and moments snatched in bed: that is possible, it often happens. But not so often if she is already a mother too, if she has by her fecundity gone a long way toward being trusted as a chaste wife. What if she is by now a formidable lady, with a grown up son into the bargain, and a daughter-in-law and grandchildren in her sights? 6. Take pity on the times we live in,

329

ne alienae innocentiae interpretationem de suis quisque
moribus trahat. Incestum posse fieri pater hoc solo vult
probare, quod filium potuit occidere.

2   "Rumor" inquit "fuit." En[33] hercules cui contra rerum
3 naturam, contra parentes liberosque credatur! "Rumor
fuit." Hoc ergo sic audiemus, tamquam si diceres: "Conscius detulit servus, nuntiavit ancilla, improvisus adstiti,
4 dum non timeor adveni"? Rogo, iudices, utrum credibi-
lius putatis incestum de matre an de rumore mendacium? Rem impudentissimam populus loquendo fecerat,
nisi pater credidisset.

5   Pessimum, iudices, humanarum mentium malum est
quod semper avidius nefanda finguntur, nec umquam[34] se
maius operae pretium putant maligni facere sermones,
quam cum incredibilia quasi deprehensa narrantur. Necesse est contentiosius loquaris quod probare non possis,
et adfirmationem sumit ex homine quicquid non habet ex
6 veritate. Est tamen hoc iniquissimum de loquacitate populi, quod plerumque accendit[35] contentio non creden-
tium famam:[36] materiam miraris rumoris, de qua nemo
7 nec sibi credit, quam qui narrat adsignat alii.[37] Rumor
res sine teste, sine indice,[38] res ex incertis improbissima,

---

33 en *Watt*[3] 58: est *codd.*: et ᔓ
34 umq- *Franc.* (*firm. Håk.*): usq- *codd.*
35 -cend- ᔓ: -cid- *codd.*   36 -am ᔓ: -a *codd.*
37 famam—alii *dist. Håk.*   38 iud- M AE δ β, *sed vd. Breij*[1]

---

31 And so, by his standards, his son could have done the same
with *him*.
32 I.e., despite the relations normally subsisting between them.
33 I.e., his believing it was more shameful still.

do not let each man judge the innocence of others by the standards of his own behavior. Here we have a father who wants to prove that incest can take place by pointing to one thing alone: that he was capable of killing his son.[31]

(2) "There was a rumor," he says. Here, by heaven, is something that deserves credence, despite nature, despite parents and children![32] (3) "There was a rumor." Shall we then take this to mean: "A complicit slave laid information, a slave girl passed on the news, I was close by at a moment they did not expect it, I came on the scene when my presence was not feared"? (4) I ask you, judges: which do you think more likely, incest in a mother or falsehood in a rumor? The people would have done the most shameful thing in the world by their gossip—except that the father believed it.[33]

(5) The worst feature of human hearts, judges, is that wicked things are always invented more eagerly,[34] and malign gossip never thinks itself better employed than when the unbelievable is being spread around as detected fact. One has to put a case more strongly when one cannot prove it, for what is not confirmed by the truth is confirmed by the man.[35] (6) But the most unfair thing about ordinary people's loose tongues is that often the flame of a rumor is fanned by the emphatic expressions of those who do *not* believe it: you cannot but wonder what foundation a rumor has when no one believes even himself on the subject, when anyone who tells the story ascribes it to another. (7) Rumor is something where there is no witness, no one laying information; it is the wickedest of un-

[34] Than truthful ones.   [35] The way a speaker puts a case is of equal importance to its factual basis.

maligna, fallax—et similis silentio tuo. 7. Quid et ipse de rumore senseris, vis breviter probem? Tormentis quaerendum putasti an verum diceret.

2 Sane sit aliqua publici sermonis auctoritas in illis, ad quae fas est populi pervenire notitiam. Video[39] cur adulteria proferantur in fabulas: explicantur per ministeria, per conscios.[40] Habent inconsulta gaudia: pars voluptatis

3 videtur esse iactatio. Facinus vero, cui, si[41] fas est ut illud humanae mentis capiat audacia, circumdatur undique nox profunda, densior caligo tenebrarum, quod nocentes suis quoque oculis vix fatentur, non servo, non creditur an-

4 cillae. Quid internuntiis, quid opus est ministeriis? Sufficit animus duorum, explicat omne filius materque secretum. Incestum tanto incredibilius est, quanto et[42] de illo plures locuntur.

5 O misera condicio sexus, cuius ipsae plerumque virtutes fabulas parant! "Cur ista nullis in publicum gaudet egressibus? Unde adversum omnes tam rigida conversatio, tam severus adfectus? Nihil concupiscit, nihil ergo deside-

6 rat? Filius possidet cuncta tempora, universos occupavit adfectus, filius matris tota iactatio est. Rogo, numquid

7 adamavit?" Mihi crede, non est nefandorum ista simplicitas. Da ut sit haec inter matrem ac filium conscientia: parcent osculis palam, abstinebunt coram patre complexibus, omnis familiaritas substringetur in publico, sermones,

39 -e Sch., sed cf. Breij[1]
40 fabulas—conscios dist. Gron.
41 om. V
42 om. A, sed vd. Breij[1]

36 Cf. 11.6.9.   37 Contrast 18.12.4.

certain things,[36] full of malice and deceit—just like your silence, in fact. 7. Do you want me to give you a short proof of what you too felt about rumor? You thought torture was needed to find out if it was telling the truth.

(2) Public talk may indeed carry some weight when it concerns matters that can come into the public domain. I can see why adulteries leak out and become matter for gossip: they are accomplished by means of slaves, of accomplices. Recklessness has its delights: flaunting seems to be essential to pleasure. (3) But a crime which—if it is possible for the audacity of the human mind to undertake it at all—is surrounded on every side by deep night, a dense black shadow, a crime which the guilty scarcely confess to their own eyes, is not entrusted to a slave or a maid.[37] (4) What need is there of intermediaries, of accessories? The intention of the pair is enough, son and mother can carry out the whole covert project by themselves. Incest becomes the more unlikely the more people speak of it.

(5) How unfortunate women are! So often their very virtues give rise to talk: "Why does this woman not take pleasure in going out? How come she is so austere in her dealings with everybody, so restrained in expressing emotion? Has she then no desires, no wants? (6) Her son occupies all her time, he has taken over all her feelings, her son is his mother's one boast. I ask, has she fallen in love?" (7) Believe me, open behavior like that is not characteristic of the unspeakably wicked. Grant an understanding of this kind between mother and son: they will be wary of kissing openly, they will abstain from embraces when the father is present; all signs of intimacy will be repressed in

occursus coram servulis libertisque vitabunt, et maximi
sceleris ardor captabit adfectare gravitatem. 8. Elige, parricida, quod voles: incestum diligens suspectum non erit,
neglegens deprehendetur.[43]

2   Sed quid ego sic ago, tamquam inauditum, incredibile
scelus locutus sit populus? Teneo in hoc sermone facinus
3 unius.[44] "Mali mariti non interest, incestum de uxore fin-
gat an credat."[45] Quid?[46] Iste ergo ‹sermo›[47] non timuit
tam nefandae rei famam, nec ad aures patris pervenire
rumor erubuit? Dissimules licet, a te malignitas accepit
ortum, te secutus est quisquis hoc ausus est narrare, pro-
4 ferre. Da bonum patrem, bonum maritum; dicturum me
putas: "Non credet"? Nesciet esse rumorem. Ite nunc,
iudices, et adhuc dubitate quis famae fuerit auctor, cuius
pater agit causam.

   9. "Speciosus" inquit "fuit." Non magis hoc facinus in
2 matre est quam crimen in filio. "Speciosus fuit." Ut hoc

43 -detur β: -ditur (-dit A) *cett.*
44 *dist. Reitz.*² 62 (*corrob. Håk.*² 143–44): post mariti *vulg.*
45 *verba personata significavi*   46 *dist. B. Asc.*²
47 *supplevi:* ergo *in* sermo *emend. Reitz.*² 62

---

38 Either way Mother is not guilty of incest: if she had taken
pains to hide it, it would not have been suspected (as it was); if
she had not taken pains to hide it, Father would have caught them
in the act (which he did not).
39 Because his behavior would be hurtful to his wife in either
case. But Father had been a *good* husband—as he implies in this
supposed disclaimer—so he would have never made up the rumor about incest; he could only believe an existing one (AS).

public, they will avoid talking or meeting in the presence of slaves and freedmen. For the passion attending this worst of crimes will strive to assume a veil of high seriousness. 8. Take your pick, parricide: an incestuous relationship that is conducted with care will arouse no suspicion; a negligent one will be detected.[38]

(2) But why do I present my case as if it were people at large who talked of an unheard of, an unbelievable outrage? In this gossip I detect the crime of a *single* person. (3) "Only to a bad husband does it make no odds whether he makes up a story of incest about his wife or believes one."[39] What? Wasn't then that ⟨gossip⟩ afraid to noise abroad something so nefarious, didn't rumor blush to reach the father's ears? You may pretend otherwise, but the malevolent tale took its rise from *you*, and whoever dared to tell it, to broadcast it, followed *your* lead.[40] (4) Suppose a good father, a good husband: do you think I am going to say, he will not believe it? He won't *know* of the rumor's existence.[41] Now go on debating, judges, who gave rise to the story: its advocate is the *father*.[42]

9. "He was handsome," he says. This is no more a crime with regard to a mother than a charge with regard to a son.[43] (2) "He was handsome." To make this a possible

[40] Father may claim otherwise (above, with n. 39), but in fact nobody would have dared to share with him such a monstrous rumor about his family: so *he* alone must have fabricated it (AS).

[41] Contrast 19.3.3. [42] Father is defending the rumor, so it follows that *he* gave rise to it. See also 18.1.1, 18.4.2–3.

[43] A son's good looks are no more a reason for his mother to commit incest with him than they are a reason to bring a charge against her son.

obici possit,[48] ut debeat, adice "et adulter et raptor; in illa
matrona maritali dolore paene percussus, in illa virgine
publica subclamatus invidia." Quamquam haec quoque
3   intra notos decurrunt iuventutis excessus.[49] Quid ais? Ab
incesto libidines coeperunt? Hoc primum umquam iuvenis admisit? Huc[50] solum argumentum sumis ex forma?
4   Dic potius: "Deprehendi iuvenem mihi venena miscen-
tem: in necem meam conscientia sceleris est armatus."
Infinitum est quantum debeat ante fecisse filius, ut de illo
5   incestum pater sibi credat. "Speciosus fuit." Quis enim
non est formosus filius matri? Amant debilitates, amplec-
tuntur illum morborum suppliciorumque pallorem, et in
vires caritatis adcrescit ipsa miseratio. Non impedit sacrae[51] pietatis animum deformitas, pulchritudo non auget;
6   amare liberos unus adfectus est. Liberi, marite, liberi non
amantur oculis: non complectitur mater ora,[52] non vultus,[53] sed est in filio matri nescioquid homine formosius.
7   Possit forsitan novitas sollicitare visus, expugnare mentes;
in matris aspectu coalescit infantia, pueritia consurgit,
iuventa subrepit: speciosum suum cotidie videt, miratur,
amplectitur. Quae tamdiu amavit, quando incipiat a

48 -sit π: -ses B[ac]: -set B[pc] V Φ   49 -cess- *Bur.*: -curs- *codd.*
50 huc *scripsi (cf. OLD²* §§2.a/c): hoc *codd., damn. Sh. B.⁴ 210*
51 sacrae *Håk.³ 138*: agre B V: (a)egr(a)e Φ
52 ora *Håk.*: ore *codd.*   53 -us A: -u *cett.*

44 Father *does* seem to hint at such allegations in 19.2.6–3.1
(though cf. 19.13.3).
45 Incest.   46 With metarhetorical allusion to other themes
(cf. *DM* 2 and 17).
47 Cf. 1.6.2. Parricide is usually regarded as the worst possible

objection, or a necessary one, add "and an adulterer and a rapist; in the case of married woman X he was nearly slain by an aggrieved husband, in the case of virgin Y he was met by shouts of popular disapproval"—though even these things come within the normal range of youthful escapades.[44] (3) What are you saying? Does concupiscence really start with incest? Was *this*[45] ever a young man's first exploit? Are his good looks the only proof you can find for *this*? (4) Say rather:[46] "I found the young man mixing a poison for me: he was armed to kill me by his bad conscience." A son has to have done an enormous amount beforehand if a father is to believe him capable of incest.[47] (5) "He was handsome." Yes: what son is not good-looking in his mother's eyes? Mothers love weaklings, they hug to themselves the pallor accompanying disease and affliction, and pity itself grows into strong affection. To a mind that feels the sacred pull of maternal love, deformity is no obstacle and beauty is no boost: love for children is of one kind only.[48] (6) Children, husband, yes *children*[49] are not loved through the eyes: a mother does not embrace their faces or their expressions. Rather, in a son a mother finds a kind of superhuman beauty. (7) Perhaps a new lover may catch the eye, take the mind over by force; but under a mother's gaze the little child grows stronger, boyhood makes him taller, manhood creeps up on him: every day she sees her handsome son, wonders at him, hugs him to her. She has loved for so long: when could she begin to

offense, but "incest is . . . an even worse crime: parricide would *precede* it" (Breij [2015, 250n300]).

[48] All mothers love their children in one and the same way, regardless of their looks.   [49] As opposed to lovers (18.9.7).

8 matre[54] desinere? Non est opus, nocentissime senex, ad
hoc nefas caritate, sed amentia, sed furore: ut in iuvene
suo mater possit concupiscere quod formosus est, oderit
oportet quod filius est, et adeo sacris adfectibus non adiu-
vatur in facinus, ut ad illud[55] nisi per oblivionem sui
transire non possit.

10. Quid, quod et hoc[56] incredibilius est, quod parem
duorum poscit insaniam, et ad incestum opus est ut ada-
2 met et filius, non ut adametur?[57] Ab utro deinde vultis
incipere preces, venire sermonem? Audebit hoc rogare
filius matrem, mater hoc impetraturam se sperabit a filio?
3 Hunc animum tuum, senex, quo cum maxime taces, si non
est callida, non maligna simulatio, de fide tanti sceleris
interrogo: an potest mater admittere quod loqui non potest pater?
4   "Speciosus fuit." Libet interrogare hoc loco omnes
5 humani generis adfectus. Placet ergo ut, si filio optigerit
indulgentior facies, vultus erectior, refugiat mater amplexus? Si virginem usque ad notabilem speciem natura
formaverit, timeat oscula pater horreatque contactum?
6 Dii deaeque male perdant tam impudentes sollicitudines,
tam nefarios metus! Prope est ab incesto, timere ne fiat.
7 Malo simplicitatem quae non vereatur infamiam, malo nudos adfectus inconsultamque pietatem. Nihil de se fingi,

[54] a matre B V AD (*def. Watt*[2] *33, Breij*[1]): amare *cett.*
[55] ill- ς: ali- *codd.*   [56] hoc π: hic *cett.*   [57] -ur ⟨tantum⟩
Golz 82 (⟨solum⟩ ς), *sed recte subaud. Håk.*[7] *128*

[50] = by forgetting, because of insanity, that she is his mother
(see again 18.9.7).   [51] "The question is splendidly rhetorical: the public must of course supply 'No' for an answer,

stop being a mother? (8) To commit this crime, you most guilty old man, one needs not affection but madness, insanity. For a mother to lust after her young boy because he is handsome, she must hate the fact that he is her *son*: she is so far from being aided to commit a crime by the holy ties of family that she could only come round to it by forgetting herself.[50]

10. What then of the fact—even less believable than the previous point—that he is requiring *two* people to go equally mad? For an act of incest the son too must fall in love, not just be fallen in love with. (2) From which of the two of them, then, would you like the propositions to begin, the chatting up to start? Will a son venture to ask *this* of his mother, will a mother have any hope of winning *this* from her son? (3) Old man, this attitude of yours that is making you silent right now, unless it is a cunning, an ill-natured pretense, is wide open to question as to the credibility of such a crime: Can a mother, I ask, do what a father cannot talk about?[51]

(4) "He was handsome." I'd like at this point to cross-examine all the feelings of humankind. (5) So, if a son has a rather winning appearance, a superior bearing, do you want his mother to avoid embracing him? If nature has made a young girl especially beautiful, is her father to fear kissing her and shrink from touching her?[52] (6) To hell with such shameless anxieties, such wicked fears! It comes close to incest to be afraid it may take place. (7) I prefer the innocent nature that has no fear of being slandered, I prefer naked feelings and unthinking affection. Let her

while in fact 'Why not?' would do equally well" (Breij [2015, 266n339]). [52] Cf. Juv. 6.50–51.

nihil credat[58] posse narrari; teneat insatiabiliter, avide.
Tanti fama non est, ut amet filium mater sollicitudine
pudicae.[59]

8   Me quidem, marite, si quis interroget, omnes matres
liberos suos, tamquam adamaverint, amant. Videbis oculos numquam a facie vultuque deflectere, comere caput
habitumque componere; suspirare cum recesserit, exul-
tare cum venerit, conserere manus, pendere cervicibus,
non osculis,[60] non conloquiis, non praesentiae voluptate[61]

9   satiari. Hoc est ergo <in>[62] tam nefanda suspicione saevissimum: incestum non potest fingi, nisi de optima matre.

10   Execrarer mehercules, iudices, si crimen istud clarius
obiecisset filio pater, si usque ad verborum processisset
amentiam. Nemini minus fas esse debet credere incestum,
quam qui propter illud paratus est filium occidere.

11. Quid, quod non credis tantum, nefande, sed quaeris? Ita tu non times monstri huius agitare secretum?

2   "Populus loquitur incestum." Sed tu nega. "Civitas infa-
mat." Tanto magis osculare unicum et coniugem, tene

3   pariter,[63] duos circa tuum stringe complexum. Pro inaudita feritas! Ita patri non sufficit non credere incestum,

---

58 -at ⊊ (*vind. Wint.*[7] *167*): -ant *codd.*
59 -citiae M γ β   60 osc- ⊊: oc- *codd.*
61 -upt- πM²: -unt- *cett.*   62 *suppl.* ⊊
63 *post* coniugem *et* pariter *dist. Reitz.*[2] *74: post* tene *vulg.*

---

53 Good mothers behave lovingly (as described) to their
sons, and so lay themselves particularly open to these suspicions
(DAR).

54 = I'd already loathe it even if a father had no more than
reproached . . .

believe that nothing can be made up, no stories told about her; let her hold him insatiably, greedily. Public opinion is not so important that a mother should love her son with the anxiety of the bashful.

(8) If you ask me, husband, all mothers love their sons as if they have fallen in love with them. You will see their eyes never leaving their child's face, you will see them smoothing his hair and putting his clothes straight; sighing when he goes out, full of joy when he comes in; joining hands with him, hanging on his neck, never getting too much of kissing him, of talking with him, of the pleasure of his company. (9) The cruelest thing, then, ‹about› such a wicked suspicion is this: incest cannot be imagined except where the mother is the best of mothers.[53]

(10) By heaven, judges, I'd loathe it if a father had reproached[54] his son with this crime too explicitly, if he had gone as far as expressing his madness in words.[55] A man who is prepared to kill his son for it ought to be the last to believe in incest.[56]

11. What of *this*, wicked man? You don't just believe, you interrogate too. Aren't you then scared to hunt down this appalling secret? (2) "They're talking of incest." It is up to you to deny it, then. "The city is slandering them." So much the more should you kiss your only son and your wife, hold them together, squeeze them both in your embrace. (3) What unheard of barbarity! Is a father then not

---

[55] Let alone in actions (see n. 56).

[56] A father who considers incest intolerable should be especially careful to gather *solid* evidence before taking action against his son—or even just accusing him verbally (cf. previous sentence) (AS).

4 quod non potest probare? Ferrem tamen adhuc suspiciones tuas, nefandissime senex, si dissimulanter indicia
tanti sceleris agitasses: observa sermones, secreta custodi,
omnium dierum noctiumque momentis sagax scrutator
insiste. Quid tibi cum abruptis, quid cum supremis? Inces-
5 tum iam credas oportet, ut torqueas.[64] At tu—pro nefas!—
verberibus, ignibus et tota crudelitatis arte scrutaris rem,
de qua non deberes interrogare servos, de qua vernilium
quoque corporum patientiam petulanter excuteres. Laminas[65] accendis, eculeos moves et parricidio suspicaris
6 incestum. Nescis quod praeceps, quod abruptum tam
nefandae diligentiae furore commoveas? Pater, qui de incesto filium torquet, non est neganti crediturus.

7 Omnium quidem, iudices, incertorum suspiciones pes-
sime semper a corporibus incipiunt, nec bene de cuiusquam moribus illam partem hominis interroges, quae non
8 animo, sed[66] dolore respondet. Nondum dico quem torqueas, quis inter eculeos ignesque ponatur; criminis[67]
argumenta[68] prius, indicia praecedant: novissimum debet
9 esse, quicquid obiter et[69] torquet[70] et punit. Fidem hominum deorumque, ne gravitatem putetis a novissimis ulti-

64 quid tibi—torqueas *post* probare (§3) *transp. Breij*[1]
65 lami- β: iam mi- *cett.* 66 sub B
67 criminis *Håk.*[2] *145*: cuius *codd.*
68 -umenta *Sch.*: -uta *codd.*
69 obiter *Hamm.*[2] *523*, et *Håk.*[2] *145*: obieret B^{ac} H: obiceret B^{pc} JO: obiret V: γ β
70 -et ς: -etur *codd.*

---

57 Because he is too biased (18.11.4).
58 = to ask questions of his body, rather than of his mind.

content to disbelieve in incest that he cannot prove? (4) Yet I should still tolerate your suspicions, you most wicked old man, if you had covertly searched out signs of such a crime: watch their conversations, look out for secret meetings, keep at it every hour of day and night, like a sleuth hot on the scent. Why do you resort to such hasty, such final measures? You must believe in incest already, if you want to employ torture. (5) Yet you (the horror of it!) use whips, fires and all the art of cruelty, to investigate something you oughtn't even to interrogate *slaves* about, something it would be sadistic of you to wring out of the endurance even of servile bodies. You heat up the plates, you bring up the racks—and you commit parricide because you suspect incest. (6) Are you not aware what a rash, what a precipitate action you are setting about in your insanely wicked punctiliousness? A father who goes as far as to torture his son concerning incest is not going to believe him if he denies it.[57]

(7) Suspicion of all uncertain matters, judges, always does worst to start from bodies: one does wrong to ask questions about a man's morals of the part of him that replies not out of reason, but out of pain.[58] (8) I do not yet say *whom* you are torturing, *who* is being placed amid the racks and the fires.[59] Let proofs, let signs of the crime lead the way: only right at the end should come what both tortures and punishes at the same time. (9) By men and gods, do not think it is a mark of high principle to begin with what should be the final and ultimate measure!

---

[59] = "[I]t is bad enough that the father uses torture, let alone that he uses it on his son" (Breij [2015, 292n406]).

[QUINTILIAN]

misque coepisse! Non habet probationem facinus, de quo
pater non potest alium torquere quam filium.

12. Video qua possis ratione defendi:[71] si omnia ante
2 fecisti, ut incestum aliter erueres. Quid ais? Interrogasti
servulos, nec[72] potuit conscius inveniri? Exquisisti ancil-
las, non apparuit ministra flagitii? Non obscena litterarum
commercia, non fatentis reprehendisti[73] nefanda[74] blandi-
3 tias? Nihil invenis maritus, dominus, pater? I nunc et dic
scisse rumorem!
4   Sed, ut torqueas, ducatur tamen quaestio per coniugis
ministeria, per filii servulos, in illa potius vilitate desaeviat.
Prius est ut repudietur uxor, ut divortio finiat[75] in domo
grande secretum. Excedit omnem immanitatem filium
ideo torquere, ut scias an innocens[76] torqueatur.
5   Unicum pater ignibus verberibusque interrogas; rogo,
quid facturus, si pernegaverit? Videlicet ut laudes, deinde
dimittas, ut[77] amplectaris perusta vitalia et laceri pectoris
6 vulnera pietati rursus admoveas? Solus superest pudor
homini qui torsit unicum, ut torquere debuerit.[78] Faciat

---

[71] *colon pos. Obr.: comma vulg.*   [72] non ς, *sed vd. Eng.*
71–72   [73] de- ς, *sed vd. Breij[1]*   [74] -da *Reitz.[2] 74 (firm.
Håk.[2] 145–46)*: -de *codd.*   [75] finiat *scripsi*: fiat *codd.*: pate-
fiat *Sh. B.[2] 216*   [76] noc- B δ, *sed vd. Breij[1]*
[77] aut *vel* <aut> ut *Sh. B.[2] 216, sed vd. B. Asc.[1] cxviii r.*
[78] ut—d. *damn. Håk., sed vd. Breij[1]*

---

[60] *Servants* are usually questioned under torture first
(18.12.2–4); if Father had none to interrogate, it means that his
case is weak (AS).
[61] I.e., despite being in so authoritative a position.
[62] This contradicts 18.7.3.

344

A crime is incapable of proof, when a father can find no one else but his son to put to the torture.[60]

12. I see how you can be defended: if you did everything beforehand to unearth incest by other means. (2) Well, did you interrogate the slaves, and no accomplice was to be found? Did you question the maids, and no helper in the crime was forthcoming? Did you not come upon any exchange of suggestive messages, any endearments indicative of wicked doings? (3) You find nothing, husband, master, father?[61] Go ahead now and say that *rumor* knew.

(4) Even if, though, you do use torture, at least let the investigation fall upon your wife's staff, your son's slaves; let its savagery be exercised for preference on those valueless bodies.[62] But first you have to repudiate your wife, to have the big secret come to an end in the house by means of divorce.[63] It is behavior beyond all enormity to torture your *son*[64] to learn if it is an innocent man who is being tortured.

(5) You, a father, question your only son with flames and lashes. What, I ask you, are you intending to do if he denies to the end?[65] Praise him, I suppose, then let him go, so that you can embrace his scorched vitals and admit the wounds in his mangled breast to your affection all over again? (6) Nothing but shame remains for a man who has tortured his only son, even if he *had* to torture him.[66] This

---

[63] Only when Mother has gone will the slaves feel free to reveal the "big secret."

[64] Rather than the slaves.

[65] Contrast 19.9.9.

[66] = even if the only thing left was to torture him.

te necesse est res ista pessimum patrem, et oderis oportet
7 filium, cui satisfacere non possis. Iam iam malo venena,
ferrum, subitos ictus improvisamque mortem. Incestum
qui non credit, torquere non debet; qui credit, statim
debet occidere.

8 Quodsi tormenta etiam filii placent, si praestanda est
satisfactio tam nefanda[79] rumori,[80] exigo ne perdas quaestionem. In media civitate, in ipsa constitue fama, advoca
illos malignos, illos loquaces, et saeculi rem exquire audi-
9 ente populo. Coram omnibus torqueri debet, de quo
locuntur omnes. Interroget quisque quod volet, suis auri-
10 bus, suis credat oculis. Cur in abditam semotamque partem iuvenis abducitur? Secretum quaestionis nec incesto
11 filio debetur nec innocenti. Dabo adhuc inter secretum
publicationemque temperamentum: advoca propinquos,
adhibe amicos, circumpone iuveni serios senes, intersint
magistratus, adsistant quibus habere possit civitas fidem.
Praestare debes aut tibi ut probare possis, si confessus
fuerit, aut filio, si pernegaverit. 13. At tu, nefande, crudelis, tollis quaestionis alteram partem: efficis ne possit am-
2 plius innocens esse qui tortus est. Quid agunt contra po-

---

79 -da V (*vind. Håk.² 146*): -do B: -di B² Φ
80 -ri *Franc.* (*corrob. Håk.² 146*): -ris B V γ β: *om.* δ

---

67 Even if it turns out that you were wrong to suspect and
torture your son, your relationship with him will be beyond re-
pair—and you will hate him (AS).   68 Killing Son on impulse, rather than torturing him, would have been preferable.
69 Cf. 19.10.3.
70 The former deserves public punishment, the latter public
apologies.

act cannot but make you the worst of fathers: you must hate a son to whom you cannot make amends.[67] (7) As things are, I prefer poison, steel, sudden blows and unforeseen death.[68] Someone who does not believe a story of incest should not use torture; someone who does should kill on the spot.[69]

(8) But if you are resolved on torture even for a son, if rumor has to be given such wicked satisfaction, I do ask you not to allow your interrogation to go to waste. Let it take place in the center of the city, in the midst of the gossip itself, summon those malicious, those talkative persons, and inquire into a thing that concerns our whole society in the hearing of the people. (9) Someone who is the talk of the town ought to be tortured in the presence of the town. Let everyone ask what he likes, and believe his own ears, his own eyes. (10) Why is the young man haled off into a hidden and secluded part of the house? Secrecy in interrogation is not the due either of an incestuous son or of an innocent one.[70] (11) But even now I will concede some compromise between secrecy and publicity: summon relatives, bring friends together, surround the young man with grave elders, let magistrates be present, let persons the city can trust be in attendance. You ought to give yourself the chance to prove your case, supposing he confesses, or your son the chance to prove his, supposing he denies to the bitter end. 13. But you, wicked and cruel as you are, are shattering the other party in the interrogation: you are making it impossible for a man who has been tortured to be innocent any longer.[71] (2) What

[71] As no witness will be available to confirm that Son had not confessed under torture.

pulum tormenta secreta? Praedico, testor: iterum dantur
malignis alimenta sermonibus, et a quaestione seposita in
maius reditur incertum. Coram omnibus torquere debet
filium pater, et qui vult absolvere et qui est paratus occidere.

3   Non vultis, iudices, ad facinus indignissimae quaestionis accedat et quod[81] ipse torsit filium pater? Adeone non
potuit libertis aut servulis necessitas ista mandari, non
4 carnifex potius adhiberi? Pater in tormentis filii non aver-
sos tenuit oculos; ipse vestes scidit, velamenta laceravit,
manibus flagella concussit, renovavit ignes et mori filium
contentione non sivit: diduxit os, quod iam suprema clau-
debant, fovit animum, ut longis cruciatibus patientia sufficeret. O dignum patrem, cui dicat innocens filius: "Feci"!
5   Non mehercules improbe mihi proclamaturus hoc
loco videor hominem, qui torquetur in matrem, debere
coram matre torqueri. Cur excluditur infelix a sua causa,
6 a sua quaestione? Adhibe speciosi cruciatibus hanc nimis
amantem, huius gemitus excipe, huius suspiria oculosque
custodi; si quod facinus admissum est, torquebis quidem
filium, sed fatebitur mater.

    14. Inrumpere me cum maxime puta in illud tuum,
parricida, secretum; inicio properanti quaestioni manum:
inhibe ictus, subtrahe paulisper ignes. Quicquid est quod

---

81 et q. *codd.*: q. et *Franc.*

---

72 Ironical.
73 Cf. 18.14.4; see also 19.1.1, blaming *Mother*'s insistence.
74 Contrast 19.11.4–5 and Introduction to *DM* 19.
75 Contrast 19.4.4.

can torture conducted in secret do to counter the general gossip? I proclaim, I assert: fresh sustenance is being given to the malicious rumors, for an interrogation held in private results in yet greater uncertainty. A father ought to torture a son with everyone present, whether he wishes to acquit or is ready to kill.

(3) Don't you agree, judges, that to the crime of an utterly unfair interrogation should be added the fact that the father tortured his son in person? Really, couldn't this so necessary[72] task have been passed over to freedmen or slaves, could not an executioner have been called upon instead? (4) The father did not avert his eyes while his son was under torture; it was he who ripped his clothes, tore his tunic, used his own hands to crack the whip and renew the flames, and in his insistence[73] would not allow his son to die: he forced open the mouth which death was already closing, kept him going, so that he could find the endurance to undergo a prolonged agony. How well would such a father deserve to be told by an innocent son: "I did it"!

(5) By heaven, I think it not improper for me to declare at this point that a man under torture to find evidence against his mother ought to be tortured with his mother present. Why is the unhappy woman excluded from her own case, from her own interrogation?[74] (6) Summon to her handsome son's agonies this woman who loves him too well, listen to her groans, keep a watch on her sighs and expressions. If a crime has been committed, you may be torturing the son, but it is the mother who will confess.

14. Imagine, parricide, that I am at this very moment bursting in on that secret spot of yours.[75] I lay hands on the interrogation as it hastens on: stop hitting him, withdraw the fires for a little. Whatever you have unearthed,

349

eruisti, profer in medium. Memento te fecisse de filio
2 propter quod tibi non debeat credi. Quid spiritum dolore
praecipitas, quid miserae intervalla patientiae pertinaci
crudelitate continuas?[82] [si][83] Frustra tibi sufficere credis
quod audieris nuntiare, proferre: incestum ut credatur,
ipse debet audiri.

3 Mirabar et ego, iudices, si tam nefanda quaestio alium
exitum potuisset habere quam mortem. Hic est parricidii
pudor, sic desinunt quae incipere non debent: facinus
quaestionis operis scelere maiore, exire tibi videris per
4 orbitatem. Scimus unde venerit ista contentio: nihil extor-
sit saevitia misero. Vincit[84] torquentem qui occiditur.

5 Iam iam non miror quod post ista non habes vocem,
verba non invenis. Unicum sine teste lacerasti, unicum
occidisti soli tibi,[85] deinde vis videri celare facinus, et in
parricidio quaeris aliunde tristitiam. Praepostera res est
6 filium occidere, deinde erubescere. Fas non est non esse

82 -uas π: -ueris *cett.*   83 *del.* (*et ante sic dist.*) *Sh. B.*[2]
217, *firm. Breij*[1]   84 -ro, vicit *Russ.*[3]
85 *levius interpunxi* (*gravius Reitz.*[2] 65.5): *post* -disti *dist. vulg.*

---

76 = let your son speak in public—for *you* cannot be believed
(see below).   77 You questioned him *in secret.*

78 The victim's breath becomes labored as death approaches;
cf., e.g., 2.18.5.

79 Cf. 18.13.4, *mori—sufficeret.*

80 Like the judges.   81 Father would have killed Son
anyway: either as a punishment, if Son had confessed the incest,
or otherwise to hide his having tortured him unjustly.

82 The modesty is the covering up.   83 The killing.

84 That made him prolong the torture (18.13.4).

85 If you are tortured to death, this proves you are innocent,

bring it into the open.[76] Remember that you have done to your son something[77] that cannot but make it impossible for *you* to be believed. (2) Why do you precipitate him into gasps of pain,[78] why do you prolong by your unrelenting cruelty the gaps punctuating his unhappy suffering?[79] You are wrong to think it enough for *you* to report and publish what you hear: for incest to be believed, he himself must be given a hearing.

(3) I too[80] would be surprised, judges, if so wicked an interrogation could have had any other outcome than death.[81] This is the modesty of parricide,[82] this is the way things end which should not start: you are trying to cover up the crime of your interrogation by doing something yet more wicked,[83] imagining you can get away with both by losing your son. (4) But we know where that insistence[84] came from: brutality extracted nothing from the poor boy. When you end up being killed, you get the best of your torturer.[85]

(5) At this point I am not surprised that after all this you have no voice, you find no words. You tore your only son to pieces without a witness, you killed your only son just for yourself,[86] and after that you want to be thought to be covering up a crime: you committed parricide, but you look for sadness from another source.[87] It is topsy-turvy to kill a son, and then blush! (6) It is not right for the

for you actually had nothing to confess. So *you* win, not your torturer (AS). Contrast 19.1.1.

[86] I.e., in private, so that only you could hear his words without making them public (18.14.1–2).   [87] You killed your own son, but you claim you cannot speak on account of a different reason for grief—and shame—i.e., incest (the *facinus* to be supposedly covered up) (AS).

notum propter quod se parricida putat innocentem. Eligas
utrum voles: aut tormenta damnes necesse est aut silen-
7 tium. Quod non debet indicari, non debet quaeri. Posses[86]
videri fortassis, crudelissime senex, silentium filio praestare, si viveret; consumpta est paterni nominis religio,
8 omni[87] pietatis sublata reverentia. Si hoc ille meruit, parum in quaestione, parum ultionis in morte est. Vindicare
vis confessionem? Traduc cadaver, et super illa vulnera
omnes pone causas. Non est eiusdem fateri cur torseris et
tacere cur occideris.

15. Quid ais, severissime parricida? Filium consumpsisti per flagella, per laminas: potes tacere?[88] Viscera de
tuis concepta vitalibus, sanguinem qui de tua fluxit anima,
non insania, non furore sed—quantum vis videri—consi-
2 lio, gravitate lacerasti: potes tacere?[89] Super vulnera unici,
super exustos[90] artus metuendus adsistis, et causas quaerente matre, quaerente populo hoc solum dicis: "Occidi."[91]
3 Contenta esse debet incerto.[92] Interrogari nunc te, marite,
credis a matre sola? Causas mortis illius reposcit sollicitudo generis humani: stant circa liberos attoniti parentes, horret invicem se caritas fraterna complecti, rupta
est illa osculorum inter soceros generosque simplicitas.

---

86 -ses *Håk., Watt*[2] 33: -sis *codd.*   87 -i *Franc.*: -is *codd.*
88 tace- *Gron.*: arde- E: age- *cett.*   89 laminas—tacere[2]
dist. Gron.   90 -ust- D (*cf. 19.6.1, 19.15.2*): -ut- *cett.*
91 incerto *tenus patrem loqui censet* B. *Asc.*[1] *cxix r., sed vd.*
Breij[1]   92 -rto ς: -rta B Φ: -sta V   *interrog. dist. vulg.,*
sed vd. Wint.[7] *168*

---

88 Sc., by you. Your silence cannot be explained as a favor to
Son, since you *killed* him in spite of any family bond.

reason why a parricide thinks himself innocent to be hidden. Choose which you like: you must either condemn your torture or your silence. What ought not to be revealed ought not to be investigated. (7) You might perhaps seem, most cruel old man, to be keeping quiet as a favor to your son—if he were alive; but the awe attending the name of father is destroyed, once all respect for family love has been wiped out.[88] (8) If your son did deserve it, there is too little revenge in torture, in death. Do you want to punish him for what he has confessed to? Then put the body on display, and on each of its wounds state the reason that caused it. It is not consistent to confess why you tortured while keeping silent as to why you killed.

15. What do you say, you sternest of parricides? You destroyed your son with whips and red-hot plates: can you remain silent? The organs conceived from your own vitals, the blood that flowed from your soul, you shredded—not in insanity, not in a frenzy, but, by your own account, after making a considered decision: can you remain silent? (2) You stand, a fearsome sight, over the wounds of your only son, over his scorched limbs, and when his mother, when the people ask why, you say no more than: "I killed him." She has to be satisfied with uncertainty.[89] (3) Do you think, husband, that you are now being questioned by the mother only? It is the anxiety of the human race that insists on hearing the motives for that death: parents stand around their children thunderstruck, affectionate brothers shrink from embracing each other, broken is that frank exchange of kisses between fathers-in-law and sons-in-

[89] In Father's opinion, of course.

4 Quousque nos cum silentii tui interpretatione committis?
Si nihil factum est, quod[93] debeat erubescere temporum
5 pudor, quid sibi volunt verba media, suspensa? Si nefas
prodigiosis simile fabulis deprehendisti, miserere, ne sis
una morte contentus. Incestam gravius odisse debes quod
et venit in forum, quod audaciam innocentis imitatur et
6 tacenti videtur irasci. Cum filium propter rumorem torseris, propter tormenta occideris, non est media res ut neu-
trum sciamus.
7 Mater quidem, iudices, innocentissima hoc complorat,
hoc ferre non potest, quod nihil parricida respondet; sed
nobis videtur iamiamque esse dicturus. 16. Non fallit nos,
nefande, quid captes: hoc, quod supra silentium trahis alta
suspiria, quod in prorumpenti videris exclamatione de-
ficere, mendacio paratur auctoritas, et in fidem erupturae
vocis adfertur ut fateri videaris invitus. Dic tamen! Par est
2 huic rei matris integritas, ut mentiaris. O quanto nunc
dolore torqueris, quod instantem non potes aliqua truci
proclamatione discutere! Non verba tibi contra miseram,
sed argumenta desunt, non voce, sed probatione deficeris.
3 Quod solum datur, relinquis infamiae, et nos cum perpetua sermonum malignitate committis. Qui interrogantem
uxorem nec damnat nec absolvit, rumore contentus est.
4 Modestiam mariti pariter et patris accipite: de muliere,

93 quo *Franc., sed vd. Breij*[1]

---

90 Contrast 19.12.2.   91 Sc., both as to the truth of the
rumor and as to what Son said under torture.
92 Cf. 19.2.5.   93 "us" (Mother and her party: see 18.1.1
and n. 4) is not expressed, but seems to be understood; cf. the
next clause.   94 Judges.

law.[90] (4) How long will you make us grapple with the interpretation of your silence? If nothing has happened of which the times should feel ashamed, what is meant by your ambiguous and hesitant words? (5) If you have uncovered a horror that resembles the prodigies of fable, for pity's sake do not be content with *one* death. You should hate the more intensely an incestuous woman for even coming into court, for assuming the bold airs of an innocent, and feigning anger at your silence. (6) You tortured your son because of a rumor, you killed him because you tortured him: it is not a matter of indifference that we are in the dark on both accounts.[91]

(7) In her complete innocence, judges, the mother laments this, this she cannot bear, that the parricide makes no answer; but to us he seems to be on the very point of speaking. 16. We are well aware, wicked man, what you are aiming at: when you heave deep sighs over your silence, when you seem to be giving way as a cry bursts forth, you are in fact looking to gain authority for your lie: it is to give credibility to words apparently about to escape your lips that you give the impression of speaking against your will.[92] But speak now! The mother's innocence can stand up to your telling a lie. (2) O how it torments you now, that you cannot use some harsh exclamation to put paid to her insistence! It is not words you lack to counter the unhappy woman, but arguments; it is not voice that fails, but proof. (3) No other course being available, you abandon us[93] to ill report, leaving us to contend with endless malicious gossip. A man who neither condemns nor acquits his wife when she questions him is obviously content with rumor. (4) Learn[94] of the respect for decency felt by one who is both father and husband: where a woman

355

quae convinci non potest, sufficere sibi putat ut incesta
5 credatur. Quis umquam tam nefandas artes, tam cruen-
tum deprehendit ingenium? Quia[94] non potest probare
6 quod dixerit, captat ut credatur quod non dixerit. Dissi-
mulas, taces, saeve, crudelis:[95] invenisti tormenta matris.[96]
7 Audi quid misera simplicissimo dolore proclamet.
"Non efficies," inquit, "callidissime parricidarum, ut non
audeam cadaver amplecti. 17. Ego vere[97] incesta sum, si
possum moderari gemitus, comprimere lacrimas. Coite in
funus, omnes liberi, omnes parentes, custodite planctus
meos, observate suspiria. Si quid feci, si quid admisi, fate-
2 bor. Ecce supra lectulum effusa feralem, laceros artus
et perustum complexa corpus, exclamo: teneo[98] unicum
meum, velit nolit invidia, meum misera formosum. Hoc
erat quod infelicissimam matrem ultra solitae caritatis exa-
3 gitabat adfectus: amabam, marite, periturum. Infames
quantumlibet hanc impatientiam, ego mihi videor de-
fuisse, cessasse, multum de laetitia, multum perdidisse de
gaudiis. Nemo umquam filium nimis amavit."
4 "Excuso tibi," inquit, "iuvenis innocentissime, quod supremis tuis nondum praestiti misera comitatum. Vivere

---

94 *an* qui?
95 *sic fere dist. Obr.: interrog. vulg.*
96 ma- *Hâk.*² 147: pa- *codd.*
97 -re *Leh.*: -ra B A δ β: -ro *cett.*
98 ⟨te⟩ ten- *Best 162*

---

95 Father.
96 Contrast 19.4.5.
97 I.e., by my behavior. Cf. 18.13.6.
98 Contrast Father at 18.15.2.

cannot be convicted, he imagines it to be enough that she be *thought* to have committed incest. (5) Who ever detected such wicked arts, such a bloodthirsty character? Since he cannot prove what he said, he tries to win belief for what he did *not* say. (6) You dissimulate, you keep silent, barbarous and cruel man: you have discovered how to torture the mother.

(7) Listen[95] to what the poor woman proclaims in her totally straightforward grief. "Most cunning of parricides, you will not," she says, "stop me venturing to embrace the corpse.[96] 17. I am truly guilty of incest if I am capable of moderating my groans, of suppressing my tears. Come together to the funeral, all children, all parents, keep watch over my laments, observe my sighs. If I have done anything, committed anything, I will confess it.[97] (2) Look, stretched on the fatal bed, embracing his torn limbs and scorched body,[98] I cry out: I am holding my only son, whether slander likes it or not, my (ah me!) handsome boy. This is what afflicted a most unlucky mother beyond the feelings of normal affection: I loved him, husband, as one doomed to die.[99] (3) Decry this passion as much as you like, I seem to myself to have failed, to have been found wanting,[100] to have lost most of my happiness, most of my joys. No one ever loved their son too much."

(4) "I ask your pardon, most innocent youth," she says, "that (unlucky me!) I have not yet accompanied you in

---

[99] An insinuation that the murder was planned long before: cf. 18.3.5.

[100] I.e., not to have loved him enough, and not to have experienced the joys mentioned next.

357

[QUINTILIAN]

quidem te defuncto continuo non debui, sed mori marito
tacente non potui. Rumpam taedium lucis invisae, si[99]
prius licuerit coram civitate manibus tuis iusta persolvere,
cum damnato supra callidissimum silentium parricida ni-
5 hil te dixisse constiterit. Ignosce quod ad iudicium istud
orbata duravi. Timui ne, si ad exitum impatientia, si praecipiti pietate properassem, faceret alium parricida de mea
morte rumorem."

[99] si *Franc.*: sed *codd.*

your demise.[101] Of course I should have stopped living straight after your last breath, but I could not die while my husband remained silent. I shall break short the ennui of this life I hate, if first I may pay due respect to your shade in the presence of the city, when, by the conviction of the parricide despite his so crafty silence, it has been established that you said nothing. (5) Pardon me, that I hung on in my bereavement until this court hearing. I was afraid that if I hurried to my end out of overwhelming passion,[102] out of headlong affection for my son, the parricide might fabricate another rumor—about *my* death."[103]

[101] I.e., by suicide.

[102] Picking up 18.17.3. Cf. 4.7.2, 17.4.4.

[103] "With the son's name not yet cleared, the mother's suicide could be interpreted as prompted by a guilty conscience" (Breij [2015, 371n667]).

DECLAMATION 19

INTRODUCTION

This declamation, on the same theme as *DM* 18, is Father's speech in his own defense. He is not on trial for torturing and killing his son, but for refusing to disclose to Mother what he learned during his interrogation.[1] While his primary goal is to account for his silence, he aims to sow suspicion that Mother was actually guilty of incest with Son, so as to shield himself from the blame for such a brutal murder.[2] Throughout the declamation, however, his argumentation is riddled with inconsistencies.

First, what happened in the torture room? In most of the speech, Father claims that he did not learn anything from the questioning (e.g., 1.1, 2.1), as Son refused to talk (e.g., 4.2–3, 15.3–5); occasionally, though, he implies that Son *may have* said something, but he refused to listen (13.5, 14.9); and at times he seems to insinuate that he *did* extort a confession from Son, which is better not revealed (14.4, 14.10, 16.2; cf. 10.10, 12.5).

Inconsistency also affects the account of Son's killing. The torture is presented both as an act of impulse (3.4–7)

---

[1] On trials for ill-treatment, see Introduction to *DM* 8.

[2] See Breij (2015, 79–81) on the ostensible and underlying goals of *DM* 18 and 19.

and as a deliberate plan; in this regard, the claim that Father aimed at protecting Son's innocence (8.8–9.1) coexists with the insinuation that Son's death was meant to shield the reputation of the whole house (5.3) and even to prevent Mother's being interrogated (10.6). The speaker nevertheless presents the torture not as a means of questioning (12.6–8) but as a punishment for Son's way of life, falling within the legitimate powers of a *pater familias* (5.4).

Finally, Mother is both praised for not interrupting the torture (4.4–5) and blamed for not being present at the questioning (11.4–5). The speaker reproaches Mother for her lack of self-restraint, as she keeps asking questions on a matter that should be veiled in silence (6.1–2), and even for her inconsistency, as she complains both of the rumor of the people and of Father's silence (1.5–2.2).

In short, it is difficult to find a coherent strategy in this declamation: the speaker is not interested in persuading the audience, but just in piling up suspicions and allegations.[3]

The speech may be analyzed as follows:[4]

PROEM 1.1–2.4
NARRATION (I) 2.5–4.9
ARGUMENTATION
Propositio causae (expanded to include an *excessus* on the inadvisability of this lawsuit) 5.1–2

[3] Cf. Breij (2015, 39–40).
[4] Breij (2015, 92–94) gives a somewhat different interpretation of the speech's structure. For the "additional narration" (*epidiegesis*) after the argumentation, see Introduction to *DM* 5, n. 4.

> *Refutatio* 5.3–10.10
> *Confirmatio* 11.1–14.10
> NARRATION (II) 15.1–7
> EPILOGUE 15.8–16.6

As already noted, the theme of this declamation must have been popular in the schools of rhetoric.[5] Quintilian informs us that Father's defense could be developed as a figured speech, a practice that he disapproves especially because it leads the accused to confirm by his defense precisely the charges that he ought to be refuting:[6] the father of *DM* 19 does exactly this, for he openly claims to have killed his son deliberately (e.g., 5.7); and this is not the only "Quintilianic" precept that he breaks.[7]

It is not likely that this speech was written by the same author as *DM* 18: although sharing a number of similarities in language, style, and rhythm, the two speeches ignore each other's main arguments and display a patently different rhetorical technique.[8] Both may be dated to the early third century AD.[9]

[5] Cf. Introduction to *DM* 18.
[6] Quint. 9.2.80; see Breij (2015, 70–77 on figured speeches in general, and 77–84 on *DM* 18–19).
[7] See in detail Longo (2021, 212–13, 218–20, 227–29).
[8] On this latter aspect, see again Longo (2021, 231).
[9] See General Introduction, §4.

Infamis in matrem II

MALAE TRACTATIONIS SIT ACTIO. Malae tractationis sit
actio. Speciosum filium, infamem, tamquam incestum
cum matre committeret, in secreta domus parte pater torsit et occidit in tormentis. Interrogat illum mater, quid ex
iuvene compererit; nolentem dicere malae tractationis
accusat.

1. Debebatur quidem tristissimae orbitatis misero pudori
ut iam taceremus omnes, et post tam prodigiosas rerum
sermonumque novitates oportuerat hoc esse novissimum
de malis infelicissimae domus, quod occidi filium pater;
sed quoniam mulier immodici semper adfectus super
cuncta, quae vel passus sum paulo ante vel feci, reatus
quoque me dolore concussit, veni petiturus a vobis ne me
scientem silentium contentioni praestare credatis: non
2 quia occidi filium taceo, sed occisus est ut tacerem. Utinam, iudices, negare possem quod occidi, utinam totum

---

¹ Cf. 18.13.4.   ² I killed him so that I didn't have to report anything after the questioning. Contrast 18.14.3–4 and see
Introduction to the present declamation.

19

The son suspected of incest with his mother II

ILL-TREATMENT IS TO BE ACTIONABLE. A handsome son was being talked of as committing incest with his mother. His father tortured him in a remote part of the house and killed him in the process. The mother asks him what he learned from the young man. He refuses to say, and she accuses him of ill-treatment.

(Speech of the father)

1. That we should now *all* keep silent ought, it is true, to have been the proper outcome of the wretched sense of shame resulting from our tragic bereavement, and after such unheard of novelties in word and deed it should have been the *final* evil afflicting a most unhappy house that I, his father, killed my son. But since a woman who has always been immoderate in her passions has, to cap all I have suffered or done in the recent past, inflicted on me the added distress of being accused, I have come to ask you not to believe that it is because I know something that I am keeping silent in response to her insistence.[1] I am not silent because I killed my son; rather, my son was killed so that I could keep silent.[2] (2) If only, judges, I could deny that I killed him, if only it were possible to restrict the

miserae necessitatis ordinem fas esset intra pectoris[1]

3 huius premere secretum! Miratur hanc aliquis patientiam
meam? Ardor ille, qui me modo impegit in filium, ipsa sui
immanitate consumptus est. Quicquid erumpere posset in
proclamationem, parricidio peractum est, in orbitate con-

4 ticuit.[2] Non habeo adfectum, nisi quo cuncta tantum patiar, audiam, feram. Utrumque de filio fieri non potest, ut
et occiderim et fatear cur meruerit occidi.

5   Quapropter, iudices, satis admirari, satis stupere non
possum quod mulier, cuius praeter optimam sane conscientiam sexus quoque maiorem malis nostris pudorem
praestare debebat, tacere non potest silentium meum.
2. Novo quin immo fabulosoque secum impatientiae genere dissentit: queritur de populo quod loquatur, de patre
quod taceat, nec contenta confessione mariti nihil se dissimulare, nihil scire reatus auctoritate testantis, mavult de

2 silentio meo facere secretum. Orbitatis istud amentia sit
an innocentia, perditus dolor viderit; ipsius animus potest
scire quid filius meus dixerit, quae me putat habere quod
dicam.

3   Fidem igitur vestram, iudices, ne vos orbitatis mise-
ratione confundat sola mater, neve maximae calamitatis
ibi tantum putetis resedisse sensum, unde vos lacrimae

---

[1] -ra pectoris *Bur.* (*firm. Håk.*[2] *147–48, Breij*[1]): -rare et oris *codd.*

[2] -ui *Gron.*

---

[3] Father now feels able only to suffer and listen, not to act or *speak*.

[4] Cf. 18.2.2.

[5] Ironic.

whole sequence of these unhappy and inescapable events to the privacy of my breast! (3) Is anyone surprised at this forbearance of mine? The passion which previously brought me into conflict with my son has been exhausted by its own fierceness. All the emotion that might have burst out into forceful expression has been used up on the killing, has fallen silent in my loss. (4) I have no feeling except the single one which enables me to endure, hear, bear everything. With regard to my son, it is impossible for me to do both—to kill him first, then to reveal why he deserved to be killed.[3]

(5) For this reason, judges, I cannot be sufficiently astonished, sufficiently amazed[4] that a woman, to whom, quite apart—of course—[5] from her perfectly clear conscience, her sex too ought to have brought a greater sense of shame to confront our common misfortunes, is unable to keep silent about *my* silence. 2. Rather, she shows her lack of self-control in a novel and hardly credible inconsistency: she complains of the people for talking and of the father for keeping silent. Not satisfied with her husband's profession, made with the authority of one giving evidence in court, that he is hiding nothing, that he knows nothing, she prefers to make a mystery out of my silence. (2) Whether this is the result of irrationality brought on by her bereavement or a sign of innocence, I leave to her desperate grief to decide. After all, she can know in her heart what my son said: for she thinks I have something to say.

(3) I beg you then, judges, not to allow the mother alone to confound you by arousing pity for her loss, and not to think that awareness of a signal calamity has taken up residence only in the place from which her tears and

gemitusque conveniunt. Mei magis debetis in uxoris
comparatione misereri, qui filium et perdidi et occidi: ego
sum infelicior ex parentibus duobus, qui quicquid, iudices,
4 ista complorat, et patior et feci. Felicem ignoratione[3] conscientiam matris, quae sufficit interrogare! Maior me impatientia, maior urit adfectus: cur filium occiderim indicare non possum, nec paenitet quod occidi.

5   Infelix senectus, misera patientia, sic quoque quam
multa dicenda sunt! Fuimus quondam, iudices, fuimus
felicissimi parentes, cum adhuc rudis unici nobis blandi-
retur infantia, duravitque domus tota prosperitas quamdiu
pariter fruebamur, pariter dileximus, quamdiu civitas de
nobis hoc solum poterat loqui, filium nos habere formo-
6 sum. Ut vero in eam adolevit aetatem, in qua corporalibus
bonis iuventus insolenter exultat, superbus atque adrogans in nullum vitae genus, non in privatos, non in publicos actus florentem duxit aetatem. 3. Dii immortales,
quantus qualisque circa iuvenem rumor ingemuit! Omnium maledictis succlamatus, omnium denotatione damnatus est, donec et ipse consensum circa se publici doloris
2 agnosceret. Inde rarus in publico, et tamquam patris occursus, tamquam civitatis ora vitaret. Non est leve conci-

---

3 -atione B^{pc} V D β (*def. Håk.*[2] *148*): -antione B^{ac}: -antiae *cett.*

---

6 Cf. 19.5.1.

7 *She* can ask questions because she does not know what happened in the torture room; *I* came out of there so overwhelmed
that I cannot talk about it.

8 Father ends the *exordium* by summarizing his position: he
cannot speak out, but the murder itself was justified.

groans demand your attention. Rather you should pity *me*
as compared with my wife, for I have both lost my son and
killed him:[6] I am the more unfortunate of his two parents,
for whatever she complains of, judges, *I* both suffer and
have acted. (4) Happy in her ignorance,[7] a mother who is
capable of asking questions! *I* am racked by a greater passion, a greater emotion: I cannot say why I killed my son,
yet I do not regret killing him.[8]

(5) Unhappy old age, wretched endurance, how much
there is to say even in these circumstances![9] We once
were, judges, yes we were the happiest of parents, when
we were charmed by the still unformed infancy of our only
son, and the house went on being entirely prosperous so
long as we enjoyed him equally, loved him equally,[10] so
long as the city could say no more of us than that we had
a good-looking son. (6) But when he grew to the age at
which youth exults arrogantly in its bodily advantages, he
became proud and overweening, and directed the years of
his prime to no pursuit—neither to a private nor to a
public career. 3. Immortal gods, picture the kind, the extent of the gossip that uttered groans over the young man!
He was decried[11] by the curses of all, condemned by everyone's pointing fingers, until even he was aware of the
unanimity of the public resentment toward him. (2) From
then on, he rarely showed himself in public, as if he were
avoiding meeting his father,[12] being seen by the city. It is

---

[9] Father implies that, despite his inability to talk, there are
things that need to be explained (cf. 18.16.1).

[10] Not so in 18.3.5.

[11] Cf. 18.9.2.

[12] Cf. 19.9.6.

[QUINTILIAN]

pere verbis in quantam civitatis execrationem, in quantam
culpam iuvenis inciderit: dictus est occidere posse patrem,
3 dictus est dignus quem posset etiam pater occidere. Quid
facerem, iudices, infelicissimus senex? Iam iam non evita-
bat fama nec patrem, iam meis auribus nemo parcebat.
4 Interrogare non audebam, dissimulare non poteram. Fallitur, quisquis me putat quicquam fecisse consilio: impetus
ac temporis ipsius nescioquis ardor explicuit. Praeparari
filio tormenta non possunt.

5   Est in miseris penatibus pars remota, seposita, profunda tenebris, tristis accessu, omnibus apta flagitiis, et in
6 qua audeat facere facinus et pater. Illo, fateor, dum me
variae cogitationes per totius domus spatia circumagunt,
quantum intellegere licuit, improvisus adveni. Et ille quidem ad conspectum meum tamquam deprehensus obsti-
puit refugitque, trepidus—puto—ne quaererem causam.
7 Inrumpo festinanter, avide, sine liberto, sine servulo, sicut
me deprehenderat temporis illius fatum, manibus, ictibus,
et quaecumque ex obviis dolor in telorum transtulerat
usus, ultra vires senectutis adgressus; ignes ex proximo
raptos, verbera quae casus obtulerat, non diviso dolore,
non per partes nec per intervalla suspenso,[4] sed semel, sed
pariter invado: pars secreti fuit ut ipse torquerem. 4. Dii

---

[4] -o π: -os cett.

---

[13] Contrast 18.8.4.

[14] Implying that Mother and Son used this hidden room for
their trysts. Cf. 19.16.2.

[15] Sc., why he was there.

[16] Without anyone's assistance. This rather circular thought (=
if I hadn't tortured him on my own, it wouldn't have been a secret)
"diverts from the question *why* the interrogation had to be secret,

372

difficult to express in words the degree of public loathing, the degree of blame into which the young man fell. It was said that he was capable of killing his father, that he deserved a *father* capable of killing *him*. (3) What was I, a most unfortunate old man, to do, judges? By now rumor was not avoiding even the father, now no one spared my ears. I dared not ask questions, I could not pretend I was in the dark.[13] (4) Anyone who thinks I did anything premeditated is quite mistaken: it was impulse, some passion of the moment that accomplished the act. One cannot make preparations to torture a son.

(5) In our unhappy house there is a remote, secluded wing, plunged in darkness, depressing to approach, well suited for all wicked deeds—a place where a father too[14] might venture to do something evil. (6) Thither, I confess it, as my varying thoughts led me round the whole area of the house, I came, so far as I could reckon, unexpectedly. For his part, as though he had been caught in the act, he was amazed to see me and made as if to flee, scared—I think—that I might ask the reason.[15] (7) I burst in hastily, eagerly, accompanied by no freedman, no slave, just as the chance of the moment took me. With more than an old man's strength I attacked him, striking him with my bare hands and anything I came across that resentment made into a weapon; I laid hands on fires snatched up from nearby, whips that presented themselves at random, not dividing up the pain, not doling it out bit by bit at intervals, but all at one time, all together: a part of the secrecy was that I should torture him myself.[16] 4. Immortal gods, what

and introduces an element of planning inconsistent with the spontaneous character of the torture as described above" (Breij [2015, 435–36n118]).

immortales, quae contumacia, quae fuit illa patientia, cum
2 domi torqueretur a patre, non invocare matrem! Non re-
pugnavit iuvenis, non opposuit manus, nullum imploravit
auxilium; mersis tantum deiectisque luminibus, tamquam
numquam[5] flagella sustinuisset, tamquam meis torqueretur oculis, omnis ictus excepit in faciem; verberibus,
ignibus laudatos vultus, velut illis irasceretur, opposuit.
3 Reddo testimonium novissimum pudori: cum iam[6] mori
vellet, occisus est.

4   Laudo, iudices, patientiam matris: cum et ipsa semper
plurimum esset domi, et ab illo secreto fortasse non longe,
intervenire noluit, interpellare non ausa est. Sed et manibus meis gratulor, quod non propinquus aliquis, non amicus inrupit: occidissem, quisquis me tunc ausus fuisset
5 interrogare pro filio. Sepelivi tamen lacera membra, funus
indulsi, ossa collegi. Non iniecit uxor lectulo manum, non
inter exequias planctibus elisisque uberibus mihi fecit
6 invidiam. Unde in hanc impatientiam prorupit, exiliut?
Domi me nihil interrogavit.

7   Possum iam, mater infelix, coram liberis ac parentibus,
possum audientibus diis hominibusque clamare: et ego
amavi filium meum—non osculis, non infirmitate, non la-
8 crimis, sed viribus, dolore, patientia. Unicum, quem, si
acie clausisset hostis, vicaria morte servassem, si subitum

---

    [5] numq- πM (*dubium, cf. ad 5.23.4*): umq- *cett.*: nusq- *Wint.*[7]
168   [6] iam 5: tam *codd.*

---

17 Contrast 18.13.5–14.1.
18 = in spite of Son's alleged guilt.
19 Contrast 18.16.7–17.2.
20 A woman's characteristic. Cf. 18.3.5.

stubbornness, what endurance not to cry for his mother when he was being tortured in his own home by his father! (2) The young man did not fight back, he did not put up his hands to protect himself, he asked for no help. Only, with eyes lowered and downcast, as though he had not undergone a single stroke of the whip, as though he was being tortured by my *eyes*, he took all the blows in the face; he put in the way of the lashes, of the fires, the features everyone praised, as though he was angry with them. (3) I pay a final tribute to his sense of shame: he was killed when he finally wanted to die.

(4) Judges, I compliment the mother on her forbearance: though she was herself always mostly at home, and perhaps not far from the secret spot, she did not choose to intervene, dare to interrupt.[17] But I congratulate my hands too that some relation, some friend did not break in on the scene: I should have killed anyone who had dared at that moment to question me on my son's behalf. (5) Still,[18] I buried the torn limbs, I granted a funeral, I gathered up the bones. My wife did not lay a hand on the bier,[19] did not try to arouse feeling against me during the rites by wailing or beating her breasts. (6) How has she come to break forth and jump into her present exasperation? She asked me no questions back at home.

(7) I can now, unhappy mother, in the presence of children and parents, I can cry in the hearing of gods and men: I too loved my son—not with kisses, not with weakness,[20] not with tears, but with strength, grief, endurance. (8) My only son, whom I would have saved by giving my life in exchange if he had been cut off by the enemy on the

cinxisset incendium, extulissem relicta meorum parte
9 membrorum, eripui malignitati, abstuli famae. Habeo
quod imputem tibi, natura,[7] pietas: rem difficillimam feci,
quod non me potius occidi.

5. Malae tractationis accusat. Adeone, uxor, tibi parum
videor dedisse poenarum post parricidium, ut[8] labores ne
lucrifaciat pater quod occidit filium suum? Non pudet
2 ergo, sic[9] irasceris parricidae? Quid tibi cum lege, quam
propter alios[10] minores accepistis adfectus? Querelas habet ista, non gemitus, et matre seposita solam complorat
uxorem.

3 Rursus ad populum vocas miserum pudorem, materiam novi rumoris accendis; perdidi ergo rationem secreti
mei: sic omnia feceram, ne quid aut quaeri posset aut dici.
4 Iam vero quid impudentius, quid indignius quam cum sibi
de liberis credunt licere tantundem, et aequum ius patris
ac matris esse contendunt, quasi nesciant nobis arbitrium
vitae necisque commissum? Non est privilegium filium

---

[7] -ae M γ β, sed vd. Håk.[2] 27–28
[8] parricidium ut Sch.: periculum et codd.
[9] sic Håk.: si codd.: si <sic> Watt[3] 58–59
[10] alios Dess.[1] 75, 92: avos B V δ: nos M E: vos AD β

---

[21] Had I done so, I would have spared myself the present sufferings and left Son to his disgrace.
[22] Cf. 18.5.2.
[23] I.e., the loss of my son, and the awareness that I killed him
myself (cf. 19.2.3).
[24] Provocatio: a parricide should stand a capital trial, while
you are just charging me with ill-treatment.
[25] Cf. 8.6.4.

battlefield, whom I would have rescued if a sudden fire had trapped him, even if I had to leave some of my own limbs behind, him I snatched from malice, rescued from disrepute. (9) O natural feelings of parental love, I have something to claim credit for from you: I did a most difficult thing—I did not kill myself instead.[21]

5. Her accusation is for ill-treatment.[22] Do you think, wife, that the penalty I have paid[23] since the parricide is so small, that you should be concerned to ensure that a father is not getting away with killing his son? Have you no shame then, is *this* the manner in which you show your anger at a *parricide*?[24] (2) What have you to do with a law that you women have been given to satisfy other, *lesser* grievances?[25] This law deals in matters for complaint, not for groans; it sets the mother aside and sheds tears only for the wife.[26]

(3) A second time[27] you summon before the people our wretched shame: you are setting ablaze fuel for a new rumor. I have thereby lost the rationale for my secrecy: I had done everything to avoid the possibility of any investigation or talk. (4) Now really, what is more impudent, what more improper than when they[28] think they have the same power[29] over their children, and claim that father and mother have equal rights, as if they were unaware that *we* have power of life and death granted us? It is not a

26 Cf. 8.6.2.

27 The first one being when she fostered the gossip of the incest: cf. 18.7.5–6.

28 Women.

29 Sc., as men.

occidere, cum fieri potest, nec quisquam tantum ideo fe-
5 cit, quia liceret. Viscera unici lacerare suffeci;[11] ignosce.
Si non potes,[12] mihi crede:[13] nemo filium suum occidit
odio; non erit tanti iuvenis invisus. Illud est in patribus
usque ad parricidium terribile, quod amant, quod suc-
6 currunt, quod sibi videntur aliter non posse misereri. Non
est quod vos ab aestimatione malorum meorum mollior
sexus abducat; maioris adfectus est filium occidere quam
7 vindicare. Desine igitur me, mulier, fatigare interrogatio-
nibus tuis. Ita tibi non videtur omnia respondere pro filio,
qui dicit: "Occidi"? Et, licet comprimantur exclamationes,
ora claudantur, nihil negat qui hoc fatetur.
8 Atquin summorum facinorum ipsa immanitas innocentia est. Filium pater non demens, non insanus occidi—
hominem extra sensus adfectusque positum, quisquis
non[14] miseretur![15]—, occidi.[16] 6. Vides senem sanguine
suo fluentem, laceratis exustisque illis sanctioribus cariori-
busque visceribus super exanimis unici corpus cruentis
manibus iacentem; horre cadaver et velut corpora, quae

11 -feci E δ: -ficit πM: -fici *cett.*
12 ignosce—potes *dist. Håk.*   13 -de V: -dere B Φ
14 non 5: nunc *codd.*   15 -rat- Φ
16 -di (*et, ante, incisum agn.*) *Håk.²* 148: -dit *codd.*

---

30 Killing a son is a prerogative of *any* father; when we *do* kill
a son, then, it is not for the sake of exercising an extraordinary
privilege, but because we have a good reason.
31 Sc., than by killing them (in this case saving Son from disgrace: 19.4.8).
32 Judges. Cf. 19.2.3.
33 Contrasting his "manly" way to love a son (by killing him)

special privilege to kill a son, when it *can* be done,[30] and no father has ever done it just because it was permitted. (5) I found it in me to rip up my only son's guts; forgive me. If you cannot, no one (believe me!) killed a son of his own out of hatred: a youth you detest will not be worth the effort. What is frightening in fathers, to the point of parricide, is that they *love* their sons, that they come to their aid, that they think they can show pity in no other way.[31] (6) There is no reason for you[32] to allow the weaker sex to keep you from making a just estimate of my troubles; it is a sign of greater affection to kill a son than to vindicate him.[33] (7) Stop, then, wearying me with your questioning, woman. Can you really not see that the complete answer on our son's behalf is when someone says: "I killed"? And even if his exclamations are suppressed, even if his mouth is kept shut, one who confesses this is denying nothing.[34]

(8) Yet, where ultimate crimes are concerned, their very savagery points to innocence.[35] It wasn't in a fit of madness, it wasn't when out of my mind that I, his father, killed my son (beyond sense and feeling is anyone who does not feel pity!), yes, *killed* him. 6. You see before you an old man awash in his own blood, lying with gory hands on the dead body of his only son after tearing and burning vitals that are more sacred and more dear;[36] shrink then

to Mother's feminine way (by demanding in court Father's punishment).

[34] For such a "counterproductive" confession, cf. Quint. 9.2.80 and above, Introduction to the present declamation.

[35] A crime so savage must be the act of a man who is not covering up anything.

[36] Sc., than his own.

caelestis exanimavit ignis, adire propius time.[17] Ad quaedam facinora sufficit claudere oculos, vultus avertere,
tacere, mirari et incredibilis calamitates relinquere suis

2   causis. Miserere, ne quid amplius quaeras, ne quid interroges. Dicturum me putas: "Parce saeculo, parce marito,
parce patri"? Tu vero parce illi, qui occisus est.

3   Novum, iudices, uxoris in marito crimen audite: silentium est, de quo queritur.[18] Solebat indignatio vestra
convicia nostra ferre non posse, et matronalis impatien-

4   tia[19] dicere videbatur: "Non parcis erga me, marite, verbis,
nullam habet nostri tuus sermo reverentiam; facile pro-
rumpis in opprobria, facile quod libet obicis, exclamas, et,
dum nimium libertati vocis indulges, potest populus ali-

5   quem de me facere rumorem." Tu, mulier, obicis mihi
rem, quae nulli umquam crimini fuit, solam in nostris
moribus innocentiam: vocem[20] repressam[21] [taciturnita-
tem].[22] Vide cur manus, cur verba peccare videantur: illis

6   infamamus, his torquemus, occidimus. Vis scire quam non
possis queri de silentio meo? Felicissima fueras, si idem
fecissemus omnes.

7   Finge me paulisper sepositis silentii causis hoc tantum

17 horre . . . time *Håk.*[2] *148–49, cf. Håk.*[2]: -eo . . . -eo *codd.*
18 querit B: queritur (*def. Håk.*[2] *149) vel* quaeritur *cett.*
19 impatientia *Watt*[3] *59 (cf.* ferre non posse): indignatio *codd.*
(*sc. e super. falso repet.*)   20 -em *Watt*[2] *34*: -e *codd.*
21 -ess- β (*vind. Watt*[2] *34*): -ehens- *cett.*
22 -tatem β: -tas *cett., secl. Håk.*

---

37 I.e., lightning: anything struck by it was considered to be
the property of the gods and not to be touched (including human
corpses, whose burial was forbidden: cf. *Decl. min.* 274).

from the corpse and fear to approach it, just like bodies deprived of life by fire from heaven.[37] In the presence of some crimes all one can do is close one's eyes, avert one's face, fall silent, be amazed, and leave disasters that cannot be believed to their causes.[38] (2) For pity's sake, inquire no further, ask nothing more. Do you suppose I am going to say: "Spare our age, spare the husband, spare the father"? No: you must spare the one who was killed.

(3) Listen, judges, to a novel charge for a wife to bring against her husband: it is silence she is making into an accusation. In the past your[39] indignation could not abide us[40] upbraiding you, and the intolerance of married women seemed to say: (4) "You do not moderate your language to me, husband, your words show no respect for me. You easily burst into abuse, you easily bring up what you like against me, easily shout, and while you indulge your freedom of speech to excess the people can produce some rumor about me." (5) *You*, woman, are accusing me of something never before made the object of a charge, the only thing that counts as innocence in the behavior of us men: the *suppression* of speech. See why hands, why words are thought to do wrong: with words we defame, with hands we torture, we kill.[41] (6) Let me show you how true it is that you cannot complain of my silence: you would have been truly fortunate if we had *all* kept silent.[42]

(7) Suppose I put aside for a while the reasons for my

---

[38] = do not pry into the causes.

[39] Addressed to married women.

[40] Husbands.

[41] = "Unlike silence, actions and words can do a great deal of harm" (Breij [2015, 468n233]).   [42] Cf. 19.1.1.

respondere: "Non prodo secretum." 7. Ex omnibus, iudices, quibus[23] humana pectora seriis gravibusque com-
plectuntur adfectibus, nullam difficiliorem quam silentii
credo virtutem, adeoque promptissimo sermone facile
delinquimus, ut constantiam tacendi neque in aliis ferre

2 possimus. Crimen hoc in me mulier vocat, quod in priscis
illis morum mentiumque rectoribus fuit prima sapientia,
quod quosdam totius vitae pertulisse patientia[24] magis illa
severa[25] miratur antiquitas, quam quod[26] temporum vices,
siderum cursus et profunda naturae velut conscia ratione

3 sanxerunt. Quae, per fidem, impotentia est effringere ri-
gens sacra dissimulatione pectus, evolvere animum, quem
supra sua secreta compositum non laetitia, non dolor, non
necessitas, non fortuita laxaverint! Quisquis de tacente
queritur, multo minus ferre poterit loquentem.

4   Nec adeo coniugali societate cuncta miscentur, ut nihil
sibi adversus hanc concordiam proprium relinquat ani-

5 mus. Est aliquis etiam a sanguine suo secretus adfectus
genusque reverentiae, ut tacenda minime velis scire caris-
simos.[27] Quaedam non possis verberibus, eculeis eruere,
et plerosque videas fortiter supra sua secreta morientis.

6 Agedum, si videtur, utrumque sexum, omnem condicionem, omnem scrutemur aetatem: nullum sine conscientia

23 *per attract.* = quae *acc. pl., cf. (Russ.*[3]) *K.-S. II.2.287–88*
24 -a *Gron.*: -am *codd.*
25 severa *Gron. (corrob. Breij*[1]): misera *codd.*: seria *Sch.*
26 qui *Wint.*[9]   27 *sic dist. Gr.-Mer.: commate Leh.*

43 I.e., as though their reason shared in the Reason of the
universe.   44 *Supra* hints at secrets being "covered up" by
people with their own bodies.

silence, and say only this in reply: "I do not betray a secret." 7. Of all the serious and weighty feelings, judges,
which human breasts embrace, I believe none presents
more difficulty than the virtue of silence: indeed, so easily
do we fall into error by overreadiness to speak that we
cannot tolerate a settled resolve to keep silent even in
others. (2) The woman calls a crime in me something that
in the eyes of those old-time guides of morals and minds
was the highest form of wisdom, something causing the
rigorous ancients to be more amazed that certain people
were able to preserve it throughout a lifetime's endurance
than that they, as though their reason had been privy to it
all,[43] laid down the alternation of the seasons, the courses
of the stars and the profound secrets of nature. (3) What
lack of restraint, for goodness sake, is needed to break into
a heart immoveable in its determination to keep a sacred
silence, to open up a mind which, once it has resolved to
keep its secrets, not happiness, not grief, not necessity, not
chance occurrences have been able to loosen! Whoever
complains of a person keeping silent will much less be able
to bear him speaking.

(4) Nor is everything so shared in the companionship
of marriage that the mind leaves itself nothing of its own
to set against this concord. (5) There is a feeling secret
even from one's own kin, a kind of reverence that makes
you wish your dearest least of all to know what must be
kept silent. Some things you could not drag out by blows,
by racks: you may see so many people dying bravely to
conceal their secrets.[44] (6) Come now, if you like, let us
examine both sexes, all classes of mankind, every period
of life: no breast is not conscious of something hidden, no

pectus, nulla vita sine causis tacendi. Si te interrogaret omnia maritus, haberes aliquid et tu quod non fatereris.

7 Et quanto silentium gravius est in sene, verecundius in marito, sanctius in patre! 8. Pudeat nos, mulier, infirmitatis: vicit nos modo iuvenis ille constantia; mori voluit ut taceremus.

2 Vides,[28] mulier, quibus interpretationibus[29] praestes tuum dolorem.[30] Diceris ideo me interrogare, quia scias[31]
3 omnia me potius pati malle quam loqui. Quis enim in hac civitate non novit taciturnitatis meae rigorem, quis ignorat qua cuncta soleam ferre patientia? Ne occisurus quidem suspiria gemitusque praemisi, nihil feci unde erupturum quandoque per[32] orbitatem patris animum aut tu praescio
4 timore sentires aut ipse periturus. Hanc nunc me iactare constantiam[33] putas, quod nihil in publico, nihil in ullo mihi permisi proclamare conventu? Ego vero non sum questus de iuvene nec tibi, nec captavi ut illum mecum et
5 mater odisset.[34] Frustra te putas extorquere accusatione posse quod mihi non ipsae calamitates, non dolor, non meditatio orbitatis expressit. Uras licet, durabo, perferam. Passus sum iam quod erat difficilius: occidi.

6 "Torsit" inquit "filium meum." Breviter, iudices, ratio reddatur: infamem;[35] quid refert an innocentem, si aliud

---

28 -e B (-es B^2), sed cf. Breij^1
29 interpreta- ς: inpatra- B: in- vel impetra- B^2 V Φ*
30 sic distinxi (cf. 19.10.3 et e.g. 5.4.5, 5.13.5): interrog. vulg.
31 scias B V δ (def. Reitz.^{2} 62.2): scis cett.
32 post Wint.^{9}, sed cf. ThlL X.1.1151.44ss.
33 -stan- Sh. B.^{2} 217 (firm. Håk.): -scien- codd.
34 -ses Franc., sed cf. Breij^1
35 dist. Håk.^{2} 150

life is without reasons to keep silent. If your husband were to question you about everything, you too would have something which you would not own to. (7) And how much more weighty is silence in an old man, more decent in a husband, more sacred in a father! 8. Let us feel ashamed of our weakness, woman: not long ago that youth surpassed us in constancy; he wished to die so that *we* might keep silent.

(2) You can see, woman, what interpretations you lay yourself open to in your grief. You will be said to be questioning me because you know that I would suffer anything rather than speak. (3) For who in this city does not know how stubbornly I keep silent, who does not know with what patience I am accustomed to bear everything? Not even on the point of killing did I send out signals of sighs and groans, I did nothing by which either you with prophetic fear or the doomed man himself might feel that the mind of a father would in the end burst forth[45] because of its loss. (4) Do you think I am boasting now of the forbearance with which I allowed myself to make no protest in public, none in any gathering? In fact I did not complain of the young man even to *you*, nor did I seek that his mother too should hate him as I did. (5) You are wrong if you think that by accusing me you can extract from me what was not elicited by my calamities themselves, by grief, by the prospect of bereavement. Burn me[46] though you may, I shall endure it, last it out. I have already suffered what was harder to bear: I killed.

(6) "He tortured my son," she says. Let the reason, judges, be stated briefly: he had lost his reputation. What

[45] = speak out.   [46] = Torture me (cf. 19.15.8–16.1).

omnibus liquet? Iuvenem cunctis pignoribus invisum, omnibus adfectibus gravem maligni fecere sermones.
7 Quid agimus, anime, quemadmodum effugimus, evadi-
8 mus? In tanta infamia nihil facere credentis est. Vis me circumire singulos, reclamare populo, cum rumore rixari? Tuae fortassis infirmitati conveniat negare; me tantum fortior adsertio unici decet: eripiendus est non contentione verborum, sed ut civitas stupeat, ut erubescat. 9. Torquere me filium putas? Invidiam facio populo: videor mihi illis verberibus lacerare famam, illis ignibus increpare rumorem. Quaestio de infami filio unam rationem habet, ut probes innocentem.
2 Dii mala prohibeant, ut noveris illum dolorem, quo potest torquere filium pater! Nihil est infelicius homine,
3 cui de unico suo mors sola non sufficit. Iuvenem, in cuius animo perdiderant nomina nostra respectum, quem cotidie necesse habebamus excusare rumori, qui inter nos formosum malebat agere quam filium, verberibus ignibus-
4 que consumpsi. Vis scire quanta tormentorum ratio fuerit? Debuit etiam tortus occidi.
5 Si tamen utique, mater, vis[36] scire causas, breviter[37] audi. Prospiciebam miser in grande quandoque facinus

---

36 vis πM E S: vis vis *cett.*
37 bre- *Håk.² 151*: le- *codd.*

---

47 Cf. 18.5.4–7, 18.11.1–4.   48 And no more.
49 From the imputations against him.   50 And therefore needs to *torture* that son to death (cf. 19.9.8–9).
51 "Father" and "son."
52 Implying that the torture elicited something serious enough to justify even the killing.

difference does it make whether he was innocent, if everyone sees it quite differently? Malicious talk made the youth hated by all his relations, a burden to all who loved him. (7) What are we to do, my soul, how are we to escape, get free? To do nothing where there is such ill report is the act of one who believes it. (8) Do you want me to go round everybody one at a time, to shout back at the people, to pick a fight with rumor?[47] It may perhaps be appropriate to a weak woman like you to deny;[48] nothing befits *me* except a stronger defense of my only son:[49] he is not to be rescued by forceful words, but in such a way as to make the city aghast and ashamed. 9. Do you think I am torturing my son? No, I am arousing feeling against the people: I see myself using those whips to lacerate gossip, those fires to upbraid rumor. Interrogation in the case of a son who has lost his reputation has only one rationale: to prove him innocent.

(2) Heaven forbid that you should know the pain which can lead a father to torture his son! Nothing is more unfortunate than a man who, for his only child, deems mere death insufficient.[50] (3) A young man in whose mind our names[51] had lost all respect, for whom every day we had to make excuses to rumor, who chose to play the beauty among us rather than the son—that is the person I destroyed with lashes and fires. (4) Do you want to know how compelling the reason for torture was? He had to be killed even after being tortured.[52]

(5) But if despite everything, mother, you want to know my motives, here is a brief explanation for you. Alas, I could see him bursting forth into a great crime one day or

prorupturum, quod otio vitam, quod desidem domi perdebat aetatem. Non peregrinationibus excolere mentem, non experiri militiam, non temptare maria, non rura colere, non administrare rem publicam, non ducere volebat
6 uxorem. Praeterea traxerat ex frequentibus castigationibus taedium patris, et in execrationem mei conscientia, quia non emendabatur, exarserat. Timebat occursus, non audebat adire conloquia: oscula convictusque fugiebat.
7 Breviter perditissimae mentis definienda mensura est: oderat me filius et timebat.

8   Filium igitur totius civitatis existimatione damnatum, quem adhuc vivere mirabantur homines, torsisse me pu-
9 tas?[38] Ego vero occidi tarde, diu. Quaestionem illud vocas? Poena, supplicium et malorum meorum exitus fuit. Nulla ratio est interrogandi hominem, cui non est fas nisi negare. 10. Quanta tamen mihi fuit et in quaestione moderatio! Non enim praecipiti raptus impulsu exsilui repente, subito, nec captus dolore caeco impatientiae meae velox
2 vulnus inflixi.[39] Non potest non ratione occidi filius, cum ante torquetur. Dedi moras, spatium, tempus indulsi.
3 Vides quantam hinc malignitatibus potuerim praestare materiam, si in illo secreto gladio tantum, si vulneribus egissem:[40] exitum fecerat iuvenis deprehensi.

---

38 -tas *Håk.*: -tatis *codd., sed 19.9.2–10.7 pater nonnisi uxorem adloquitur*   39 -flixi *Gron.*: -duxi β*: -dixi *cett.*
40 materiam—egissem *sic dist. Wint.*[7] *168*

---

53 Sc., to greet me: in fact, he shunned me altogether (cf. 19.3.2).   54 Mother (here and below).
55 Again (cf. n. 34), contrast Quintilian's view on such admissions (9.2.80) and see Introduction to the present declamation.

other, because he was wasting his life in idleness and his youth in laziness at home. He did not care to cultivate his mind by foreign travel, to try a military career, to confront the seas, to look after our country estates, to go into politics, to take a wife. (6) What is more, he had from frequent reproofs become fed up with his father, and had flared up into cursing me out of a bad conscience, because he wasn't mending his ways. He feared meeting me, he did not dare to come and talk to me: he avoided kissing me[53] or being in my company. (7) To take a brief measure of his depraved state of mind: my son hated me—and feared me.

(8) Do you[54] think, then, that I *tortured* a son who was condemned in the eyes of the whole city, whom men were astonished was still in the land of the living? No: I *killed* him, slowly, taking my time.[55] (9) Do you call that an interrogation? It was, rather, a punishment, an execution, the way out of all my troubles. There is no point in questioning someone who can do nothing but deny.[56] 10. Yet how restrained I was even in the interrogation! For it was not that I was taken over by a headlong impulse and flew at him suddenly, unexpectedly; it was not that I was seized by the blind pain of my passion and inflicted a swift wound. (2) A son cannot but be killed for a reason, when he is tortured first. I gave him delays, I granted him breathing space and time. (3) If in that secret place I had just resorted to a sword, to stabbing, you can see how much material I might have given to the malevolent: he would have died the death of a youth caught in the act.[57]

[56] Contrast 18.12.5.
[57] Cf. 18.12.7.

[QUINTILIAN]

4   Non est igitur, mulier, quod mihi facias duplicatae
questionis[41] invidiam: idem est[42] quod torsi et occidi; sola
5   est huius necessitatis ratio de morte. Illud est parricidium,
filium torquere victurum. Putas iuvenem vivere potuisse,
6   cui iam non poterat nisi morte succurri? Quem contra
malignos[43] sermones adserere coeperam, non reddidi rursus infamiae, neque in oculos et ora vulgi de secreto patris
emisi. Providentia mea[44] tibi quoque, mater, ne in hunc
7   interrogareris,[45] eripui.[46] Ille vero non fuit post tormenta
laturus vitae pudorem, ut interrogaretur a singulis, ut
negaret. Verum, mulier, adfectibus tuis renuntiandum est:
ad totius domus nostrae pertinere innocentiam credidi, ne
se ipse potius occideret.

8   Sentit, iudices, mulier ad ius querelae suae nec quod
torserim, nec quod occiderim pertinere, itaque[47] quaerit
9   quid mihi dixerit ille, de quo nescit an dixerit. Quid ais,
mater impatiens? Ita in morte filii tui nihil aliud ad te
pertinet, quam quid locutus sit? Ita, si respondero, remit-
10 tis parricidium, tormenta non obicis? O inconsultam mu-
liebrem semper amentiam! Quid iuvenis in tormentis
dixerit, tamquam ignoret, interrogat; nihil me comperisse
non credit, tamquam sciat quid dixerit.

---

41 que- *Håk.*[2] *151*: quae- *vulg.*: *nutant codd.*   42 idem est
M (*cf. 19.12.7* quisquis—occideretur): idem D: id est *cett.*
43 malig- ς (*def. Dess.*[1] *92, Breij*[1]): mag- *codd.*
44 -ia -ea ς: -iam -eam *codd.* (*def. Reitz.*[2] *62.2 ut acc. exclam.*)
45 -gareris *Wint.*[7] *168–69* (-geris *Sch.*): -getur *codd.*: -garetur
Gron.   46 providentia—eripui *post* negaret (*§7*) *transp. Breij*[1]
47 itaque E (*def. Håk.*): ata (*mox* illeque *pro* ille) B: ita B[2] *cett.*

---

58 Father claims he merely prevented Son from committing
suicide out of shame, in the best interest of their whole house.

(4) There is then no reason for you, woman, to try to
arouse hatred against me by making a twofold complaint:
my torturing him and killing him are one and the same
thing; the only logical conclusion to this inevitable process
is death. (5) *Parricide* means torturing a son who is going
to *live*. Now do you think the young man could have gone
on living, when he could no longer be helped except by
dying? (6) Having begun to defend him in the face of
malign gossip, I did not send him back into ill repute,
dispatching him from a father's secret place to the gaze
and tittle-tattle of the commons. Thanks to my foresight,
I snatched him away from you too, mother, to prevent your
being interrogated to give evidence against him. (7) As for
him, he was not after his torture going to endure the
shame that his living on would involve—being interrogated by all and sundry, having to deny. For all your animosity, woman, you have to be told the truth: I thought it
was in the interests of the innocence of our *whole* house
that he should not be allowed to kill himself instead.[58]

(8) The woman, judges, realizes that it is irrelevant to
the rights and wrongs of her complaint either that I tortured or that I killed.[59] That is why she asks what he said
to me, though she does not know if he said anything. (9)
What are you saying, impatient mother? Does nothing
really concern you in the death of your son other than what
he said? Will you really, if I reply, condone the parricide,
stop reproaching me for torturing him? (10) O the stupid-
ity of women, illogical to the bitter end! She asks what the
young man said under torture, as if she did not know; she
does not believe I found out nothing, as though she knew
what he said.

---

[59] Her charge is merely that he kept silent.

11. Fidem communis sanguinis, fidem communium
malorum, ne parricidii me velis agitare secretum, ne cala-
2 mitatibus nostris gravem facias innocentiam tuam! Viderit, quid meruerit iuvenis[48] ille; ego iam possum suprema
revereri, et post exitum unici revertor in patrem. Maior
defunctis liberis praestanda reverentia est, nec quicquam
minus convenit adfectibus patris,[49] quam si insultare vi-
3 deatur occiso. In gratiam me cum filio reduxit orbitas,
iram nostram mors severa composuit. Quin immo recogi-
tanti mihi totum secreti illius ordinem subit tacita miseratio,[50] quantam ego debeam reverentiam filio quem potui
torquere solus, quem potui solus occidere.
4 Perseveras, cogis, instas? Invicem te, mulier, interrogo,
cur, si tanto opere volebas scire quid interrogarem, quid
ille loqueretur, non inruperis in quaestionem, quam nullis
ministris, nullis custodibus vallaverat pater. Quanto melius, mater, ipsum adisses, quanto fortius interrogasses
5 una, quanto tibi plura dixisset! Quis te, mulier, adfectus
abegit, tenuit, exclusit? Agnosco verecundiam tuam: timuisti, credo, ne, si in illo secreto fuissemus omnes, occidisse filium diceretur et mater.
6 Instas tamen et miseri senis ora diducis?[51] Puta me hoc

[48] viderit—iuvenis *dist. Str.[10] 129.124*
[49] pa- ⋜: ma- *codd.*
[50] *levius dist. vulg.*: *gravius Håk.*
[51] did- ⋜: ded- *codd.*

---

[60] I.e., the blood that mingles in our son.
[61] I.e., do not aggravate our problems by stressing your innocence: the only reason why your reputation is now intact is that
I killed Son.

11. In the name of our shared blood,[60] of our common troubles: do not wish me to stir up the secret of the murder, do not make your innocence bear hard on our calamities![61] (2) No matter what the young man deserved: I can now revere his end, going back to be a father after the death of my only son. More respect is to be paid to children when they are dead, and nothing less befits the feelings of a father than seeming to revile a child he killed. (3) Bereavement has reconciled me to my son, a ruthless death has allayed my anger. In fact, as I look back over the whole sequence of events in that private spot, an unspoken pity steals up on me, at the thought of all the respect I owe a son whom I found it in me to torture alone, to kill alone!

(4) Do you keep on at me, force me, pressure me? In return I ask you, woman, why, if you so wanted to know what I was asking, what he was saying, you did not burst in on an interrogation that the father had not walled off by any servants, any guards.[62] How much better, mother, it would have been for you to have approached him! How much more urgently would you have questioned him if you had joined in, how much more he would have said to you! (5) What feeling, mother, drove you away, held you back, kept you out? I understand the reason for this restraint of yours: you were afraid, I believe, that, if we had all been there in that private place, the mother too would be said to have killed her son.

(6) Do you nevertheless press me and try to force open

---

[62] Contrast 18.13.5 and see Introduction to the present declamation.

[QUINTILIAN]

solum dicere: ex maximi facinoris colluctatione[52] veniens,
quid audierim nondum scio; totus adhuc sum in parricidio[53] meo, et post mortem unici omnia, quibus laceratus,
7 occisus est, in animum meum tormenta redierunt. Est
quidem difficile ut aliquem pati pudorem parricida videatur, verumtamen stuporem, amentiam;[54] et[55] in silentium[56] orbitate defeci: ablata est mihi omnium verborum
fides, omnis sermonis auctoritas, nec habet causam lo-
quendi, cui non potest credi. 12. Desine, mulier, interrogare: filium, quem occidit,[57] pater nec absolvere nec
accusare iam debet.

2 "Quid" inquit "dixit, cum occideres?" Miseram parricidii innocentiam, quod hoc me non potestas, non magistratus, non propinquus aliquis, non amicus, non ille
semper loquax populus ac malignus interrogat! Quiescitis,
3 tacetis; me infelicem, numquid scitis omnes? Puta me,
mulier, hoc tibi respondere: non habent incredibilia vocem, quaedam maiora sunt quam ut illa capiat modus sermonis humani. Tu vero crede nihil aliud fuisse quam fu-
4 rorem, insanisse me puta.[58] Videbam quae non fiebant,
audiebam quae nemo dicebat. Hoc solum non insanientis
5 habui, quod tacebam. Finge me respondere: nihil dixit,

---

[52] colluctati- M[2] (*vind. Dess.[1] 93*): coniuncti- B: -ctati- V ψ* P:
commutati- A S: co- veniens *om.* δ   [53] *post* p. *desinit* V
[54] -rem -iam *Sh. B.[1] 79*: -re -ia *codd.*
[55] *cf. ThlL V.2.892.77ss.*
[56] -ium *Håk.[2] 151 coll. 18.2.3:* -io *codd.*
[57] *distinxi: post* pater *vulg.*   [58] -ta C[2]: -to *codd.*

---

[63] He knows he has lost credibility, having tortured his own
son to death (cf. 18.14.1)—and without any witnesses (cf.
18.12.8–11).

the lips of a wretched old man? Imagine that all I say is this: coming from the traumatic stress of an utmost crime, I do not yet know what I heard; I am still completely bound up in my parricide, and after the death of my only son all the torments by which he was torn apart and killed have come back to my mind. (7) It is certainly difficult for a parricide to be thought to feel any shame, but not bewilderment, senselessness; indeed, it is because of my bereavement that I have relapsed into silence: nothing I say can be believed,[63] my words have forfeited all authority, and one who cannot be believed has no reason to speak. 12. Stop questioning me, mother; a father should neither acquit nor accuse a son once he has killed him.[64]

(2) "What," she inquires, "did he say when you were killing him?" O the unhappy innocence of parricide, that I am being asked this not by a person in power, not by a magistrate, not by some relative, not by a friend, not by the people, ever garrulous and malevolent![65] You are quiet, you are silent; unhappy me, maybe you all know the truth already? (3) Suppose, woman, I make you this reply: incredible things have no voice, some things are too great for the limits of human language to cope with them. But you must believe that it was nothing more than a fit of frenzy, must suppose I went mad. (4) I saw what was not happening, I heard what no one was saying. All I had left of a sane man was that I kept silent. (5) Suppose I reply:

[64] By acquitting him, he would admit that he killed him for no reason; by accusing him, he would bring public dishonor to his whole family.

[65] Implying that they all may already know (see below, "You are quiet etc.," addressed to all and sundry). Contrast 18.15.3.

nihil locutus est. Non credis? Atquin multo minus credi-
tura quid dixerit.

6   Accipe, mulier, brevem veramque rationem, cur in
quaestione iuvenis occisus est:[59] torquebam nec interrogabam. Si qua ad aures tuas ab illa quamvis remota domus
parte perlata vox est, meus gemitus fuit, meorum visce-

7   rum dolor. Quaeris cur nihil dixerit? Quia non habuit quod
scire vellem, quod audire deberem. Nihil aliud quaestio
illa captavit quam silentium, quod praestare vita non poterat. Quisquis in tormentis occiditur, ideo tortus est, ut

8   occideretur.[60] An tu quaestionem illam fuisse credis, qualis vernilibus corporibus adhibetur? Ideo enim eculeos
movebam artifex senex, tendebam[61] fidiculas ratione sae-
vitiae, ut leviter sedibus suis remota compago per singulos

9   artus membra laxaret?[62] Consumptus est spiritus silentio
sui, et verbera ignesque animum pariter vocemque cluse-
runt. Videbatur mihi premere gemitus, tenere suspiria, et
sic nihil dixit, tamquam torqueretur ab homine qui sciret.
13. Miraris hanc in filio contumaciam, in iuvene patientiam? Patri torquenti non potest aliter responderi, quam
ut mori malit quam confiteri.

2   Quod sufficit igitur interrogantibus respondeo, mulier:
occidi. Fallitur, quisquis expectat ut obiciamus illa com-

---

[59] *de usu indicativi vd. Breij*[1]
[60] quisquis—occideretur *post* adhibetur (*§8*) *transp. Breij*[1]
[61] -nde- *Gron.*: -ne- *codd.*
[62] *interrog. dist. Suss.* (*praeeunte Du Teil 376*)

---

[66] = believe me if I told you what he said.
[67] I.e., aimed at having them *talk* (cf. n. 68).

he said nothing, spoke nothing. Don't you believe me? Yet you would still less believe what he said.[66]

(6) Here, woman, is the short and true reason why the young man was killed during the interrogation: I was torturing, not asking questions. If any sound came through to your ears from that part of the house, remote though it was, it was my groaning, the grief inside me. (7) You ask why he said nothing? Because he had nothing I wanted to know, nothing which I ought to have heard. That interrogation aimed at nothing more than silence, which his survival could not provide. Anyone killed under torture is tortured precisely in order to be killed. (8) Do you think the interrogation was of the kind applied to the bodies of household slaves?[67] Did I really, an aged virtuoso, move up the rack and tighten the cords with methodical savagery in order that the frame of his body, easily displaced, might loosen the limbs joint by joint?[68] (9) No: his spirit was destroyed by *his own* determination to keep silent, the lashes and fires closing off breath and voice at the same time. He seemed to me to be suppressing his groans, to be holding back his sighs: he said nothing as if he was being tortured by someone who already knew the truth. 13. Are you surprised that a son was so stubborn, that a young man showed such endurance? When his father is the torturer, a son can only reply that he prefers to die rather than confess.

(2) Therefore, woman, this is answer enough for those who ask: I killed him. Anyone who thinks I will make the

[68] Sc., to the point that he would no longer be able to keep silent. No: I tortured him so that he would *not* speak, but die.

3   munia. Ego vero proclamo non luxuriosum, non amore meretricis infamem; nihil ille delinquebat quomodo liberi solent. Monstrum erat inenarrabile, quod nollem deprehendere, quod ferre non possem.

4   Miratur aliquis quod non abdicaverim, nec notissima ultione patrum fuerim tantum expulisse contentus? Tuus, mulier, nefarius, tuus inconsultus non permisit adfectus. Filium, cui contra severitatem meam ignoscebas, quem mecum odisse non poteras, secuta fuisses abdicatum.

5   Finge iuvenem dixisse nescioquid; ego audire nihil potui. Non enim potestatis alicuius more consederam, nec torquentibus aliis agebam iudicem pater.[63] Ego tunc
6 cuncta et passus sum pariter et feci. Non vacabat aures praestare verbis, excipere gemitus, aestimare singultus; avocavit me contentio, dolor, orbitas, parricidium. Omnia facta sunt festinatione praecipiti. Idem patris adfectus est torquere ut scias, occidere ut nescias.

7   "In meam" inquit "infamiam taces." Ita nunc primum laboras, misera, de fama, et post unici mortem pertinere
8 ad te coepit quid loquantur homines? Scilicet filius impensus est ut erubesceres, ut male audires. Adeone hoc captanti non erat satis rem totam commisisse rumori? 14. Ego vero me famae tuae, mulier, opposui, et inter matrem filiumque medius parricidium feci, unicum occidi, ne quid

---

63 pater *Gron.* (*def. Breij[1]*): patrem pater B: patrem Φ

---

69 Cf. 19.2.6–3.1 and contrast 18.9.2; also (Corcella [2021], 96–97]), from the Libanian corpus, *Decl.* 27.10–11 and 49.24.
70 Metarhetoric.   71 Father had acted hastily, gripped by the urge both to know Son's secret and to kill so as to keep it hidden: two sides of the same emotion.   72 Ironic.

customary accusations is mistaken. (3) In fact, I assert that he was *not* a philander or notorious for the love of a harlot; he did *not* do anything wrong of the kind children usually do.[69] No: his was an unspeakable abomination, one that I did not wish to find out, one that I could not tolerate.

(4) Is anyone surprised that I did not disown him, content just to banish him—the most familiar type of fatherly punishment?[70] It was your affection, woman, wicked and ill-advised as it was, that tied my hands. You forgave our son in the face of my severity, you did not feel able to join me in hating him: and you would have gone away with him, if I had driven him out.

(5) Suppose the youth did say something: I could hear nothing. After all, I was not in session like some civil authority, I was not a father sitting in judgment while others carried out the torture. On that occasion I suffered everything, did everything, at once. (6) There was no time to lend my ears to his words, to take in his groans, to weigh up his sobs; I was distracted by stress, grief, bereavement,—parricide. Everything happened in headlong haste. For a father it is a sign of the same emotion to torture in order to know, to kill in order not to know.[71]

(7) "You are keeping silent to discredit me," she says. Poor woman, are you only *now* worrying about gossip? Only after the death of your sole child does it begin to matter to you what people are saying? (8) Of course[72] our son was sacrificed just so that you could blush, just so that you could be slandered.—Now if that was my aim, would it not have been enough to leave it all to rumor? 14. In fact I pitted myself against the talk about you, woman, and, caught between mother and son, I committed parricide, killed my only son, so that people might not say anything

[QUINTILIAN]

aliud loquerentur homines. Alioquin si hoc capto, quod
putas, quousque taceo, in quod tempus differo illam,
2 quam me putas premere, vocem? Ecce reatus, iudicium,
pronuntiatio:[64] ego tamen scire me nego. Egregiam rationem malignitatis: locuturus adversus uxorem feci ne mihi
crederetur!
3   Fateor igitur: nihil ad certum indubitatumque perduxi.
Hoc est quin immo, propter quod ad mortem usque
contendi: non explicant tormenta quaestionem, quae occi-
dunt.
4   "Quid" inquit "dixit?" Felicem te, misera, si nescis!
5 "Quid dixit?"[65] Ita non es contenta conscientia tua? Non
sufficit quod non habuit ille quod negaret, quod fateretur?
6 Poscis verba quaestionis, cogis, extorques? Testor: tu fa-
7 cis ne possis negare quod dixero. "Quid dixit?" Parasse
se parentibus venenum? Negas. Proditionis agitasse sermones? Negas. Tyrannidis inisse consilium? Negas, et
8 quicquid dixero, negabis. O bonae conscientiae incauta
simplicitas! Ita non times ne coactus loqui multa fingam,
multa componam? Si potes scire, mulier, an mentiar, scis
9 quid dixerit. "Quid dixit?" Nihil. "Quid dixit?" Omnia:
maledixit saeculo, fecit temporibus invidiam, detestatus
est patrem, conviciatus est matri. "Quid dixit?" Plus quam

64 -ntiatio *Obr.*: -ntio *codd.*
65 si—dixit *dist. Obr. (firm. Håk.² 152)*

---

73 Sc., to be issued at the end of the trial.
74 If my reason to keep silent was only to foster further gossip
against you, I would talk *now*, when I am facing a verdict.
75 Had I really wanted to make insinuations about my wife,

400

further. On the other hand, if I am aiming at what you suppose, how long am I still to keep silent, to what time am I to put off saying what you think I am suppressing? (2) Here we have an accusation, a law case, a verdict:[73] but even now I say I do not know.[74] What a remarkable refinement of malevolence, that when intending to defame my wife I made sure I should not be believed![75]

(3) I confess therefore: I did *not* bring the matter to a sure end, leaving no doubt behind. That indeed is why I went on till he died: tortures that kill do not resolve an investigation.

(4) "What did he say?" she says. Poor woman, you are lucky if you do not know! (5) "What did he say?" Aren't you then content with what you know in your own heart? Is it not enough that he had nothing to deny, nothing to confess? (6) Do you insist on the words he spoke under torture, force them out of me, extort them? I tell you: you are putting yourself into a position where you cannot deny what I shall say. (7) "What did he say?" That he prepared poison for his parents? You deny it. That he talked of treason? You deny it. That he plotted a tyranny? You deny it; and whatever I say, you will deny it. (8) O, the reckless naïveté of a good conscience! Aren't you afraid, then, that if I am forced to speak I may make up a lot of things, concoct a lot of things? If, woman, you can know whether I am lying, you *know* what he said. (9) "What did he say?" Nothing. "What did he say?" Everything: he cursed our age, he cast aspersions on our times, he execrated his father, he abused his mother. "What did he say?" More than

I wouldn't have maintained such a persistent—and thereby counterproductive—silence.

10   interrogabam. Vicisti, mulier, obstinationem meam; audi
breve succinctumque responsum, quid dixerit: quod quaeris, quod[66] putas.
    15. O si quis in illam vos secreti nostri potuisset adhi-
bere praesentiam! Vidissetis novum genus quaestionis.
2   Stabam senex furiis monstrosae feritatis accinctus, manibus exertis, hinc ignibus, hinc verberibus armatus. Super
ora, super oculos iacentis adsistens clamabam: "Furiose,
demens, tace!"; et ille, velut exustis amputatisque per quae
3   dolor exit in verba, fuit adtonitus, amens. Quotiens admo-
tis ignibus ad aliquam corporis partem totum pectus imposuit! Quotiens hiatu oris avide flammas adversus exeuntia
4   verba collegit! Cum vero iam totus calor verberibus expul-
sus viribus novissimi doloris erumperet, pertractis[67] ab
ima pectoris parte suspiriis brevissime collecti spiritus,
ille, quo redditur anima, singultus fuit similis exclamaturo
5   nescio quid, quod et tu fortassis audires. Occupavi, fateor,
et advocatis, quas iam consumpseram, viribus, manibus,
telis totoque corpore pariter adnisus, antequam mentire-
6   tur, occidi. Misera temporis illius recordatio! Deficientem
in manibus meis filium vidi, aspexi ora pallentia, frigidos
anhelitus, interrupta suspiria et animam magno silentio
exeuntem. Non tamen tormenta laxavi, non subtraxi
7   restinxique[68] flammas. Miserere, mulier, ne quaeras amplius vocem huius adfectus. Filium, qui moriebatur, occidi.

---

[66] -od . . . -od 𝔖: -id . . . -id *codd.*
[67] -actis B[pc] (*def. Breij[1]*): -actatis B[ac] Φ*
[68] -tin- 𝔖: -trin- *codd.*

---

[76] Judges.
[77] Mother.

I was asking. (10) You have defeated my obstinacy, woman; hear a brief, a concise reply about what he said: what you are looking for, what you think.

15. O if only someone could have brought you[76] to be present at our private scene! You would have seen a novel kind of interrogation. (2) An old man, girt in the furies of prodigious cruelty, hands outstretched, armed on one side with fires, on the other with whips, I stood over his face and eyes as he lay there, and cried: "Be silent, you crazy madman!"; and he, as though the passages through which pain finds its way out into words had been burned and cut away, was thunderstruck, out of his mind. (3) How often, when the flames were directed at some part of his body, did he put his whole breast in their way! How often, opening his mouth wide, did he eagerly draw in the flames to counter the words that were trying to come out! (4) But when now all his vital warmth, expelled by the flogging, burst forth, under the pressure of his final agonies, as sighs were drawn from deep within his breast by the breath collected for a brief moment, the gasp by which the soul is rendered up made him resemble someone about to utter some cry—that you[77] too perhaps might have heard. (5) But I was too quick for him, I confess, and summoning up the strength I had already used up, applying the force of my hands and weapons and my whole body, I killed him before he could tell a lie. (6) Unhappy the memory of that time! I saw my son passing away in my grasp, I saw the pale face, the cold gasps, the broken sighs and a soul leaving the body in a great silence. Yet I did not slacken the torture, I did not remove and extinguish the flames. (7) Have pity, woman, do not ask any further for words to express what I felt then. I killed my son as he was dying.

403

8   Non perdidi tamen, non perdidi unici mortem, fortuna, non perdidi: iam me non interrogat nisi sola mater.
Consiste agedum, mulier, loco meo, et in habitum paterni
furoris accincta admove eculeos, flagella, laminas; praedico, testor: aliter non possum loqui, aliter mihi non potest
credi. 16. Quamquam, miserrime iuvenis—fas est enim
iam tuos alloqui manes—, exprimere mihi vocem nullus
poterit dolor. Quantum volet laceret, vel occidat; vincere
2   me tormenta docuisti. Si tamen fas est cogitationis memoria tractare verba miserae quaestionis, cur me coram populo magis interrogas? Eamus, uxor, in illam desolatam
domum, in illud iam patris filiique secretum; ibi me inter-
roga, ibi, ubi torsi, ubi occidi, ubi adhuc forsitan filii tui
3   vaga per maestos penates anima discurrit. Porrigat aliquis
imaginem iuvenis occisi, ponat in sinu matris illas vestes,
4   quibus ipsa iuvenem misera comebat. Eamus ad tumu-
lum, misceamus supra busta lacrimas. Ibi aut tacebimus
pariter aut invicem confitebimur.
5   Iam iam miser mori possum: explicui[69] te, sollicitudo,
pietas. Non scribo tabulas, testamento suprema[70] verba
6   non credo.[71] Et ego moriar in tormentis meis. Illud tantum

---

[69] -i *Håk.*[2] 152: -it *codd.*
[70] -ma M: -mo M[2] *cett.*
[71] *gravius dist. Håk.*[2] 152

---

[78] I.e., get no benefit from (DAR).
[79] If Son had survived, he would, like Mother, be questioning
Father now (DAR).
[80] It used to be the place for the illicit meetings of Mother and
Son (19.3.5 with n. 14); but *now*, since Father tortured and killed
Son there, it has become *their* place.

(8) But I did not waste, I did not waste[78] the death of my only son, no, fortune, I did not waste it: now only his mother questions me.[79] Come now, woman, stand in my place, and girded with a father's frenzy bring up the racks, the whips, the plates; I proclaim, I bear witness: I cannot speak in any other way, I cannot be believed in any other way. 16. On the other hand, most wretched youth—for it is proper now to address your ghost—, no pain will be able to drag speech out of me. Let her tear me as she will, or kill me: you have taught me to overcome torture. (2) But if it is possible to go over in my mind the words I remember from that unhappy interrogation, why do you prefer to question me before the people? Let us go, wife, to that desolate house, to that place that is now[80] the secret haunt of father and son. Question me there, there where I tortured, where I killed, where perhaps the wandering shade of your son still flits through the grieving mansion. (3) Let someone hand over[81] the picture of the young man who was killed, place in the mother's lap those clothes with which she would personally deck (unhappy lady!) the youth out. (4) Let us go to the tomb, let us mingle our tears over the grave. There we shall either keep silent together or confess to each other.

(5) *Now* I can die,[82] unhappy me! I have brought you to fulfillment, my anxious fatherly love. I do not write my will, I do not entrust my last words to a testament. I too shall die amid my torments. (6) This alone in my last

[81] To her.
[82] I.e., in peace, having done my duty as a father by preserving the reputation of the family.

novissimis precibus a te, civitas, per liberos, per[72] coniuges, ⟨per⟩ parentes,[73] a te, uxor, per occisi iuvenis umbram peto:[74] a te, mater, ne quid amplius quaeras, ⟨a⟩ te,[75] fama,[76] ne dicas.

[72] per AD β: ferre B δ: ferre per E
[73] ⟨per⟩ parentes *Reitz.*[2] 72 (*corrob. Breij*[1]): paterne B δ: per natos γ β
[74] *colon pos. Dess.*[1] 96: *comma vulg.*
[75] ⟨a⟩ te *Wint. ap. Breij*[1]: in ψ: tu *cett.*
[76] -a ς (*vind. Dess.*[1] 65, 96 *ut vocat.*): -am *codd.*

prayers I ask of you, my city, by children, by spouses, ⟨by⟩ parents, and of you, my wife, by the shade of the young man who was killed: of you, mother, that you inquire no more, and ⟨of⟩ you, rumor, that you say no more.

FRAGMENTS

INTRODUCTION

The Church Fathers Lactantius and Jerome attribute to "Quintilian" a number of passages that do not appear either in the *Institutio oratoria* or in the two collections of pseudo-Quintilianic declamations handed down to us.[1]

In the first case (Fr. 1), Lactantius quotes a short sentence from "Quintilian in *The Fanatic*," presumably a declamation. We have no information on such a piece, besides what we can gather from the context of this quotation: Lactantius is criticizing the foolishness of the cults of Cybele and Bellona for the acts of self-mutilations they require of their followers (the *fanatici*); the "Quintilianic" speech, thus, must have concerned someone performing ritual practices of this kind. The case may have been that of a son disowned by his father, or of a father accused of *dementia* by his children, for taking part in these rites; alternatively, we may think of a "fanatic" son killed by his father, who is then charged with ill-treatment by the mother.

[1] Only explicit quotations of, or specific references to, lost "Quintilianic" speeches will be considered in the following pages (substantially based on Stramaglia [2017]). In addition to these instances, a larger number of allusions to, and quotations from, the preserved *Major Declamations* have been detected in the works of authors from the fourth century onward, and especially Jerome; for full references see Stramaglia (2006, 557–59, 561–63; 2017, 200n27).

The second fragment (Fr. 2) comes from a declamation
on a theme known from both Greek and Roman sources,
The Veiled Head: a father is suspected of incest with the
wife of his son; Son finds his wife with a lover, whose face
is veiled. Two alternative outcomes are attested: either
Son lets the lover go, refuses to reveal the latter's identity
when asked by Father, and is therefore disowned;[2] or Son
kills his wife while sparing the lover, is charged with murder and asks Father to represent him in court, but Father
refuses.[3] Obviously, we cannot know whether the "Quintilianic" declamation adopted one of these two versions or
some other variation on the theme.

Very little can be made of the third fragment (Fr. 3).
Here Lactantius states that women are often all too ready
to absolve themselves for their infidelities, considering
them nothing but requital for their husbands' affairs; then
he quotes a *sententia* he ascribes to Quintilian, mentioning
a man who neither keeps away from others' wives nor
concerns himself with the chastity of his own. This sentence does not occur in the *Institutio* or in the surviving
"Quintilianic" declamations; Lactantius must have drawn
it from a speech that circulated in his time under the name
of Quintilian, then disappeared without leaving further
trace. The speech might have involved "a debate on *mala
tractatio* or *iniustum repudium*."[4]

The fourth text (Fr. 4) shows that a "Quintilianic" *con-*

[2] Thus [Hermog.] *Inv.* 4.13.18 Patillon; Fortunat. *Rhet.* 1.7
(p. 73.14–16 Calboli Montefusco).

[3] Cf. Calp. Fl. 49.

[4] Translated from Rizzelli (2021, 350).

troversia entitled *The Child Who Was Born Black* existed by the late fourth century. We know the subject of this declamation from the collection of Calpurnius Flaccus:[5] a Roman married woman is accused of adultery after giving birth to a black son. Jerome does not quote a specific passage from the speech, but he mentions one of the arguments it exploited in defense of the woman: the birth of a son who does not resemble his father does not necessarily prove the infidelity of the mother, since it can be due to a particular thought she had in her mind at the moment of the conception.[6]

Finally, there is an epigram that Jerome quotes twice, ascribing it once to "Fabius" (Fr. 5a), once to an unnamed "most eloquent orator" (Fr. 5b). It has been questioned whether "Fabius" is in fact Quintilian, since Jerome does not refer elsewhere to him by his *nomen* only; yet the use of both *Fabius* and *Quintilianus* is attested in mentions of Quintilian (also with reference to declamation) by Ausonius[7] and cannot be ruled out in Jerome. It has been observed that twice in the *Institutio* Quintilian makes a point that may have inspired Jerome in this quotation—namely, that art is best judged by artists;[8] yet Jerome is very clear

[5] Calp. Fl. 2.

[6] This was a traditional opinion, attested by Plin. *HN* 7.51–52 and other ancient sources (full bibliography in [Santorelli-] Stramaglia [2015, 288n64]; add Fermi [2014]); this argument is not exploited in the extant excerpts of Calpurnius Flaccus (on which see now Dimatteo [2019b, 99–102] and Lentano [2020, 89–91]).

[7] Cf. Auson. *Prof. Burd.* 1.2 and 1.16 (*Quintilianus*) vs. 1.7 (*Fabius*).

[8] Quint. 2.5.8 and especially 12.10.50.

in ascribing to *Fabius* not the general concept (which, in itself, was traditional)[9] but the specific *epigram* he cites, which is not found in the *Institutio*. It therefore seems certain that this too was a *sententia* drawn from a speech that Jerome knew as Quintilianic and that was subsequently lost.

It may be objected that the "Quintilianic" fragments under discussion could derive from the large section of the *Minor Declamations* not preserved by the manuscript tradition.[10] This hypothesis cannot be entirely excluded. But we have no hard evidence that any author of the fourth or fifth century knew the excerpt-like *Minor Declamations* at all;[11] whereas it is a fact that, during that period, various *fully* developed *controversiae* circulated under the name of Quintilian, nineteen of which were gathered by Dracontius in his collection of what we now know as the *Major Declamations*. Jerome was able to quote from some of the pieces handed down to us in this collection and could well have known others that have not been preserved;[12] the same may be true of Lactantius. It should be noted, finally, that titles such as *The Fanatic*, *The Veiled Head*, and *The*

---

[9] The formulation goes back as far as Anacharsis (sixth century BC): cf. *Apophth.* A 42a–f Kindstrand.

[10] I.e., declamations 1–243: see General Introduction, §1. Three of these fragments were in fact printed as *Fragmenta incerta* of the *Minores* by Winterbottom (1984, 291; comments on p. 595).

[11] Some scholars detect an allusion to *Decl. min.* 260.10 in Lactant. *Div. inst.* 5.9.8, but this is highly doubtful: see Stramaglia (2017, 199–200).

[12] For references see Stramaglia (2017, 200n27).

Child Who Was Born Black in their Latin wording are short, enigmatic, and intriguing, like those of our *Major Declamations*; the titles of the *Minor Declamations*, on the contrary, are not meant to tickle the reader's interest but to point out the facts of the case, in a pragmatic way.

We do not know why the "Quintilianic" pieces mentioned by Lactantius and Jerome were not preserved. The very existence of these fragments, however, proves that what we call the *Major Declamations* did not include *all* the speeches that circulated over the centuries under the name of the great master. It is possible that the "editor" of our collection, Dracontius, selected only the pieces that he considered useful for his purposes; yet the varying degree of technical mastery and refinement displayed in the individual speeches leads one rather to think that Dracontius included in his anthology all the speeches he *could* get hold of, whatever their merits or shortcomings.[13]

[13] On Dracontius and the process that led to the formation of our collection of the *Major Declamations*, see General Introduction, §5.

FRAGMENTA[1]

1 Lactant. *Div. inst.* 1.21.16–17 (edd. Heck-Wlosok)

Ab isto genere sacrorum non minoris insaniae iudicanda sunt publica illa sacra, quorum alia sunt Matris, in quibus homines suis ipsi virilibus litant . . . , alia Virtutis, quam eandem Bellonam vocant, in quibus ipsi sacerdotes non alieno, sed suo cruore sacrificant. Sectis namque umeris et utraque manu destrictos gladios exserentes currunt, efferuntur, insaniunt. Optime igitur Quintilianus in Fanatico, Istud—*inquit*—si deus cogit, iratus est.

2 Lactant. *Div. inst.* 5.7.6–7 (edd. Heck-Wlosok)

ideo potentiores esse iniustos permisit [sc. Deus], *ut cogere ad malum possent, ideo plures, ut virtus esset pretiosa, quod rara est. Quod quidem ipsum Quintilianus egregie ac breviter ostendit in* Capite obvoluto: Nam quae—*inquit*—virtus esset innocentia, nisi laudem raritas dedisset?

---

[1] *ad fragmenta seligenda edenda enarranda vd. fusius Str.*[13]

FRAGMENTS

1

Just as crazy as religious practices like this are to be judged well-known public rites: some dedicated to the Mother, where men offer up their own sexual organs . . . , others to Valor (also called Bellona), in which the priests themselves sacrifice with their own blood, not that of others—for they slash their shoulders and run about carried away by madness, an unsheathed sword in each hand. Hence Quintilian's excellent remark in The Fanatic: If a god compels that sort of thing, he is angry.

2

[God] let the unjust be more powerful in order that they might be able to compel others to evil; he let them be in the majority in order that virtue might be precious because it is rare. This precise point was made strikingly and briefly by Quintilian in The Veiled Head: For what kind of virtue would innocence be, if its rarity had not made it praiseworthy?

3 Lactant. *Div. inst.* 6.23.30–31 (edd. Heck-Wlosok)

nulla est tam perditi pudoris adultera quae non hanc causam vitiis suis praetendat, iniuriam se peccando non facere, sed referre. Quod optime Quintilianus expressit: homo—*inquit*—neque alieni matrimonii abstinens neque sui custos, quae inter se natura conexa sunt.[2] *Nam neque maritus circa corrumpendas aliorum coniuges occupatus potest vacare domesticae sanctitati, et uxor, cum in tale incidit matrimonium, exemplo ipso concitata aut imitari se putat aut vindicare.*

4 Jer. *Quaest. Hebr. in Gen.* 30.32–33 (p. 48, 16–23 de Lagarde = *CCSL* 72, p. 38)

Nec mirum hanc in conceptu feminarum esse naturam, ut quales perspexerint sive mente conceperint in extremo voluptatis aestu quae concipiunt, talem sobolem procreent, cum . . . Quintilianus in ea controversia, in qua accusabatur matrona quod Aethiopem pepererit, pro defensione illius argumentetur hanc conceptuum esse naturam, quam supra diximus.

5a Jer. *Ep.* 66.9.2 (*CSEL* 54, p. 659, 7–8 Hilberg[2])

Felices—*inquit Fabius*—essent artes, si de illis soli artifices iudicarent.

---

[2] quae—sunt *item ac superiora "Quintiliano" deberi ostendit Rizz.* 346–48

3

*there is no adulteress so utterly shameless that she does not
plead, as cover for her vices, that by sinning she is not
doing an injury but repaying one. Quintilian put this very
well:* a man who neither keeps out of the marriages of
others nor guards his own—two things connected by nature. *For a husband who spends his time leading other
men's wives astray can find no room for moral behavior at
home, and a wife who is saddled with a husband like that
is herself spurred on by his example and thinks she must
either follow suit or take revenge.*

4

*Nor is it surprising that such is the nature of women at the
moment of conception, that those who conceive generate
offspring in the likeness of the persons they saw or imagined in the paroxysm of their pleasure; for . . . Quintilian,
in the* controversia *where a married woman was being
accused for bearing a black child, uses in her defense the
argument that the nature of conceptions is as I have just
described it.*

5a

Fabius says: Happy would be the arts, if it were only artists
who made judgments on them!

5b Jer. *In Is.* 16.pr. (*CCSL* 73a, p. 641, 1–2 Adriaen =
p. 1625, 1–2 Gryson *et al.*)

Egregia disertissimi oratoris sententia est: Felices essent
artes, si de illis soli artifices iudicarent.

5b

Excellent is the epigram of a most eloquent orator: Happy would be the arts, if it were only artists who made judgments on them!

INDEXES

The following indexes are keyed to the English text of introductions, translations, and notes by volume and page number. Numbers in bold signal that a topic appears in, or is implied by, the theme of a declamation; further appearances in the same declamation are not included. Common words (e.g., *controversia*, declamation) are not recorded.

a
INDEX OF NAMES

423

INDEXES

426

adultery, 3.207, 329, 333, 337,
412–13, 419

aggravating circumstances,
2.129n25

astrology, 1.xvii, xix, **161**; 2.145–
47, 215

bees, beekeeping, 1.xviii, xxi,
xxii n41; **3.85**

blindness, 1.xv, xviii, xxi, **2**, **53**;
2.2; **3.221**; alleviated by the
support of others, 2.47, 51–
53; caused by excessive weeping, **2.2**, 252n17, 265n38,
271; **3.221**; compensated for
by other senses, 2.45;
equated to death, 1.64n20,
89; exposes to insults,
1.20n35, 85; increases affection toward parents, 1.79; in-
hibits the intrusion of strong
emotions and vices, 1.20n30,
79–81; 2.24; lighter for a
woman than for a man, 2.47;
prevents from weeping,
1.47n104, 109n121

burial. *See under* funerals

cannibalism, 1.xvii; **3.3**

chastity, 1.114, 117, 119, 121,
129, 133, 137, 139, 151;
3.183, 207, 314, 319, 323,
329

citizenship, Roman, 1.xxxiv; 2.3,
48n86

collusion (of a party with its opponent: *praevaricatio*), 1.129;
2.55; 3.147n7, 227n8

cosmology, 1.204n71, 205;
2.283–85

damage: harm to the state,
1.xxiii; **3.3**; to property, 1.xvi,
xxv, xxviii; 3.4, **85**

debt-slavery, 1.xxxiv, 151

disability, 1.xxi, **2**, **53**, 191; **2.2**;
as an argument to demon-
strate innocence, 1.3–4, 7, 17,
58n4, 61, 75–77, 103. *See also*
blindness

doctors. *See under* medicine

domestic council, summoned to
consult on difficult decisions,
1.85, 89; 2.125, 142n49;
3.314, 347

excusatory circumstances,
1.131, 245, 251, 281; 2.39–41,
55, 59, 137, 149, 253, 313;
3.59–61, 71, 239

429